DEMOCRATIC
CIVILITY

DEMOCRATIC CIVILITY

The History and Cross-Cultural Possibility of a Modern Political Ideal

EDITED BY

ROBERT W. HEFNER

Transaction Publishers

New Brunswick (U.S.A.) and London (U.K.)

This book is printed on acid-free paper that meets the American National Standard for Permanence of Paper for Printed Library Materials.

Library of Congress Catalog Number: 97-47003
ISBN: 1-56000-364-2
Printed in the United States of America

Library of Congress Cataloging-in-Publication Data

Democratic civility : the history and cross-cultural possibility of a modern
  political ideal / edited by Robert W. Hefner.
      p. cm.
  Includes bibliographical references and index.
  ISBN 1-56000-364-2 (alk. paper)
  1. Civil society. 2. Democracy. 3. Multiculturalism. 4. Pluralism
(Social sciences) I. Hefner, Robert W., 1952–   .
JC336.D42   1998
321.8—dc21   97-47003
                                                          CIP

Contents

Preface

In the summer of 1993, the Institute for the Study of Economic Culture (ISEC) at Boston University inaugurated a four-year program on Civil Society and Civic Values. The program was intended to work in several educational fora, sponsoring research and conferences, running faculty seminars, and publishing books on the relationship between the economy, civil organizations, and democratic change. Though at the time there had already been a small flood of literature on civil society, the Institute's director (Peter L. Berger) and I hoped that ISEC's history of research into modern markets, politics, and transcultural exchange might offer a useful vantage point on problems of democracy and civil society today.

This book is the fruit of one of the most interesting of those collaborative endeavors, a Working Group on Civil Society and Civic Culture that met over two weekends in the spring and fall of 1995. The original Working Group consisted of sixteen individuals from the United States and Europe. Funds to bring them together came from a grant by the Bradley Foundation to support ISEC's Programs in Democracy and Civil Society. I wish to express my gratitude to the Foundation for their generous support. Four members of the Working Group, Peter L. Berger, Adam Seligman, John Hall, and myself, had earlier been involved in another ISEC project on civil society, a faculty summer seminar on democracy and civil society, held at ISEC during June-July of 1994. Our goal in that earlier seminar was to assess whether cross-cultural and multidisciplinary methods might better illuminate contemporary democracy's challenges. To our delight, we found that this comparative effort did offer some novel insights.

Buoyed by our summer experience, we decided to extend this dialogue with the formation of the Working Group in 1995. We added to the initial core of four a larger group of scholars engaged in comparative research on problems of democracy and civil organization. Our goal in these two meetings was not to reach methodological or ideological consensus. Readers of the present volume will note more than a few differences of political commitment among contributors. The attempt to bring together scholars of different persuasions was necessary, I felt, because challenges to democracy in the post-Cold War era raise serious questions about the received nostrums of Left and Right. We are not living through an end to ideology; but we may be witness to a significant refiguration of the central ideological questions of our time. In such circumstances there may be wisdom in listening to viewpoints other than one's own, and recognizing that courage is not always found on just one side of a divide. In addition, of course, the central premise of democratic civility is that engagement across social barriers is a constructive feature of culture and politics, if managed with critical sensitivity. One only has to peruse the literature on democracy and society to realize that, though academic discourse pays homage to diversity, efforts toward its achievement in conferences and published work is regrettably rarer—especially, it seems, when it comes to matters of democratic theory!

For reasons of thematic coherence, the disciplinary scope of this volume came to include sociology, anthropology, and politics. This emphasis allowed us to create a volume that seeks to speak across all three fields; in so doing, it also attempts to redraw some of the conventional lines of debate. Sociologists and political scientists have made progress toward developing a framework within which to think about the political and ethical foundations of civil democracy. However, to assess the generalizability of this framework, we felt a need to draw on the resources of anthropologists and sociologists working at the margins of the Western world.

My hope is that readers of this volume will discover in these essays something of the excitement of our multidisciplinary exchange. They will also discover, however, something of its difficulty. After almost two years of interaction through meetings and correspondence among members of the Working Group, the gap between contributors interested in the Western genealogy of the idea of civil society and those attempting to decenter its insights across cultures remains a daunting one. This tension is one of the most vexing in contemporary political theory, and its resolution will require a deepening of the multidisciplinary experiment attempted in this book.

I want to express my deep gratitude to Dr. Irving Louis Horowitz at Transaction Publishers, who ushered this volume through the review process with intelligence and consideration. I would like to think that this volume pays tribute to Dr. Horowitz's understanding of the seriousness of the challenge facing social and political theory today.

The Working Group and this volume would not have been possible without the tireless support and critical input of the ISEC Director, Peter L. Berger. Peter's engaged interpretive sociology has been an inspiration to all of us in this project. I hope that in some small way this volume can repay our collective debt to him.

Robert Hefner
Boston University

Introduction

1

On the History and Cross-Cultural Possibility of a Democratic Ideal

Robert W. Hefner

Few questions more clearly preoccupy our era than that of how to facilitate civil, free, and democratic interaction among the citizens of multicultural societies. In recent years, the importance of this challenge, the challenge of democratic civility, has become globally apparent. In the late 1980s and early 1990s, we were witness to a transformation of international politics more fundamental than any since the end of the Second World War. The collapse of European communism, the break-up of the Soviet Union, programs of economic restructuring, and efforts to advance human rights and the rule of law throughout the world–these and other developments seemed to mark a new era in global politics, characterized by widespread demands for civic rights and democratic participation.

These same events gave rise, however, to furious debates as to whether the culture and organization required to fulfill such aspirations were realizable across the diverse nations of the world. A few well-positioned Western analysts responded with an unhesitating affirmative to this question. In the immediate aftermath of the Cold War, in particular, one heard that we had transcended the central ideological struggles of this century, and arrived at "the end point of mankind's ideological evolution and the universalization of Western liberal democracy as the final form of human government."[1] This "end of history" was so decisive, it was asserted, that from this point on all serious political discussion would take place within the cultural horizons of liberal democracy.

Other observers responded to the new world order, however, by rejecting such universalist effervescence. As prodemocracy voices in their countries grew louder, conservative rulers in East Asia, Africa, and the

3

Middle East announced that human rights and civil democracy were premised on "Western" values incompatible with their own. In Western circles, a few high-ranking policy experts made similar pronouncements (though for different political motives), declaring democracy incompatible with many non-Western cultural traditions. In one of the most celebrated of these prognoses, the Harvard political scientist Samuel Huntington forecast a coming age of international turmoil, in which the grounds for conflict will no longer be ideological or economic, as during the Cold War, but "civilizational." The clash of civilizations, Huntington warned, "will dominate global politics," and make the achievement of an international consensus on democracy and peaceful coexistence highly unlikely.[2]

Not surprisingly, the scope of Huntington's generalities incited a chorus of criticism, not least of all from specialists on China and the Muslim world, the two regions singled out as most likely to clash with the West. Disappointment with Huntington's pronouncements was perhaps greatest among Muslim proponents of democratic reform. Having struggled for years to refute Islamist radicals' claims that the West views Islam as the enemy, democratic Muslims found themselves in the awkward position of having to explain how one of America's most influential policy advisors seemed to have identified Islam in just such terms. Questions of reception and historical accuracy aside, the really interesting thing about Huntington's remarks was that they revealed just how much the heady triumphalism of the post-Cold War era had given way to growing doubts about democracy's generalizability.

The bittersweet anxiety of the age was not confined to commentaries on ex-communist or non-Western societies. During these same years, numerous writers began to voice concerns about the health of Western democracy. To borrow a phrase from Jean Bethke Elshtain, there was talk of the "deepening emptiness" to public life, "a kind of evacuation of civic spaces."[3] Declining electoral participation and a lack of civility across cultural and ideological divides were cited as primary expressions of our crisis. Similar statements of concern, of course, had been a commonplace of Western politics since the 1960s, if not earlier. However latter-day versions of the lament showed something new. Rather than being the clarion call of a disaffected few, the plaint was heard across the ideological spectrum, from home-spun conservatives to the left-liberal avant garde.

This cultural anxiety was heightened by a number of very real social changes. In Western Europe, immigration and the transformation of nations into multiethnic societies provoked heated debates over the range of cultural pluralism compatible with received ideas of nationhood and citizenship.[4] A similar debate over nation and immigration took place in the United States, which found itself in the throes of an immigrant wave second only to the "great immigration" that transformed American society between 1890 and 1910. The American debate quickly became part of a broader "culture war" over abortion rights, school prayer, affirmative action, and, most generally, the identity politics of ethnic and life-style minorities.[5] Even in Canada, by most measures one of the most successfully multicultural societies in the world, disputes over Québecois independence and Native American rights raised questions about the viability of Canadian democracy and the rights of cultural minorities within any political union.

Under these and other influences, and in the span of just a few years, the attitude of Western policymakers toward democracy's future went from breezy confidence to edgy uncertainty. Interestingly, however, this wave of concern had a salutary effect on empirical studies of democracy. Whereas during the 1970s and 1980s political theory had been dominated by decontexualized debates over democracy's first principles, democratic theory now took a more sociological or anthropological turn. There was a heightened awareness of the multicultural nature of the contemporary world, and the need to attend to this pluralism when considering democracy's prospects.[6] As the problem of pluralism loomed larger, there was a parallel expansion of interest in the kinds of cultures and organizations that, to adapt Robert Putnam's now-famous phrase, "make democracy work."[7] What conditions encourage democratic participation and civil tolerance? Can ideas of human rights and democratic participation take hold in cultures whose ideas of personhood are premised on values other than those of liberal individualism? Is Western democracy really threatened by the twin trends of cultural separatism and the "continuing erosion of civic engagement?"[8] The attention these questions attracted showed that, for students of comparative politics, the social conditions of democracy's possibility had become the order of the day.

Conditions of a Modern Possibility

Perhaps no phrase has figured more prominently in this literature on the social prerequisites of plural democracy than has "civil society." Though writers differ on its details, most describe civil society as an arena of friendships, clubs, churches, business associations, unions, human rights groups, and other voluntary associations beyond the household but outside the state. This tissue of social ties, civil theorists assume, mediates between the household and the state so as to provide citizens opportunities for learning democratic habits of free assembly, noncoercive dialogue, and socioeconomic initiative. In so doing, it is implied, civil society is the key to balancing private interests and public solidarity.

Defined in so preliminary a manner, it is hard to understand why the concept of civil society seemed new to so many people. Stripped to its definitional shorts, the idea shows little more analytic muscle than the long-familiar reflections of the French observer of nineteenth-century American society, Alexis de Tocqueville. Drawing on ideas first developed by Montesquieu, de Tocqueville too had regarded intermediary associations as vital ingredients for a healthy democracy. He observed, "No countries need associations more–to prevent despotism of parties or the arbitrary rule of a prince–than those with a democratic social state." He also commented that Americans had "carried to the highest perfection" the democratic habit of pursuing goals in common effort and independent of the national government.[9] In reflecting on what made American democracy work, Tocqueville highlighted the role of small-town government and churches. These institutions, he suggested, drew Americans away from the narrow concerns of their private lives into public projects where they learned habits of the heart conducive to democratic compromise and a sense of civil good.

Some might argue that today's discussions of civil society add little to de Tocqueville's observations. But this has not prevented born-again enthusiasts of the idea from providing breathless accounts of civil society's ameliorative powers. A healthy civil society, certain sociological promoters insist, can counterbalance the power of the state and moderate the appetites of rulers. Republican political philosophers claim civil society is where citizens learn the habits of participation and toleration vital for democracy.[10] For enthusiasts of a free market bent, civil associations are said to deliver social services without trapping citizens in welfare dependency.[11] For writers on the post-Marxist left, civil society is trumpeted as a means to deepen democracy.[12] All in all, and varying according to the school of thought with which it is associated, civil society has been attributed the power to create countervailing forces, eliminate anomie, increase enterprise, strengthen the family, radicalize democracy, reduce teenage pregnancy, and inculcate republican virtue.

Rarely has so heavy an analytic cargo been strapped on the back of so slender a conceptual beast. The contradictory uses to which the idea of civil society has been put make a cool assessment of its utility difficult, to say the least. But the contributors to this volume are intent on just such an assessment. While acknowledging that the concept has acquired a conceptual polymorphousness, the authors in this book share the conviction that the idea of civil society can be given sociological precision, and that it is an important ingredient in any effort to understand the conditions of modern democracy's possibility. The authors also agree that, to realize its promise, the concept of civil society must be more firmly tethered to its sociological and cross-cultural moorings, and analyzed in relation to real social worlds. Deployed in this manner, the concept becomes less stratospheric in its pretensions, but more realistic in its insights.

None of this is to say that the problem of civil society should be stripped of normative concerns. On the contrary, one of the attractions of the concept is that it is, as John Hall has put it, a "package deal," linking the ideals of freedom, equality, and tolerance to the structures and institutions thought to make such a political culture possible.[13] The problem, then, is not that normative issues are somehow inimical to empirical analysis. It is instead that much of the theoretical writing on civil democracy has been more concerned with summarizing technical debates among professional philosophers than it has been in demonstrating whether those ideas inform actual people's political actions. Similarly, disputes over different versions of civil democracy have sometimes been conducted without asking whether the high principles in question can ever be socially realized. Finally, much of the debate has been conducted within a philosophical framework of uniquely European provenance, without bothering to ask how much of the framework is transferrable to non-Western societies—or, equally important, whether such a framework does justice to the variety of Western political experiences.[14]

Commenting on some of these problems a decade ago, the political theorist John Keane rightly observed that theories of civil society "could benefit from critical encounters with the pluralist trends within contemporary philosophy."[15] In the years since his essay, the concept has benefitted from just such a dialogue in the works of such leading pluralist philosophers as Charles Taylor and Will Kymlicka. However, a few admirable exceptions aside,[16] the dialogue with pluralism has yet to take the final step, which is to engage not merely Western philosophers, but peoples and cultures grappling with the question of whether civil and democratic ideals can be made their own.

It is just such a pluralist dialogue that we attempt in this volume. Urging the concept of civil society toward greater sociological realism, our central concern is the compatibility of democracy and civil society with plural polities and cultures. In addressing these issues, we speak to a broader debate over the form and meaning of civil democracy.[17] Engaging and, at times, transcending its conceptual compass, the essays provide five lessons on this debate, and on the enduring challenge of civility in democracy.

From Pluralist Cages to Democratic Civility

Since its initial stirrings in ancient Greece and Rome, Western political theory has developed as if the communities to which it applied were culturally homogeneous entities with securely agreed borders. Though both ancient Greece and Rome developed from simple republics into multicultural empires, their political theories remained premised on a vision of close-knit communities sharing language, culture, and religion. Surprisingly, this homogenizing bias persisted in the democratic theory that emerged in the West in the eighteenth and nineteenth centuries. As the political theorist Michael Walzer has put it, liberal writers were "ready enough to acknowledge a plurality of interests," but they were "strikingly unready for a plurality of cultures. One people made one state."[18]

To unravel the problem of pluralism in comparative democratic studies, then, it is useful to begin by reminding ourselves that pluralism is by no means a uniquely modern problem. Though Durkheimian stereotypes of traditional societies imply otherwise, societies in which people from varied religious, ethnic, linguistic, and racial backgrounds lived within and across the confines of one political order have existed since prehistoric times.[19] Similarly, such "traditional" states as Mughal India, the Ottoman empire, West African Asante, and Majapahit Java all incorporated a diverse array of peoples and cultures, and were involved with a social and economic macrocosm extending far beyond their borders. Though often established through conquest and domination, most of these societies went on to develop more pacific arrangements to facilitate tolerable interaction among the varied groupings which comprised their whole.[20]

Indeed, in matters of pluralism, premodern Western Europe–with its Christian church, Roman legal heritage, and politics of kingdom and manor—was considerably less pluralistic than many of its imperial counterparts in East Asia, West Africa, or the Muslim Middle East.[21] Moreover, Europe's relative homogeneity was not merely the consequence of natural circumstances, but reflected a history of sometimes violent suppression of religious, ethnic, and cultural differences. With its antiheresy campaigns, mass killings of witches, and chronic inaccommodation of Muslims and Jews, premodern Europe can claim no special cultural genius in the problem of pluralism.[22] If this generalization is true for the premodern era, however, the same cannot quite be said for all recent European experiments in civility. In the early modern era a few regions in Western Europe attempted to develop forms of political cohesion that showed a cultural distinctiveness indeed.

In its most general sense, political civility concerns the public discourses and practices through which cohesive interaction among the members of a plural society is facilitated in ways other than (but sometimes complementary to) political domination. In most societies, and certainly in those we too simply label "premodern," political civility was premised on categories and hierarchies that classified populations into large social blocks defined in terms of religion, ethnicity, tribe, gender, caste, or some other ascriptive quality.[23] Typically these categories were the basis on which people were assigned differential rights of participation in the social and political order. To borrow a image from John Hall's essay below, this premodern tradition was a civility of "social cages." Hall's image is normatively supercharged, and overlooks the fact that, as F.G. Bailey has recently emphasized, such systems of cohesion relied on a "civility of indifference" as much as exclusionary groupings.[24] This criticism acknowledged, Hall's basic point is well taken, in the sense that most premodern states premised their politics on an idealized segregation of social groups. By contrast, after the European Enlightenment efforts were made to formulate political ideals of a "civic" nature, grounded on the triplicate values of freedom, equality, and tolerance in public interaction.[25]

Of course, history teaches us that, in practice, these Enlightenment experiments in democratic civility failed to extend rights of participation to whole categories of people, including, most famously, women, the propertyless, and racial and ethnic minorities. It is also clear that, to this day, no Western political system has ever managed to bring political practice into absolute conformity with civic ideals.[26] Political practice is, of course, never merely execution of the rule; and in the case of these Enlightenment experiments, other interests competed with civic ideals to structure politics in sometimes contradictory ways. These qualifications acknowledged, the fact remains that the effort to conjoin rights of democratic participation with tolerance and equality represented a novel formula for political integration, and is the basis of the values we know as *democratic civility*.

Indeed, though its principles may be violated or ignored, democratic civility is not an ideological illusion or mere tool of hegemonic control. On the contrary, it is an idea that has mattered in modern history, and mattered greatly. Postmodern and Foucauldian theories greatly oversimplify our world when they assert that modern politics has involved no more than the ever-greater intrusion of a "panopticon" state into the public sphere and our private lives. Modern Western history has witnessed repeated struggles to extend rights of political participation to excluded social groupings. Even more remarkably, as we all know, in this century civil democratic ideals have spread throughout the world with a speed and intensity that mark them as among the most important "globalizations" of our time. Whereas a century ago civil ideals were foreign to most of the world's political cultures, today ideas which bear at least a family resemblance to those of democratic civility have their supporters in almost every corner of the globe. Here, then, is a development as world transforming as the emergence of modern capitalism or nationalism, yet of which we have an astoundingly incomplete grasp.

Unfortunately, one of the things that we *do* know, and know all too painfully, is that the diffusion of civil democratic ideals by no means guarantees their effective implementation in governance and society. Ideas of civil democracy may have a contagious popularity, but their realization in real-world politics remains problematic, to say the least. However, the difficulty surrounding their social institutionalization only makes all the more intriguing the question of how these modern political ideals ever came into existence, and why so many people in different corners of the globe today rally to (vernacularized variants of) these ideals. It is these points, among others, on which the essays in this volume have much to say.

Maculate Conception

Much has been made of the fact that the modern ideals of democratic civility first appeared in the West. Sometimes this seemingly innocent observation is linked to a more sweeping claim, to the effect that the emergence of civil democracy depended upon a constellation of values and institutions unique to the West. By implication, it is some-times argued, civil democracy is unlikely to take hold in societies that lack this heritage, unless, that is, the tiger can somehow change its stripes to a Western dress.

Though such culturalist accounts of democracy's possibility have enjoyed a renewed popularity in recent years, their central claim is problematic. Their identification of just what is "Western," first of all, appears highly selective, overlooking the fact that democratic and egali-tarian values are even today not the only ones animating Western cul-ture, and not that long ago were far from secure. Equally seriously, such a culturalist approach overlooks a basic lesson from the sociology of knowledge, namely that ideas originate in the minds of individuals, but their institutionalization in public life depends not only on the bril-liance of their message, but a complex "political economy of mean-ing," whereby some ideas are publicly amplified, while others are suppressed.[27] To understand the conditions of democratic civility's pos-sibility, therefore, requires that we attend to the interaction of culture and social structures that first facilitated just such an ascent. Having done so, we can then ask whether a similar process might be occurring in the non-Western world today.

John Hall's essay in this volume moves to tackle these questions di-rectly. He shows that, in Western Europe, the development of a *culture* of democratic civility depended upon the prior emergence of a variety of civil-societal *structures*. Building on (but also amending) the analyses of Max Weber and Ernest Gellner,[28] Hall observes that a number of things in early Western Europe converged to begin the weaving of a civil social fabric. Western Europe was unusual in that from early on it was charac-terized by a relatively broad dispersion of powers, popular liberties, and legal structures. Underlying all these characteristics is the trait Hall iden-tifies as most important for civil society, "societal self-organization," that is, the ability of people to regulate their affairs without interference from state authorities *or* societal hierarchies.

Following Weber, Hall argues that European society's self-organi-zation was in the first instance facilitated by the absence of any pan-European imperial structure in the aftermath of the Roman Empire. The resulting "pluricentric" political map, as Hall has described it,[29] was in part the product of the ecological fragmentation of the European continent, which made lasting control of Europe's scattered regions difficult. But it was also related to the military and administrative vigor of the local state systems which survived in the aftermath of Rome.

Contrary to the pattern of imperial China, once established, Europe's regional states proved skilled at resisting those who dreamed of restoring imperium.[30]

Western Europe enjoyed other advantages in matters of societal self-organization. Unlike the states of classical Islam, early on Western Christianity institutionalized a separation of ideological and political power, and this separation also helped to decenter power away from the state. The Church *was* deeply involved in public and political matters. Christian norms facilitated trust and collaboration across Western Europe's expanse, and Church representatives provided vital legal services for merchants and lords. However, while Byzantium witnessed numerous Caesaropapist pacts, the Western Church concluded that its interests were better served through a strategic collaboratation with many local states rather than full institutional union with one. The Church's interest in defending its own authority thus worked to limit the power of secular states.

Another precedent for Western European civil society was the fact that by the time that, in the late Middle Ages, kings were willing and able to centralize power, they faced a well-entrenched array of countervailing forces. The Church and feudal lords enjoyed extensive rights to property and influence, and both groups were reluctant to relinquish their privileges. In addition, in a few parts of late medieval Europe, the growth of commerce and towns had created wealthy centers of independent activity. Faced with assertive burghers and a restless peasantry, centralizing kings in Eastern and Central Europe forged an unholy alliance with the feudal aristocracy, preserving the bondage of the manor and destroying the dynamism of towns. In Northwestern Europe, however, rivalries among centralizing rulers led a few kings to conclude that they could best enhance their power by distancing themselves from the landed aristocracy, and allowing merchants and towns a measure of liberty. Inasmuch as they prospered, the towns offered the state new revenues, thereby providing kings with a decisive advantage over their rivals. The "multipolarity" of Europe's state system also allowed merchants unhappy with their treatment to take up residence elsewhere, as happened with France's Huguenots. The resulting formula–enhanced royal power through urban liberties and economic initiative–further strengthened the legal-mindedness of Western European society.

Critics of this historical sociology might well counter that it shows a retrospective selectivity. One might ask, Where in this account do we locate Europe's persecution of the Jews, bloodshed between Protestants and Catholics, colonialism, nineteenth-century class conflict, and the twentieth century's wars of nation and race? Hall has addressed many of these concerns. In this volume, for example, he notes that civil society gained "self-consciousness" in the fight against "politico-religious unification drives" in the aftermath of the Reformation. He also argues eloquently that European civil society effectively collapsed in the late nineteenth century, largely as a result of the unwillingness of ruling elites to feel the winds of change and allow the entry of popular classes into state politics. This failure to integrate these social classes, he argues, also underlay Europe's world wars. Hall therefore sees the violence of the nineteenth and twentieth centuries as a product of elite blunder rather than failure of the European system as a whole, which otherwise enjoyed extensive civil organization and freedoms.

One could suggest a less rosy reading of this same historical evidence, however, and draw from it a different but important lesson. European history shows that the qualities of societal self-organization we associate with civil society did indeed have deep precedents, but well into the twentieth century they were insufficient to stabilize European politics around an enduring and society-wide pattern of participation, freedom, and tolerance. Civil organization there was, but democratic civility there was not.

The multipolar state organization that facilitated urban commerce and the Protestant Reformation also allowed Europe's religious wars to rage unresolved for decades. On this point, Europe compares rather poorly with imperial China, which showed a much better ability to domesticate religious difference.[31] Later this structural vulnerability facilitated the explosive development of colonialism and ethnonationalism, culminating in a war in which one of the world's most affluent societies annihilated a vital segment of the continent's citizenry. In short, it could be argued, Europe's multipolarity and self-organization ensured a measure of liberty for some people, but it also created a highly unstable arena for imperial and national rivalries, with decidedly uncivil consequences at home and abroad. Relative to society and politics as a whole, Western Europe for most of its history achieved an only *segmentary* civility, not a democratic one.

In his chapter on Romania, Dan Chirot provides a poignant illustratation of the broader theoretical point in question here, this time in an Eastern European setting. The issue, again, concerns exactly why structures and associations that look "civil" at a segmentary level do not automatically scale up into a *culture* of democratic civility in state and society as a whole. Chirot explains that, in the 1930s, Romania was emerging briskly from its status as one of Europe's most backward locales. As late as 1937 it held its freest ever parliamentary elections. Labor unions, student groups, literary societies, theater groups, and chambers of commerce also flourished at a level never before seen. There was also substantial industrial progress, and agricultural productivity was on the rise. Benefitting from mass education, even the peasantry was organizing, and perhaps 5 percent of the peasants and artisans in villages and small towns had converted to an independent-minded Protestantism. In short, Romania seemed to be developing the pluricentrism and self-organization Hall associates with civil society.

But this ever-expanding grid of grass-roots association could not create a culture of civility in the political arena as a whole. Romania's activist intellectuals, Chirot points out, were unhappy with this seemingly prosperous state of affairs. Too many of the owners and managers of industry were non-Romanians; too many wealthy were Jews. Like so much of Europe, Romania in the 1930s was feeling the breeze of another "globalizing" current, European anti-Semitism. By 1937, the fascist Iron Guard had gained ground among Romanian workers in Transylvanian cities, where the divide between Romanian workers and non-Romanian bosses was particularly pronounced. Bright young nationalist romantics like Mircea Eliade rallied to the Guardist ideology of racial communalism, antiliberalism, and self-pitying victimization. By contrast, the liberal democratic opposition had no significant social base, as radical nationalists dominated universities, schools, government administration, and the military. In short, Romania showed promising "sprouts of civil society," but the impact of civil associations remained segmentary, incapable of effecting an overarching cohesion. The problem was that political parties mediated the relationship between state and society. And, in the end, they would prove more decisive than churches and business organizations in turning state politics in an uncivil direction.

These and other examples in no way deny John Hall's larger point as to the prevalence of self-organization in European society prior to the modern era. And that self-organization may indeed have developed to a greater degree than in many parts of Asia or Africa. (Though, as my chapter on Indonesia suggests, I believe there were areas of the world with a self-organization rivaling that of early modern Europe, though most were eventually destroyed by the centralizing violence of European colonialism). However, modern Europe's troubled history provides a first and largely cautionery lesson on democratic civility. The dispersion of powers and the counterbalancing of forces associated with civil society are indeed preconditions for democratic civility. Left to themselves, however, they create no more than a segmentary pattern of participation and social freedom. The achievement of broader citizen equality, participation, and tolerance requires at least two other things: the scaling up of civic values into a certain kind of state, and a broadly based political culture. As we shall see, these two influences are not reducible to societal self-organization, but have a political and sociological integrity quite their own.

Civil Society Against the State?

An observer unimpressed by this small library of recent writing on democracy and civil society might rightly ask, Where *did* this idea of civil society come from, and is it really relevant to the political challenges of our day? Such skepticism is well founded. After all, from a historical perspective, the reappearance of the idea of civil society in academic and political circles is a matter of no small irony. Originating in Northwestern Europe in the seventeenth and eighteenth centuries, the phrase had long since ceased to fire the imagination of real-world political actors. Indeed, by the early years of this century it had been relegated to the dusty shelves of Western academia. Or so it seemed until the revolutions of 1989–1991 swept communist parties from power throughout Eastern Europe.[32] In the aftermath of the communist collapse, there arose a new generation of Eastern Europeans, confident of little more than that they wanted prosperity, did not want communism, and believed that both goals might be well served by promoting this curious entity called civil society.

Some critics of Western-style democracy and culture have warned that the promotion of civil society would disseminate a culture of self-centered individualism around the world. But the usages to which civil ideals were put revealed no such consistency of meaning. The concept was assigned widely differing meanings and employed in contradictory political actions.[33] The variation in usage was by no means arbitarary, however; indeed, it offered insights into problems confronting struggles for democratic citizenship in various parts of the world.

In the case of Eastern Europe, it is important to remember that the idea of civil society had in fact been revived well prior to the 1989 revolutions, in the last years of the Cold War. Its earliest promoters included poets, writers, clergy, academics, and labor leaders involved in the struggle against, to borrow John Keane's apt phrase, the "command states" that dominated this region.[34] Among this diverse group only a few professional academics were interested in the bookish genealogy of the civil society idea. What ordinary people found appealing was the phrase's promise of something of which they felt themselves long deprived. Civil society evoked images of freedom to speak and associate without fear. It conjured up images of a public life in which the words and actions of ordinary citizens would be duly acknowledged by the state. It spoke, in short, to a painful absence in Eastern Europeans' lives.

There was a bittersweet irony to Eastern Europeans' embrace of the civil society ideal. Many of the concept's promoters had first encountered the phrase in state-mandated courses on Marxism. Marx *did* have a good deal to say about civil society. The irony lay in the fact that, for him, civil society is the sphere of bourgeois satisfaction, which he portrays as private and, for the most part, rather selfish. The conventional rendering of "civil society" in Marx's German is *burgerliche Gesellschaft*. In eighteenth-century Germany, the phrase drew on the ambiguous referents of the first word's root, *burger*, which blends the meanings of both citizen and bourgeois, political participation and economic self-interest. In invoking civil society, Marx shifted the weight of the *burgerliche* away from its connotations of participatory citizenship toward the latter economistic referent. Thus, in Marx's eyes, the privacy of civil society was above all the privacy of economic self-interest; it represented a freedom for a few premised on exclusion and exploitation of the many. Not surprisingly, in Marx's communist utopia, civil society would be transcended and replaced with a *polis* of universal and undifferentiated citizenship.[35]

It was a symptom of the depth of their disaffection that so many Eastern Europeans resisted official canons and heard civil society as a positive ideal. The ideal struck deftly at the pretensions of the Eastern European regimes. Though, by the end of the communist era, the actual effectiveness of their control varied from country to country, these states retained the right of the party to command society. Theirs was an authority of denials: denial of a legal and political difference between state and civil society; of rights of free association and speech; of economic initiative other than that under party control; and of public values other than those franchised by the state. In the official scheme of things, the whole of social life was, to borrow Charles Taylor's image, "satellized" to the state.[36] By the time of communism's collapse, of course, many regime spokespersons had ceased to believe in the official slogans of the vanguard party and mobilizational state. But the principle of the party-state remained, and could be conveniently deployed against societal forces threatening state domination.

In the face of such a domineering state, it is not surprising that Eastern European activists sometimes articulated their desire for civil society in antistatist and even antipolitical terms.[37] At times they spoke as if what were required for civil decency was not just the dismantlement of the totalitarian state, but an abolition of politics itself. The appeal of such a naively privatist ideal is of course not something unique to Eastern Europe. As Tocqueville first remarked, it has been an intermittent feature of populist imaginings in, among other places, the United States.

Whatever its social logic, the situation that unfolded in postcommunist Eastern Europe indicates just why this antipolitical impulse is, in the end, so antithetical to the decency and freedom enjoined by civil ideals. Throughout Eastern Europe, the unity enjoyed by the dissident community when in opposition gave way in the early postcommunist era to a cacophony of voices. Disputes over state programs pitted secularists against the religious, libertarians against welfare-state social democrats, fiery anticommunists against careful constitutionalists, and, everywhere it seemed, dealmaking insiders against democratic reformers. In a few countries, like the former Yugoslavia, leaders turned ethnonationalist slogans against their rivals, and succeeded in seizing control of the state. Once in power, they used the machinery of state to suppress other claimants to power, destroying the social decency for which people had yearned. Postcommunism proved to be neither as easy nor as civil as many had imagined.[38]

In this there is an important if painful second lesson on civil society and the state. However seductive the temptation to flee the public for the pleasures of the private, modern freedoms are thoroughly dependent upon citizen participation in, and effective guarantees by, a civil state. In this sense, and contrary to some of its sloganeering characterizations, there is no zero-sum opposition between civil society and the state.[39] On the contrary, as Dan Chirot and John Hall both illustrate in their essays, a civil democracy requires a state that is both strong and self-limiting. It must be self-limiting in the sense that it does not monopolize society's powers, drawing all vital personnel, services, and enterprise back into itself. Such a civil state is most likely to develop in the context of countervailing institutions, and a wide dispersion of informal powers, cultural and economic as well as political. However, as illustrated in Chirot's essay, this kind of state is also dependent upon political leadership that demonstrates an effective commitment to the twinned values of citizen participation and civil tolerance.

A civil state must also be strong. It must be strong because society itself is not always civil, and the state provides safeguards of last resort for freedoms of speech, association, and initiative. It is a banal but important truth that, contrary to certain libertarian imaginings, these freedoms are not "free" in the sense that they are the spontaneous outcome of independent human association. Democracy always depends upon something larger than itself. The recent history of Afghanistan and Rwanda shows all too painfully that a weak or crippled state can be an invitation to factionalist butchery rather than untrammeled liberty. Democracy and civility can be menaced as much by uncivil *societal* forces as they can the state.

Indeed, democratic civility is only imaginable within the horizons of an effectively functioning modern state. This is so because, in its modern form, democracy is premised on the civil ideals of universal freedom and citizen equality. To the degree they are at all, these ideals can be realized only on the basis of ongoing collaboration between an engaged citizenry and a state capable of protecting rights across the whole of its territory. As Michael Mann and Anthony Giddens have both demonstrated, premodern states may be capable of explosive bursts of power, but they lack the infrastructure for a uniform, enduring, and, therefore, equitable administration across their expanse.[40] From our modern vantage point, this should not seem surprising. Even in today's strongest civil democracies, the willingness and capacity of the state to guarantee civil security for all citizens is at best partial. As in some of America's violence-plagued cities, some citizens may find themselves deprived of life and liberty, often at the hands of their hateful or criminal neighbors in "civil" society.

In the final days of Eastern European communism, it is not surprising that dissidents might overlook arguments like these on the fragile interdependency of state and civil society. It was all too easy to imagine that freedom could be achieved through a flight from the political into the delights of the private. Indeed, in some countries the concept of civil society lost its appeal early on in the postcommunist era, as the once-united dissident coalition dissolved, citizen engagement declined, and problems of practical government became painfully apparent.[41] As illustrated in Daniel Chirot's essay on Romania, a wave of "ethnic" and "religious" hatred swept across parts of the region, manipulated by rival factions within the political elite.[42] The worst such cases provided a doleful reminder of our second principle of modern civility: that democratic civility requires the legal vigilance and regulatory safeguards of an engaged citizenry *and* a civilized state.

Globalization via Localization

While events in Eastern Europe unfolded with their own logic, the deployment of civil society slogans in the region's prodemocracy movements attracted the attention of activists and intellectuals in other parts of the world. Indeed, with the related notion of democracy, the diffusion of the phrase "civil society" became one of the more dramatic examples of the much celebrated process of cultural "globalization."[43] The usages to which the concept of civil society was put, however, illustrated that cultural globalization is never merely a matter of untransformative diffusion, but a process in which the item transferred is shaped as much by local context and usage as it is its culture of origins. Context and usage are in turn affected by the way in which a cultural item (like the idea of civil society, or democracy, human rights, etc.) is drawn into social and political rivalries. All this again illustrates that cultural globalization is thoroughly dependent upon local articulation.

As Robert Weller explains in his essay, in China the phrase "civil society" caught on despite enormous problems of cultural translation. Weller observes that Confucianism in China left little ideological room for a distinction between state and society, "except in the way that fathers can be distinguished from sons." As late as the nineteenth century, there was still no plausible way to translate civil society into Chinese. Indeed, even today, the term is translated through a variety of "awkward neologisms." It goes without saying that these would make many Western professors of civil theory nervous.

But all is not culturally relative, nor is the popularity of the phrase a simple effect of Western cultural hegemony, as China's leadership might suggest. Illustrating once again that globalization works through complex contextualizations, Weller shows that some of the referents of civil society made the passage quite well from the West, because, one might say, elements of them were already "there" in Chinese social practice, though in an as yet unamplified form.[44] Despite the lack of official precedents for democratic civility, China has long had an array of horizontal ties beyond the family. Though this social precedent had never been elaborated into an explicit ideology of civic associationalism (official or populist), its networks and values existed at the interstices of public life. In Weller's excellent phrase, it was "an undeveloped possibility." Not coincidentally, it was also the sort of thing that activists in Chinese and Taiwanese new social movements could invoke to provide cultural resonance for their democratic appeals. Theirs was an effort to recover, amplify, and redirect what had previously been submerged in the myriad practices of everyday life.

The example provides a general lesson on the cross-cultural prospects for civil-democratic ideas. At first glance, the China example seems to confirm the pessimism of some cultural relativists about the impossibility of meaningful translation across distant cultures. In translating the values of civil society, "awkward neologisms" remain approximations at best, and miniature acts of cultural imperialism at worst. However, under closer inspection, or, perhaps one should say, from a practical rather than culturalist perspective,[45] things do not look nearly so bad. Viewed from the ground of everyday practice rather than the dizzying heights of official canons, the normative diversity of even traditional societies is far greater than most sociological models imply.[46] As in Weller's China, Chirot's Romania, and Hefner's Islamic Indonesia, there are always "undeveloped possibilities"–values and practices that hover closer to the social ground and carry unamplified possibilities. These low-lying precedents may not appear in high-flying discourse. Nonetheless, they are in some sense "available" for engagement and reflection, even if they have long been overlooked in public formulations. Under conditions of cultural globalization or cross-regional transfer, some local actors may seize on exogenous idioms to legitimate and elevate principles of social action (such as equality, participation, etc.) already present in social life, if in an undeveloped, subordinate, or politically bracketed manner.

In commenting on such complex processes, it would be a mistake to say that what is happening here is "Westernization." Occidentalist cheerleaders might want to portray it as such, and speak of a victory for Western values. Native conservatives might see it similarly, and condemn yet another instance of spiritual pollution. But what is really in question in such circumstances is a far more complex interaction between the local and the (relatively) global. For local actors, the global is meaningful because it resonates with something local. Under circumstances of a "global ecumene,"[47] people in different societies can meaningfully aspire to ideals that bear a family resemblance to those we describe as civil democratic. Awkward neologisms may abound but, as Weller's example demonstrates, so too do commonalities of situation and aspiration.[48]

The example of Muslim Indonesians provides us with one more illustration of the complexities at work in such cross- and intracultural dialogue. Unlike some of their Middle Eastern counterparts, Muslims in Indonesia have a long history of intellectual and organizational pluralism. This pluralist precedent originated in part in the fact that Islam was introduced to the region, not by world-conquering potentates, but through a network of trade and city-states that resembled, if anything, the multicentric polities of early modern Europe. This politically dispersive pattern was reinforced rather than diminished in the colonial era. The Dutch policy of a strict separation of Islam and state pushed Muslim institutions away from state and into society, where they helped to create a remarkable Islamic tradition of grass-roots association and civic independence. In this century, movements of Islamic reform have complicated but not done away with this intellectual and organizational pluralism. New social organizations and "Islamic intellectuals" have only added to the pluralist stew.

Despite these precedents for pluralism and association, however, some (happily, a minority here in Indonesia) in the Muslim community remain ambivalent about civil democratic ideals. They insist that their religion enjoins them to look away from their immediate historical experience and back to an imagined golden age, when religion and state were one. They thereby deny the truths of their own practical history, and miss a rich opportunity to scale up its organizations and meanings. The future of Indonesian Islam will be determined in large part by this struggle between two visions of Islamic politics.

In his discussion of the Islamist Welfare Party in contemporary Turkey, Resat Kasaba provides a related illustration of the fragile politics of the amplification process. Turkish Islam, too, has a proud tradition of associational independence with many characteristics we could regard as "civic." As in our earlier European example, however, the Turkish case shows that by itself a tradition of independent association can guarantee little more more than a segmentary civility. Kasaba shows us why this is the case for Turkish Islam. Many of the religious organizations for which Turkey is well known had an internal organization that was restrictive and authoritarian. Some tended to isolate their member-

However, as communist regimes in Eastern Europe teetered toward collapse, and as the full extent of their deformation of democratic ideals became apparent to even the most stalwart apologists of Leninism, writers on the democratic Left began to ask more boldly whether the abuses of state-socialism were not themselves implicit in Marx's ideas on state and civil society. These critics took issue with Marx's obsession with seizure of state power as the key to emancipation, seeing the resulting effort to unite political, economic, and cultural power in one structure as an invitation to tyrannical abuse. They also rejected Marx's essentialization of class as the always-dominant line of exclusion and inequality in society, emphasizing instead that religion, ethnicity, gender, and race can also serve as fault-lines for inequality. Finally, and most relevant for our present discussion, they repudiated Marx's "hatred of civil society, presumed to be identical with capitalist domination," insisting that civil society could be a line of defense not only for elites but for all citizens.[51] Through these and other critiques, a self-consciously "post-Marxist" Left emerged. Uncomfortable with an even residual identification with Marxism, some among these critics dropped the post-Marxist label in favor of a phrase they felt conveyed the positive content of their principles: radical democracy.

The phrase "radical democracy" does indeed express the ambitions and ambiguities of this stream in the contemporary revival of civil democractic theory. Rejecting Marx's critique of civil society, radical democrats insist that the Western Left must develop a new position on liberal democracy. In a preface to an important collection of writings, for example, the French political philosopher Chantal Mouffe takes many of her colleagues on the Left to task for denouncing liberal ideals and for romanticizing revolution. "If the Left is to learn from the tragic experiences of totalitarianism it has to adopt a different attitude toward liberal democracy, and recognize its strengths as well as reveal its shortcomings.... [T]he objective of the Left should be the extension and deepening of the democratic revolution initiated two hundred years ago."[52]

As illustrated by this quotation's reference to Enlightenment-era revolutions, Mouffe and her colleagues distance themselves from the antinormative postures fashionable among some postmodernist writers.[53] Some among the latter, she observes, see the heterogeneity of culture as so exhaustive as to render judgments as to the merits of one set of political values over another impossible. The ethical grounds for criticizing even as odious a figure as Adolf Hitler thus become unclear:

"Such an extreme form of pluralism, according to which all interests, all opinions, all differences are seen as legitimate, could never provide the framework for a political regime. For the recognition of plurality not to lead to a complete *indifferentiation* and *indifference*, criteria must exist to decide between what is admissible and what is not."[54] In another widely cited essay, Erik Olin Wright has made a related point, arguing that the "postmodernist rejection of 'grand narratives'" and "emancipatory values" encourages a cynical corrosion of democratic and egalitarian ideals.[55]

One need only add that the general insight here is relevant for a broader range of democratic thinkers than radical democrats alone. At the heart of all civil democratic visions lies the idea that, even as we legitimate pluralism, in practice not everything can be relativized. Though, as John Hall and Adam Seligman both imply in their essays, democratic civility enjoins a mild relativism on some values, it retains an unambiguous commitment to others, including the values of freedom, equality, and tolerance-in-difference. The nonrelativist commitment worries some anthropologists and non-Western intellectuals, who are rightly concerned that democracy and civil society may be premised on a narrowly individualistic ethical base.[56] However, as the case studies in this volume illustrate, it would be a serious mistake to take liberal philosophy as the best guide to the values of civil-democratic practice. Even in the the United States over the past century, civil democrats have struck different balances between individual and group rights, and among the triplicate values of equality, freedom, and tolerance. Just how much this variation "relativizes" democratic values is a problem to which I return below.

The difficulties involved in achieving a practical as opposed to philosophical balance among civil democracy's values is aptly illustrated by radical democracy itself. What makes the radical democrats' position "radical" is that they seek to extend the liberty and equality associated with citizenship beyond their usual range of application in liberal democracies. Freedom and equality are to be promoted in a full range of social spheres, not just in the formal domain of, say, electoral politics. In keeping with this activist understanding of citizenship, radical democracy places great emphasis on the creative role of "new social movements" in democratic life. These include the women's movement, gay and lesbian rights, environmentalism, multiculturalism, and movements for other groupings regarded as heretofore excluded from mainstream politics and society. Though it is sometimes argued that radical democrats invoke new social movements as functional equivalents of Marxism's proletariat, there is an important difference. For radical democrats, the demands of these movements represent not irrecuperable contradictions in the political system, but shortcomings that may be reformable through a deepening of the democratic commitment to equality and justice. Rejecting Rousseauian utopianism, radical democrats work within the political system to open it to more inclusive participation.

Conservative- and left-liberals often react to radical democratic projects with unease, fearing that the highlighting of group identities through which radical democrats promote greater inclusion may, despite itself, be corrosive of the values of individual dignity and group equality. This unease illustrates a larger tension, one endemic to all versions of civil democracy. The principles of liberty, equality, and tolerance in plurality are highly general, to say the least. As first principles, they come with no instructions as to how they might be balanced in the endless assortment of policies and programs a citizenry must devise. This would not be a problem, of course, if the principles always worked in synergistic harmony, the promotion of one necessarily enhancing the others. However, the past century of debate over liberal democracy shows clearly that these first principles come with no such compatibility guarantee. Principles of private property may promote a broad dispersion of individual liberties under some circumstances, but be corrosive of freedom and equality under others. Affirmative actions to promote the collective well-being of one disenfranchised group may run up against principled objections that individual opportunity must take priority over concerns for collective equality.[57] Similarly, demands for gender and sexual equality may excite opposition among minorities who insist that efforts to promote sexual rights within their temples and mosques violate the minority subculture's rights to equal protection and self-determination.

These are not just minor blemishes in the radical version of liberal democracy, but tensions endemic to the the democratic tradition as a whole. In radicalizing democracy, radical democrats only make this general tension more apparent. Not surprisingly perhaps, radical democrats are not always quick to point out this tension in their program. Indeed, when citing pluralism as a primary value, seeking its extension to "the widest possible set of social relations,"[58] some radical democrats seem unaware of just how quickly the radicalization of pluralism can relativize other civic values, such as liberty and equality. Not all people protected by pluralism clauses will agree that liberty and equality should also be maximized. Similarly, radicalization of popular political participation is itself no guarantee that the resulting political order will be civil or free, as the treatment of minorities in modern democracies has repeatedly illustrated. Freedom, equality, and plurality come with no guarantee of triplicate compatibility.

Problems of this sort have been at the heart of debates over affirmative action for scheduled castes in India, over the rights of Muslims to educate their children apart from mainstream in Britain and France, and over abortion and sexual freedom in the United States. In the face of this unnerving complexity, one might be tempted to limit one's defense of pluralism to aggrieved minorities regarded as "good" pluralists–which is usually to say the kind that agree with one's own politics. Thus, in supporting equality and inclusiveness, radical democrats readily cite new social movements committed to the defense of gays, women, and progressively inclined ethnic minorities. Typically absent from the list are Christian evangelicals, orthodox Jews, and conservative Muslims. Yet representatives of these last groups could make a credible argument that they too have been unfairly marginalized from the political mainstream.

In short, the fact that civil democracy does not inalterably specify the relative balance among its principles is a source of chronic tension in civil democracies. But it is this very quality that underscores the importance of our fourth lesson on democratic civility. For it is precisely at this point, at what seems to be the most vexing of impasses in democratic practice, that a commitment to democratic civility becomes most important. Civil theory may not offer a final definition of the good, or a definitive resolution of the proper balance among its first principles. Yet it is this inability to absolutize that makes all the more imperative the establishment of a sphere of uncoerced association, speech, and exchange in which different ideas of the good can be debated and tried. As Michael Walzer has put it, civil society can serve as this "setting of settings" in which people are free to experiment, associate, and debate.[59] From there, the results of such experiments may be communicated to other citizens, and, in at least some cases, to the policies of the state.

However, not all the fruits of civic participation can or should be conveyed upward to the institutions of the state. Just as there is a fragile mutuality of state and civil society, there must also be a buffer. However nostalgic some might feel for the imagined conviviality of the

Greek *polis* or early America, the first fact of modern life is its vast scale and dizzying plurality. On this, our modern social differentiation, there is no going back. This is not to deny that there may be wisdom in restoring a different balance between domestic privacy and citizen participation, as radical democrats, communitarians, and not a few republican conservatives have argued. But efforts to effect a new balance cannot abolish the space between government and civic association, for it is on just this space that the dynamism of modern society, and our practical freedom, depend.

If the vigor of the Greek *polis* must elude our politics, it need not be lost in our civic life. Churches, women's groups, political clubs, environmental organizations, sports leagues, union halls, and ordinary friendships may afford us just such intimacy and empowerment. As modern citizens, Michael Walzer reminds us, our emotional life is mostly "lived in private—which is not to say in solitude, but in groups considerably smaller than the community of all citizens." [60] A similar argument was made more than twenty years ago in an essay that confounded the nostrums of Left and Right. Peter L. Berger and Richard Neuhaus argued that modern government and business are destined to remain impersonal and vast, but the associational networks of civil society afford opportunities for meaningful self-expression, and "people-sized institutions."[61]

None of this provides a definitive resolution of civil-democracy's axiological conundrum. But it is that impossibility that gives special urgency to our twin freedoms of public debate and civil privacy. The enduring tension between these two freedoms is inevitable in our world, and is another reason some among us feel democratic civility must be defended.

Democracy's Embedding: Civic Thick or Procedural Thin?

That civil democracy requires culture and organization to be realized in actual life is a premise that strikes most sociologists and anthropologists as so patently obvious as to be trivial. For scholars in these disciplines, it is a commonplace of analysis that all societies require some minimal consensus to smooth social interaction. In recent years anthropologists, sociologists, and other researchers have recognized that culture is far more unbounded, heterogenous, and uncentered than once thought, and subject to force and contestation. While these insights have complicated our understanding of culture, they have done little to diminish the analytic confidence that, like fish in water, every politics, including civil democracy, requires a culture.

Though sociologists and anthropologists share this conviction, the fact remains that characterizing the culture and organization conducive to civic democracy has proved difficult. In part this reflects the fact that, given the division of academic labor, the recent revival of interest in civil society and democracy began in the field of political philosophy. There is nothing wrong with this, but, as noted above, it has meant that much writing on civil democracy has been less concerned with sociological realism than it has debating the relative grounds for one imagined liberalism as opposed to another.

Recently, however, some political theorists have taken their colleagues to task for this putatively irrealist bias. One sustained example of just such a critique is the debate between so-called communitarians and liberals. (The contrast is somewhat misnamed because, in the larger scheme of things, most communitarians are philsophical liberals, though of a republican or "civic-virtue" sort).[62] Communitarians' arguments are varied, but in general they agree in faulting mainstream liberals for identifying the grounds for civil politics in such culturally anorexic terms as to imperil democracy's health. Thus communitarians claim that liberal theory' s emphasis on individual rights, to the exclusion of social "goods," leads liberals to tolerate developments in our laws, marketplace, and morals which over the long run corrode the virtues on which a decent and participatory government depend. Though this critique is by no means peculiar to them,[63] communitarians oppose what they see as this trend toward ethical laissez faire. For them, the idea of civil society is a clarion call for heightened citizen education and participation. At a more theoretical level, communitarianism also takes issue with the idea that all variants of civil democracy are equally individualistic, suggesting instead that extreme variants of philosophical individualism misrepresent the variety of normative traditions informing the practice of Western democracy.[64]

One of the earliest and best-known examples of this critique was Alasdair MacIntyre's *After Virtue*. In this book, MacIntyre attacks mainstream liberalism for having forgotten the wisdom of the ancients, namely that good politics and a good life depend on people's socialization into a "tradition of the virtues." An effectively republican tradition, MacIntyre explains, must be embodied in stories, rituals, religions, and practices into which individuals are drafted (so to speak), and through which they learn the habits of civic virtue. Indeed, MacIntyre adds, a good life and good politics are operable *only* inasmuch as such a deep and enduring ethical consensus is fostered. The fact that, with their individualist biases, mainstream liberals today slight such ethical tuition, MacIntyre warns, dooms us to a coming age of "barbarism and darkness."[65]

Like many professional philosophers, MacIntyre bases the bulk of his argument, not on a detailed excursion into the words and actions of everyday life, but on readings of contemporary political philosophy. This makes him vulnerable to the charge that he has confused liberal political theory, which does tend to be individualistic, with liberal political practice, which need not always be. In a subtly argued critique, Bernard Yack has taken issue with MacIntyre on just this point. Had MacIntyre taken time to look at real-and-existing liberal societies, Yack asserts, he would have realized that they are replete with stories, traditions, and mythologies through which liberal ideas become embodied in a community's social imagination. In effect, Yack claims, MacIntyre has unwittingly replicated his discipline's bias, taking liberal theorists too much at their word:

> [I]f man is, as MacIntyre insists, 'in his actions and practice as well as his fiction, a story-telling being,' then we should expect men and women to turn theories, even liberal theories which insist on impersonal and antitraditional criteria, into the basis for new stories. This is precisely what has happend. The French turned liberty from tradition into a female figure, symbolic of the Republic's virtues and energy. American colonists turned Lockean liberal principles into didactic stories with which to educate their children.... According to MacIntyre's own conception of human behavior, we must assume that it is only to the extent that liberal theories have generated stories that they have shaped our character and practices. The Enlightenment attack on tradition could never have succeeded without itself "becoming tradition."[66]

Whatever MacIntyre's intent, it is hard to deny the logic of Yack's critique. MacIntyre and some other communitarians read too quickly from liberal philosophy to liberal practice, assuming a continuity that need not exist. However, having said this, it is clear that Yack's argument does not deflect those critiques that assert that recent trends in Western societies are undermining the values and associations on which a civil democracy depends. MacIntyre may have stretched himself thin in generalizing from liberal philosophy to practice. Having uncovered this logical shortcoming, however, Yack cannot turn around and conclude that democracy is necessarily in good health. This latter claim is an empirical issue, not merely logical, and its justification demands a good deal more than anecdotal evidence on the encultured nature of liberal values.

Indeed, this is precisely the point at which another scholar identified (too simplistically) with the communitarian viewpoint has entered the fray. In his, *Democracy and Discontent*, Michael Sandel returns to the argument of his earlier writings, to the effect that today's liberal theory (unlike its incarnation in the time of, say, Thomas Jefferson) is premised on the idea of the "unencumbered self." Sandel's characterization of liberal actors as "unencumbered" is based on the MacIntyre-like assertion that liberal theory assumes that individuals formulate their interests and values in isolation, and, as a result, concludes that we need not concern ourselves with creating social environments that foster democratic virtues. Such a view is not only sociologically implausible, Sandel argues, but, inasmuch as it becomes the basis for legal-political policy, dangerous. Among other things, it leads to a formalistic emphasis on right procedure rather than the fostering of the good, leaving the public sphere prey to less high-minded actors in the media and marketplace. Sandel characterizes the resulting ethically empty politics as a "procedural republic." [67]

Having revisited this earlier analytic claim, Sandel's new book takes us through an intriguing array of examples from contemporary America's courts, marketplace, and political life to show that, time and time again, policies have been formulated on the basis of an ethically "thin" proceduralism corrosive of civil decencies. Critics might counter that no more than a proceduralist emphasis is possible in a society as pluralistic as today's America. Whether this is convincing or not, the argument that communitarian arguments conflate liberal philosophy with practice cannot be applied to Sandel's weighty analysis. Yack's elegant defense aside, the jury remains out on whether liberal practices in places like America do, indeed, live up to civil-democratic ideals.

Arguments of this sort often strike philosophical teetotalers in sociology and anthropology as of little relevance to their concerns. However, from a sociological and cross-cultural perspective, the debate offers insights that get right to the heart of just why philosophical genealogies of democratic ideas are not versatile enough to allow us to assess democracy's cross-cultural possibilities. The lesson is that, having inspired researchers to go out and examine the actual practice of Western politics, the liberal-communitarian debate has inadvertently produced a small mountain of evidence showing that people in Western democracies engage politics on the basis of values, motives, and attachments more varied than the elegant models of liberal philosophy. Thus though Yack is right to say that the French popularized liberal ideals by turning Liberty into a handsome female form, what his account leaves out is the fact that, once socially embedded in this way, democratic institutions come to depend upon associations and values more varied than those of philosophical individualism alone. This complicates rather seriously our question of just how much cultural and associational variation is compatible with a civil-democracy.

This general concern runs through all the essays in this volume, but is especially central to four. In her chapter on the family and civil society, Brigette Berger argues that that there has been a macro-institutional bias to liberal and democratic theory, focusing on markets and public politics to the neglect of the intimate sociabilities of the family. Berger argues that the family has always been involved in the nurturing of sensibilities on which our ideals of individual dignity and civic responsibility depend. The family, she writes, is the "launching pad into the public world"; as a result, the destabilization of its structures has serious implications for society as a whole. Berger is careful to point out that the kind of family she has in mind is not peculiarly Western. However her argument raises complex historical and cross-cultural issues, which can only be resolved if social and political theorists realize that they too have a stake in efforts to revive the much-neglected field of comparative family studies.[68]

The author of one of the decade's most influential books on the idea of civil society,[69] Adam Seligman turns in his chapter to this same issue of the values and organizations compatible with civility and democracy. For Seligman, the central issue in the idea of civil socity is the "proper mode of normatively constituting the existence of society–whether in terms of private individuals or in the existence of a shared public sphere." Voicing concerns similar to communitarians (though pessimistic about communitarian projects), Seligman argues that there is a tendency in contemporary Western society to blur the border between the public and private. By itself, a critic of Seligman might argue, there is nothing wrong in this; indeed, the "publicization" of the personal can serve deeply just causes. In earlier times, for example, the treatment of slaves, the physical abuse of wives, and a host of other injustices were defended on the grounds that these were purely "private" concerns. They were opened to critique only inasmuch as their private status was challenged.[70]

However, when Seligman speaks of the blurring of the private and the public, he has a different dynamic than this in mind. For him, one of the greatest threats to civil democracy is that the assertion of formal equality in the political sphere will undermine our ability to share a public sociability. It is as if the constant drone of individualistic equality makes us deaf to the music of the public sphere. Yet–and here Seligman seems close to MacIntyrian themes–private virtues cannot be sustained without public nurture. The scale of this ethical conundrum leaves Seligman pessimistic about the prospect of a civil societal revival. The projection of the private into the public, and the resulting devaluation of the public sphere, Seligman argues, is related to the very structures of modernity, including the pluralization of life worlds and the complexity of modern social roles. As in his earlier book, Seligman is deeply troubled by our plight, but confident only that we seem fated to growing ethical confusion.

Focusing on religion and civil ethics in America, Robert Wuthnow raises much the same concern, but comes to a more optimistic conclusion. Like Seligman, he is concerned that what he calls an exaggerated "inner pluralism" weakens our ability to make sound ethical judgments. However Wuthnow posits a different dynamic to the problem than that Seligman describes. He sees our ethical problems as originating, not in the projection of the private into public life, but in our participation in radically divergent social communities. Their pluralism is so great that at times it seems we are in danger of losing our moral balance.

Wuthnow illustrates the tensions he has in mind through a person he encountered in his ongoing research on American religion and society, a twenty-six-year-old disabilities counselor who describes herself as a "Methodost Taoist Native American Quaker Russian Orthodox Buddhist Jew." Without knowing more about her, Wuthnow writes, we might be tempted to doubt that this woman can be trusted to comport herself in a coherent and civic manner. The counselor's inner pluralism contrasts dramatically with the unitary moral self on which most liberal theory is premised; yet, Wuthnow argues, she embodies an only modestly exaggerated version of a cognitive pluralism widespread among us. She is also representative of more general postmodern trends in contemporary American religion that include denominational switching, institutionalized eclecticism, and syncretism. However, unlike Seligman's prototypical egoist (who resembles, if anything, Robert Bellah's Sheila from *Habits of the Heart*),[71] Wuthnow's counselor does not suffer from isolation or excessive self-preoccupation. Indeed, Wuthnow sees sunlight through the clouds, suggesting that this inner pluralism may yet nurture civic values. The key, Wuthnow insists, is not whether we settle comfortably in a homogeneous community or embrace a single grand narrative, but simply whether our social lives draw us into public engagements that encourage us to think long and hard about common problems. Though he stops short of a definitive conclusion, Wuthnow clearly implies that we are not as lacking in moral compass as many social critics imply.

The fourth of the essays on democracy's compatibilities, the chapter by Anton Zijderveld, draws us forcefully back into comparative concerns. Zijderveld illustrates brilliantly just how remote most philosophical characterizations of liberal politics have been from real-and-existing democracies. Philosophical readers may be surprised to learn that until recently the Netherlands—an origin-point for many Western ideas on republican freedom and economic liberalism[72]—had a political system organized around state-supported social "pillars." This arrangement lay at the heart of Dutch democracy, and was premised on a more "socialized" concept of personhood than acknowledged in philosphical liberalism. The pillars were vertical social structures based on the Netherlands' four major religious groupings: Roman Catholics, Orthodox Protestants, Liberal Protestants, and secular humanists. Recently, efforts have been made (not least of all by Zijderveld himself) to get the state to recognize a fifth pillar for the Netherlands' small Muslim community. As Zijderveld points out, the pillars are social and not ecclesiastical organizations, each of which is headed by a nonclerical administrative board. Originating in the last century's struggles among Dutch religious communities, today the pillars administer funds provided by the state for religious education and other social services.

At its origins the pillar arrangement was socially emancipatory and democratic—at least inasmuch as it provided the Roman Catholic and Orthodox minorities with protections from the majoritarian tyranny of liberal Protestants. In actual operation, however, the structure was controlled by pillar leaders in a way that was, as Zijderveld puts it, "rather authoritarian and elitist," even though it allowed a "remarkable social and political pacification." Moreover, the impact of the pillars was not confined to churches and religious schooling. Zijderveld observes that "even the labor market" was informally organized around these social pillars. In short, democratic civility was facilitated by arrangements at the national level that were vertical, collectivistic, and, it seems, not all that "liberal."

The combination of the de-churching of Dutch society, which began in the 1960s, and baby boom anti-authoritarianism has recently made the pillars less popular and brought about a "concomitant rise of a typically modern individualization." These and other developments were related to the growth of the Dutch welfare state, about which Zijderveld has much to say. From our comparative perspective, however, what is so fascinating about the Dutch example is that civil values were fostered here in a highly contextualized manner, defined in terms of a complex and changing balance of social attachments and power.

Is there a larger lesson in this example? In one sense, the Dutch case illustrates our earlier (lesson three) observation that the practice of civil democracy is premised on a congeries of values, the precise balance of which is never indefinitely secured. The pillarized structure of Dutch sociopolity promoted certain civil values (civic peace, religious tolerance, and the formal equality of religions) by quietly looking the other way on others (political participation and equality between elites and masses). But there is a larger and more original lesson in this example. To borrow terms from Adam Seligman's discussion, we can say that the civic ideals of equality, freedom, and tolerance are of a highly generalized and abstract nature. Despite their abstract nature, however, the realization of these ideals for ordinary citizens is neither formal nor abstract, but grounded on local values and relationships. Indeed, civic ideals are nowhere realized through their magic wand absolutization to all social spheres. If the latter were possible, civil democracies would show none of the variation that they do in their relative balance of freedoms, responsibilities, and group versus individual rights. The unimaginable might become possible: Americans and British would agree on gun-control policies. As the Netherlands example illustrates so well, however, democratic societies differ greatly in the balances they strike and the values they embed. The precise balance depends not on an invariant set of political principles, but on compromises negotiated by representative elites during critical moments of institution-building. Here is an insight that should reassure cross-cultural researchers worried that civil democracy is compatible with only one set of social values, those of a hyperindividualistic liberalism.

Hence we arrive at a fifth and final lesson: that democratic civility depends upon cultural and institutional embedding, the precise structure of which varies from society to society. This variation is inevitable because democratization is not merely a matter of philosophical principles, but of negotiating and structuring worlds. Philosophical absolutists might see this as a fatal flaw in real-and-existing democracy, wondering how civil democracy can flourish if freedom, equality, and tolerance are not maximized in all societies and all social spheres at all times. Inasmuch as situational compromises may allow the denial of civil rights to some people, this *can be* a serious problem. The failure of America's founders to resolve the question of slavery during the Constitutional Convention was one such weighty event, and, as Chirot points out, this small inconsistency in practice allowed for a radical deformation of rights for America's not-quite-citizens, its African-Americans.

Granted, we might say, real-and-existing democracies are never as simple as philosophers' models. But clearly this cannot mean that every ideology and social organization is equally compatible with democratic civility. What range of social "embeddings" and ethical "encumberments" is compatible with civil democracy? The reigning wisdom in policy circles on this matter seems fairly clear: laterally organized civic associations are more conducive to democratic values than are vertically organized networks. In a pioneering study of civic traditions in modern Italy, Robert D. Putnam emphasizes that civic organizations helped democracy grow in the north of the country by fostering norms of reciprocity, improving information flow, reducing opportunism, and, in general, heightening people's trust in each other and political institutions. For Putnam, then, "networks of civic engagement" are a "social capital" vital to the effective functioning of civil democracy and markets. By contrast, Putnam observes, vertical networks of patron-clientage may be capable of providing goods and services, but they do so in a way that discourages trust between superiors and inferiors ("the subordinate husbands information as a hedge against exploitation") while encouraging destabilizing rivalries among patronage cliques.

These are important insights, and resonate strongly with the Tocquevillian tradition in democratic studies. However, at the risk of impiety in the face of an original study, the evidence of the studies in this book suggests a more complex conclusion than Putnam's. First, and most basic, not all laterally organized organization are necessarily democracy enhancing. Quite simply, there are civil and uncivil "civil" associations. Organizations like the Klu Klus Klan and extremist militias in the United States may well have the characteristics of rank-and-file participation associated with civil organizations, but still be intolerant and dangerous.

What these uncivic associations illustrate is that our models have too simplistically assumed that the decisive determinant of an organization's ethico-political influence is its internal structure—horizontal or vertical, participatory or elitist. Thus, we hear "the more horizontally structured an organization, the more it should foster institutional success in the broader community," conversely, "Membership rates in hierarchically ordered organizations...should be negatively associated with good government."[73] Horizontal groupings are democracy-good, it seems, vertical ones democracy-bad. However, as the Oklahoma bombers (who, reports say, did *not* "bowl alone"), extremist cults, and other horizontalist nasties remind us, lateralism does not guarantee civility. Associational culture and leadership matter once more.

If horizonalism is not all good, verticalism is not all bad. As in the Netherlands, some vertical structures may not only coexist with civic organizations, but, by preserving the peace or building bridges over troubled waters, actually help to strengthen civility and democracy. The key to determining just when and where verticalism is good is the values and procedures through which it operates, especially those that regulate interaction between lower- and higher-level actors. Putnam and others quite rightly remind us that patron-clientage is corrosive of civility and trust. But not all vertical structures are of a clientalist sort. Some can strengthen democracy if they operate in transparent and procedurally responsive fashions. This is to say that it is the culture and context of verticality that is decisive, not its mere form.

The same is true in a different way for horizontal organizations. Some small-scale organizations, even "horizontal" ones, seem to be ideal mediums for the virus of intolerance. The influence of horizontal associations may be more democratic, however, where their organization is premised on open and rights-regarding principles. Where associations overlap in complex or countervailing manners—so that the members sitting side by side on one occasion find themselves looking at each other from across an organizational divide on another—the moderating influence of membership may be all the greater. The logic of such a situation is simple: When your colleagues in one enterprise are your rivals in another, you have a strong incentive not to demonize members of the second association, because such acts will have an unpleasant effect on your relationship. Inasmuch as civic associations have countervailing memberships *and* democratic principles and procedures, they may contribute significantly to a culture of democratic civility. As Jose Casanova shows in his chapter, it is just such an cross-cutting weave of social memberships that is defusing ethnic tensions in the contemporary Ukraine.

Zijderveld and Chirot's studies also illustrate a related point: that an exclusive focus on local-level associations overlooks the crucial influence of higher-level structures and leadership on democratic processes. Chirot's essay stresses the importance of the international environment in which civil and political struggles unfold, noting (with Hall) that the collapse of communism in Eastern Europe was more critically influenced by elite struggles in Moscow than it was local civil society. Political elites exercise a decisive influence on civil society, but their role is especially critical during times of regime transition, when the terms are being set for future political games.[74]

There is a final paragraph to this fifth lesson on democratic civility. It is that the realization of civil-democratic values is, by its very nature, ever unfinished. This is so not merely because the ideals of civil democracy are unevenly applied and at times in tension. That is part of it. But the indeterminacy also reflects the fact that societies change, so that the balance of forces that underlay one civil compromise (such as the pillar system in the Netherlands) shifts and people perceive old arrangements in a new and unfavorable light. Thus, the pillar system is no longer popular among Dutch youth because it is seen as authoritarian rather than protective of their religious rights (in which they have lost interest). Or, similarly, Western gender prototypes once seen as immutable have been found wanting by some in light of contemporary egalitarian ideals.[75] The controversies that result from such critical reexamination can tear a society apart. However, with the right dose of democratic civility, the instability can also be a source of strength, demonstrating civil democracy's ability to accommodate new interests, new personnel, and new ideas of the good.

Conclusion: From Civil Society to Democratic Civility

For those who had placed their hopes in civil society as the key to democracy and civility, the recognition that it cannot quite guarantee either may sound like a counsel of despair. Faced with authoritarian regimes or the loss of democracy's vitality, well-meaning people in many parts of the world pinned their hopes for decent politics on this appealing little idea. Civil society seemed to offer a kinder and gentler road to democratic renewal. The road passed through friendships, women's groups, houses of worship, press freedoms, business associations, and legal aid rather than violent and uncertain struggles for state power. If this is no longer enough, what is to be done?

A less pessimistic perspective on this point would return to our earlier observation that democratic civilities depend in the long run upon a virtuous circle of culture and organization. This is a familiar point in the literature on democracy and civil society, one aptly summarized, for example, in Robert Putnam's assertion that in assessing democracy's supports there can be no priority of "structure" over "culture." We err even in framing the question in such a bipolar way, Putnam quite rightly observes, because civic "attitudes and practices constitute a mutually reinforcing equilibrium."[76]

This is an important point, but the five lessons provided by the studies in this book reveal its underlying complexity. Seeking to improve on philosphers' singular emphasis of ethical individualism, recent sociological writing has asserted that it is not ethical individualism per se, but horizontal structures of participation and exchange that best guarantee civility with democracy. This associationist explanation improves on the philosophical account by reminding us that democratic culture depends not only on abstract ideas but on values sustained in a certain way of life. Another benefit of the sociological view is that it acknowledges a more complex balance of civic and individual goods than emphasized in the often Hobbesian world of philosophical liberalism.

Nonetheless, on the evidence of the studies in this book, this associationalist model still risks a simplifying flight of sociological imagination. Civil association is necessary but never sufficient to guarantee a civil-democratic politics. Equally important is that this self-organization be part of a broader pattern of political pluricentrism, in which no single social class or organization asserts monopoly control over the social, political, and moral resources of society. Only in such pluricentric polities, our second lesson on democratic civility showed, is the state likely to display that delicate balance of strength and self-limitation that allows it to work with rather than against civil participation. Finally—and perhaps most overlooked in contemporary accounts of civil democracy—for this balance of state and society to endure, its norms must be elevated into a constitutional charter that enshrines equality, participation, and tolerance as principles of law, in a manner that protects them from political vicissitudes and socializes them among the public at large. Without this larger "mutually reinforcing equilibrium," civil association may do no more than create a segmentary civility, in which only a few are granted the dignity of a free public life.

Though some have argued that such a constellation of culture and institutions can only be achieved in the West, the third lesson from this book suggested that the contrast between the West and the rest is too monolithic. Though, historically, Westerners were among the first to enunciate modern variants of civil-democratic ideals, from the outset the principles were understood in varied ways. The West looks less monolithic—and less uniformly individualistic—from the diverse perspectives of the Netherlands' pillars, nineteenth and twentieth century movements for voting rights, American struggles over race, or, most unhappily, the modern destruction of European Jewry. Conversely, in non-Western settings, civil democratic ideals have appeal not because Taiwanese and Muslim democrats want to imitate the West, but because the ideals are versatile enough to respond to local needs.

In its most general form, that to which democratic civility responds is the simple desire for participation and self-determination. This desire is neither unique to our age nor universal. However, social change has become so pervasive in our era that people in many places have been drawn to variants of civil ideals to provide an ethical compass amidst the ongoing flux. No single "determinant in the last instance" can explain the breadth of this diffusion. On the contrary, all evidence suggests the appeal of dignity and participation arises through varied circumstances and combinations: as settled villages give way to mobile urbanizations; as kinship collectivities become optative ties of family; as mothers become "working" mothers; as economies of command become competitive; as public voices become multiple. Plural in its organizations and meanings, there is no single modernity; nor is there but one form of civility-in-democracy. However, the restructuration of life worlds characteristic of our era is so massive and aspirations for dignity and participation so widespread that, more than any time in human history, large numbers of people find themselves drawn to these ideals we call civil democratic. In actual usage, of course, the precise social referent of such ideals varies. So too does the balance societies strike between public and private goods, and individual and collective rights. But this only shows that it is contextual and hybridizing processes, not imitation or untrammeled diffusion from afar, that is the real key to our much misrecognized notion of democracy's "globalization."

It is for reasons of this sort, after all, that American-style denominationalism is taking hold in, of all places, the Ukraine (chapter 8), whereas it did not take hold anywhere in Western Europe. It is not that, by some bizarre genealogy, the Ukraine has an ancient affinity with the culture of the United States that France and England do not. It does not. What is pushing the Ukraine toward a pattern of religiosity like that of the U.S. is the fact that the balance of religious groupings "on the ground" has created an impasse and opportunity. No single religious body can impose its will on the whole. The structure of this impasse, Casanova tells us, bears a striking resemblance to circumstances obtaining in the U.S. at the time of the nation's founding. And the compromise toward which Ukrainians seem to be stumbling does as well. The convergence here is product neither of ancient association nor American hegemony, but of a creative resolution of historically convergent problems.

Indeed, our last two lessons on democratic civility suggest that a not dissimilar process of adjustment and localization has always taken place in Western societies themselves. The principles of civility and democracy are highly generalized, and their synchronization in political practice never finished. As affirmative action debates in the United States show, much of democracy's creative dynamic centers on just this tension, as to which balance of freedom, equality, and tolerance in difference is most fitting for the age. The outcome of such debates is determined not by the eternal flame of unchanging ideas, but by recontextualized understandings of general truths, and an ever-changing balance of societal forces committed to their meanings.

Rather than a counsel of despair, the complexity of the influences sustaining democratic civility should encourage a realistic if guarded optimism. For those thirsting for democratic decencies, the real message of despair is that democracy's fate was sealed hundreds of years ago, as some recent studies of civic traditions have argued. Fortunately, the evidence of the studies in this book suggests a less paleopolitical conclusion. It is not the ancient beat of associational drums that determines democracy's rhythms, nor some inimitable archaeology of philosophical ideas, but a thoroughly contemporary circle of organizations and values. In practical terms, this means that democracy and civility can be advanced through strategic interventions at any number of points in the democratic circle—by building civil associations, supporting countervailing institutions, diffusing wealth and decentralizing economic initiative, strengthening the judiciary, defending a free press, and, always, fostering political leadership committed to these very goals. Even in the smoothest-running systems, democracy is not all or nothing, but eclectically incremental.

The situationalist argument I am making here should not be misunderstood. Cultural and organizational precedents matter, and matter deeply. Enormous efforts may be made to insure that new ideas conform to civilizational precedents, especially where, as with Islam and other world religions, the precedent is identified as divine. While acknowledging this truth, however, we must politely disagree with those who portray politics as so thoroughly dependent on ancient huddles and instincts as to deny the reality of many modern peoples' aspirations. In our global ecumene, all societies face problems of civility in plurality; and all have at least some citizens who believe that ideals of equality, participation, and tolerance may aid their resolution. Where societies stumble, the evidence suggests it is not because of primordial urges, but present-day imbalances in democracy's circle.

The evidence of these studies leads me to a final, normative observation, one with which I am not sure all my fellow contributors would agree. It is that we supporters of civil and democratic principles must show greater confidence in their practical relevance. That confidence has nothing to do with the alleged occidental origins of democratic ideals, a mythic charter that, I have suggested, only clouds the issue by telling non-Westerners that their own experience is not what is most deeply relevant to democracy's possibility. Rather than selective genealogies, our democratic confidence should be based on the conviction that, in the end, the appeal of freedom, equality, and tolerance-in-plurality is not narrowly circumscribed, as argued by prophets of the new civilizational relativism. The ideals respond to circumstances and desires widespread in our world.

This is not to say that the outcomes of today's struggles are guaranteed. Ours will remain an age of democratic trial, and, for better or for worse, the verdict of history will vary. But of this we should feel certain: that aspirations for dignity and civility are not civilizationally circumscribed, but will remain a powerful force in world culture and politics for years to come.

Notes

1. Francis Fukyuama, "The End of History?" In *The National Interest* (Summer 1989), p. 4. See also his more nuanced, *The End of History and the Last Man* (New York: The Free Press, 1992).
2. Samuel P. Huntington, "The Clash of Civilizations?" *Foreign Affairs* 72:3 (1993): 22–49. Huntington has expanded and refined this argument in a recent book. However his pessimism as to the likelihood of Western conflict with certain societies (especially Islamic) has, if anything, deepened. See *The Clash of Civilizations and the Remaking of World Order* (New York: Simon and Schuster, 1996), especially pp. 209–65.
3. The quotation is from Elshtain's remarkable *Democracy on Trial* (New York: Basic Books, 1995), p. 5.
4. On the cultural challenge of Muslims in France, see Jocelyne Cesari, *Etre musulman en France: Associations, militants et mosquees* (Paris: Karthala & Ireman, 1994), and Bruno Etienne, ed., *L'Islam en France* (Paris: Editions du

CNRS, 1990); for contrasting evaluations of British attitudes towards Muslims (and vice versa), see, Talal Asad, "Multiculturalism and British Identity in the Wake of the Rushdie Affair," in Asad, *Genealogies of Religion: Discipline and Reasons of Power in Christianity and Islam* (Baltimore, Md.: Johns Hopkins, 1993), pp. 239–68; and Pnina Werbner, "Allegories of Sacred Imperfection: Magic, Hermeneutics, and Passion in *The Satanic Verses*," in *Current Anthropology*, vol. 37, special issue supplement (Feb. 1996), pp. 55–86.

5. See James Davison Hunter, *Culture Wars: The Struggle to Define America* (New York: Basic Books, 1991).

6. Students of social theory will rightly observe that concern for the conditions of democracy's possibility is a *renewed* interest, not one created from scratch, since many of these same issues underlay modernization theory in the 1960s. However there is an important difference in the way this interest was developed in the two periods. Though the best modernization theorists were aware of the world's cultural diversity, they had a greater confidence in the generalizability of Western developmental models, and a simpler understanding of just what those models involved. Social and political theory in the 1970s was marked by, as Anthony Giddens has put it, the loss of this orthodox consensus and a momentary diminution in comparative inquiry. When the issue of democracy across cultures reemerged in the late 1980s, it benefited from debates that had complicated our understanding of the state, nationalism, and the concept of culture.

7. Robert D. Putnam, *Making Democracy Work: Civic Traditions in Modern Italy* (Princeton, N.J.: Princeton University Press, 1993).

8. The latter question is at the heart of Robert D. Putnam's provocative little article, "Bowling Alone: America's Declining Social Capital." In *Journal of Democracy* 6:1 (January 1995): 65–78.

9. Alexis de Tocqueville, *Democracy in America*, two volumes, translated by George Lawrence and edited by J.P. Mayer (Garden City, N.Y.: Doubleday, 1969), p. 192.

10. An intelligent example of this genre is Mary Ann Glendhon and David Blankenhorn, eds., *Seedbeds of Virtue: Sources of Competence, Character, and Citizenship in American Society* (Lanham, Md.: Institute for American Values, Madison Books, 1995).

11. See for example, David G. Green, *Reinventing Civil Society: The Rediscovery of Welfare without Politics* (London: Institute of Economic Affairs, Choice in Welfare Series No. 17, 1993); and Gregg Vanourek, Scott W. Hamilton, and Chester E. Finn, Jr., *Is There Life After Big Government? The Potential of Civil Society* (Indianapolis, Ind.: Hudson Institute, 1996).

12. See Paul Barry Clarke, *Deep Citizenship* (London: Pluto Press, 1996), and Ernesto Lacalu and Chantal Mouffe, *Hegemony and Socialist Strategy: Towards a Radical Democratic Politics* (London: Verso, 1985).

13. John A. Hall, "In Search of Civil Society." In Hall, ed. *Civil Society: Theory, History, and Comparison* (Cambridge: Polity Press, 1995), p. 2.

14. For a critique of this narrow usage and an illustration of what it obscures in a non-Western setting, see Jenny B. White, "Civic Culture and Islam in Urban Turkey," in Chris Hann and Elizabeth Dunn, eds., *Civil Society: Challenging Western Models* (London: Routledge, 1996), pp. 143–54.

15. John Keane, "Introduction." In Keane, ed., *Civil Society and the State: New European Perspectives* (London: Verso, 1988), p. 28.

16. Three of the more notable are Chris Hann and Elizabeth Dunn, eds., *Civil Society: Challenging Western Models* (London: Routledge, in Conjunction with the European Association of Social Anthropologists, 1996); John W. Harbeson,

Donald Rothchild, and Naomi Chazan, *Civil Society and the State in Africa* (Boulder, Colo.: Lynne Rienner Publishers, 1994); and Augustus Richard Norton, ed., *Civil Society in the Middle East*, two volumes, (Leiden: E.J. Brill, 1995, 1996). With its unusually rich combination of history, ethnography, and philosophy, the last work remains the single best sourcebook on the problem of civil society in a non-Western context.

17. For reasons that will become apparent later in this introduction, I prefer to use the term "civil democracy" rather than "liberal democracy" when referring to the political institutions through which the modern ideals of equality, dignity, and tolerance are realized. My intent in doing so is to underscore that civil values are compatible with a wider range of real-and-existing social orders than implied in, most notably, certain philosophical discussions of Western liberalism. Some of the latter imply that democracy is only viable in cultures that affirm strong variants of ethical individualism. Yet in practice, the range of ethical traditions within which real-and-existing democracies have co-evolved even in the West—and, increasingly, the non-Western world—is more varied than such accounts imply, as is the relative balance of group and individual rights.

18. Michael Walzer, "Pluralism: A Political Perspective," in Walzer, *What It Means to be an American: Essays on the American Experience* (New York: Marsilio, 1996 [1980]), pp. 53–77. The philosopher Will Kymlicka takes a slightly different perspective on the pluralism problem in Western liberalism. He argues that liberalism's neglect of cultural diversity has been especially characteristic of postwar writing, observing that some nineteenth- and early twentieth-century liberal theorists did discuss the problem of ethnic minorities and multinational states. See Will Kymlicka, *Multicultural Citizenship: A Liberal Theory of Minority Rights* (Oxford: Clarendon Press, 1995), p. 49. Kymlicka may be right about professional philosophers, but the central strain in Western policy circles has clearly been closer to that described by Walzer.

19. The effort to go beyond Durkheim's legacy and acknowledge the unboundedness and internal complexity of even "traditional" societies has been a central theme in recent anthropological writing. See, for example, the essays in Adam Kuper, ed., *Conceptualizing Society* (London: Routledge, 1992); and in Richard Fardon, ed., *Counterworks: Managing the Diversity of Knowledge* (London and New York: Routledge, 1995). For outstanding demonstrations of the unbounded and pluralist nature of "tribal" Africa, see Igor Kopytoff, "The Internal African Frontier: The Making of African Political Culture," in Kopytoff, ed., *The African Frontier: The Reproduction of Traditional African Societies* (Bloomington: Indiana University Press, 1987), pp. 3–84; and Terence Ranger, "The Local and the Global in Southern African Religious History," in Robert W. Hefner, ed., *Conversion to Christianity: Historical and Anthropological Perspectives on a Great Transformation* (Berkeley: University of California Press, 1993), pp. 65–98.

20. The issue of the world religions' role in integrating multiethnic empires is discussed in S.N. Eisenstadt's "Introduction: The Axial Age Breakthroughs—Their Characteristics and Origins," in Eisenstadt, *The Origins and Diversity of Axial Age Civilizations* (Albany: State University of New York Press, 1986), pp. 1–25, and in my "World Building and the Rationality of Conversion," in Hefner, ed., *Conversion to Christianity*, pp. 3–44.

21. Readers will note a significant tension between my account of Muslim pluralism here and in chapter 12 and that of John Hall in this volume.

22. As a field of inquiry, the comparative study of pluralist civility is still in its infancy. As the field takes shape, however, it is clear that the discussion of Euro-

pean civility will have to acknowledge the awesome achievement of Norbert Elias's, *The Civilizing Process: The History of Manners and State Formation and Civilization*, translated by Edmund Jephcott (Oxford: Blackwell, 1994). For a discussion of civility in China, see Robert Weller's essay in this volume.

23. In making such a generalization, it is important *not* to fall back into nineteenth century dichotomy of "traditional" vs. "modern" society, with the assumption that premodern societies were essentially the same. While some premodern societies do invoke principles of hierarchy like those Louis Dumont has described in classical India, others show a nuanced pattern, blending hierarchical with egalitarian themes. Charles Lindholm has recently examined one such complex blend, that of the premodern Muslim Middle East. He shows that there a strong ethic of male equality coexisted with relationships of authority and subordination. See Lindholm, *The Islamic Middle East: An Historical Anthropology* (Oxford: Blackwell, 1996). For a textual analysis of related problems, see Louise Marlow, *Hierarchy and Egalitarianism in Islamic Thought* (Cambridge: Cambridge University Press, 1997).

24. F.G. Bailey, *The Civility of Indifference: On Domesticating Ethnicity* (Ithaca, N.Y.: Cornell University Press, 1996).

25. This is not to say that this was the only or dominant form of political civility in Enlightenment Europe. As my argument will make clearer later, modern Europe contained (and still contains) rival ideological traditions, among them hierarchical corporatism and romantic nationalism (the two of which sometimes worked in unison). In determining which of these rival ideologies was to be amplified and which suppressed, structural developments in European economy and society would play as critical a role as the popular force of cultural ideas. See Chirot in this volume for a related argument.

26. Some of the most insightful literature on the exclusions operative in European civil society has originated in response to Jurgen Habermas's rather idealized characterizations of the eighteenth century "public sphere." Of special note are Nancy Fraser's, "Rethinking the Public Sphere: A Contribution to the Critique of Actually Existing Democracy"; Mary P. Ryan, "Gender and Public Access: Women's Politics in Nineteenth-Century America"; and Geoff Eley, "Nations, Publics, and Political Cultures: Placing Habermas in the Nineteenth Century"; in Craig Calhoun, ed., *Habermas and the Public Sphere* (Cambridge, Mass.: MIT Press, 1992), pp. 109–42, 259–88, and 289–339 respectively. The work to which they direct their critique is Jurgen Habermas's much read, *The Structural Transformation of the Public Sphere: An Inquiry into a Category of Bourgeois Society*, translated by Thomas Burger (Cambridge, Mass.: MIT Press, 1989).

27. See Dale F. Eickelman, "The Political Economy of Meaning," in *American Ethnologist* 6 (1979):386–93.

28. Especially relevant to Hall's approach are Ernest Gellner, *Conditions of Liberty: Civil Society and Its Rivals* (New York: Penguin Books, 1994), and "Flux and reflux in the faith of men," in *Muslim Society* (Cambridge: Cambridge University Press, 1981), pp. 1–85. For Max Weber, see *The City* (New York: The Free Press, 1958).

29. John A. Hall, *Liberties and Powers: The Causes and Consequences of the Rise of the West* (Berkeley: University of California Press, 1985).

30. Cf. Daniel Chirot, *Social Change in the Modern Era* (San Diego, Cal.: Harcourt Brace Jovanovich, 1986), esp. pp. 11–56; and E.L. Jones, *The European Miracle: Environments, Economies, and Geopolitics in the History of Europe and Asia*, second edition (Cambridge: Cambridge University Press, 1981).

31. For insights into why this might have been so, see David K. Jordan and Daniel L. Overmyer, *The Flying Phoenix: Aspects of Chinese Sectarianism in Taiwan* (Princeton, N.J.: Princeton University Press, 1986), and David K. Jordan, "The Glyphomancy Factor: Observations on Chinese Conversion," in Hefner, ed., *Conversion to Christianity*, pp. 285–303.

32. The post-Marxist literature on new social movements and civil society emerged earlier, in the early 1980s, anticipating the general revival of interest in civil society which was to occur a few years later. See, for example, Claus Offe, "The New Social Movements: Challenging the Boundaries of Institutional Politics," *Social Research* 52: 4 (1985): 817–68; and Alberto Melucci, "Social Movements and the Democratization of Everyday Life," in Keane, ed., *Civil Society and the State*, pp. 245–60.

33. See for example, Michael Buchowski, "The Shifting Meanings of Civil and Civic Society in Poland," and Steven Samson, "The Social Life of Projects: Importing Civil Society to Albania," in Hann and Dunn, *Civil Society*, pp. 79–98 and 121–42.

34. John Keane, "Introduction," in Keane, ed., *Civil Society and the State*, p. 2.

35. One of the finest critiques of Marx's ideas on civil society remains Jean L. Cohen's *Class and Civil Society: The Limits of Marxian Critical Theory* (Amherst: University of Massachusetts Press, 1982); for a more sympathetic assessment of Marx's views, see Keith Tester, *Civil Society* (London: Routledge, 1992).

36. Charles Taylor, "Invoking Civil Society," in Taylor, *Philosophical Arguments* (Cambridge, Mass.: Harvard University Press, 1995), p. 204. Cf. Ernest Gellner, *Conditions of Liberty: Civil Society and Its Rivals* (New York: Penguin Press, 1994).

37. A theme explored in Gyorgy Konrád's, *Antipolitics* (London: Quartet, 1984).

38. Katherine Verdery's discussion of Romania is paradigmatic in this regard of much of multiethnic Eastern Europe. By promoting a chauvinistic patriotism, Romania's conservative nationalists forced supporters of civil society onto the defensive, obliging them to adopt nationalist slogans and, in so doing, undermining their appeals for multiethnic civility (particularly as regards Rumania's Hungarian minority). See *What Was Socialism, and What Comes Next?* (Princeton, N.J.: Princeton University Press, 1996), pp. 115–29. The Romanian case makes an interesting contrast with the Ukraine, as discussed by José Casanova in this book.

39. This point is also illustrated in Robert Putnam's *Making Democracy Work*, p. 176. See also Chris Hann, "Introduction: Political Society and Civil Anthropology," in Chris Hann and Elizabeth, eds., *Civil Society*, p. 7.

40. See Michael Mann, *The Sources of Social Power*, vol. I, *A History of Power from the Beginning to A.D. 1760* (Cambridge: Cambridge University Press, 1986), especially pp. 518–541; Anthony Giddens, *The Nation-State and Violence*, volume 2 of *A Contemporary Critique of Historical Materialism* (Berkeley: University of California Press, 1987), pp. 35–60; and John A. Hall, "Introduction," in *States in History* (London: Blackwell, 1986), pp 1–21. For a Southeast Asian illustration of the uneven power of premodern states, see Anthony Reid's masterful, *Southeast Asia in the Age of Commerce, 1450–1680*, volume 2, *Expansion and Crisis* (New Haven, Conn.: Yale University Press, 1993).

41. On the fracturing of the opposition and the decline of the civil society ideal in postcommunist Poland, see W. Wesolowski, "The Nature of Social Ties and the Future of Postcommunist Society: Poland after Solidarity," in John A. Hall, *Civil Society: Theory, History, Comparison* (Cambridge: Polity Press, 1995), pp. 110–35, and, for Hungary, Andrew Arato and Jean L. Cohen, "Civil Society and the

Public Sphere," paper presented at the Institute for Advanced Study, Boston University, October 28, 1995.

42. The scale of this conflict gave rise in some circles to the simplistic view that the violence was merely an explosion of long suppressed "primordial" tensions. For a better account, see John R. Bowen, "The Myth of Global Ethnic Conflict," in *Journal of Democracy* 7:4 (October 1996):3–14.

43. For an excellent discussion of the contemporary globalization of a related political concept, see Richard A. Wilson's *Human Rights, Culture and Context* (London: Pluto Press, 1997).

44. My discussion of cultural "amplification" and "dampening" has parallels to two otherwise unrelated bodies of research: the model of cognition and culture elaborated in the cross-cultural psychiatry of Arthur Kleinman, as in his, *Rethinking Psychiatry: From Cultural Category to Personal Experience* (New York: The Free Press, 1988), and Peter Evans' discussion of the "scaling up" of social capital in his, "Government Action, Social Capital and Development: Reviewing the Evidence on Synergy," in *World Development* 24:6 (1996): 1119–32.

45. For illustrations of the interactionist understanding of culture and practice underlying this model see Anthony Giddens, *The Constitution of Society: Outline of the Theory of Structuration* (Berkeley: University of California Press, 1984); Maurice Bloch, "From Cognition to Ideology," in Bloch, *Ritual, History and Power: Selected Papers in Anthropology* (London: The Athlone Press, LSE Monographs on Social Anthropology No. 58, 1989), pp. 106–36; and Arthur Kleinman, *Rethinking Psychiatry*, pp. 18–76.

46. A point touched on from a different perspective by Fredrik Barth in his, "Toward Greater Naturalism in Conceptualizing Societies," in Kuper, *Conceptualizing Society*, pp. 17–33.

47. This phrase is from Ulf Hannerz's delightful, *Transnational Connections: Culture, Peoples, Places* (London and New York: Routledge, 1996).

48. For an affirmation of the possibility of such democratic convergence in the Muslim Middle East, see Dale F. Eickelman and James Piscatori, *Muslim Politics* (Princeton, N.J.: Princeton University Press, 1996), and Augustus Richard Norton's introduction to *Civil Society in the Middle East*, vol. I.

49. Probably the most important among the early works on radical democracy was Ernesto Laclau and Chantal Mouffe's *Hegemony and Socialist Strategy: Towards a Radical Democratic Politics* (London: Verso, 1985).

50. On the way in which capitalist politics and ethics vary according to their social "embedding," see Gordon Redding in this volume, as well as Redding and S.R. Clegg, eds., *Capitalism in Contrasting Cultures* (Berlin: Walter de Gruyter, 1990); and Robert Hefner, "Introduction," in *Market Cultures: Society and Morality in the New Asian Capitalisms* (Boulder, Colo.: Westview Press, in press).

51. The quotation here is from Jean L. Cohen's, *Class and Civil Society*, p. 29. As this work's publication date indicates, to say that the effluorescence of the post-Marxist left was facilitated by the crisis in Eastern Europe is not to imply that the intellectual foundation was not laid earlier. The democratic left's rejection of Marx's analysis of civil society began earlier, during the 1970s in the pages of such journals as *Telos* and *Dissent*, and of course in the writing of the leading European pioneer of post-Marxist democracy, Jurgen Habermas.

52. Chantal Mouffe, "Democratic Politics Today." In Mouffe, ed., *Dimensions of Radical Democracy: Pluralism, Citizenship, Community* (London: Verso, 1992), p. 1.

53. But the postmodern label can be misleading. Self-proclaimed postmodernists tend to agree with Francois Lyotard's assertion that ours is an era marked by the loss of "grand narratives" and metaphysical absolutes. However, while some

interpret this as a denial of any possibility of judging one ethicopolitical option superior to another, others, such as the influential American philosopher Richard Rorty, see this situation as a confirmation of the pragmatic utility of nonmetaphysical understandings of the ideals of tolerance, pluralism, and freedom. See for example, Richard Rorty, *Objectivity, Relativism, and Truth, Philosophical Papers,* vol. 1 (Cambridge: Cambridge University Press, 1991), especially pp. 175–22. For a sympathetic but intelligently critical review from a more universalist perspective, see Norman Geras, *Solidarity in the Conversation of Humankind: The Ungroundable Liberalism of Richard Rorty* (London: Verso, 1995).

54. Mouffe, "Democratic Politics Today," p. 13; emphasis in the original.

55. Erik Olin Wright, "Preface: The Real Utopias Project," in Erik Olin Wright, ed., *Associations and Democracy: The Real Utopias Project*, vol., I (London: Verso, 1995), p. xi.

56. See for example Richard A. Wilson's *Human Rights, Culture and Context* for a critical but balanced anthropological reflection on this issue.

57. The fact that there has been intense debate in places like the United States over issues of individual opportunity and group justice (as in the controversy surrounding affirmative action) should serve as a reminder that, contrary to some philosophical portrayals, real-and-existing democracies acknowledge collective as well as individual goods. It is nonetheless true that the modern language of individual rights, with its image of the "autonomous agentic individual," has made discursive legitimation of such concerns more difficult in courtrooms and other public fora. For a discussion of how such an individualized model of personhood poses problems of integration in the contemporary West, see Adam Seligman, *The Idea of Civil Society* (New York: The Free Press, 1992).

58. Mouffe, "Democratic Politics," p. 14.

59. Michael Walzer, "The Civil Society Argument." In Chantal Mouffe, ed., *Dimensions of Radical Democracy*, pp. 98.

60. Walzer, "The Civil Society Argument," p. 99.

61. Peter L. Berger and Richard John Neuhaus, *To Empower People: From State to Civil Society* (Washington, D.C.: AEI Press, 1996), p. 164.

62. On this point, for example, see Charles Taylor, "Cross Purposes: The Liberal-Communitarian Debate," in Nancy L. Rosenblum, ed., *Liberalism and the Moral Life* (Cambridge, Mass.: Harvard University Press, 1989), pp. 159–82.

63. Among others, for example, Francis Fukuyama has recently made an extended critique of neoclassical variants of liberalism, arguing that they promote an atomistic individualism that undermines the morality on which liberal democracy and market economies depend. See his, *Trust: The Social Virtues and the Creation of Prosperity* (New York: The Free Press, 1995).

64. This distinction is sometimes overlooked in otherwise sound sociological and anthropological discussions of democracy and human rights. A proper anthropology of civil democracy would begin by invoking the first principle of practice theory, namely that the canonical truths used to legitimate practice are not necessarily the best indicators of the norms guiding social practice itself.

65. Alasdair MacIntyre, *After Virtue: A Study in Moral Theory*, second edition (Notre Dame, Ind.: University of Notre Dame Press, 1984), especially pp. 255–63.

66. Bernard Yack, "Liberalism and Its Communitarian Critics: Does Liberal Practice 'Live Down' to Liberal Theory?" In Charles H. Reynolds and Ralph V. Norman, eds., *Community in America: The Challenge of* Habits of the Heart (Berkeley: University of California Press, 1988), pp. 151–52.

67. Michael Sandel, *Liberalism and the Limits of Justice* (Cambridge: Cambridge University Press, 1982), and "The Procedural Republic and the Unencumbered Self," *Political Theory* 12 (1984): 81–96.
68. This is the point of departure for much recent comparative research on gender, kinship, and modern politics. Among many fine anthropological studies, see the essays in Sylvia Junko Yanagisako and Jane Fishburne Collier, eds., *Gender and Kinship: Essays Toward a Unified Analysis* (Stanford, Cal.: Stanford University Press, 1987); from the perspective of political theory and history, see Nancy Fraser's "Rethinking the Public Sphere," and Joan Landes, *Women and the Public Sphere in the Age of the French Revolution* (Ithaca, N.Y.: Cornell University Press, 1988).
69. Seligman, *The Idea of Civil Society.*
70. Since the last century, the contesting of the boundary between public and private has been central to arguments in favor of women's rights. More recently, it has also figured in the debate over the relevance of religion for public ethical concerns. See Jose Casanova's *Public Religions in the Modern World* (Chicago: University of Chicago Press, 1994).
71. Robert N. Bellah, Richard Madsen, William M. Sullivan, Ann Swidler, and Steven M. Tipton, *Habits of the Heart: Individualism and Commitment in American Life* (Berkeley: University of California Press, 1985).
72. On the formative role of Dutch writers in the early modern development of European republicanism, see Martin van Gelderen, "The Machiavellian moment and the Dutch Revolt: the rise of neostoicism and Dutch republicanism," in Gisela Bock, Quentin Skinner, and Maurizio Viroli, eds., *Machiavelli and Republicanism* (Cambridge: Cambridge University Press, 1990), pp. 205–23.
73. Putnam, *Making Democracy*, p. 176.
74. This theme is developed in Guillermo O'Donnell and Philippe C. Schmitter's, *Transitions from Authoritarian Rule: Tentative Conclusions about Uncertain Democracies* (Baltimore, Md.: Johns Hopkins University Press, 1986).
75. On the changing nature of the American family, see Rayna Rapp, "Toward a Nuclear Freeze? The Gender Politics of Euro-American Kinship Analysis," in Collier and Yanagisako, eds., *Gender and Kinship*, pp. 119–31.

Part 1

Western Genealogies

2

Genealogies of Civility

John A. Hall

For perhaps a full decade, "civil society" has had about it an air of excitement. This is not surprising. For the concept was taken as a banner by those wishing to be free, in Latin America and in Eastern Europe, and it was further invoked by Marxisant thinkers in the West seeking a nonstatist social theory of the Left.[1] Still, there was always vagueness as to exactly what the notion implied. Was it an ideal or a set of institutions—perhaps, indeed, a noble hope rather than a possible reality? Further, was the concept necessary, that is, did it contain anything that went beyond "liberalism" and "democracy"? Was the notion really desirable, finally, especially in Eastern Europe where it seemed to be associated with the crassest of marketist ideologies? The most recent critical voices, which have these considerations at the center of their attention, have tended to be exasperated.[2] Fashion can mean that a topic is dropped as quickly as it is taken up, and this may be about to happen to the notion of civil society.

This essay seeks clarity in these muddied waters. I argue that the concept in question should not suddenly receive the cold shoulder. For one thing, it is possible to specify what we imply and should mean by civil society, and to do so without that endless reference to the history of political ideas that seems to have been almost mandatory amongst those who have debated this topic. For another, this is the term which best helps us understand what it is that can make our social world decent and desirable. If the paper begins by establishing a definition of civility, it then seeks to underwrite it by genealogical analysis. A first claim is that civil society emerged only in the Occident. It is as well to highlight immediately the certain fact that this does not lead to Eurocentric self-congratulation: for the second claim is that the pedigree of civility in the West was deeply flawed, with recovery from disaster being more the result of luck than of any social inevitability. The final part of this slightly polemical essay seeks to examine—and to assess the likely success of—routes to civil society based on imitation.

Definition

The method of immanent critique so favored by German philosophy can be very irritating. If no clearly stated position follows suggestive critical exegesis then confusion usually reigns. For this reason, I begin with a bald definition bluntly stated. Nonetheless, there is a great deal to be said for setting a definition in context. Hence, initial abstraction is followed by analysis of alternatives: demonstrating the problems of those alternatives lends credence to the definition proposed.

Civil society is an ideal that is capable of social embodiment. It is a form of societal self-organization which allows for cooperation with the state whilst enabling individuation. It should be stated firmly that the creation of a modern capitalistic economy does not guarantee that society will be civil, for all that specifiable links exist between commerce and civility. Further, civil society is not the same thing as liberalism or democracy: it has its own qualities, and these can usefully be encapsulated by saying that it is civil society which makes liberalism and democracy truly desirable. Finally, civil society has a complex relation to that abstraction termed modernity.

The most obvious alternative to this view conceptualizes civil society simply as societal self-organization. Brilliant recent work by Grzegorz Ekiert on post-communist Poland speaks in this spirit of a revival of civil society seen in the creation of a huge number of interest groups.[3] Interestingly, this revival does not in itself delight the author: endless claims between militant groups might yet lead to anarchy rather than to a mature political society. This hesitation suggests that Ekiert's use of the term civil society may be mistaken. A moment's thought makes it quite obvious that this skeptical consideration should be applied to other cases. The exceedingly solidaristic self-organization of Mafiosi, whether in Sicily or, by process of emulation, in Moscow, quite obviously has the capacity of destroying liberal regimes; equally, the manner in which members of these organizations are controlled is far removed from any connotation of the word civil. Again, tribal self-organization can both destroy organized states and so control human beings as to rule out any possibility of individual self-determination and moral growth.

The analytic point to be derived from all this is simple: the self-organization that is part of a civil society has a particular character. Differently put, mere social activism resulting in a war of all against all can be very far removed from the condition of civility.[4] Two distinct reasons for this general judgment lurk in the background; they deserve to be distinguished and highlighted.

On the one hand, intellectual provincialism makes many forget that the pleasures of settled existence depend upon the rule of law being guaranteed by effective state power. The intellectual roots of this blindness derive from nineteenth-century England. A thinker such as Herbert Spencer could imagine a hugely moral social world based wholly on contracts between individuals[5]; this view, itself derived from the ethos of neoclassical economics, was taken over wholesale by Karl Marx, whose phrase "the withering away of the state" characterized the general point most evocatively. The fact that the twentieth century has seen viciously effective states which ignored the rule of law provided experience that seemed to underwrite this antistatist ethic. But if despotism is a danger, so too is anarchy. Those who talk of the desirability of the destruction of the state, whether in nineteenth-century England or twentieth-century America, overgeneralize on the basis of the pacific consensus which marks their social world. This is provincial because it takes no account of bastard feudalism or of Beirut in its worst days, thereby failing to provide safeguards against any further such savageries. Social forces which destroy a liberal state or prevent it operating efficiently do not contribute to a civil society: that term should be reserved for societal self-organization which cooperates with a responsible and responsive state. A paradox involving trust needs to be noted at this point. When a political elite surrenders some control it can generate an increase in state power, for those who feel the state to be their own are likely to help rather than to hinder its endeavors.[6] At the most abstract level, what the history of the late twentieth century forces us to notice about the states of liberal democracy is that they have greater strength than those of more authoritarian social systems.[7]

On the other hand, social forces which cage and control the individual, limiting room for moral autonomy, are equally opposed to what is implicitly meant by civil society. The all-powerful tyranny that closed groups can exert over every aspect of daily life, from clothing to the choice of marriage partner to the details of belief, is antithetical to any concept of civility. Positively put, a civil society is one in which individuals have the chance of at least trying to create their own selves.

This means that the membership of social groups must be voluntary and overlapping, for it is, as Erving Goffman demonstrated, in the complex interstices of social life that individuality often resides.[8] Further, there is likely to be an elective affinity between civil society and fashion: for all the fripperies to which the latter can be prone, it remains the area in which many can experiment with and try on new conceptions of their selves. The most general point underlying all of this is that a civil society will be one in which difference is allowed, accepted and even encouraged—albeit, within limits which will be specified in a moment.

A second alternative manner in which civil society has been conceived is not opposed to the first, but its main thrust is far more aggressively sociological.[9] Civil society in this view is seen as the inevitable and automatic concomitant of the socioeconomic logic of capitalism. This view has been particularly warmly endorsed by many who lived in state socialist societies. The pioneer of Polish "shock therapy," Leszek Balcerowicz, gave the essence of the idea when proclaiming his indifference to the fact that much privatization was in effect piratization. For such theorists, what matters fundamentally about capitalism is that power is in different sets of hands, the presumption being that there is a strong link between societal pluralism and political liberty.

This view is not nonsensical, and there is certainly much to be said for insisting that a civil society must rest upon a separation of economic and political power. But a condition of existence is not the same thing as a causal agent—and with regard to cause the general view in question is exaggerated. Specification with reference to the historical record will demonstrate this; whilst key detailed considerations on this point can best be made later, it is worth classifying immediately three stages in the history of the relations between capitalism and civil society.

There is sense, to begin with, in the limited claim that there was, as Adam Smith stressed, an elective affinity between civil society and the first emergence of commercial society. On the one hand, strong and autonomous group organization itself helped the emergence of commercial society. On the other hand, that initial emergence did much to strengthen civil society. Perhaps most important was that large interpretation encapsulated in Samuel Johnson's dictum that "a man is never so innocently employed as when he is making money": differently put, economic interest was held to be relatively benign and thereby capable of curtailing the depredations consequent on no-holds-barred power seeking.[10] More generally, both Smith and Johnson endorsed civil society as an ideal quite as much as a set of institutions. They praised a world of refinement, polish, and manners—with Smith interestingly opposing Rousseau's call for a return to the unitary simplicity of precommercial Sparta.[11]

Still, no absolute and necessary link exists between capitalism and civility. Most importantly, old regimes soon sought to imitate the economic success of their competitors, and to that end *planned* capitalism from above. Authoritarian capitalism of this sort was often far from civil. To the contrary, the presence in many such regimes of socialist working classes made their bourgeoisies the slavish friend of authority. Archetypical in this respect were Wilhelmine Germany and Imperial Japan, states whose contours were to be repeated by Korea and much of Latin America in much of the postwar period. These were worlds which did not allow for the emergence of "loyal oppositions" within the elite whilst equally excluding the people.

In very recent years, it has become apparent that much authoritarian capitalism has fared badly. By this is meant that economic development by means of import-substitution, as in Latin America, has performed terribly in comparison to East Asia's style of escorting initially protected industries on to the world market.[12] State retreat in Latin America and in Eastern Europe most certainly does not guarantee the emergence of civil society, but it does allow political space within which it may develop. And the fact that late industrial society as a whole, that is, in East Asia as much as in Eastern Europe and Latin America, is known to depend ever more on the activities of the information classes may at least improve the chances both for the emergence and the maintenance of civil society.

A final issue needing to be confronted is that of the status of the definition offered. Given that there is no necessary social evolutionary logic pushing forward civil society, a question anyway deserving consideration comes decisively to the fore. Is civil society a universal ideal, attractive to all human beings once it has been expounded and explicated? Or is the notion of civil society, rather, merely a Western dream? These questions necessarily raise the crucial issue of relativism and rationality. In this matter, it can be said at once that the proponents of civil society have enemies on both sides, being opposed to the absolutism of some universalisms as much as to blanket relativism. These enemies need to be examined before the analytic question can be answered.

Civil society is based on a recognition of difference and diversity. Varied attitudes can be involved here. Some welcome diversity enthusiastically, whilst others put up this with resignation. A still more sophisticated attitude is that of those who think that a good deal of truth can be discovered, but are reluctant to force feed human beings into accepting every detail of a morality. This was the position, for example, of the narrator of Proust's *In Search of Lost Time*: seeing a young boy about to waste years, as he had wasted them himself, along the false trails of "society" and art, Marcel refuses to intervene—on the grounds that moral learning can only take place through making one's own mistakes. A key analytic point derives from this. That type of holistic liberalism represented by Durkheim in which socialization is all encompassing and all effective is not at all the same thing as a civil society. A civil society will allow the individual room in which to experiment, doing so most of the time from a position of mild relativism—that is, one which doubts the presence of a single set of universal rules about every aspect of behavior.

Mild relativism needs to be distinguished from blanket relativism. To say that the recognition of difference is *shared* and the decision to live together with diversity *mutual* is to note a background consensus that enables civility to flourish. Such limits to diversity are necessary. The consensus in question should of course be minimal, including most obviously respect for the rule of law and abhorrence of violence, whilst its characteristic style will be that of ironic and affectionate amusement at the foibles of humanity within the resulting settled world. All this can be put more bluntly. The diversity that is acceptable to a civil society is that within a particular world with its own boundaries. Civil society is a social world rather than a mere space in which every sort of difference is negotiated. This point is of such importance that it deserves to be highlighted by means of two analogies. There is a resemblance, to begin with, with the position being argued and conclusions that ought to be drawn about the famous claim that the ideological age had ended.[13] The insistence that others were ideological but that we were not was terribly mistaken: the point about liberalism was that it was an ideology, albeit a peculiar one given that it did not seek to fill out the world completely, and that it deserved defense as such. Equally, philosophies of science which suggest that cognitive power rests only upon systematic doubt deserve to be criticized for forgetting the shared background consensus as to how doubt is to be dealt with, that is, by means of empirical testing—as to whose usefulness there is no doubt whatsoever.

The twentieth century has seen ideocracies that are opposed to the ideal of civil society, thereby making it crystal clear that modernity can have many faces. Insofar as this is so, civil society *is* but one option amongst others, that is, an ideal born in the West which faces alternatives. This lends the existence of anyone endorsing civil society a certain schizophrenia. On the one hand, awareness of enemies makes explication and analysis important in an internal sense: it makes it possible to understand ourselves, so that what we value can then be the better defended. On the other hand, recognizing that civil society is a world amongst others puts on the agenda the desirability of finding rational grounds by means of which to choose one world rather than another. Most ultimate defenses of civil society of this sort tend to be negative, to stress the failure of alternatives and the fact that there is some connection between civil society and prosperity. Such defenses have power but are unlikely to persuade everyone, not least given flaws to the pedigree that will be considered. In the final analysis, I suspect that civil society can only be defended in Kantian terms, that is, on account of its respect for the individual. Whilst not impossible, it is only fair to say that producing transcultural argument on this point is notoriously difficult—and a subject best treated on a different occasion.

Birth

Gore Vidal once suggested that the deepest meaning of *Creation*, his magnificent novel about the origins of the world religions and ethics, was that agrarian civilizations before the advent of the great monotheistic creeds were the most tolerant in the history of mankind.[14] There is some justification for this view. On the one hand, the logistics of agrarian civilizations meant that they had no capacity to penetrate let alone to police the thoughts of the tribes and peasant communities over which they ruled. On the other hand, monotheism brought in its train the potential for—and, with Christianity once Constantine had converted, the enthusiastic and vicious practice of—intolerance, for all that the principle of universal salvation envisaged and allowed the incorporation of all human beings into society for the first time. Nonetheless, the classical agrarian civilizations were not civil societies. The inability of the state to penetrate social life is not at all the same thing as the creation of social practices which make state-society interactions civilized. Differently put, civil society has everything to do with the modern world in which such interaction is necessary.

As the origins of that modernity lie within Europe, it accordingly makes sense to turn to it immediately. The explanation of that presence is followed, however, by remarks insisting that civil society did not emerge in the other great civilizations. It is worth emphasizing that the account cannot be accused of any easy orientalism given that the next section describes the horrors unleashed by European civilization in the twentieth century.

The deepest roots of civil society in Europe result from the way in which the removal of the centralized authority of Rome placed power in several sets of hands. What is most striking in comparative perspective is the separation between ideological and political power. This separation has its origins in Jesus's injunction to deliver to Caesar what was Caesar's, but to give to God what was God's—a remark that amounts to saying that Christianity's concern was with spiritual salvation rather than political order. Christianity later refused to provide ideological justification for Rome, and it found thereafter that it could survive and prosper without benefit of an imperial polity. Once it realized that it could not itself create a theocracy, fear of concentration of power in the hands of a secular emperor led the church to encourage kings whom they made more than *primus inter pares* by ritual anointing and the singing of the *Laudes Regiae*. If those policies were conscious, very different activities by the church may have done as much to encourage state formation in Europe. The church's greed for land seems to account for that breaking up of the obligations of an extended kinship network[15]: if the way in which this resulted in a family pattern responsive to Malthusian pressures is well known, the manner in which its atomization of society made for easier state building may be quite as important. Nonetheless, it would be a mistake to imagine that royal power became unfettered as the result of these two forces. Rather, state building took place within a field of preexistent social forces. Kings were faced with feudal nobilities whose property rights were firmly established, as of course were those of the church. In these circumstances kings sought to enhance their powers by granting autonomy to towns; these became islands within the feudal sea in which new ideas and practices could develop. All in all, this was an acephalus world in which liberties were both widespread and firmly codified in a legal system that privileged corporate rights.

This vesting of power into separate bodies might have led to a static society, in which different sources of power merely blocked any common enterprise. This did not happen, with European society in consequence gaining a restless dynamism that changed the pattern of world history. Trust and cooperation was initially made possible by the sense of unity provided by Christian norms;[16] shared membership in a civilization certainly helped to revive and deepen economic interaction even within the medieval period. However, cooperative relations *within* states became of ever greater importance. European rulers did not, as was the case elsewhere, conquer a society which they then had little real interest in organizing. To the contrary, state-society interaction necessarily became ever more intense due to endless competition in war consequent on multipolarity; given the preexistence of social relations, royal activism necessarily depended upon cooperation and coaxing quite as much as upon sheer coercion.[17] The need for monies for war led to the practice of calling assemblies of the estates of the realm, that is, of church, nobility and townsmen—to whom were even added in Sweden and Norway representatives of the peasantry! Such assemblies took over tags of canon law—"what touches all must be agreed by all" and "no taxation without representation"—that made European states essentially rule bound. Of course, the fact that there were several such states was of enormous importance. A measure of internal decency was encouraged once it was realized that foul treatment to key social elements might encourage them to move and thereby to enrich a rival state, as clearly happened when the Huguenots were expelled from France. The presence of avenues of escape supported both economic and political liberties.

This account is slightly exaggerated. Central and Eastern European history took a turn away from social diversity in the fifteenth and sixteenth centuries, as nobles and kings allied against towns and independent peasantries.[18] In Northwest Europe, in contrast, states remained rule bound even during absolutist rule in the seventeenth and eighteenth centuries; equally, multipolar pluralism was sufficiently well entrenched as to rule out all attempts—whether by popes, emperors or monarchs—at re-creating imperial unity. Nonetheless, it is crucial for my argument to note that civil society gained in self-consciousness from the experience of fighting against politico-religious unification drives. What mattered most of all was the rise of toleration. Attempts at suppression of the religious diversity created by the Reformation failed because Charles V's imperial pretensions were destroyed by balance of power politics. The principle of *cuius regio, eius religio* enshrined in 1555 at the Treaty of Augsburg seemingly allowed for diversity and difference, at least between states. But the principle was not really accepted and internalized, as the brutality of the Thirty Years War so decisively demonstrated. The Westphalian settlement of 1648 is a better marker of development in European attitudes, since it went beyond affirming the principle enshrined at Augsburg to the attempt to take religion out of geopolitics altogether, one mechanism towards which was the insistence that existing religious groups within states should be allowed to worship as they saw fit. As it happens, this marker too was incompletely observed, as is obvious once we remember that Locke's advocacy of toleration was written a generation later, with Montesquieu's chapters in *The Spirit of the Laws* accepting religion as long as it was not allied to fanaticism coming a full century later. But even if there is no absolutely decisive single marker, the change itself remains obvious. The long religious wars of Europe could not be won by either side for the forces of pluralism could always defeat any drive to politico-religious unification. Facing endlessly destructive stalemate, an extraordinary switch in attitudes took place: if agreement on detailed matters of belief could neither be reached nor imposed, a background consensus, to tolerate religious difference, was a viable alternative.[19] If toleration was at first merely accepted as a sour grapes philosophy, that is, one imposed by circumstances beyond one's control, it came to be valued: put differently in the spirit of Marx, a civil society in-itself, that is, a society in which negative resisting power was high, became a civil society for itself.

The initial breakthrough to civilized acceptance of difference in Europe obviously predated capitalism, with Montesquieu insisting later that the spirit of toleration then facilitated the triumph of capitalism. But capitalism did have something to do with the establishment of a political culture of civility in England—an event deserving notice since it underlines the creative importance of stalemate. It is important initially to recall that soft political rule was not always present in England; to the contrary, it was an historical achievement. Seventeenth-century England had been prey to civil war, treason trials, regicide, conspiracy, and the sundering of families. The very sudden move to political stability between 1675 and 1725 seems to be best explained by this traumatic experience. In a condition of continuing stalemate, in which neither side was capable of outright victory, it suddenly began to make sense, as it had to those divided by religion in early modern Europe, to try to live together—the successful accomplishment of which then fostered a culture of civility. For all that this political achievement was genuinely autonomous, it was nonetheless aided by economic factors. For one thing, the stalemate itself resulted from negative resisting power in society being widely spread. For another thing, the acceptance of

party alternation in government was eased by the presence of a growing economy, that is, of a source of remuneration other than that derived from political power. Differently put, separate patterns of power
reinforced each other, making any full account of the creation of civil
society necessarily multicausal in character.[20]

Civil society reached an initial apogee in eighteenth-century Britain.[21] Historically new levels of self-organization were made possible
by the spread of periodicals, coffee houses, and associations, all of which
were underwritten by a vibrant commercial society. Individualism flourished within this world. The modern novel, allowing discussion and
thought about new types of social identity, attests to this fact.[22] Related
to this and of still greater import was the birth of the first consumer
society.[23] Political innovation marked the age quite as much as these
basic social forces. John Wilkes stands as exemplar of the emergence
of popular politics, concerned at one and the same time with popular
representation and the interests of the English nation.

No similar set of developments marked the world outside the occident.
To analyze the social portfolios of a set of different civilizations, that
is, to understand the different directions taken elsewhere, is an immense
task and one that is certainly impossible here. Nonetheless, it is worth
saying something about the ideas and institutions of three other civilizations: the intent is that of underlining—rather than of explaining—
the claim made, namely that civil society did not emerge endogenously
outside the occident.

At the ideational level, little evidence can be found of interest in a
shared world within which difference is respected.[24] Islam certainly
stands utterly opposed to this.[25] What is most noticeable about this religion is the supreme confidence with which it offers a total set of injunctions designed to apply to politics as much as to matters of salvation.
The great tradition of this religion was not flexible enough to adapt
itself to different political regimes, as was Christianity, let alone keen
to allow for toleration. At first sight, the Hindu-Buddhist synthesis of
Indian civilization seems the exact opposite of this, essentially tolerant
in the relativism of its insistence that there are many ways in which to
find salvation. But this position is equally hostile to the notion of civil
society. That Western notion depends upon a *shared* world within which
differences are accepted; Indian civilization stands in contrast to this
for the brute reason that difference is absolute, with the shadow of an
untouchable being such as to pollute a member of the higher castes. It
may well be that Confucianism, whose ethic of politeness superficially

so resembles the British upper-class insistence that "manners maketh man," stands closest to the Western notion. But that oriental ethic never faced ideological rivals, rather preferring to retreat from power at any moment when its standards were temporarily placed in question. Mannered self-restraint may well be important in Chinese civilization but, in the last analysis, this was not occasioned by nor necessary for the management of ideological difference—let alone as a shell designed to allow human individuation.

There are of course myriad, complex and varied relations between ideologies and institutions, making the following comments about the latter alone especially arbitrary.[26] Still, the extent to which the social patterning of the major non-Western civilizations stands opposed to civil society is very striking. The certainty and completeness of Islam gave no room to mundane politics, and this so weakened states as to occasion an endless cycle in which corruption was always replaced with a new despotism; the fact that this was allied to perpetual external military threat from tribes ruled out of court limited, civil politics. The organization of Indian civilization by means of caste made states quite as weak—with the prospects of a short tenure of power again occasioning predation upon rather than cooperation with the forces of society. Chinese civilization did depend upon a long-lasting state, but the difficulty here was that the co-incidence of political and ideological power left no room for societal organizations which could balance centralized power. Of course, in all these civilizations, there was intense social organization. But such organization was either privatized or directed against the state: social actors faced states which were either short-lived and predatory or long-lasting and cohesive—and tended in any case to be caged by kinship based organizations. In every case, social patterning was far removed from the notion of civil society.

Flaws Revealed—And Repaired

It is impossible to leave an account of civility at this point. For the first consolidation of civil society was followed by the great ideological surge of the French Revolutionary period. The attempt to install unitary virtue in this period was so catastrophic that it merits a detailed analysis which space does not allow for in this essay. In any case, the politics of the citizen were interpreted, by Stendhal as much as by Marx, as opening a progressive era. Differently put, the idea of civility remained a program for the enlightened members of many European

middle classes. Hence a still more pressing question than that of analyzing the Terror is that of discovering why this promise was not ful-
filled, that is, why civil society collapsed so totally at the end of the
long nineteenth century. The key to explanation lies in the differential
character of European states. Bluntly, such states need, as a minimum,
to integrate both classes and diverse national identities if they are to be
stable and successful; civil society before the French Revolution had
not faced these challenges, which is to say that its sense of propriety
and refinement was the creation and property of the few. The crucial
issue that needs to be squarely faced is then whether civility is necessarily at odds with the entry of the people onto the political stage. The
answer to that question is negative. Whilst it is certainly true that "the
people" can behave brutally, the likelihood that they will do so depends
heavily on the extent to which they have been excluded from political
participation. For we should not romanticize exclusion. Gentleness is
not bred by being locked out; rather, exclusion encourages alternative
certainties which foster political viciousness. All this can be put in a
different manner. The tragedy of European civilization is that political
elites who might have modernized their polities failed to do so. The
lesson these diehards learned from the behavior of the Jacobins was
wrong: they sought to batten the hatches down rather than to modernize by inclusion. Let us see in turn how exclusion affected class and
nation in the period before disaster; the analysis of recovery that follows this will do much to highlight the analytic argument—for it will
demonstrate that inclusion moderates political life.

The impact of regime on working class behavior is particularly con-
spicuous. The best starting point for analysis is the realization that there
has been very great variation in levels of class consciousness amongst
different working classes. At one end of a scale of militancy in the
years before 1914 can be placed the accommodationist working class
of the United States and at the other the revolutionary workers of St
Petersburg, with British labor loyalty and German socialist militancy
standing between these poles.[27] In a nutshell, these working classes did
not share a single essence, rather they had very distinctive existences.
Variation is best explained in political terms, not surprisingly given
that social movements gain their character as the result of their interactions with particular states. In general, liberalism diffuses social conflict, whereas autocracy and authoritarianism concentrates it. Russian
workers had no choice but to "take on" the state since it prevented
them organizing their own trade unions;[28] in contrast, American work-

ers organized their class conflict at the industrial level, whilst remaining loyal to a political system which had given all white males the vote by the 1830s.

Two general points need to be noted in all this. Most immediately, the variation in levels of militancy among working classes allows generalizations to be made about ideologies. The United States has, famously, had no socialism, and precious little welfare spending to boot; this is a rather monotone social world, whose considerable successes have been achieved without having to face much social diversity. This contrasts with the situation of most European countries in which struggles for citizenship by labor movements led to considerable social diversity backed up by welfare systems. Russian revolutionary workers—or, rather, about the intellectuals who used their movement as a means to accede to power—created an alternative moral universe utterly opposed to civility in every form. When socialism was scientific and total, it had no room for difference and no time for doubt: enemies had to be destroyed rather than tolerated. Secondly, bourgeoisies lacked an essence quite as much as did proletariats. Where the English middle classes, facing the limited claims of a moderate working class lacking universal suffrage, consistently sought to extend civility, their German colleagues, faced by socialists with the vote, allied with ruling elites, thereby abandoning their best hopes and re-enforcing reaction.[29] Middle classes were thus opportunistic, friends to civil society only so long as their interests were not threatened from below. This variable character reflects the fact that they were often unable to control traditional elites; at a putative peak in the history of capitalism, the logic of politics was determined by others. If middle classes were scarcely brave, it remains important to stress the skill with which others acted upon them: Bismarck deliberately introduced a generalized suffrage so as to replace their hope with fear.

The same analytic categories can be applied to nations. Under a liberal regime, there is a good deal of evidence to suggest that nations, whether real or imagined, will rest content inside the borders of an existing multinational state. It is doubtful that the Austrian monarchy was doomed by its nationalities problem. By this I have in mind a rather particular Hapsburg enterprise, one that would have adopted the Kremsier reform proposals of 1849—the key clause of which asserted that:

> All peoples of the Empire are equal in rights. Each people has an inviolable right to preserve its nationality in general and its language in particular. The equality of rights in the school, administration and public life of every language in local usage is guaranteed by the state.[30]

Had this been enacted, different nationalities may not have sought to escape the empire. It is noticeable that even the nonliberal Dual Monarchy did not look set to fall apart after 1867, despite the tensions amongst the southern Slavs caused by forcible Magyarization. The elements of the monarchy were clearly unable to agree, but geopolitical facts—above all, the realization that small independent states sandwiched between Russia and Germany would be insecure—remained, and key groups, particularly the Czechs, did not yet look as if they were prepared to risk going it alone. The whole matter is best described with reference to Albert Hirschman's classic distinction between exit, voice, and loyalty: when it is possible to have voice inside a system, exit loses its attraction.[31] Once again the nature of political regime matters: the great ages of nationalism—in the sense of secessionist movements determined to have their own political roofs—have involved separation from authoritarian polities.

But this was a road not taken. The monarchy wished to continue to be a great power at a time when geopolitical conflict was entwined with and enhanced by demands for imperial possessions. In these circumstances, nationalist demands tended to become vicious: self-imagining in integralist ethnic terms led to absolute intolerance to those deemed not to be part of the new collectivity. It is very important, and much too often forgotten, that such absolutist certainty came to characterize extant states as much as secessionist movements. Above all, the respectable middle class employed by the German state, from government officials to "Fleet Professors" such as Max Weber, formed a radical right at once proud of Germany's achievements yet critical of the ancien regime which had excluded it from power on the grounds that it failed forcibly to represent the national interest. If integralist, ethnic imagining directed against the Poles was one deleterious consequence of this situation, a more important one was that the radical Right sought to cage its upper classes. Such nationalism can be better understood by comparing it to two other potential identities, those of the internationalists and of the nationally bounded.[32] Capitalists can inhabit international society, but their control over foreign policy has always been weak. In contrast, the statesmen of international society, whose sharing of norms allows the give and take of realism to work properly, often do control foreign affairs. They cease to do so when pressured from inside their nation-states. Little of that pressure comes in the majority of cases from the people, mere national actors caged by their nation-states without having their own distinctive geopolitical ideas. Nationalist actors do have such ideas, and their narrow privileging of national interest can make the game of realism much harder to play.

It was always possible that European multipolarity would bring disaster rather than progress once industry had been applied to war. Nonetheless, there can be no doubt but that the failure to integrate classes and nations contributed to the outbreak of war in 1914. In particular, German leaders wished for a success in order to appease a semimobilized society, but the pressures of the radical Right augmented disastrous geopolitical miscalculation. Of course, the war released revolutionary forces, in defeated Russia and Germany, that brought unimaginable horror to the world. This may make it seem perverse to insist that the flaws in civil society, at least in Western Europe, were repaired after 1945. But such is the case. The complete failure of European states has been followed by miraculous reconstruction.[33] Understanding the contours of this success will accentuate the analytic argument being made: just as there was nothing inevitable about the emergence of civil society, so too has the miracle of recovery rested on factors as much conjunctural as structural.

Most immediately, recovery was made possible by the outcome of the Second World War. To begin with, if the sheer fact of winning the war meant the destruction of the extreme Right, the United States also helped undermine the extreme Left. The promotion of centrist parties, particularly those of Christian Democracy, was far from difficult: the allies were essentially knocking at an open door, since wholesale conversion to a new order based on social redistribution had already been made.[34] Further, the United States provided a model of how to overcome internal social struggles. The politics of productivity, soon to be (loosely) described as Keynesian, meant that zero-sum redistributive conflicts could be avoided.[35] Finally, the American presence—together with an insistence on placing power above national self-determination—solved Europe's security dilemmas, thereby making genuine interdependence based on trade rather than imperialism's search for self-sufficiency the norm of economic life. Nonetheless, the United States did not realize its dream, that of Britain, divested of its colonies, creating a united, eventually supranational capitalist Europe capable of its own defense. Militarily, the United States was forced into becoming an "empire by invitation," that is, it accepted the initiative proposed by Bevin to found NATO, and thereby to lend troops whose hostage status was designed to ensure that European defense could not be ignored.[36] Economically, the near collapse forced the United States to endorse

France's attempt to lead in a Europe that would be opposed to multilateral norms. French bureaucrats sought to control Germany less by force than co-operation—for exactly that was involved in a decision by each country to give up national control of the geopolitically significant industries of coal and steel. But if one element to most initiatives towards European integration have had as an element the control of Germany, another has been that they served the interests of other states. Arrangements were put in place, to adapt the terms of Polanyi,[37] that cushioned market forces, that is, that allowed for some protection of society in order that the market might work: thus the historic achievement of the Common Agricultural Policy has in fact been to remove farmers from the land.[38]

European states now provide stable homes for civil society. Two sides of what is a single coin need to be stressed. On the one hand, such states have more nearly integrated their people into a settled way of life, marked by welfare provisions and continual economic growth, than ever before. On the other hand, these states now exist within a larger frame, meaning that zero-sum, no-holds-barred, beggar-my-neighbor competition has ceased: one way of measuring the extensiveness of this frame is that huge increase in intra-European trade which has created genuine interdependence. Regular meetings within the context of shared objectives has created a very particular, partially institutionally integrated society of states. All this deserves encapsulating in a formula. Many European states sought from the end of the nineteenth century to be everything, to become complete power containers, worlds unto themselves. This policy went disastrously awry. European states have finally become successful because doing less means that they achieve more.

All of this amounts to saying that major European countries are not now driven by any narrow nationalism. Liberalism has been cemented both by international agreement and by political and social inclusion, that is, by states becoming, in one sense, genuine nation-states. But what about the more obvious connotation of the term nation-state? What of the argument that secessionist nationalism might cause problems in Europe? Will European states which contain more than a single nation fragment?

Secessionist nationalism in the West *is* novel in seeking to remain within the international market. Nonetheless, economistic accounts mislead in suggesting that there will be an increasing number of secessions by rich regions blessed with some national symbol.[39] Far more

important than economic advantage is the nature of the political regime. If the great ages of nationalism involved separation from
authoritarianism, equally there have been very few exits from liberal
systems. It is customary in this connection to mention Norway in 1905
and Ireland in 1922—with the liberalism of the British state towards
Catholics at the end of the nineteenth century being very much open to
question. Further, the geopolitics of the contemporary West make it
possible to encourage and to add to liberalism. The long peace entails a
diminished need for centralized and unitary states, making it possible
to allow for the introduction of federal and consociational deals capable of appeasing discontent.[40] The European Union goes beyond this
in insisting on liberal treatment towards national minorities. Given voice,
as argued, exit is unlikely. This political sociology of nationalism in
the contemporary West is supported by obvious examples. Positively,
the Spanish state was able to contain its nationalities problem by a
combination of democratic opening and asymmetrical federalism.[41] The
British state provides a negative pole. Scottish nationalism is on the
increase for the very obvious reason that the Scots have voted for parties other than the one that actually governed them for the last fifteen
years—with that party going out of its way, moreover, to abolish "socialist" local government, most recently in Strathclyde. Were the British state less dreadfully sleepy, prepared to allow assemblies now that
a unitary geopolitical force is less needed, separatist sentiments would
die in tandem with the maintenance of a set of national identities; if the
increasing centralization of the British state continues, as is possible, it
may yet—incredibly—breed serious nationalist challenges.

A final comment about the extent to which civil society is now secure in the West can best be made by first highlighting the character of
the argument made about European recovery. Liberalism and economic
success have been present at the same time, supporters of each others'
achievements—with the shared ideology of welfare and full employment facilitating national policy coordination. Still, one wonders which
factor in the abstract is the more important. In this connection, it is
worth noting that those who felt that social achievements, and in particular corporatist arrangements, were most crucial often asserted that
liberal capitalism would suffer major instability were they to be removed. At least in the short term, this has not proved to be the case:
unemployment has risen, the welfare state been attacked and corporatism
in part discredited without much reaction. Of course, many have continued to further their interests within economies that have continued

to grow, making any final resolution of the issue perhaps impossible. Still, the result of the Cold War should make us realize that consolidated liberal regimes are, against the expectations of many academics and commentators who wrote in the 1970s about the ungovernability of the West, extremely stable. Differently put, statist power systems that seemed to be built of iron proved to be both feeble and brittle: the strength of liberalism, in contrast, resides in its ability to diffuse conflict throughout society. In a nutshell, civil society does seem secure in the West, even if the ability to exercise its rights have been somewhat diminished.

Imitation

Let us turn from—or, rather, put flesh on—these abstract considerations by straightforward analysis of the chances of extending civil society in the different political economies of the modern world. Let us begin with the East, and then turn to the South.

Hindsight makes us realize that communist power systems rested, as noted, on feet of clay.[42] Lenin had once remarked that the absence of self-organizations under tsarism would make it hard to really penetrate society. The prescience of this insight was most spectacularly seen in the manner in which this historical project came to an end. Civil society had been so destroyed—by bolshevism still more than by tsarism— that a reforming elite could find no partner with whom to make pacts, so as to conduct a controlled decompression of political life.[43] In consequence, the name of the game in this part of the world is now democratization rather than liberalization. Many scholars accordingly suggest that the reform plans of most elites are likely to be blocked by instant democratic pressures.[44] Such reform is of course desperately needed since all of this world is involved in a double transition, to democracy and the market—with some of it adding to this basic nation-building as well.[45] The chances for the emergence of a civil society look dim in the face of such an historical agenda.

Pessimism can be overdone. Depoliticization has resulted from absolute disenchantment with the past, leaving a good deal of steering room for elites to push through economic reforms. There may be little to fear from movements from below:

> [I]t also follows that it is entirely possible to have pluralism and a wide variety of small groups competing for influence without ever pulling large numbers of people into political life...if states remain strictly liberal and do not grant organizational

advantages to large groups, it may well be possible to maintain pluralism without extensive mass movements. If, for example, workers are free not to join unions, many will simply not join.[46]

Further, postcommunist societies have no equivalent of Latin America's powerful landed elite. Revolution destroyed the old classes, whilst those nomenklatura members who did not enter business are now very clearly defeated—except, of course, for those who have retained power by changing their colors, that is, by moving from communism to nationalism. All in all, the amount of resistance from within the elite to radical change is historically abnormally low. Most important of all, however, is something that has nothing to do with the legacy of communism, namely geography. Many Eastern and Central European states are extremely happy to have policies directed by experts associated with the European Union. The desire to return to Europe means that there is considerable resistance to the re-introduction of authoritarian incivilities.

If these factors lend advantage, it remains important to stress that depoliticization is not the same thing as the consolidation of civil society. The absence of positive faith in a regime can lead at any time to the emergence of symbolic politics, and in particular to trust in one's ethnic group. It is worth recalling at this point Tocqueville's comment about the legacy of divide and rule politics for continuing hatred of classes since it helps us to understand the virulence of postcommunist nationalism:

> It was no easy task bringing together fellow citizens who had lived for many centuries aloof from, or even hostile to, each other and teaching them to co-operate in their own affairs. It had been far easier to estrange them than it now was to reunite them, and in so doing France gave the world a memorable example. Yet, when sixty years ago the various classes which under the old order had been isolated units in the social system came once again in touch, it was on their wore spots that they made contact and their first gesture was to fly at each other's throats. Indeed, even today, though class antagonisms are no more, the jealousies and antipathies they caused have not yet died out.[47]

The fact that there are perhaps twenty-five million ethnic Russians outside the borders of Russia, many of whom face new and nationalizing states,[48] is of course hugely dangerous—especially give that the Russian elite is divided, with some being very reluctant to abandon empire so as to allow economic interdependence to flourish. More generally, a country is only strong when an orderly civil society works with the state. At present, most states in former communist countries may have autonomy but this scarcely makes up for the absence of linkages with

society. The lack of self-organization of society may be impeded, interestingly enough, by the legacy of excessive egalitarianism: differently
put, the striking of bargains—that is, the practice of normal, civil politics—only becomes possible once interests have become conscious and
organized.

It is already apparent that there will be diverse national outcomes to
these post-communist dilemmas. Countries which broke firmly with
the communist past,[49] which are physically close to the European Union,
which have civil traditions and histories of social self-organization,
and which have already undertaken basic nation-building may well be
able to establish civil societies. Against the hopes that can be entertained for the Czech Republic, Hungary, Poland, Estonia and Lithuania,
Slovenia, and perhaps even Slovakia have to be set the fears and pessimism that inevitably rise up when one looks further East. In this connection it is well worth noting the contrast between the post Soviet
Russian situation and that which is developing in the remaining great
communist power. China's reversal of Soviet policy, that is, its emphasis on perestroika *before* glasnost, looks set to create a proto-civil society, that is, a socially differentiated society in which interests are well
articulated. If elite skill can engineer a political opening, civil society
may thereby have a good chance of being consolidated.

The chances of Latin America achieving civil society are poised on
a knife edge. For all that the transition to civil society is far less complicated than it is in postcommunism, the fundamental difficulty that
remains is recognizable from that world. Populism and clientelism were
modes of inclusion controlled from above, that is, they had little to do
with societal self-organization.[50] In addition, redistributive policies—
which, given gross social inequality, are needed if civil society is to
have meaning—may lead to resistance on the part of the established
elite. Against the obvious pessimism engendered by these considerations can be set three factors which point in the opposite direction.
Firstly, fights within the elite of many countries have become moder-
ated and civil as the result of brutal trauma.[51] The determination to
keep conflict within bounds in countries such as Argentina and Chile,
where memories of the vicious consequences of extremes are sufficiently fresh, is such as to induce considerable self-discipline. Differently put, the seemingly endless oscillation between military rule and
democracy is a sort of stalemate; realization that this is so might well
lead to something better. Secondly, the chances for civil society are on
balance improved by the historic rejection of import substituting in-

dustrialization. The possibility of a rise in levels of economic growth and an increase in connections to the external world will both lend support to civil society. Thirdly, genuinely popular movements of the poor have recently emerged, most notably during the last period of military rule. As yet, it is too early to be certain that these new social movements will remain free from state interference. What remains desperately needed is the creation of a modern party system—that is, of parties at once independent of the state apparatus and under the control of well-articulated interests in society.[52] It is worth noting in this connection that East Asian societies, whose marked economic growth has given them both wealth and sufficient social differentiation to support a civil society, suffer quite as much from the absence of a party system. Trust within the political elite is limited, with the current president of South Korea seemingly seeking legitimacy by means of open populism.

If one can hope, with more or less conviction, for the spread of civil society in the social worlds considered, foreboding seems natural when considering other political economies. Adherence to the ideal of civil society in modern India, amongst popular sectors as well as within the elite, is very remarkable; but this exists within the social context of caste—which still cages huge numbers with awful efficiency. Still, India may well be set for a period of economic growth whilst its insistence on allowing minorities linguistic and social rights may continue to keep separatist tendencies in check.[53] In contrast, the insistence in Africa on trying to create unitary and homogenous nation-states has proved to be disastrous.[54] If encouragement can be found in the fact that there is now a general realization that this is so, and a corresponding interest—not least in South Africa—in consociational and federal arrangements, there can still be no doubt but that the scale of economic, social and national problems provide an awesome challenge to the possibility of the spread of civil society, despite interest shown in the idea by many African intellectuals.

Standing apart from everything that has been said to this point is Islam. If it is a terrible mistake to essentialize Islam, that is, to neglect Islamic intellectuals attracted to the notion of civil society, it is impossible to ignore the hostility shown by militant Islam at the end of the twentieth century to the ideals of civil society. These tensions are apparent in contemporary Turkey, despite the legacy of Ataturk's secularism, in the spectacular rise of the Islamist party Refah. But that is as nothing compared to the situation in much of the rest of the Middle East and North Africa. It may be that the power of fundamentalism, its stress on Puritanism and literacy, owes something to it being attuned to modernity—for all that, *pace* Gellner,[55] in practice it has proved a poor puritan ethic for development purposes. But whatever the explanation for the secularization-resistant quality of this world religion, what is hugely striking is the manner in which the completeness of its vision lends it enormous power when confronting massive social problems. If a foretaste of that power was seen in Iran in the last two decades, Algeria at the time of writing and potentially Egypt in the future look set to provide further evidence of a social world utterly foreign to that whose contours have been mapped here.

Conclusion

Clarity may be enhanced by concluding with a summary of the points made. My principal contention has been that civil society is more than the presence of strong and autonomous social groups: only a special type of societal self-organization, moderate, cooperative and permeable, makes a society civil. This form of society, born in Europe, was not somehow pre-ordained by the logic of history. To the contrary, its social moorings were weak and conjunctural, as was spectacularly evident in the collapse of Europe in the twentieth century and in the fact that recovery then owed much to intervention from the outside—that is, from the United States whose rather homogenized culture makes it something less than an exemplar of the concept in question. Scepticism was shown to the view that civil society is now set to conquer the world. Non-Western civilizations do not have the ideal at the center of their ideological repertoires, and anyway face social problems so debilitating as to rule out of court softer social and political life. Civil society is accordingly unlikely to spread outside parts of Central Europe and of Latin America.

Notes

1. J. Keane, ed., *Civil Society and the State* (London: Verso, 1988).
2. K. Kumar, "Civil Society," *British Journal of Sociology*, 44 (1993): 375–401; and C.M. Hann, "'Philosopher' Models on the Carpathian Lowlands, " in J.A. Hall, ed., *Civil Society* (Oxford: Polity Press, 1995), pp. 158–82.
3. G. Ekiert, "Resurrection of Civil Society and Politics of Discontent in Post-Communist Poland, 1989–1994," Conference Paper, McGill University, Department of Sociology, October 1994, pp. 1–32.
4. E.A. Gellner, *Conditions of Liberty: Civil Society and Its Rivals* (London: Hamish Hamilton, 1994).

5. J.D.Y. Peel, *Herbert Spencer* (London: Heinemann Educational Books, 1971).
6. J.A. Hall, "Understanding States'," in J.A. Hall, ed., *The State* (London: Routledge, 1993), pp. 1–17.
7. J.A. Hall, *Coercion and Consent* (Oxford: Polity Press, 1994), chapters 2–3.
8. J.A. Hall, "Sincerity and Politics," *Sociological Review*, vol. 25 (1977): 535–50.
9. This view has received fine recent codification by one of its initiators, S.M. Lipset, in "The Social Requisites of Democracy," *American Sociological Review*, 59:1: (1994): 1–23.
10. A.O. Hirschman, *The Passions and the Interests* (Princeton, N.J.: Princeton University Press, 1977).
11. M. Ignatieff, *The Needs of Strangers* (London: Chatto and Windus, 1985); C. Blum, *Rousseau and the Republic of Virtue* (Ithaca, N.Y.: Cornell University Press, 1986).
12. D. Zhao and J.A. Hall, "State Power and Patterns of Late Development," *Sociology* 28 (1994): 211–29.
13. D. Bell, *The End of Ideology* (New York: Collier Books, 1962).
14. G. Vidal, *Creation* (London: Heinemann, 1981).
15. J. Goody, *The Development of the Family and Marriage in Europe* (Cambridge: Cambridge University Press, 1983).
16. M. Mann, *Sources of Social Power*, volume 1: *From the Beginning to 1760 AD* (Cambridge: Cambridge University Press, 1986), chapter 10.
17. J.A. Hall, *Powers and Liberties* (Oxford: Blackwell, 1985), part 1.
18. D. Chirot, ed., *The Origins of Backwardness in Eastern Europe* (Berkeley: University of California Press, 1989).
19. H. Kamen, *The Rise of Toleration* (London: Weidenfeld and Nicolson, 1967).
20. J.H. Plumb, *The Growth of Political Stability in England, 1675–1725* (Harmondsworth: Penguin, 1969).
21. P. Langford, *A Polite and Commercial People* (Oxford: Oxford University Press, 1989).
22. I. Watt, *The Rise of the Novel* (Harmondswroth: Penguin, 1963).
23. N. McHendrick, J. Brewer, and J.H. Plumb, *The Birth of a Consumer Society* (London: Europa Press, 1982); C. Campbell, *The Romantic Ethic and the Spirit of Modern Consumerism* (Oxford: Blackwell, 1987).
24. M. Carrithers, M. Collins, and S. Lukes, eds., *The Category of the Person* (Cambridge: Cambridge University Press, 1985).
25. P. Crone, *Slaves on Horses* (Cambridge: Cambridge University Press, 1980); Ernest A. Gellner, *Muslim Society* (Cambridge: Cambridge University Press, 1981).
26. For an attempt at a general comparative account, see my *Powers and Liberties*.
27. M. Mann, *Sources of Social Power*, volume 2: *The Rise of Classes and Nation-States* (Cambridge, Cambridge University Press, 1993), chapters 15, 17, and 18.
28. T. McDaniel, *Autocracy, Capitalism and Revolution in Russia* (Berkeley: University of California Press, 1988).
29. D. Geary, *European Labour Protest, 1848–1945* (London: Methuen, 1984).
30. A. Sked, *The Decline and Fall of the Hapsburg Empire, 1815–1918* (London: Dent, 1989), p. 143.
31. A.O. Hirschman, *Exit, Voice and Loyalty* (Cambridge, Mass.: Harvard University Press, 1978).
32. Mann, *Sources of Social Power*, volume 2, chapters 20–21 and passim.
33. A. Milward, *The Reconstruction of Western Europe, 1945–51* (Berkeley: University of California Press, 1984); A. Milward, *The European Rescue of the Nation-State* (Berkeley: University of California Press, 1992).

34. C. Maier, "The Two Postwar Eras and the Conditions for Stability in Twentieth-Century Western Europe,",*American Historical Review* 86 (1981): 214–32.

35. C. Maier, "The Politics of Productivity," *International Organisation* 31 (1977): 607–33.

36. G. Lundestad, "Empire by Invitation?" *Journal of Peace Research* 23 (1986) 263–7.

37. K. Polanyi, *The Great Transformation* (Boston: Beacon Press, 1944).

38. Milward, *The European Rescue of the Nation-State*, passim.

39. The most brilliant such account is T. Nairn, *The Break-up of Britain* (London: New Left Books, 1977).

40. J. McGarry and B. O'Leary, "Introduction," in J. McGarry and B. O'Leary, eds., *The Politics of Ethnic Conflict Regulation* (London: Routledge, 1993), pp. 1–40.

41. J. Linz and A. Stepan, "Political Identities and Electoral Sequences," *Daedalus*, 121 (1992): 123–39.

42. J.A. Hall, "After the Fall," *British Journal of Sociology*, 45 (1994): 525–42.

43. R. Bova, "Political Dynamics of the Post-Communist Transition," *World Politics*, 44 (1991): 113–38.

44. A. Przeworski, *Democracy and the Market* (Cambridge: Cambridge University Press, 1991).

45. C. Offe, "Capitalism by Democratic Design?" *Social Research*, 58 (1991): 865–902.

46. E. Comisso, "Property Rights, Liberalism and the Transition from 'Actually Existing Socialism'," *East European Politics and Society* 5 (1991), p. 184.

47. A. de Tocqueville, *The Old Regime and the French Revolution* (New York, Anchor Books, 1955), p. 107.

48. R. Brubaker, "Aftermaths of Empires and the unmixing of peoples," *Ethnic and Racial Studies*, 18 (1995): 189–209.

49. I am indebted on this point to discussion with Anatoly Khazanov.

50. N. Mouzelis, *Politics in the Semi-Periphery* (London: Macmillan, 1986).

51. T. Karl, "Dilemmas of Democratization in Latin America," *Comparative Politics*, 22 (1990): 1–21.

52. F. Hagopian, "After Regime Change," *World Politics*, 45 (1993): 464–500.

53. D. Laitin, *Language Repertoires and State Construction in Africa* (Cambridge: Cambridge University Press, 1992).

54. B. Davidson, *The Black Man's Burden* (New York: Random House, 1992).

55. Gellner, *Muslim Society*.

3

Between Public and Private:
Towards a Sociology of Civil Society

Adam B. Seligman

Over the past few years the idea of civil society has had a rather strange and a-symptotic history. For at the same time that its value as an analytic concept or political slogan has declined in the countries of East Central Europe, it has been picked up in the West, used (and often misused) by writers on both the political right and the left to legitimize their own social programs and has entered academic discourse with a vengeance that is somewhat disquieting. One cannot pick up a periodical or book in the social sciences these days without coming across the notion of civil society used in every context imaginable and imbued with as many meanings are there are authors: Civil Society in Nigeria, in China, Globalization and Civil Society, The birth, rebirth, or death of Civil Society, Civil Society and Democracy in Latin America, in the Middle East, On the Path to Civil Society, Israel: From Mobilized to Civil Society, Foucault, Habermas and Civil Society, Civil Society and political economy, Civil Society and Shanghai society, Civil Society and the civil service, and apartheid and postapartheid, Civil Society and communism, and capitalism, and liberalism, and post-communism, Civil Society in America, in Siberia, in the Enlightenment, in Russia, Civil Society and the Family, and the State, Civil Society and Client-ilism, and Heteroglossia in Bakhtin, and CD-Rom...and one awaits the article on Civil Society and the Carburetor. The list goes on and on in an endless litany of titles that take us no further towards understanding the term or its possible relevance for our contemporary predicament (in either the West or the East, or Asia, Africa or the Middle East for that matter).

This inflation in the use of the term can, on the whole, be attributed to the dual influence of self-interest and market forces. When it is used it is often in the pursuit of certain, very circumscribed, interests—of scholars as well as political actors. Academics, as is well known, are always eager to assimilate the latest catch-phrase, this year's "paradigm" and as anything with "civil society" in the title seems to sell well the phrase (if not the concept) continues to appear in article after article with little care taken to delineate its meaning, historical, philological, or sociological attributes. Among social activists a similar logic holds. In the countries of Eastern Europe, the history of the revolutions of 1989 are being reinterpreted through what are essentially "whiggish" lenses which present the intellectuals as the major dramatis personae who gradually mobilized society against a totalitarian State under the rather abstract banner of "civil society." In the West a somewhat similar dynamic holds. Indeed and just as the slogan arose in Eastern Europe in the 1980s as a cudgel to batter the totalitarian State, it has emerged in the 1990s in Western Europe and in the U.S. by critics of the existing political order to press home their claims. Interestingly (and in a way that should be a warning to us all) the idea of civil society is used by political groups and thinkers on both the right and the left and though in Europe in general it is most often the province of the left, in the U.S. it has been appropriated by both groups to advance their political agenda.

Thus, for right-of-center thinkers as well as for libertarian followers of F. Hayek, the quest for civil society is taken to mean a mandate to deconstruct many of the powers of the state and replace them with intermediary institutions based on social voluntarism. For many liberals, civil society is identified with social movements, also existing beyond the state. And while many of the former refuse to recognize that voluntary organizations can be of a particularly nasty nature and based on primordial or ascriptive principles of membership and participation that put to shame the very foundations of any idea of civil society; the latter are blind to the fact that the achilles heel of any social movement is its institutionalization which—one way or the other—must be through the state and its legal (and coercive) apparatus. In the meantime both communitarians and liberals continue to assimilate the idea of civil society to their own terms, invest it with their own meanings and make of it what they will. Right, Left, and Center, North, South, East, and West, civil society is identified with everything from multiparty systems and the rights of citizenship to individual voluntarism and the spirit of community.[1]

That any concept could be invested with such varied and often contradictory meanings should make us suspect of its usefulness within the social sciences (if not in politics). One way to address this state of affairs is of course simply to indulge in the requisite historical, philosophical, and sociological research in an attempt to understand the term. This is however a project which we cannot undertake in the short space of this essay. Rather, I suggest, let us look at those two components and the problem of their synthesis which make up the very idea of civil society and, I submit, allow it the very diverse interpretations to which it has been subjected. These are the ideas of the public and the private.

For if constitutive of civil society is some sense of a shared public (as I believe all would agree)—so is the very existence of the private. It is after all the very existence of a free and equal citizenry—of that autonomous, agentic individual—of the private subject that makes civil society possible at all. The public space of interaction is a public space only insofar as it is distinguished from those social actors who enter it as private individuals. Where there is no private sphere, there is, concomitantly, no public one—both must exist for sense to be made of either one.

It is precisely this tension between public and private, as constitutive of civil society that I wish to develop. For civil society is, most essentially, that realm where the concrete person, that particular individual, subject of his or her own, wants, caprices, and physical necessities—seeks the attainment of these "selfish" aims. It is that arena where the "burgher" as private person seeks to fulfil his or her own interests. Civil society is thus that arena where—in Hegelian terms—free, self-determining individuality sets forth its claims for satisfaction of its wants and personal autonomy.

These are of course well-known perspectives on civil society—drawing on the traditions of Ferguson, Smith, and, most especially, Hegel.[2] Indeed, what, I wish to claim, stood at the core of all attempts to articulate a notion of civil society lay the problematic relation between the private and the public, the individual and the social, of public ethics and individual interests, individual passions, and public concerns. More pointedly, the question of civil society was, and still is how could individual interests be pursued in the social arena and, similarly, the social good in the individual or private sphere. What is ultimately at stake in this question is, moreover, the proper mode of *normatively* constituting the existence of society—whether in terms of private individuals or in the existence of a shared public sphere.

The answer to these problems hinges on the conception of the public arena—as simply a neutral space where individual interests are played out, or, alternatively, as a realm of value in itself. If the former, the public space cannot be envisioned as a constitutive sphere of ethical validation. If the latter (positing the public sphere as *the* realm of value) the individual or particular lose their autonomous status.

It is this problem that I wish to pursue in the following essay through two very different modes of inquiry. First I will review (very schematically) two classical early-modern attempts to bring the contradictory demands of public and private life into harmony with one another and then, in view of the failure of these attempts I will offer a modest—and much more sociologically orientated—proposal for understanding the problem of public and private as it exists in contemporary, modernist cultures.

Civil Society between Public and Private

As I do not wish to review here the whole history of classical political economy I will present only two examples of previous attempts to square the contradictory demands of public and private and will bring illustrations from Hegel and Adam Smith as only two representative figures—of different strands of this classical tradition. What I wish to emphasize is how Hegel's notions of ethical solidarity based on the unity of public right with private ethics find a strong resonance in the earlier tradition of the Scottish Enlightenment (of "natural sympathy," moral affections and "sociability"). I will take only one example, though a centrally important one: the phenomenon of property exchange which takes place in the market, is itself, in the writings of both Hegel and Adam Smith, imbued with a value that subsequent Marxist and utilitarian theories have, in different ways, occluded.

In Hegel's writings it becomes clear that the individual need for recognition (and hence existence) is attained through the recognition of property. Indeed, for Hegel property in the realm of civil society takes the place of love in the realm of the family.[3] Through both (as different moments in the actualization of the spirit) a universal will is constructed through recognition, and as Hegel observed at the end of part I of the Jena lectures: "The will of the individual is the universal will—and the universal will is the individual. It is the totality of ethical life [*Sittlichkeit*] in general, immediate, yet [as] Right."[4] It is, according to Hegel, precisely through the mutual recognition involved in property exchange that the individual as self-consciousness (*fur sich*) is constructed, which—one may add—is the closest we can come to an ethical realm in a world defined by the mutual exchange between different entities (as opposed to the ideal self of the Greek polis, undifferentiated from community). In this latter-day world, the realm of ethics is constructed in and only in the mutual recognition which defined civil society. What we find in Hegel is thus a substantiation of both private and public in the mutual exchange of individuals in the public and civil arena.

Strangely congruent with this notion is the idea found in Adam Smith's (1759) *The Theory of Moral Sentiments* which argues that the moral basis of individual existence is the need for recognition and consideration on the part of others. "To be observed, to be attended to, to be taken notice of with sympathy, complacency and approbation" are for Smith the driving force of "all the toil and bustle of the world...the end of avarice and ambition, of the pursuit of wealth."[5] Thus, as tellingly pointed out by A.O. Hirshman, economic activity itself is rooted, in *The Theory of Moral Sentiments*, in the noneconomic needs for sympathy and appreciation.[6] It is for Adam Smith our interest in "being the object of attention and approbation" that leads to the complex of activity which defines economic life.[7] What is common to both perspectives, albeit in different ways, is the idea of the arena of exchange (of civil society) as rooted in a sphere of values predicated on the mutuality of individual recognition.

In terms of a theory of civil society what both attitudes would indicate is an approach to the public realm—to the sphere of commodity exchange—as something well beyond a neutral arena where a "universal subject" (owner of commodities) acts out their individual interests. Rather, both Hegel and Adam Smith, albeit with different stresses, maintain that interaction itself as the matrix of individual existence.

For Hegel however this public validation of individual selves would ultimately lead to the overcoming of civil society in the apotheosis of the universal State (the public sphere par excellence), while for Smith it would, finally, unravel (see below) in a glorification of individual conscience and private existence. And while this is not the place to enter into an analysis of either thinker, the broader dynamic of that contradiction which adheres to the attempt to synthesize public and private within the idea of civil society does deserve our attention.

For the selfsame validation of the individual in and through the social which we have seen in the realm of exchange was, according to Habermas, at the essence of the legal-normative structure as well. Thus he points out:

> The criteria of generality and abstractness that characterizes legal norms had to have a peculiar obviousness for privatized individuals who, by communicating

with each other in the public sphere of the world of letters, confirm each other's subjectivity as it emerges from their sphere.... These rules, because they are universally valid, secure a space for the individuated person; because they are objective, they secure a space for what is most subjective; because they are abstract, for what is most concrete.[8]

Here then we enter into the crux of those contradictions which in essence define the idea of civil society. For whether in the realm of commodity exchange, or of legal sanctions, it is precisely the generalized, formal, and abstract nature of the rules governing intercommunicative action that afford the particular individual his universal social status (in the meeting of particular wills). This, then, is the paradox at the core of modern civilization—an ethical solidarity (of, if we follow the Scottish Moralists, "natural sympathy" and "moral affections") in the public realm achieved through the universalization of abstract reason in terms of particular subjects.

That "metaphysical equality"—which defines the public nature of individual existence in the modern era and pertains to the equality of citizens is, as we see, dependent on the workings of a universal abstract reason. Both are essential components of the idea of civil society.[9] For if, on the one hand, the arena of civil society, of law and exchange was not viewed as simply a neutral space of interaction but was rather, that arena where the private (particular) was itself constituted and so shared in the attributes of some ethical—or transcendental (if not transcendent) validation, on the other hand, the very establishment of this ethical space was based on abstract, instrumental reason, orientated towards the individual parts rather than to the social whole. In fact Habermas's whole analysis of *The Structural Transformation of The Public Sphere* in the nineteenth century traces precisely this awareness (expressed albeit in class terms) of the reduction of the public sphere to an arena of private interests, incapable of representing the social whole (an insight that, by the way, was prefigured by Smith's own turning away from any belief in the salutary effect of public opinion by the end of the eighteenth century).

In the ideal classic modernist vision, society or the public sphere, is thus posited as a realm of value, indeed precisely as that arena where those individuals, existing in formal equality were constituted. In this reading, the public and private spheres, as matrices of social life, stood, however, in tension with one another. For if the public sphere was the locus of ethical solidarity, it was so, precisely because in it, the individual as particular was validated in his (and unfortunately then, not her) individuality.

The Unraveling of Civil Society

As we can see, the demands of the formal equality of citizens—based on instrumental reason—are ultimately (or at least seem to be) irreconcilable with the continued existence of a locus of (ultimate) value rooted in the public sphere. The focus of conflict is here between a public or socially constituted source of value and the very terms of ethical validation in modernity—defined by formal equality and, ultimately, by instrumental rationality (as a component of procedural justice). The latter continually vitiating the existence of the former. For the more the terms of equality—between autonomous subjects—are realized in the public sphere, the less this sphere itself need retain its qualities as source of value.

In slightly different terms, that individual autonomy, upon which the subject/citizen rests is validated in the public sphere of civil society. However, the very terms of this existence are those of instrumental-legal-rationality. A rationality of means and not of ends (this is hardly surprising as the *end* is each and every individual subject). Consequently, the more this rationality is realized in the sphere of public life, the less common ground remains between the individual subjects.

The resulting devaluation of the public sphere is what is behind so many of the current jeremiads in the West—of left and right both—which go under the heading of civil society. Whether the term itself provides any solution to the problem is another matter entirely (and if we follow the thought of either Hegel or Smith, not to mention Hume or Marx, the answer would seem to be in the negative). For the contradiction between public and private is an age-old one, one that informs the very project of modernity itself. In the annals of Western political thought and practice, it has taken many forms and has been expressed in many ways, from Benjamin Constant's juxtaposition of ancient and modern definitions of liberty to Isaiah Berlin's explication of the difference between positive and negative liberty.[10] Indeed, we may look to the very different traditions of "civic virtue" and "civil society" as embodying two almost contradictory orientations toward the public and private as alternative loci of value, virtue, and the public good.[11] In the former tradition the public good is one which overrides all private goods and rests, ultimately, on the overcoming of self-interest for public concerns. This however is not simple public spiritedness, but a vision of humankind which sees in the public arena the only possibility to realize and fulfill the self-identity of the private citizen. By contrast, the ethical idea in the civil society tradition became for many thinkers ultimately a private one, which, while acknowledging the necessity of public validation was finally realized only within the hearts, minds, and acts of exchange of individual social actors.

Indeed in the writings of Smith himself (especially in the move from the first to the sixth edition of *The Theory of Moral Sentiments*) the public nature of individual validation gives way to a much more private locus of virtue and ethical realization.[12] In this move the idea of the "impartial spectator," the "great inmate of the human breast" as adjudicator of competing moral goods ultimately breaks with the naive anthropology of Ferguson and Shaftesbury, with all ideas of innate sympathy as well as with any allegiance to collective norms and mores, what well may be termed in the language of republican citizenship, with the "latent community" as repositories of virtue.[13] Rather than any facile identification with public opinion and a "propriety" rooted in common standards and social morality, the impartial spectator is (in the sixth edition of *The Theory*) internalized. As the "man within" takes the place of the "man without"—or public opinion—as the source of virtue a new much more private and individual foundation is posited for the pursuit of the public good and virtue casts off its moorings in the public sphere. Henceforth the realm of virtue (and hence value) was to be located in the individual citizen himself, that citizen for whom the abstract and impersonal laws of justice (*pace* Habermas above) provided the necessary framework for interaction and exchange.

In many respects these two visions of political life and of the public good—focused on the public and private realms respectively—continue to resonate in the debate between liberal and republican (or communitarian) versions of citizenship. Liberal (or what Charles Taylor has called "procedural") liberal theory views society as an assortment of morally autonomous individuals, each with his and her own concept of the good life, with the function of society being limited to ensuring the legal equality of these individuals through a procedurally just (or fair) process of democratic decision making in the public sphere.[14] This tradition is concerned with insuring the continued operation of universally valid principles of justice (or right) rather than with imposing any particular moral vision on the individual social actors who make up society.

Republican versions of citizenship (including many currently being aired in Eastern and East Central Europe) posit, by contrast, a conception of society as a "moral community" engaged in the pursuit of a common good, whose ontological status is prior to that of any individual member. In this reading the terms of selfhood no less than those of community are transformed, as—following Sandel's critique of Rawls—there can exist no "radically situated" or "unencumbered" self free from the morally binding and constituting ties of a particular community.[15]

What I am suggesting can be learned from these debates and from the fact that many of its leading advocates use the idea of civil society in their polemics is that the current popularity of the idea of civil society among politicians and well as scholars stems from its assumed synthesis of one of the most fundamental contradictions of modern life—that between the public and the private. The very diverse meanings and valences attributed to the term stem moveover from its own ambiguity and essentially from the fact that—as I hope I have, however schematically indicated—rather than overcoming the opposition it subsumes it within the logic of modernity itself. No wonder then that the most interesting of contemporary uses are prescriptive and political—caught however within a procrustean bed whose dimensions are at least as old as the eighteenth century.

Given this situation I would suggest that rather than seek to overcome this opposition—within the realm of normative political theory—we would do much better to try to understand the problematic relation of public and private in historic terms with analytic categories taken more from the realm of sociology than from political philosophy. In the following sections of this essay I will thus offer an alternative understanding of the problem of civil society—that is of the problem of public and private—in terms of a very specific set of meanings that have come to define the private realm in modern Western societies, those centering on the individual and of the moral autonomy of this individual.

Sociological Perspectives on the Public and the Private Spheres

When attempting to understand the problem of public and private it is useful to begin with the very diverse and sometimes opposing meanings and definitions attributed by different theorists to these concepts. One glaring example of this type of divergence among existing perspectives can be found in Hannah Arendt's conception of public and private—which in her reading begin in fact to disappear in modernity with the "rise of the social," a concept which in her usage subsumes the very distinction that had previously existed (in antiquity for example) between public and private realms.[16] This very compelling account stands in contradiction to that of most other theorists, from Marx, Constant, and down to Habermas, all of whom see in the eighteenth century and the beginnings of modern capitalist culture the very origins or emergence of that distinction between public and private realms whose demise Arendt posits in the selfsame period.

Or, to take, yet another example, Norberto Bobbio's now classic essay on "Public and Private/The Great Dichotomy" where he classifies these concepts in relational terms of inequality vs. equality and of relations between the parts and the whole vs. relations among parts.[17] His scheme would appear something as follows:

Public	Private
unequal	equal
relations between parts and whole	relations between parts
God	brothers
State	kin
Family	friends
citizens	enemies

Here of course we have the beginnings of a fascinating cross-cutting categorization, but one laden with problems as soon as we leave the field of political philosophy and enter the minutia of daily life. Thus, relations between God and man while certainly unequal and pertaining to the relations of the part to the whole are also, often, defined within the privacy of conscience and in many circumstances the privacy of a home or other secluded space (at least since the Protestant Reformation). So too the family has, in modernity, entered into the private realm as, for that matter, has the state penetrated into the regulation of private lives and agendas. On the other side of the balance, the relation between brothers are characterized by equality only in some cultures and not in others (primogeniture being a good example of the inequality reigning between brothers). In tribal societies kin systems may be ordered according to principles of equality or hierarchy and one does not take analytic preference over the other. Friendship too, as an informal relation between equals is a most modern phenomenon with vast variations across cultures and historical periods. What does remain of Bobbio's definitions is the crucial (somewhat Hegelian) and thought provoking identification of the public with the relation between the parts and the whole, and the private with the relations between the parts. This however is still a far cry from enabling us to understand how these definitions and relations are played out in different cultural settings and, of central importance, in our own culture of modernity and/or postmodernity. It will however, be a distinction we shall have reason to return to in our own analysis of the changing terms of public and private in the contemporary world.

How different moreover such an interpretive model stands from the one sociological attempt to chart out the dimensions of private and public and to provide a preliminary classification of these phenomena. I am referring here to the work by Benn and Gaus, who distinguish public from private along the axes of: (a) access (i.e., pubic or private space); (b) agency (i.e., capacity of actor in his/her act as defining intentionality of action; (c) interest (at the root of action—public or private).[18] However, and as the authors themselves admit, this scheme of analysis does itself presuppose the very liberal distinction between public and private spheres which it aims to categorize or define. As such it reflects as well the very modern and Western sets of assumptions on the private realm as founded on the moral autonomy and economic agency of the individual social actor.

Indeed, this identification of the private realm with the individual is an essential aspect of the way publicness and privateness are constructed in the West and one to which we should pay a bit closer attention. It is, I wish to claim, this moral valuation of the individual that has, since the seventeenth century come to define our very ideas of the private realm as well as our evaluation of it in respect to those realms deemed more public in nature. In fact, the moral or ethical elevation of the private over the public (as that arena where virtue, morality and conscience are realized) emerged, I will argue, concomitantly with the growing, Western realization of individual agency and autonomy.

Needless to add, these conceptions stand at the core of Western liberalism as it developed from the writings of Hobbes and Locke in the seventeenth century.[19] The sharp turn away from any Aristotelian (Christian or otherwise) conceptions of human nature (or essences) to one privileging individual responsibility and agency, beyond we may note, any metaphysically assured community of interests, stands, after all, at the root of what Alasdair MacIntyre has termed the "enlightenment project" of modernity, and as such, at the core of its social categories as well.

Thus we may note at the outset that the very construction of that eighteenth-century "publicness" that was theoretically articulated by Habermas and admirably charted by the work of historians such as Robert Chartier (on the development of a literary culture in eighteenth-century France) or Sarah Maza (on the increasing public nature and representation of private court cases in the same period) had its compliment in the very definition and isolation of the private as a realm of value that we find in the writings of Philip Aries and other Annaliste historians.[20] Not surprisingly both realms can be seen as defining themselves concomitantly and in mutual recognition. Ultimately I would argue, both rested on the newly emergent *idea* of the individual and of individual agency as coming to exist beyond the normative expectations of, what we would term, social status and role.

Necessary for this development was, of course, a reformulation of the reigning terms of sociability (and of the laws governing such sociability). Indeed and as Aries himself has noted "the entire history of private life comes down to a change in the forms of sociability."[21] Inherent to this eighteenth-century change in the terms of sociability was the gradual transformation of the meaning of the private from that which was hidden and withdrawn (either on the cause of shame or the *imperia arcana* of royal justice for example) to what pertains only to the individual. To be sure both meanings continue to be used today, often contributing to much confusion in our understanding of the phenomena. Yet an understanding of the modern distinction between these realms, and of its specificity in terms of other forms of social organization rests, I would maintain, on an appreciation of this historical dynamic. The oft-remarked upon lack of a "publicness" (in the Habermasian sense) in premodern European culture (allowing for such exceptions as Renaissance co-fraternities in Italian city-states for example) rests on a conception of privateness as that which was hidden and beyond the gaze of a society where the public itself (the whole) was constituted solely in transcendent terms (the *corpus mysticum* of the Church, universal and apostolic). Only the disembedment of the whole (society) from this transcendent matrix allowed that differentiation of realms through which the idea of public and private in their modern senses emerged. In this differentiation a new whole (in Bobbio's sense) was constituted which turned on the very privileging and valorization of private selves that the new definition of privateness involved. This was, for example, reflected in the development of modern natural law theory, as manifest in the quote from Habermas above.

The Private, the Individual, and the Role of Complexity

The emergence of a private sphere as increasingly identified with the idea of the morally autonomous individual arose, I would argue, very much as a "Durkheimian" social fact out of the growth and prolif-eration of social roles that came to characterize polities and societies in Western Europe. In the following I will in fact seek to link these two developments, of role complexity and the growth of individual identi-ties as providing the background to the problem of public and private realms as we experience them today.

Analytically, this process involved the multiplicity of roles and so the unique configuration of role sets that becomes every "individual identity." Connected to this is the developing propensity to negotiate the contents and expectations involved in each role. Moreover these developments allow the crucial possibility to judge one role (or role set) from the perspective of another (or others). As the person becomes a vector of more and more roles the very idea of the individual be-comes a means to specify the unique aggregation of roles that each social actor bears. This very multiplicity of roles carries with it the potential for mediating and blurring the boundaries between roles in a singular manner and for the progress of an almost infinite self-reflexiv-ity as each role can become the archimedean point from which others can be judged, negated, modified, and so on. Connected to this process (and facilitating its progress) is that fact that as roles and role-sets pro-liferate within social formations the boundaries between the roles be-come more permeable and the moves from one to the other less structured by formal (ritualized) criteria. There is then not only more negotiability in the definition of each role but, crucially, in the moves from one to the other. This too becomes a process that each social actor negotiates alone, in private, rather than within the confines of norma-tive group-held injunctions.

While these analytic traits characterize social formations from Papua, New Guinea to Los Angeles, USA, the degree of differentiation between roles, as well as the specific type of roles defined are crucial variables in the development of individual and collective identities. Thus and while some notion of the individual and of the private sphere as separate from the group exists in all societies known, there is little doubt that the type of individualism (which sees in the individual the locus of the moral and political orders, the fount of agency and intentionality, a transcendental subject invested with transcendent rights) which we associate with West-ern European civilization (i.e., that civilization that developed from the Judeo-Christian and Greco-Roman foundations) is a relatively unique phenomenon. It is moreover one which came to invest the private sphere with a unique and moral priority.

While the uniqueness of this phenomenon has been studied by scholars ranging from Max Weber and Marcel Mauss down to contemporaries such as Charles Taylor and, in a very different mode, Louis Dumont, the above-noted perspectives on role open some imposing questions for existing traditions and understanding of Western individualism and its concomitant ideas of the private sphere as realm of value.[22] For, and to a great extent, these traditions see Western individualism as rooted, in one form or another, in the soteriological assumptions of Christian belief. That is to say, the very positing of a monotheistic creator G-d and—especially with Christendom—the "personal" relation of the "individual" to the G-dhead are, to large extent, the foundation of our notions of individualism and of the transcendent subject. At present I am not concerned with specifying either the precise origin of such beliefs (whether in the Jewish idea of creation in the image of G-d or in Christian doctrines of grace) nor in the varieties of its development and transformation (in Kantian ideas of the transcendental subject for instance). All those aware of this tradition of sociological thought can easily delimit its contours. What I am interested in exploring however is the notion that it is not in Christianity per se, that is in its soteriological doctrines, that the origin of modern individualism is to be found, but rather in the specific differentiation, division and definition of roles that it brought to the cultural, political, social and economic arenas that is perhaps at the core of our own understanding of the individual.[23]

Let us, for arguments sake take only three historical periods that have, in the past, been seen as critical points in the development of Western ideas of the individual: Late Antiquity, the Renaissance, the Protestant Reformation. All have been identified with the development of Christian individualism through the refinement of Christian salvational doctrines. Is it not possible that the individualism that we identify with these eras is an outcome not solely of the changing content (soteriology) of religious civilization but of its changing form (in the nature of group affiliations).[24] Thus while Late Antiquity is the period of the emergence of Christianity as a world-historical religion with its own salvational dogma of grace—it is also the period of the emergence of a whole new set of roles and role definitions identified with Christianity (as for example in the transformation of sexual relations from a public matter to the private concern of the individuals).[25] This is, after all, the central dynamic behind the replacement of kinship identities with membership in a sacramental community.[26] Similarly, the positing of the City of God provided a most central counterfactual reality from which the City of Man could be judged, negated or affirmed. It injected a dimension between social reality and ontological reality (through of course the redefinition of the later in terms of transcendence) that gave to the former a lability and negotiability not hitherto existent.[27] However the argument I wish to make is that perhaps it is less in transcendence itself, and more in the radical breaking and making of social bonds that accompanied it, that the origins of Christian individualism is to be found.

The development of early Christianity saw, after all, the construction of a new "moral community" of believers differentiated from the societies in which they lived and united by bonds of exclusive communal fellowship.[28] These groups of early Christians, scattered across the Roman Empire, were united by social ties of a charismatic nature. Cutting across existing solidarities of kith and kin, the message of the early Church was one of a social solidarity rooted only in a shared experience of the sacred. In the words of Saint Paul: "There is neither Jew nor Greek, there is neither bond nor free, there is neither male nor female: for ye are all one in Christ Jesus."

Early Christianity thus presented an alternative locus of social identity and of community that was rooted in the experience of grace. The bond established between communal members was one rooted not in primordial givens, but in an immediate connection to the fount of transcendental order. The new locus of communal solidarity and of the moral order was epitomized in St. Paul's rejection of the "ascriptive confines of Jewish ethical monotheism."[29] This redefinition of the terms of community in the experience of grace and a direct relation to the source of cosmic order and salvation (and not in legal prescriptions or primordial networks) allows us to speak of the early Christian ties of community as essentially a reformulation of existing roles and role definitions within the social world of Late Antiquity.

These new roles were those of members of a new corporate body (the Church) which subjected the *nova creature* to the new laws of regenerate man. What this new *congregatio fidelium* implied however was precisely a transformation of the terms of the *fidelis* "now subjected as far as his social and public life went, to the law as it was given to him, not the law as it was made by him. The consequences of the incorporation was that his *fidelitas*, his faithfulness, consisted precisely in his obeying the law of those who were instituted over him by divinity."[30] The very absorption of the individual in and by the new corporation of the Church was thus a transformation of those social bonds, roles, and role-expectations that had hitherto defined the social world.

We may note a similar emergence of role differentiation and the development of individual identities, especially in the refinement of ideas of conscience and agency which characterized what has been termed the renaissance of the twelfth century.[31] Not or not only the recovery of spiritualism in that era—but the establishment of new social groups through which it emerged is responsible for the growing individualism of that period. The very differentiation of corporate bodies engendered by the papal revolution (investiture conflict) together with the development of myriad new roles as group identities proliferated in this era were all central to the development of ideas of an inner life and of intentionality (as opposed to just action) as an aspect of the individual agency and morality (Abelard). In fact, this period was characterized not solely by the growth of different group identities (of which the new corporate identity of the clergy was by far the most important) and by the increase in horizontal mobility as the immediate family differentiated itself from wider kin groups—but by the very emic recognition of different orders of knights, clerics, priests, married men and women, widows, virgins, soldiers, merchants, peasants, and craftsmen—each with their different talents, institutions and roles in society (central here was the growth of different religious orders).[32] All these developed concomitantly with the growth of individual and private modes of self-expression through the revival of the religious tradition of autobiography, confessional literature, courtly love poetry as well as the emergence of legal differentiation, of a legal corpus no longer bounded by custom or Germanic tribal ideas of honor and fate.[33] This later development stressed the legitimacy of enacted, objective law over the consensual mold of tradition and custom. In so doing the new legal system of the twelfth century set up a generalized conceptual legal system that broke with existing group (clan and household) loyalties and posited new corporate definitions of what were, essentially, new social roles and role expectations.[34]

In a manner reminiscent of both the development of early Christianity and foreshadowing the Protestant Reformation of the sixteenth century the twelfth century was thus also characterized by a convergence of a specific set of structural and symbolic features. All coalesced around a greater appreciation of individual identities as central and focused, interestingly enough, on the ideas of agency or voluntarism and the workings of conscience. As Benjamin Nelson noted, "The extraordinary stress on the responsibility of each individual for the activity of his will and the state of his soul attained its height in the High and Later Middle Ages."[35] It was, we may note, not simply Abelard in his *Ethica seu Seito te Ipsum* (*Ethics: or Know Thyself*) and *Sic et Non* (*Yes and No*) who stressed inward intentionality in the conceptualization of spiritual life. Such a reorientation was evinced in the writings of others, the school or Laon for example and upheld even by such of Abelard's critics as Bernard of Clairvaux. Its institutionalized expression was in the decree of the Fourth Lateran Council of 1215 to require an individual confession for communicants at least once a year. As Colin Morris has noted "the attempt to make intention the foundation of an ethical theory is a striking instance of the contemporary movement away from external regulations towards an insight into individual character; a movement which finds its widest expression in the acceptance of private confession as the basis of the Church's normal discipline."[36] Its other institutional expression was in the developing science of casuistry and the proliferation of "specialized treatises tracing the obligations of conscience in the here and now, spelling out how individuals were obligated to act in every case they encountered in the conduct of their lived.... In these works conscience extended into every sphere of action, ranging over the whole moral life of man."[37]

Not surprisingly the new valorization and indeed representation of a self apart from social roles saw too the valorization of personal relations not so defined. Hence, there emerged tentative and nascent ideas of friendship (albeit still within the boundaries of the Church) on the one hand. And on the other, the conceptualization of love advanced by the troubadours, both of which, in Morris's terms, "desired to make personal experience and personal relations the focus of life," through, it should be added, the process of self-discovery and analysis.[38]

Of crucial sociological importance is the fact that these developments all took place against a backdrop of increasing structural differentiation. Central to this increasing complexity of the system were: (1) the separation of the nobility from the rest of society through its increasing tendency to be defined in hereditary terms; (2) the growth of commerce and of cities with the vast degree of internal differentiation among the different urban orders that characterized their growth; (3) the post-Gregorian Church which not only freed episcopal elections (and elites) from political impingement but "created a clergy that was set apart much more radically than before from ordinary Christians."[39] In fact, and as Caroline Bynum has noted, the Gregorian Reform not only separated the clergy from the laity (most especially through the campaign for clerical celibacy) but led to a vast proliferation of new institutional (and sometimes only semi-institutional) religious orders or roles—most formidably in the development of the friars (for men) and in the creation of new roles for women, such as the begunie which was, in its essence, "opposed to complex institutional structures."[40]

Note then the very "Durkheimian" correlation between the development of individual identities together with the ever-growing complexity of social organization and its roles and role- expectations. The same period which sees the "fundamental religious drama" relocated into the self is the period that sees a proliferation of religious orders, vocations, "callings," and "lives." The same period that saw a growing literature of private passion and theories of love, of, in R. Southern's terms, "the enlargement of the opportunities of privacy, in the renewed study of the theory of friendship, of conscience and of ethics" is also a period marked by a greater social differentiation, complexity, and distinction in the forms of social life.[41]

Moreover, as Bynum has noted, this period was characterized not only by a proliferation of the forms of institutionalized religious life as well as a greater degree of social differentiation in other realms. But, by an intense awareness of this differentiation, an "urgency, unlike anything we see in the early Middle Ages, about defining, classifying, and evaluating what they termed 'orders', or 'lives' or 'callings' (which includes what we would term both voluntary religious associations and social roles)."[42] Only, we would claim in this developing complexity of social identities (what sociologists so infelicitously term role incumbencies) could a sense of individual identity flourish. Central to this individual identity as it developed in the West was the idea of conscience (expressed most saliently in this period in the idea of intentionality in religious life) and the gradual construction of a private realm, beyond formal role obligations, where such intentionality and conscience came to the fore, whether in the rites of courtly love, the developing genre of correspondence between friends or in the individual Church confession.

The importance of the Protestant Reformation, especially of its sectarian variants in the developing idea of conscience is so well studied as to need almost no explication. Through it and in Benjamin Nelson's words there developed "a new integration of life, both personal and political through the rearrangement of existing boundaries.... [O]lder maps were redrawn, fixing new co-ordinates for all focal points of existence and faith: religion-world, sacred-profane, civil-ecclesiastical, liberty-law, public-private. [In this rearrangement] new scope and authority were given to the Inner Light, sparked by the Holy Spirit. This was the Holy Spirit within each individual and within groups."[43]

Here then the return to Augustinian piety, the breaking with the sacraments and mediating structures of the Church (as well as its symbols—of the Virgin Mary and the different saints) to reassert unmediated access of the believers to the deity within what became the private space of individual conscience.[44] But here too, the radical, painful, often violent breaking of established group identities and the re-establishment of new group solidarities and new role definitions (through, among Puritans for example, the whole covenantal theology).[45]

The new bonds forged under sectarian Protestantism were, in essence, a recasting of the bonds of "community" as a shared tradition, into new bonds of "communality." These bonds of a new "communion," in Herman Schmalenbach's sense, were to be the basis of the new communities forged by religious virtuosi throughout European societies.[46] The social restructuring of the bonds of communality (and we may note of authority) was, in essence, part of the restructuring effected by the Reformation in general, but specifically in ascetic Protestantism of the relation between the Church and the World. Within medieval Catholic Europe, the only "life-calling" legitimized in sacred terms was that of the monastic orders. As noted by Weber and others, the importance of the Reformation lay precisely in its "endowment of secular life with a new order of religious life as a sphere of 'Christian opportunity.'"[47] It was thus only with the Reformation that secular callings were given a religious legitimation and were perceived as possible paths to salvation.

Famously, within the Puritan context, these religious orientations took a particularly intense expression.[48] There developed new forms of religious expression, as well as of communal bonds, both characterized by a break with existing models of social organization. More than in any other social act, the drawing up of "covenants" between and among Puritans in Tudor England provided the basis for the reworking of the terms of social life in line with a new model of social organization.[49] In the covenanted communities and the "gathered churches" of the later sixteenth and early seventeenth century, diverse groups of English Puritans laid down, as it were, the blueprint for a fundamental reorganization of the principles of collective life.[50]

The institutional aspects of this new conception of social order have been attested to by historians from William Haller and Patrick Collinson to William Hunt and J.G.A. Pocock and we need only summarize them here.[51] On one level, they were manifest in a new mode of religious expression characterized by lay preaching, "prophesysings," as well as what later would be termed an "enthusiastic" religiosity of popular piety and noninstitutionalized manifestations of grace.[52] On the level of social organization, the covenanting of communicants implied primarily a break with existing solidarities of both Church and neighborhood.[53] Covenanting together, the Puritans also covenanted themselves off from the major existing institutional loci of solidarity—the Church, village, or parish—and so of those social identities which prevailed in English society.[54] The withdrawal from existing loyalties both national and ecclesiastical to the Church of England and the growth of a new set of commitments, loyalties, and identities to the individuals covenanted together in pursuit of a new spiritual and moral life was a fundamental element in the construction of new loci of social life and individual identity.[55]

Interestingly enough as Puritan communities underwent a process of institutionalization in the late seventeenth and early eighteenth centuries the privileging of conscience and individual agency in the definition of the moral life (i.e., as an attribute of virtue) became a constitutive component of many such communities. Perhaps more than anyone else, Margaret Jacob has developed this argument in respect to English Unitarians, Dutch Collegians, and the increasingly secular French Freemasonry. Perhaps the central tenet of these groups religiosity was, as Andrew Fix has described in his study of the Dutch Collegians, the fact that they "rejected the authority of ecclesiastical institutions and based religious life on the individual believer and his inner ability to know religious truth."[56] By the second half of the seventeenth century this conception, wedded to a belief in the workings of natural reason in the apprehension of truth, led to an emergent belief in the "principle of individual conscience."[57]

Jacob's own work has in fact stressed the role of religion—or more properly a particular form of privatized Protestantism which developed among certain groups of elites—in the construction of that private and individual sphere oriented around personal autonomy which we identify with bourgeoise culture: "At the heart of this experience lay the encouragement it gave the individual to conceptualize and to experience himself and herself as an ethical being equally engaged in the private and public spheres."[58]

This new ethical being emerged as the universal subject who, *qua* individual, became the new locus of solidarity, orientated around new definitions of moral autonomy and economic agency. Portentously and as Stephen Darwall has explained in his recent work on seventeenth and early eighteenth century moral philosophy, "the most significant developments of this period was the fashioning of the concept of autonomy *in tandem with* philosophical speculation about moral obligation" (emphasis in original).[59] Here too we see the necessary concomitance of doctrines of agency and action together with ideas of moral obligation and the workings of conscience.

Though circumscribed within the religious realm and limiting our understanding of agency to the phenomena of conscience we have, I hope, seen how the moral valuation of the private and of the individual agent who stood at its core developed (albeit haltingly) in periods of greater structural differentiation to become, with capitalism and the culture of modernity constitutive of both our political principles as well as individual selves.

Finally of course, and beyond Christian civilization proper we may look to eighteenth-century bourgeois society with its doctrines of civility and moral individualism—those beliefs given philosophical form by Kant and embedded within our own sociological understanding by Durkheim. Here of course, the idea of the individual sheds its religious garb and is no longer constituted by relations with the transcendent but achieves its meaning in the autonomy of the individual conscience. Here too, contemporary social thinkers, from Adam Ferguson in the eighteenth century to Benjamin Constant and Alexis de Tocqueville in the nineteenth, all noted the importance of what we would term, role differentiation to the making of bourgeois culture.

In all periods we witness a number of similar, related and central developments: (a) the breaking of existing group bonds and their replacement with new ones—including new roles and new definitions of existing roles; (b) the move from fewer roles to more roles and more complex and multitudinous role-sets and status-sets; (c) the move from more rigid, publicly sanctioned modes of role transition (and definitions) to ones less anchored in public constraints (tribal, civic, fraternal and later, confessional boundaries between roles are replaced by actor orientated ones)—as for example with sexual practices among early Christians, twelfth-century religious orders, or the "internalization" of conscience among late seventeenth century Puritans and the role of civility—as opposed to honor—in the discourse of the Scottish moralists.[60] In all the idea of the individual emerged slowly as did the idea of a private sphere. Both would of course only begin to be fully articulated in the eighteenth century when, not surprisingly the tension between them and more public, legally sanctioned modes of interaction and expression became apparent. Perhaps most accessible in the literature of the period we find resonances of this tension in works such as Defoe's *Roxana*, Richardson's *Clarissa,* and Fielding's *Amelia* all of which are mid-eighteenth-century novels, dealing with the needs of the hero and heroine to come to terms with new distinction between public and private, between law and morality, essentially between formal relations regulated by public law and search for new basis of individual trust and a matrix of interpersonal relations beyond contract and law. As succinctly stated by John Zomshick "In Fielding law and virtue remain divergent."[61] And in this divergence lies, we might add, the developing tension between public and private existence as they became apparent in this period.

Trust and the Problem of Indeterminacy

It was to a great extent some awareness of the above developments (if phrased in different terms) that led the eighteeth-century moral philosophers to posit a personal or private sphere of friendship and trust (as opposed to interest) as one of the unalterable benefits of "commercial" (what we would term, modern) society.[62] In so doing they were in effect noting those changing terms of sociability remarked upon above. For in premodern and feudal society bonds of personal affinity were rooted in codes of status and honor while in the court societies extant from the sixteenth century they were tied to a personalized politics of court status. Freed from the constraints of calculation and interest the private sphere became in the eighteenth century a realm where the personal nature of individual relations (i.e., friendship) was freed from concerns of social station. Thus and just as the idea of the morally autonomous individual emerged through the myriad of new and impersonal role relations in the public sphere so did the very idea of the private, which came to be conceived as a realm of trust and mutuality existent apart from the legally defined relations of the public sphere.

However and while the idea of civil society emerged as a way to bridge the two worlds of public and private, of interest and trust, we have seen how the realm of the private—founded on individual conscience—took a certain moral priority, constituting, with Smith for instance, the true residency of virtue (or with Immanuel Kant, the realm of the ethical). Here however a new dynamic evolves. For the very emergence of a realm of trust as an (ideal) potentiality of true mutuality also makes of trust something problematic. Just as the potential for trust emerges when social expectations are no longer determined by legally sanctioned public norms so does the potential for mistrust. With the greater ability to negotiate social behaviors and expectations an element of risk enters these relations that was, to a great degree absent when such behavior was embedded within strictly defined normative codes (of court society for example, not surprisingly the bête noir of the Scottish moralists).

Indeed, and if we follow Giddens' framework and contrast trust (between individuals) to confidence (in abstract system—as two modes of negotiating risk,) we see that where relatively strict definitions of role behavior apply, the mutuality of roles is embedded, as it were, within the overall social system.[63] One needn't develop trust within particular role sets as the relationship between role incumbents is structured by the existence of an overriding systemic logic. Rather than trust between individuals what anchors the mutuality of the relationship is confidence in the system. The specific normative values of said system are of course variable. They can be organized around the certainties of kinship (honor), of a transcendental religion (faith), or the logic of market exchange and the principles of abstract, rational and universal rights of the individual (contract)—which inform the system of modern social relations.[64] In the latter case however the issue of trust does become a problem. The move, if you will, from faith (confidence + sacrality) to trust which brings with it a heightened degree of indeterminacy also fundamentally transforms the nature of social relations, engendering in modernity the very particular distinction and tension between public and private which has become a hallmark of modern civilization. Thus, and in ideal-typical terms, modern societies are characterized by the existence of two types of (institutionalized) relation, those defined by public, formal, relatively determined (and often, indeed, increasingly legally defined) roles and those defined by negotiable, labile, and relatively indeterminate role expectations. The specificity of modernity is precisely the emergence of a realm of interaction that, while not defined by strict legal coordinates and collective desiderata, is nevertheless seen as a repository of value: the realm of the private.

The institutionalization of this duality in the frame of social relations engenders a host of problems that are unique to modern social formations. One of the most interesting of these problems is the difficulty modern societies—especially the United States—have with the existence of ambiguity, both conceptually and, more importantly in the field of human relations.[65] For without a shared world of life experience—and with public trust replaced almost solely with confidence in universalistic, univocal and abstract systems (of increasingly instrumental nature) as the basis of social life—ambiguity becomes intolerable and often unacceptable. The existence of situations of interpersonal indeterminacy becomes not something to be navigated through but an aspect of life to be restricted to the greatest extent possible. Perhaps, many of the most "burning" of contemporary issues revolving around political correctness, new norms of inter-personal behavior, the almost obsessive concern with explicating (often legally) gender roles and role expectations is to be viewed in this light.

Indeed, the modern distinction between public and private which increasingly relegates the realm of value (or more properly ultimate value) to the sphere of private (individuals and relations) and the problems of indeterminacy and ambiguity which ensue define both the uniqueness and some of the unique problems of contemporary Western and most particularly, American cultures. This form of representing social life stands after all in stark contrast to other forms of social organization where the private realm, when existent, was defined solely in negative terms of either that which was not public or, often that which was secret, hidden from public view. Here of course the paradigmatic statement on this relation between public and private was that offered by Arendt in terms of the meaning of the private (the *oikia*) in classical thought.[66] Similarly, work carried out by anthropologists in tribal and relatively undifferentiated societies points to the strong correspondence of private with that which is hidden or secret in those societies.[67] This situation changes rapidly in modern social formations where the very institutionalization of the rights of man and citizen (as public values) increasingly leaves the realm of the private as the paramount realm of value and meaning (and in fact, ethical action).[68] Aspects of this trend were however present already in the eighteenth century and can be found in the foundation texts of political liberalism as well as in the thought of the Scottish Moralists. So for example, and as we have seen above, the very idea of civil society contains a stress on the private realm as that of value and ethical action as opposed to the public stress of other political traditions such as those of civic virtue for example.

Within this developing dynamic of public and private and the increasing relegation of meaning and value to the realm of the private the problem of trust takes on an added dimension. It becomes in some sense a defining problem of modernity as it is only in the negotiation between private realms—that occasioned by trust—that shared value can emerge. The problem of shared value (or lack thereof—which is precisely what stands at the core of current debates between communitarians and liberals on the definition of the public good) brings us in fact, rather directly to the problem of the collectivity; of defining its boundaries, criteria of membership and participation and, most especially, modes of representation. It is this problem, or set of problems, which stands behind much of what is currently termed "the culture wars" and it is with an attempt to explicate these in terms of the public private dilemma that I will end this essay.[69]

To appreciate the sociological aspects of this debate we should return to the distinction made by Norberto Bobbio between relations between parts (private) and between the parts and the whole (public). What will in fact be argued, is that whereas Bobbio's distinction holds for premodern and classical modern culture where the public realm was one which included the relation between different individual identities (and structures or institutions) and the representative social whole—the very logic of modernity, resting on the idea of the individual as moral absolute, fundamentally transforms this set of relations. For with the terms of representation increasingly being defined by the autonomous, rights-bearing individual, the representation of the public sphere (and so of relations between public and private) becomes increasingly problematic. This problem is essentially that noted by Luhmann of the part (the private/individual) supporting the whole (the public/collective).[70] With the realm of value relegated to the sphere of the private it increasingly difficult to represent (especially when we consider the moral or value laden aspect of every representation) the collective whole, the realm of the public. In this sense and very tersely we may note that the loss of honor (as a category of public value) represents the triumph of the private. However, and contrawise, such a radically constituted private cannot support itself, cannot in fact, represent itself which is the situation at present. Bearing in mind the legal aspects of any process of representation one particularly salient illustration of this process (and one not unconnected to the loss of honor) can be found in the field of family law where, as Mary Glendon has noted "the emergence of new legal images of the family...stress the separate personalities of the family members rather than the unitary aspect of the family."[71] Quoting the 1972 Eisenstadt vs. Baird court decision which stressed that "the married couple is not an independent entity with a mind and heart of its own, but an association of two individuals each with a separate intellectual and emotional makeup" she argues that the new family law "holds up self-sufficiency [of individual members] as an ideal and is "somehow degrading and implicitly denying the importance of human inter-subjectivity."[72] Thus, even the legal idea of the family as a social and moral institution has been replaced by those discreet and particular individuals who comprise it. The case of the family and its legal representation (or lack thereof) is but one aspect of a trend whose inherent logic is diametrically opposed to the type of communal affirmation characteristic of the communitarian tradition noted above.

The sociological consequences of this situation are, I would claim, of a dual and related, even if seemingly contradictory nature and of great importance to understanding the current and reigning confusion in matters pertaining to the public and the private. The one is the phenomena of projecting the private into the public realm as an attribute of representation. The other phenomenon is the reimposition of public definitions onto the private realm. This dual moment being in a sense the core dynamic of what Arendt referred to as the "rise of the social" and the loss of all distinction between public and private realms.[73]

As illustrations of the first we may think of the inordinate importance awarded to the drinking or fornication of public officials in the U.S. or of talk shows dedicated to sexual infidelities, incest or penile implants, or for that matter, the bumper stickers one passes on the highway proudly proclaiming the owners to be the parents of a child on the honor list at some elementary or middle school. And while the last case may leave us wondering why the validation and recognition of the child's accomplishments within the private circle of the family is not sufficient (or perhaps nonexistent, or as I believe tied to the changing nature of the family) the former leaves us wondering why the most weighty of public matters (such as the confirmation of a Supreme Court justice) are debated almost exclusively in terms of personal sexual ethics.

And if in the former set of cases the public realm seems to be reduced to a movie screen for the projection of private lives and interests, it is, to great extent the logic of the latter development which defines much of what we refer to so often as multiculturalism (a development which classical liberals view with some approbation, marking as it does an attack on that distinction of realms which stands at the heart of the liberal political philosophy and *lebenswelt*). Behind the development of multiculturalism (and much of present struggles over political correctness) stands in fact the defining premise of modernity—of value as an aspect of the private. The multitude of private realms, each a value in itself, can however no longer be negotiated without the imposition of public, normatively standardized role definitions. Without a shared universe of expectations, histories, memories, or affective commitments no basis of trust can exist. In a situation of radically incommensurate life-worlds (or even their potentiality) that trust necessary to negotiate role expectations and social behaviors is lacking. What is beginning to emerge in its place is the increasingly public definitions of roles and expectations (defined, most saliently in this country, through its legal culture). In the absence of trust, indeterminacy becomes intolerable, hence the daily promulgation of "speech codes," housing association regulations, smoking laws, and other forms of formal regulation (and sanctions) of interpersonal behavior. This logic however goes much further than simply interpersonal relations. The world of private philanthropic foundations is, for example, currently being reorganized to meet standards of "diversity" and "multiculturalism"—that is a subversion of their private purpose (of aiding let us say artistic excellence, expression, and performance) in the name of currently salient public desiderata.[74] The fact that much of this is framed in terms of collective identities (ethnic, gender, or even of sexual preference) is, I argue, indicative of the fragility of collective representation based solely on the private. It is a return of collective identities rather than individual selves as modes of representing public culture.

It is this dynamic which explains so much of the contradictory features of modern social and political life in the United States. Not only increasing regulation from the top (as social actors can no longer negotiate their own role behavior) but a rise of affective group identities from the bottom. The politics of gender, of sexual preference, the whole multicultural agenda and the very strong feelings it evokes both among it adherents as well as from its more conservative opponents, points, I would claim, to a reemergence of group identities that take the place of those individual identities which we had come to equate with the progress of modernity. Ethnicity, race, gender, sexual preference, "new age," and so on, are not simply separate interests akin to corporate groups acting in the public arena. Nor are they simply what is so tellingly termed "life-styles." They are rather life-styles which represent a mode of identity contrary to those classic ideas of the individual that we associate with bourgeois political forms and were indeed essential to that mode of social organization. Perhaps indeed we will be left with the forms of political life devoid of their content. What this may mean for the organization of society is of course an open question.

Notes

1. Daniel Bell, "American Exceptionalism Revisited: The Role of Civil Society," *Public Culture* 95 (1989): 38–56; Edward Shils, "Was is eine Civil Society?" in K. Michelski ed., *Europa und die Civil Society* (Stuttgart: Kult Cola, 1991), pp.13–52; Vladimir Tismaneau, *Reinventing Politics: Eastern Europe After Communism* (New York: The Free Press, 1992); Amitai Etzioni, *The Spirit of Community* (New York: Crown Publishers, 1993).
2. Adam Ferguson, *An Essay on the History of Civil Society*, Edited by Fania Oz-Salzberger (Cambridge: Cambridge University Press, 1995 [orig. 1782]); Adam Smith, *The Theory of Moral Sentiments* (Indianapolis: Liberty Classics, 1982); G.W.F. Hegel, *The Philosophy of Right* (Oxford; Oxford University Press, 1952); G.W.F. Hegel, *Hegel and the Human Spirit: A Translation of the Jena Lectures on Philosophy of Spirity (1805–1806)* (Detroit: Wayne State University Press, 1983).
3. Hegel, *Philosophy of Right*, pp.105–155; *Jena Lectures*, pp. 99–118.
4. Hegel, *Jena Lectures*, p.118.
5. Smith, *Moral Sentiments*, p.50.
6. Albert Hirschman, *The Passions and the Interests* (Princeton; Princeton University Press, 1977), p.109.
7. Smith, *Moral Sentiments*, p.50.
8. Jurgen Habermas, *The Structural Transformation of the Public Sphere* (Cambridge [Mass.]: MIT Press, 1989), p. 112.
9. This reading, is of course a central one in Western political thought, at least since Immanuel Kant. The "troika" of reason, equality, and a shared public sphere was first articulated by Kant in the late eighteenth century. For Kant reason, more concretely practical reason, was realized in the juridical community of citizens and as such represented the crowning achievement of human freedom in the modern world. Central to the whole Kantian conception of practical reason was, moreover, the existence of a shared public arena where the workings of reason were substantiated. As Hannah Arendt has made clear, the category of the "public" was central for the Kantian synthesis of reason, equality and freedom. It was, for Kant, within the public arena of critical discourse that reason and equality, and with them the preconditions for the "kingdom of ends," were validated. On these perspectives see, John Laursen, " The Subversive Kant: The Vocabulary of Public and Publicity," *Political Theory*, 14 (1986): 584–603; John Rundell,*The Origins of Modernity* (Madison: University of Wisconsin Press, 1987); Susan Shell, *The Rights of Reason*, (Toronto: University of Toronto Press, 1980); Hannah Arendt, *Lectures on Kant's Political Philosophy* (Chicago: University of Chicago Press, 1982).
10. Benjamin Constant, "The Liberty of the Ancients Compared to that of the Moderns," in Constant, *Political Writings* (Cambridge: Cambridge University Press, 1988), pp. 308–28; Isaiah Berlin, "Two Concepts of Liberty," Berlin, *Four Essays on Liberty* (Oxford: Oxfrd University Press, 1969), pp.118–72.
11. Adam Seligman, "Animadversions upon civil society ad civic virtue in the last decade of the twentieth century," in John Hall, ed., *Civil Society: Theory, History and Comparison* (Oxford: Polity Press, 1995), pp. 200–23.
12. J. Dwyer, *Virtuous Discourse: Sensibility and Community in Late Eighteenth Century Scotland* (Edinburgh: John Donald, 1987), pp. 54–61.
13. Smith, *Moral Sentiments*, pp. 110, 134–35.
14. Charles Taylor, "Cross Purposes: the liberal-communitarian debate," in Nancy Rosenblum, ed., *Liberalism and the Moral Life* (Cambridge, Mass.: Harvard University Press, 1989), p. 52.

15. Michael Sandel, *Liberalism and the Limits of Justice* (Cambridge: Cambridge University Press, 1982); M. Sandel, "The Procedural Republic and the Unencumbered Self," *Political Theory*, 24 (1984): 81–96; Quinten Skinner, "The Republican Ideal of Political Liberty," in Bock, Skinner, and Viroli, eds., *Machiavelli and Republicanism* (Cambridge: Cambridge University Press, 1990), pp. 293–309.

16. Hannah Arendt, "The Public and the Private" in her *Human Condition* (Chicago: University of Chicago Press, 1958), pp. 22–78.

17. Norberto Bobbio, "The Great Dichotomy" in his *Democracy and Dictatorship* (Minneapolis: Minnesota University Press, 1989), pp. 1–21.

18. S.I. Benn and G.F. Gauss, *Public and Private in Social Life* (New York: Croom Helm, 1983), pp.3–27.

19. For these perspectives on liberalism see: Pierre Manent, *An Intellectual History of Liberalism* (Princeton, N.J.: Princeton University Press, 1994); Stephen Darwall, *The British Moralists And the Internal 'Ought' 1640–1740* (Cambridge: Cambridge University Press, 1995).

20. Roger Chartier, *The Cultural Origins of the French Revolution* (Durham, N.C.: Duke University Press, 1991); Sarah Maza, *Private Lives and Public Affairs: the Causes Celebres of Pre-revolutionary France* (Berkeley: University of California Press, 1993); Philip Aries, *Centuries of Childhood* (New York: Random House, 1962); Philip Aries and George Duby, eds., *A History of Private Life,* vols. 1–5, (Cambridge, Mass.: Harvard University Press, 1987–1991).

21. Phillipe Aries and George Duby, eds., *Passions of the Renaissance: History of Private Life,* vol. 3, (Cambridge, Mass. Belknap Press, 1987), p. 9.

22. Max Weber, *The Protestant Ethic and the Spirit of Capitalism* (New York: Scribners, 1958); Max Weber, *Economy and Society* (Berkeley: University of California Press, 1975), p. 1204; Marcel Mauss, "A Category of the Human Mind: The Notion of the Person, the Notion of Self," in M. Carrithers, S. Lukes et al., eds., *The Category of the Person* (Cambridge: Cambridge University Press, 1985), pp.1–25; Charles Taylor, *Sources of the Self* (Cambridge, Mass.: Harvard University Press, 1989); Louis Dumont, *Essays on Individualism: Modern Ideology in Anthropological Perspective* (Chicago: University of Chicago Press, 1986).

23. On this connection see, Rose Laub Coser, *In Defense of Modernity: Role Complexity and Individual Autonomy* (Stanford, Cal.: Stanford University Press, 1991).

24. Ernest Troeltsch, *The Social Teachings of the Christian Churches*, vol.1 (New York: Harper and Row, 1960), pp. 39–89.

25. Peter Brown, *The Body and Society: Men, Women and Sexual Renunciation in Early Christianity* (New York: Columbia University Press, 1988).

26. On these perspectives see: Peter Brown, *The Making of Late Antiquity* (Cambridge, Mass.: Belknap Press, 1978); Sheldon Wolin, *Politics and Vision* (Boston: Little Brown and Company, 1960).

27. Dumont, *Essays on Individualism.*

28. See Wolin, *Politics and Vision*, 95–140; Charles Cochrane, *Christianity and Classical Culture* (New York: Oxford University Press, 1957); Peter Brown, *The Making of Late Antiquity*, pp. 56–77.

29. Wolfgang Schluchter, *The Rise of Western Rationalism* (Berkeley: Univeristy of California Press, 1985), p. 152.

30. Walter Ullmann, *The Individual and Society in the Middle Ages* (Baltimore, Md.: Johns Hopkins University Press, 1966), p. 9.

31. Following précis is based on, R.W. Southern, *The Making of the Middle Ages* (London: Hutchinson, 1953); Catherine Bynum, "Did the twelfth century Dis-

cover the Individual?" *Journal of Ecclesiastical History* 31 (1980): 1–17; C. Bynum, *Jesus as Mother: Studies in the Spirituality of the High Middle Ages* (Berkeley: University of California Press, 1982); Walter Ullmann, *The Individual and Society in the Middle Ages* (Baltimore, Md.: Johns Hopkins University Press, 1966); Harold Berman, *Law and Revolution The Formation of the Western Legal Tradition* (Cambridge, Mass.: Harvard University Press, 1983); Marie D. Chenu, *Nature Man and Society in the Twelfth Century* (Chicago: University of Chicago Press, 1957).

32. Bynum, "Did the twelfth century."
33. Peter Brown, *Society and the Holy in Late Antiquity* (Berkeley: University of California Press, 1982), pp. 302–32.
34. Berman, *Law and Revolution*, pp. 103, 145, 149–51.
35. Benjamin Nelson, "Self Images and the System of Spiritual Direction in the History of European Civilization," in Nelson, *On the Road to Modernity: Conscience, Science and Civilizations, Selected Writings by Benjamin Nelson*, Toby Huff, ed. (Trenton, N.J.: Rowman and Littlefield, 1981), p. 43.
36. Colin Morris, *The Discovery of the Individual 1050–1200* (London: SPCK, 1972), p. 75.
37. Nelson, *Modernity*, p. 45. See also, D. Odon Lottin, *Psychologie et Morale Aux XII ET XIII Siecles,* Tome II (Louvain: Abbaye Du Mont Cesar, 1948), pp. 104–350.
38. Morris, *Individual*, p. 118.
39. Bynum, *Jesus as Mother: Studies in the Spirituality of the High Middle Ages* (Berkeley: University of California Press, 1982), p. 11.
40. Bynum, *Jesus as Mother*, p. 15.
41. Southern, *The Making of the Middle Ages* p. 221.
42. Bynum, *Jesus as Mother*, p. 89.
43. Benjamin Nelson,"Conscience and the Making of Early Modern Culture: The Protestant Ethic Beyond Max Weber," *Social Research* 36 (1969) 16–17.
44. Adam Seligman, "Innerworldly Individualism and the Institutionalization of Puritanism in the Late Seventeenth Century New England," *British Journal of Sociology* 41: 4 (1990): 537–57; A. Seligman, *Innerworldly Individualism: Charismatic Community and Its Institutionalization* (New Brunswick, N.J.: Transaction Publishers, 1994).
45. William Hunt, *The Puritan Movement: The Coming of Revolution in an English Country* (Cambridge, Mass.: Harvard University Press, 1985); David Little, *Religion, Order and Law: A Study of Pre-Revolutionary England* (Chicago: University of Chicago Press, 1984); Patrick Collinson, *The Puritan Character: Polemics and Polarities in Early Seventeenth Century Culture* (Los Angeles, Cal.: William Andrews Clark Memorial Library, 1989); William Haller, *The Rise of Puritanism* (Philadelphia: University of Pennsylvania Press, 1972); Avihu Zakai, *Exile and Kingdom* (Cambridge: Cambridge University Press, 1992).
46. Herman S. Schmalenbach, "The Sociological Category of Communion," in Talcott Parsons et al., eds., *Theories of Society* (New York: The Free Press, 1961), pp. 331–47.
47. Talcott Parsons, "Christianity and Modern Industrial Society," in E. Tiryakian, ed., *Sociological Theory, Values and Sociocultural Change* (New York: Harper and Row, 1967), p. 51.
48. Much has been written on the institutional implications of Puritan religiosity. For some of the more relevant analyses see Michael Waltzer, "Puritanism as a Revolutionary Ideology," *History and Theory* 3 (1963): 59–90; George Mosse,

"Puritanism and Reasons of State in Old and New England," *William and Mary Quarterly* 9 (1952): 67–80; G. Mosse, "Puritan Political Thought and the Case of Conscience," *Church History* 23 (1954): 109–25; G. Mosse, *The Holy Pretense: Christianity and Reasons of State from William Perkins to John Winthrop* (Oxford: Basil Blackwell, 1957); C. and K. George, "Puritanism as History and Historiography," *Past and Present* 41 (1968): 77–104; C.H. George, "Protestantism and Capitalism in pre-Revolutionary England," *Church History* 27 (1958): 351–366; W. Lamont, "Puritanism, History and Historiography," *Past and Present* 44 (1969): 133–46; Jerald Brauer, "The Nature of English Puritanism: Three Interpretations," *Church History* 23 (1954): 99–108; Gordon Marshall, *Presbyters and Profits: Calvinism and the Development of Capitalism in Scotland 1560–1707* (Oxford: Clarendon Press, 1980).

49. On the centrality of the covenant in the lives of the Puritans see, Patrick Collinson, "Towards a Broader Understanding of the Dissenting Tradition," in C. Cloe and M. Moody eds., *The Dissenting Tradition* (Athens: Ohio University Press, 1975), pp. 3–38. On the relation of covenant theology to Calvinist doctrine see: Everett Emerson, "Calvin and Covenant Theology," *Church History* 25 (1956): 136–44; Perry Miller, *Errand into the Wilderness* (New York: Harper and Row, 1964), pp. 48–98; J. Moller, "The Beginnings of Puritan Covenant Theology," *The Journal of Ecclesiastical History* 14 (1963): 46–67. Further theological issues are explored in Klaus Baltzer, *The Covenant Formulary* (Philadelphia, Pa.: Fortress Press, 1971); C. Burrage, *The Church Covenant Idea: Its Origins and Development* (Philadelphia, Pa.: American Baptist Publication Society, 1904). Different political aspects of the covenant are developed by S.A. Burell, "The Covenant Idea as a Revolutionary Symbolic: Scotland, 1596–1635," *Church History* 27 (1958): 13–58; David Zaret, *The Heavenly Contract: Ideology and Organization in Pre-Revolutionary Puritanism* (Chicago: University of Chicago Press, 1984).

50. The extent to which the covenants regulated the lives of those who entered into them, especially in maintaining the symbolic and physical boundaries of the new community is evinced in the 1642 Independent Covenant presented by John Bastwick and reproduced by Michael Tolmie, *The Triumph of the Saints: The Separate Churches of London 1616–1649* (Cambridge: Cambridge University Press, 1977), p. 196. See also Michael Watts, *The Dissenters* (Oxford: Oxford University Press, 1978), pp. 30, 31, 41, 42, 55, 56.

51. Haller, *The Rise of Puritanism*. In addition to the above noted references see: Michael Knappen, *Tudor Puritanism: A Chapter in the History of Idealism* (Chicago: University of Chicago Press, 1939).

52. For these aspects of Puritanism see: Geoffrey Nuttal, *The Holy Spirit in Puritan Faith and Experience* (Oxford: Basil Blackwell, 1946); Norman Pettit, *The Heart Prepared: Grace and Conversion in Puritan Spiritual Life* (New Haven, Conn.: Yale University Press, 1966). For a less theological and more historical view see Hunt, *The Puritan Moment*, p. 94. For the importance of this form of religious expression among the separatists see Watts, *The Dissenters*, p. 26. For a general history of Christian enthusiasm see Ronald Knox, *Enthusiasm: A Chapter in the History of Ideas* (Oxford: Oxford University Press, 1950). For a discussion of its changing temper in the seventeenth century see Michael Heyd, "The Reaction to Enthusiasm in the Seventeenth Century," *Journal of Modern History* 53 (1981): 258–80.

53. Just how drastic this "dichotomizing" of society was is a matter of some historical debate, though there is a relative consensus among historians that by the early decades of the seventeenth century it was radically more evident than in

the Elizabethan period. By this later period the desire to make the community of the godly "real and visible" led to palpable tensions between the community of the gathered Church and the rest of the "Christian nation." Recent discussion of this problem can be found in Patrick Collinson, *The Puritan Character*.

54. A slightly different view is offered by Patrick Collinson in his *The Elizabethan Puritan Movement* (Berkeley: University of California Press, 1967), see especially the idea of *ecclesiola in ecclesia*, p. 375.

55. Avihu Zakai, "The Gospel of Reformation, the Origins of the Great Puritan Migration," *Journal of Ecclesiastical History* 37 (1986): 14. Impressive discussions of this process whereby new loci of community were formed within the overall Puritan movement and its separatist tradition can be found in Collinson, "A Broader Understanding," pp. 3–38; Watts, *The Dissenters*, pp. 14–26; Tolmie, *Triumph of the Saints*, 1977; Haller, *The Rise of Puritanism*. The tension formed within society by the growth of Puritanism is amply attested to in such satires as "Zeal-of-the-land-Busy" in Ben Jonson's *Bartholomew Faire* (London: Cass, 1964), or in the 1633 *Declaration of Sports*, which explicitly ordered the Puritans "to conform themselves or to leave the country" if they would not abide "our good people's law for recreation," for which the king's pleasure decreed "that after the end of divine service our good people be not disturbed, letted or discouraged from any lawful recreation, such as dancing, either men or women; archery for men, leaping, vaulting, or any other such harmless recreation, nor from having of May-games, Whitsunales, and Morris-dances; and the setting up of May-poles and other sports therewith used." Cited in S.R. Gardiner, ed., *The Constitutional Documents of the Puritan Revolution 1625–1660* (Oxford: Clarendon Press, 1906), p. 101. A good understanding of the social importance of the local games, rites and feasts (with which the Puritans broke) can be found in V.A. Kolve, *A Play Called Corpus Christi* (Stanford, Cal.: Stanford University Press, 1966); James Mervyn, "Ritual Drama and Social Body in the Late Medieval English Town," *Past and Present* 98 (1983): 3–29; Peter Laslett, *The World We Have Lost* (London: Methuen and Co., 1965). Other aspects of the Puritan break with established authority can be found in J.F. New, *Anglican and Puritan: The Basis of their Opposition 1558–1648* (Stanford, Cal.: Stanford University Press, 1964). Comparative perspectives on ritual among Protestants and Catholics on the continent can be gained from Natalie Z. Davis, "The Sacred and the Body Social in Sixteenth Century Lyon," *Past and Present* 90 (1981): 40–70. Further perspectives on the Puritan aversion to the *Declaration of Sports* can be found in W. DeLoss, *The Fast and Thanksgiving Days of New England* (Boston: Houghton Mifflin Co., 1895), pp. 1–27.

56. Andrew Fix, *Prophecy and Reason: The Dutch Collegians in the Early Enlightenment* (Princeton: Princeton University Press, 1991), p. 118.

57. Fix, *Prophecy*, p. 119.

58. Margaret Jacob, "Private Beliefs in Public Temples: The New Religiosity of the Eigtheenth Century" *Social Research*: 59 (1991), p. 64.

59. Darwall, *The British Moralits*, p.17.

60. Marvin Becker, *The Emergence of Civil Society in the Eighteenth Century* (Bloomington: Indiana University Press, 1994).

61. John Zomchick, *Family and the Law in Eighteenth Century Fiction: The Public Conscience in the Private Sphere* (Cambridge: Cambridge University Press, 1993), p. 52.

62. Alan Silver, "Two different sorts of commerce—Friendship and Strangership in Civil Society, " forthcoming in J. Weintraub and K. Kumar, eds., *Public and Private in Thought and Practice* (Chicago: Chicago University Press).

63. Anthony Giddens, *The Consequences of Modernity* (Stanford, Cal.: Stanford University Press, 1990). See also Niklas Luhmann, *Trust and Power* (New York: John Wiley, 1979), pp.24–31.
64. In a fascinating study of the Frafras in Ghana, Keith Hart (1988:186–93) has shown how a society moving between "faith" and "confidence," between "status" and "contract," and between "custom" and "law"—that is between different systems of systemic confidence in role expectations based alternatively on pre-market and market relations—must develop structures of trust to continue functioning. His study provides important insight on just how trust emerges in the absence of systemically defined role-expectations.
65. Donald Levine, *The Flight from Ambiguity* (Chicago: University of Chicago Press, 1985), pp.20–43.
66. Hannah Arendt, "The Public and the Private" in Arendt, *The Human Condition* (Chicago: University of Chicago Press, 1958), pp. 28–32.
67. See Martin Krygier, "Publicness, Privateness and Primitive Law," pp. 307–41 and L. and J. Haviland, "Privacy in a Mexican Indian Village" pp.341–61 both in R. Benn and G. Gauss, eds., *Public and Private in Social Life* (Boulder, Colo.: Westview Press, 1987).
68. Adam Seligman, "The Representation of Society and the Privatization of Charisma," *Praxis International*, 13 (1993):68–84.
69. James Hunter, *Before the Shooting Begins* (New York: The Free Press, 1994).
70. Niklas Luhmann, "The Representation of Society Within Society," *Current Sociology*, 35 (1987):101–6.
71. Mary Glendon, *The Transformation of Family Law* (Chicago: University of Chicago Press, 1989), p. 102.
72. Glendon, *The Transformation*, pp. 103, 297.
73. Arendt, *The Human Condition*, pp. 38–49.
74. Robert Brustein, "Culture By Coercion," *The New York Times*, November 29, 1994, p. A21.

4

A Reasonable Role for Religion?
Moral Practices, Civic Participation, and Market Behavior

Robert Wuthnow

In this chapter I want to develop an argument about the role of religion in civil society that runs against the grain of much contemporary thinking on the subject. The conventional wisdom has been shaped by an image of conflict as the seat of the problem. If the question is asked, how much conflict can civil society withstand before it flies apart, then any strong religious commitments that promote conflict must be viewed negatively, as least as far as the preservation of civil society is concerned.

But posing the question this way is unhelpful for two reasons. The first is that conflict is not necessarily inimical to a strong civil society; indeed, the American democratic system has often been strengthened by the presence of contending groups who come together in the political arena to work out their differences. The second is that ideologically motivated reports of escalating conflict in American society are themselves gross distortions of prevailing evidence. An exhaustive effort to examine the extent of and trends in polarization in American culture, in fact, suggests no evidence of worsening ideological conflict, even when a wide variety of issues and a number of ways of examining polarization are considered; as its authors conclude, "There is no support for the proposition that the United States has experienced dramatic polarization in public opinion on social and cultural issues during the past two decades. Variance in most measures has not increased. Neither has bimodality in response. Nor have attitudes become more constrained by ideology or...by group identity."[1] These authors conclude, as have

113

other researchers, that the controversy over abortion is itself the single exception to the rule and that the debate over it has probably been permitted unduly to influence perceptions of other cultural conflicts.[2]

The alternative way of framing the question of civil society focuses on a more subtle kind of shift that may be taking place in commitments and in personal identities. This shift has sometimes been evident among public figures. For example, journalists covering the Clinton White House were quick to observe the president's tendency to speak in different registers, borrowing from the pious Baptist traditions of his native Arkansas on one occasion, using the polished speech of a Rhodes scholar on another occasion, periodically falling into trendy jargon from the recovery movement, and often resorting to the technical political language of a calculating administrator. Some argued, just as critics had of Ronald Reagan, that it was difficult to know which president was present at any given moment.[3]

Such observations, I believe, challenge us to think hard about the changing relationships among character and morality, on the one hand, and on the other hand the civic values on which democratic government and market economies are based. Put simply, the growing diversity of American culture means that many of us now appear to have unstable selves and this development in turn leads us to wonder who can be trusted and on what basis civic discourse can be conducted.[4] If American democracy is in sore need of renewing itself at the end of the twentieth century, the reason may not be that we are pursuing our self-interests too much, as some have argued, or that we are spending too little time participating in voluntary associations, as others contend, but that there is a kind of wimpishness, to draw reference to yet another recent president, that somehow undermines our ability to form compelling commitments and to convince ourselves that our leaders and our fellow citizens are trustworthy. In the worst-case scenario, the moral fabric unravels less from blatant conflicts over socially accepted norms and more from the suspicion that none of us holds deep enough convictions to anchor us when we face challenges individually and as a people. Indeed, it is this prospect that has led some observers to call for spiritual renewal in American culture, an appeal to which zealots and totalitarians are often more than willing to pay heed.

But if presidential politics renders these examples less than satisfactory, consider an ordinary citizen interviewed recently for a project on spirituality: a twenty-six-year-old disabilities counselor, the daughter of a Methodist minister, who describes her religious preference as

"Methodist Taoist Native American Quaker Russian Orthodox Buddhist Jew." She herself is bemused by this string of adjectives, and without knowing more about her we are tempted to wonder: Can this woman be trusted to live stably and reliably and to bring up her children as responsible citizens? She appears to have so many religious identities that all or none are likely to matter little when the chips are down. Interesting as she might be, she raises doubts about how seriously religion can be taken when it becomes a mixture of everything, and she contrasts sharply with the unitary moral self on which most conceptions of democracy have been based. To the extent that she merely exaggerates the inner pluralism present to one degree or another in many of our contemporaries, we might assert with Richard Rorty: "We have become so open-minded that our brains have fallen out."[5]

This example also usefully illustrates a relationship between values and society that is often missed by critics who argue that America is in jeopardy because of moral or spiritual indifference. Were the problem, as William Bennett has asserted, that "the enervation of strong religious beliefs...has de-moralized society," then it would be likely to find twenty-six-year-olds disclaiming faith in religion at all, and opinion polls would show that belief in God, prayer, and participation in religious services has dropped off dramatically. In reality, these indicators have remained relatively stable.[6] The claim that democratic and economic life in America would be strengthened by more prayers in classrooms and more teaching of biblical injunctions to children is not necessarily refuted by such evidence. Yet, the very trends that critics attempt to correlate with diminishing spirituality (rising crime rates, drug use, child abuse, gang membership, and the like) have occurred despite constant rates of church going, virtually universal belief in God, and somewhat elevated levels of belief in heaven and hell.[7] The situation to which these examples draw attention is rather one in which personal commitment remains high, and yet is changing in a way that raises questions about the kind of people we are becoming, especially in terms of moral and religious character and its consequences for public life.

I want to focus on three questions: (1) Can moral practices play an animating and sustaining role in bridging the demands of democratic participation and market forces? (2) Can religious inclinations provide a reasonable basis for such moral practices? And (3) are religious institutions changing in a way that may be undermining those practices? The first question is deliberately framed in broader terms than might be needed for a consideration of religion itself. The reason for doing this is that religion is indeed likely to matter little to the life of our society if moral deliberation of any kind has become superfluous; conversely, understanding the place of such deliberation can suggest a role for religion, even if religion is not presently fulfilling that role. The second question brings religion into the discussion largely in institutional terms and as it is generally conceived in discussions of its political and moral implications. Against this background, we can understand more clearly how recent changes in spirituality may be altering the public place of religion. In order to bring the discussion to a more normative conclusion, I suggest in closing that the idea of practice itself may provide the key for keeping the public role of religion vital despite changes in its character.

Moral Practices

Speaking of moral practices is always troublesome because the very term suggests that some activities are to be set apart from others that are either immoral or amoral. Such a distinction plays well with certain economistic views of the marketplace that regard it as separate from moral considerations and from liberal conceptions of democracy that emphasize procedural rationality and little else. I wish to distance the present argument from those views, however, by conceding that there is a great deal about markets and democracies that is, in one usage of the term, moral. A long tradition of sociological theory, starting with Max Weber and Emile Durkheim, running through Talcott Parsons, and continuing in the recent work of Alan Wolfe, Amitai Etzioni, Viviana Zelizer, and others, has argued that economic behavior is composed of trust, loyalty, and other binding moral obligations, as well as sheer exchanges of goods and services. The embedding of economic transactions in such moral relationships shapes the meaning of these exchanges, and economic transactions in turn reinforce certain understandings of what is moral. The same is true of democracy, especially if it is conceded that government inheres in the *legitimate* exercise of power, rather than only the application of coercive force.

Still, it does not follow from these ways of thinking about moral obligations that markets and democracies subsume all that is meant by morality or that economic and political relationships are essentially capable of producing all the moral considerations on which a good and decent social order is based. Corruption in business and in politics reminds us of the weaknesses of these institutions as self-policing moral entities. Whistle-blowers may not be rewarded monetarily or politically, and the moral considerations required to decide what kind of society we *should* aspire to are not necessarily generated by the economic and political means of attaining our goals. Without denying the moral behavior built into social institutions, therefore, we cannot escape the fact that morality must also be considered in other ways.

A preliminary sense of how to resolve this issue can be drawn from Dewey's distinction between "customary" and "reflective" morality.[8] The former depends on force of habit, on doing things the way they have always been done. Dewey describes it as the morality of the tribe, the ancestral home, the parental rules that have never been questioned. Reflective morality, in contrast, emerges from conscious deliberation. It "springs from the heart, from personal desires and affections, or from personal insight and rational choice."[9] It often requires criticizing existing customs and institutions from a new point of view.

Customary morality is of considerable importance because it often provides a reliable guide in matters of right and wrong. In principle at least, long-established norms about telling the truth, not stealing from one's neighbors, and the like, still pertain appropriately to most people in most situations. Customary morality also serves a positive function in everyday life simply by permitting us to *avoid* thinking about some things. Dewey suggests there is something "sick" about a person who goes through life questioning the morality of everything. But customary morality becomes a negative force when people let institutionalized norms make their basic decisions for them. The economic realm can of course be a strong source of customary morality, as can established governmental and legal procedures.

Reflective morality requires conscious effort on the part of the individual. It involves questioning one's behavior, knowing what options are available, thinking through the consequences of various choices, and recognizing one's responsibility to choose wisely. It comes into play most visibly when people are faced with choices about their basic values and how to realize these values in their daily lives. Indeed, Dewey goes so far as to say that an immoral decision is one that has been made unreflectively, while a moral act takes the form of a well-considered judgment. Saying "I meant well" (when things turn out badly) is not a good excuse, Dewey asserts, because the person probably did not really pause to reflect on what he or she was about to do.

Unlike customary morality, which can often be articulated in simple moral dictums, reflective morality cannot be codified in terms of absolute rules. It is instead a matter of theory, process, and character. Theory—or perhaps better, "outlook"—is a frame of reference, a set of beliefs and values that inform the individual's thinking. It includes a conception of individual freedom and responsibility, an understanding of the importance of reflection itself, and an awareness of the need to balance self-interest with the needs of others. Process is the ongoing act of reflection itself. It is not so much a matter of making airtight, logical choices, but of bringing one's outlook into conscious engagement with one's experience and behavior. It requires individual soul searching, but is also a social activity, benefiting from formal education, reading, and interacting with others. "Character" signals the fact that reflective morality is integrally rooted in the self. This means moral worth is ascribed less to single, discrete activities than to longer-term patterns of behavior. It also means that morality and the self are fundamentally intertwined in a mutually reinforcing, and hopefully upward, spiral of development. In short, moral reflection is conducive to personal growth.[10]

For our purposes, it is also useful to consider Charles Taylor's more recent discussion of "strong evaluation."[11] Daniel Weinstock provides a helpful definition: "A strong evaluator is an agent capable of second-order reflection upon her desires, whose practical deliberation is guided by `a language of evaluative distinctions' identifying certain types of actions as base, noble, courageous, etc., rather than simply by calculations of the probable outcomes associated with the pursuit of given desires."[12] It is unnecessary to engage Taylor's controversial claim that strong evaluation is *essential* to self-identity; that there is *some* relationship between strong evaluation and the self, nevertheless, seems incontrovertible. Certainly, as Taylor notes elsewhere, strong evaluation "can be the basis for attitudes of admiration and contempt."[13] That is, reflecting on our desires and bringing values to bear on our deliberations forms the basis both of how we think of ourselves as moral beings and in many instances how those who observe us evaluate our behavior.

Strong evaluation is similar to Dewey's reflective morality, while making calculations of the probable outcomes of our behavior leaves moral obligations largely implicit or embedded in institutional life itself, similar to the way Dewey conceives of customary morality. A preliminary sense of how these distinctions relate to my initial observations about unstable selves is evident in the connection Taylor draws between strong evaluation and character. When people deploy multiple languages and appear to have multiple identities, how we feel about those disclosures is likely to depend on the type of reflective morality that entered the deliberative process.

I will return to the question of *practice* after discussing religion, but it is worth mentioning here that practice as strongly evaluative or deliberative activity is a more restricted category of behavior than "social practice" in either Alasdair MacIntyre's or Jeffrey Stout's usage, although both consider the idea in a context of discussing moral orientations.[14] To take a favorite example in this literature, playing chess may well be a social practice that reinforces moral behavior (and character) insofar as it teaches teamwork, discipline, responsibility, and even courage. Indeed, Stout may be correct in asserting that a good way of teaching children to be virtuous is to encourage them to play chess (or soccer). But moral practice in Dewey's or Taylor's sense is behavior explicitly involving reflection upon the criteria by which one evaluates the moral worth of one's activities.

We come, then, to the question of whether moral practices have a significant place in animating and sustaining either democracy or markets. Intuitively, we may of course believe that moral deliberation is an important part of character formation in children and that it cannot hurt for it to be present in Congressional hearings or in corporate boardrooms, but we should not be hasty about saying that such practices are significant, especially if we are sociologists. This is because sociological theory has placed far more emphasis on the embeddedness of morality in institutions than on discrete moral deliberation. According to this view, markets and democracies work well because they allow many different moralities to be embraced without substantially interfering with social relationships, and yet provide safeguards that punish the worst violations of common human decency.

Against standard sociological wisdom, I want to suggest that at least three arguments for the significance of moral practices can be adduced, and that any of the three should be provisionally compelling, depending on one's theoretical perspective. The first argument emphasizes a pragmatic orientation toward morality and can be derived directly from Dewey. Philosophical pragmatism, unlike the implicit pragmatism practiced in everyday life, urges that thoughtful deliberation about personal and collective goals and about the rightness or wrongness of those goals be included in social life. While it remains skeptical toward the possibility of finding one right answer as a result of such deliberation, it asserts that democracy and moral deliberation have much in common because both require faith that human betterment can be approximated through an experimental process of working together and engaging one's own faculties to the fullest. Rorty's insistence on the essential and yet provisional nature of morality, George Kateb's assertion that people must think their own thoughts—but think them *through*—in order to contribute to democracy, and Robert Bellah's Deweyian arguments about attentiveness to social institutions are all variations of this argument.[15]

The second argument pertains mostly to the relevance of moral deliberation to democracy and can be supported by Rawlsian deontological liberalism as well as by Taylor's more ontological communitarianism. It contends that there is a complementary relationship between the cultural diversity that democracy aims to uphold and moral reasoning. On the one hand, democracy that ensures freedom of thought and that imposes only standards of fair treatment on diverse subcultures permits a kind of free market of ideas and values to prevail, and this very pluralism forces people to think through their moral positions to a greater extent than if only one totalistic world view were present. On the other hand, moral deliberation contributes to the maintenance of democracy because it, in itself, is a form of civic participation, and it connects considerations of virtue with public policy, among which are concerns about the very democratic structures that ensure freedom to engage in moral deliberation.

The third argument is similar to the second, but starts with considerations of the market and then extends them to civil society more generally. It observes that markets tend to promote diversity by giving people freedom to cultivate their own life-styles and tastes. It also emphasizes that contemporary markets depend increasingly on the production and processing of information; and in this, they contribute to the availability of ideas for moral deliberation (as in the publishing of books and newspapers or the support of universities). It also recognizes that markets are embedded in social institutions and thus are never entirely structured by their own autonomous rationality. Markets and civil society more generally, therefore, require an ongoing discussion of the values toward which social behavior is oriented.

It will be evident that these arguments supply relatively minimal reasons for supposing that moral deliberation makes a difference to civil society. They do not, for instance, presuppose that moral absolutes exist and should be discussed for their own sake or that people necessarily are elevated by or have an intrinsic responsibility to focus on these absolutes. Each argument, however, implicitly accepts that conventional morality may be embedded in political and economic institutions, and yet asserts the need for special efforts to be made individually and collectively to reflect explicitly on considerations of goodness, truth, and virtue. Times and places for these efforts to take place can be located in families, schools, corporate offices, and government agencies. Insofar as such efforts may need to be set apart from everyday life and given an explicit connection with supreme values, religion is also a location in which moral deliberation may be practiced.

The Role of Religion

For the moment, I want to restrict the discussion to those institutionalized expressions of religion that we normally refer to as established or organized religion, but will use the term "religious inclinations" to avoid some of the problematic connotations of "belief," "values," or "world views," while retaining a focus on individuals. As with our discussion of moral practices, it will be useful to acknowledge that religious organizations may seem at first glance to be an important place in which moral deliberation takes place, and yet closer consideration gives ample reason to be skeptical about the significance of this activity for either the polity or the economy. On empirical grounds, evidence from recent research on the role of religion in decisions about work, professional ethics, and money provides reason to doubt that religion plays much of a role in public thinking about these secular issues.[16] Religiously inclined people seem to differ little from their counterparts in their understandings of these issues or in the nature of their economic behavior. Indeed, evidence suggests that religious people readily absorb norms of the workplace that encourage them to think about morality in ways that depart from sacred teachings. Other reasons for skepticism about the relevance of religion include evidence that religion has become therapy, functioning to make people feel better about whatever they do, rather than guiding them morally. Many arguments have been put forth as well suggesting that democracy and markets are deontological and thus that religion should be excluded from public debate. Whatever one may think of these arguments, enough evidence exists concerning the difficulties of bringing religious arguments to bear on public life that doubt about their efficacy is certainly well founded.

If the foregoing arguments about moral practices are take seriously, religion nevertheless remains a relevant consideration. Empirically, some evidence suggests that religion serves, at least for small minorities, as a kind of counterculture to the marketplace and to government agencies, variously encouraging its adherents to help the poor, work for social justice, talk about ways of living true to their faith in the workplace, or banding together to protest government policies.[17] In political philosophy, more room is granted for religion than is sometimes recognized. Rawlsian liberalism, for instance, asserts the value of an overlapping consensus based on multiple traditions and protected by a shared commitment to fair treatment and open discussion.[18] Although this conception of democracy imposes limits on religious behavior, it is fundamentally concerned with achieving a stable social order in which competing religious traditions are in fact permitted freedom to exist. Communitarian arguments generally go a step further in asserting that conceptions of truth shared by dominant religious traditions are themselves the moral basis for democracy and in attempting to find a balance between norms of fair treatment and procedures that encourage the vitality of religious communities. Paradoxically, postmodern relativism that denies the value of grand metanarratives posed either by religion or by science has also created conceptual space in which religious communities, as locally plausible sources of meaning, can occupy a legitimate space in public life. Congregations in virtually all denominational traditions have implicitly seized on the importance of local knowledge by asserting that they provide communities in which faith is realized and through which civic responsibility is enhanced. If, as Robert Putnam has suggested, team bowling is preferable to bowling alone because team members may occasionally voice concerns about their communities, then worship services and Bible study groups should also be seen as agents of the collective conscience.[19]

So much attention has been paid to the communal aspect of congregations in recent years that it is important to observe the assumptions that can be made about religion's role in nurturing a certain moral conception of the self. Some discussions of religious communities adopt a kind of associational logic which suggests that little happens to the self at all; rather, communities simply expose people to social networks and encourage them to play organizational roles. These discussions, however, miss the moral connections that are taken for granted in deeper understandings of religion and of democracy alike. On the religious side, congregations are assumed to be agents of moral socialization and, following Erikson, Piaget, Kohlberg, and others, these influences are assumed to be ongoing throughout life. Change is expected, personal reflection is part of this change, and there is nevertheless strong personal continuity over the life course. Implicitly the congregation tends to be regarded as an all-encompassing community to which people belong and from which they derive a primary sense of identity. Although it is sometimes acknowledged that congregants participate in other communities as well, congregations depict themselves as the only communities in which the true self and the highest values are reinforced. Treatments of democracy are at least compatible with some of these assumptions because they also argue that certain conceptions of the self are important, especially a unitary self that can be treated as a continuous entity for legal purposes, and that assumes deep responsibility to play out its various social roles in a consistent manner.[20]

Multiphrenic Sprirituality

It should be obvious that standard arguments about religious communities, their participation in public life, and their conception of the unitary self run counter to—or at least have failed to consider—what happens when people adopt a more fluid style of spirituality. Following Kenneth Gergen's discussion of the saturated self that is torn in such multiple directions that it loses its center, we might speak of multiphrenic spirituality as the kind of religious orientation that is rooted in participation in more than one religious community and that draws its moral inspiration from a variety of sources.[21] Although multiphrenic spirituality characterizes only some of the American population to an extreme degree, and fails to pertain to some people at all, it appears to be an apt description of a prominent trend that includes denominational switching, church hopping (and shopping), institutionalized eclecticism and syncretism in many congregations, and a growing variety of spiritual stimuli, ranging from recovery groups to New Age bookstores to angel books and spirit guides.

The twenty-six-year-old woman I mentioned earlier fits this pattern of multiphrenic religious identity. The labels she uses to describe her spirituality have specific referents: she was raised Methodist, attended synagogue regularly with one of her friends, joined a Quaker meeting in college, was baptized in an Orthodox church during a trip to Russia, practices Buddhist meditation, and participates about once a month in a Native American sweat lodge ceremony. Her multiphrenic spirituality reflects both the opportunities and the pressures that American social structure generates at the end of the twentieth century. Her parents were college-educated professionals who held steady, well-paying jobs and were able to send their daughter to a prestigious university. She enjoyed the freedom to take liberal arts courses that were not narrowly career oriented and was given the opportunity in college to travel and to construct an independent major organized around her own interests. Five years after graduation she is unmarried but is in what she describes as "a very committed partnership," and she works part-time in a job that offers few employment benefits and little job security but also gives her flexibility to plan her work day and her activities as she chooses. The job puts her in daily contact with African Americans, which is a new experience for her, and it gives her time to pursue her interests in weaving and to do volunteer work. Unlike her mother, who worked as a hospital administrator, she is relatively unconstrained by bureaucratic structure and virtually all her commitments are tenuous.

Her religious commitments, in fact, are her strongest links with institutional practices and traditions. Their multiplicity actually *overdetermines* her identity, making her the virtual opposite of Bellah's "Sheila," who had such a privatized conception of spirituality that she named her faith "Sheilaism."[22] This woman does not suffer from the isolation that worries Bellah and she is not forced to look inside herself for answers because she believes only in a cosmic self as an ultimate authority. By most accounts, she appears to be religiously conventional, attending Sunday services at a small-town Methodist church nearly every week and participating regularly in a fellowship group at the church. Yet her multiple religious preferences carry the idea of religious pluralism to such an extreme that she is singular in her approach to spirituality. As she talks about it, she professes confusion and its ambiguities are evident in her speech. "I use different words," she says, "you know, God, father sky, mother earth. I feel like the symbiosis of the creator and the created, the masculine and the feminine being in both of the creator and the created. In some ways I feel like I'm open to anything, but there are definitely things that resonate most for me at different points. For example, at present I could not just be goddess focused, because both are essential. I'm wandering all over the place."

Her open-mindedness provides a tangible illustration of Rorty's concern about "wet liberals" who believe in everything and thus in nothing. She is the kind of person who would certainly arouse distrust were she to run for elected office and the instability of her religious commitments raises questions about how such commitments, multiplied by a hundred million, may be influencing the character of American democracy. She may not raise these questions very seriously for people who believe that religion isn't relevant to the democratic process at all, and she may be regarded as a temporary aberration who will settle down in a year or two, have children, get a steady job, and return to the more predictable Methodism of the past. Yet there is plenty of evidence in studies of the labor market that she may be part of the growing number of people who will not be assimilated into long-long careers and who will work from home or as independent contractors and who will also be skeptical of grand narratives about the self, religion, modernity, or truth.

In one respect, multiphrenic spirituality may be largely irrelevant to questions about civic or economic participation. Thomas Jefferson remarked that it made little difference whether his neighbor believed in twenty gods or in no god.[23] His reasoning was that democracy could be indifferent to specific expressions of religion because all religions pointed to features of human nature that could also be observed philosophically and scientifically and that these features were shared by everyone and could be agreed upon by everyone. If nature's laws inspire less confidence now than in Jefferson's day, there is nevertheless reason to agree that multiphrenic spirituality does not substantially undermine common values because people with diverse religious identities still believe in treating others fairly and with respect, value love and common human decency, and are animated with a kind of "fellow feeling" that comes from living on the same planet and recognizing common ecological constraints on human life.

In another respect (to which we will want to return), multiphrenic spirituality may be a positive contribution to civic life. If, as Rawls and others suggest, a reasonable approach to public life takes into account the likelihood and desirability of people changing their minds, then someone who changes her mind about religion, and does so repeatedly, may be deemed a thoughtful, unbigoted person who can be persuaded by new evidence and who can respond to new circumstances.

Nevertheless, shifting sands are not a good foundation on which to build public trust and they raise doubts about the solidity of our convictions. If governments and employers count on people to have unitary selves, then multiphrenic spirituality that encourages people to juggle a pantheon of sacred values may run against the stability of these institutions. And if congregations do not serve as sheltering communities in which the plausibility of a single set of beliefs is upheld, but function more as bazaars where people can shop for convictions to tide them through the day and then trade them in for other commitments tomorrow, religion in its institutional forms may also be contributing something rather different to public life than our theories have supposed.

I want to suggest that the idea of *practice* holds the key to thinking about how people with multiphrenic selves may be able to participate effectively and in a morally responsible way in the civic and economic arenas. The critical issue is not whether people change their minds, even if they do so frequently, and it is not whether they draw inspiration from many different sources, rather than one; it is whether or not they take their spirituality and their moral concerns seriously enough to spent time reflecting on them, deliberating over them, and connecting them with their behavior. Put simply, practice should not be conceived in opposition to theory, but in contrast with flakiness. Practice is the effort that goes into having good reasons for what one believes and that demonstrates the seriousness of these beliefs by thinking about them and incorporating them into everyday life. Practice generally takes place in dialogue with other people, but it shifts attention from community to activity. Strong practice, just as strong evaluation, may indeed be achieved at the intersection of several communities instead of through submersion in any one community.

Several of the most important features of practices can be illustrated by looking more closely at our twenty-six-year-old woman. For one, practices are deliberate and reflective. It is revealing that this woman speaks of her spirituality as a "practice" and that she devotes considerable energy to it and to thinking about it. She says she prays a lot during the day as a way of "holding someone in my heart." Prayer is a specific activity that nevertheless blends with her commitment to "the wellness of people around me." In comparison with other people interviewed in the same project, she is considerably more serious about her spirituality, not simply in saying she takes it seriously but also in giving evidence that she has thought long and hard about it, come up with good reasons for identifying herself as she does, and devoting time to it on a regular basis.

In addition, practices adhere to the person and are thus understood in terms of personal development. This woman expresses her spirituality in multiple terms because she believes her experiences have had a cumulative impact on her thinking. She recognizes the discontinuities, but also constructs these as developmental processes. She sees continuity with her parents' religious values and a continuing ("formless") effect of her Methodist upbringing. She observes that her interest in Quakerism came from writing a paper on it for a college project that required participant observation, which she found gave her an opportunity for self-reflection. Her encounter with Russian Orthodoxy has more of an epiphanal quality, stemming from a chance encounter with a young Russian man, but she participated in it long enough to feel that she gained an inside perspective. Each phase of her spiritual development, she says, added depth to the previous phase. Unlike someone who simply follows the latest fads, she actually has developed a strong sense of self and is able to make informed choices about her religous commitments on this basis. The stories that people like her can tell about their practices are, therefore, ways of forging biographical continuity and establishing their own trustworthiness.

She also illustrates that practices are embedded in institutions, deriving some of their shape from these institutions, and forging moral bonds between individuals and institutions. This woman's journey has been of her own design; yet, at every juncture it has been connected with institutions: her church, a synagogue, the Russian Orthodox church, the college she attended, the job she holds, and the Native American activist group she has joined. With the last of these she has actually participated in a number of political activities, including some peace and environmental meetings in Washington. The fact that most of the institutions in which she participates are porous, however, means that she has to exercise discretion in how she participates and she has freedom to participate simultaneously in several. Her congregation is not an encompassing community from which she derives her identity, but a node in a network of activities that she chooses to combine in her own way.

And finally, practices have both a private and a public dimension. In her case, spirituality is intensely inner, but also a way of reinforcing her commitment to the environment and to the cause of world peace. She is a better citizen because of her spirituality, even though she has drawn from a variety of sources.

Practices have come to be featured in moral philosophy and in social theory because they provide a more realistic way of thinking about moral reasoning in the cultural and social circumstances in which we live. Practices require a lot of faith, but depend very little on certainty that absolute truth exists or that one is approximating it. Practices also recognize that commitments pull people in multiple directions and that few people settle comfortably into any single community, religious or otherwise, or stay there very long. Practices take the varied inputs supplied by the marketplace and protected by democracy and reflect on how these inputs should be put together.

If practices are conceptually appealing, they are nevertheless difficult to sustain. Democratic structures provide space in which to think about moral and spiritual values, but procedural concerns also inhibit full and frank discussion of these values, let alone their implementation. Indeed, these structures require individuals to do much of the work of developing their own practices because organized efforts quickly run into political constraints. Markets give opportunities for exchanging new ideas and information, yet markets also impose their own expectations, encouraging people to take everyday reality for granted rather than questioning it too much, and drawing more and more people into vicious cycles of working and spending that leave little time for reflection on higher values. Even religious organizations cannot be expected to reward many kinds of practices because it is in their interest to create loyal Methodists rather than Taoist Jewish Methodists.

Practice, moral and spiritual, is thus a subject that needs encouragement if it is to contribute valuably to civic society. Hucksters who sell cheap grace and who encourage facile spirituality need to be challenged, just as totalitarians do when they sell religious bigotry. But if all this sounds too serious, it is also well to remember, as Rorty reminds us, that moral commitment "does not require taking seriously all the matters that are, for moral reasons, taken seriously by one's fellow citizens." Indeed, it "may require trying to josh them out of the habit of taking those topics so seriously."[24] With good humor and prayer, religion can indeed play a reasonable role in contemporary life.

Notes

1. Paul DiMaggio, John Evans, and Bethany Bryson, "Have Americans' Social Attitudes Become More Polarized?" Working Paper, Department of Sociology, Princeton University, 1995.
2. See also Michael Hout, "Abortion Politics in the United States, 1972–1994: From Single Issue to Ideology," Working Paper, Survey Research Center, University of California, Berkeley, 1995.
3. Michael Paul Rogin, *Ronald Reagan, the Movie and Other Episodes in Political Demonology* (Berkeley: University of California Press, 1987).
4. My interest in trust parallels that of Francis Fukuyama, *Trust: The Social Virtues and Creation of Prosperity* (New York: The Free Press, 1995), and Adam Seligman, *The Problem of Trust* (Princeton, N.J.: Princeton University Press, 1996).
5. Richard Rorty, "On Ethnocentrism: A Reply to Clifford Geertz," in *Objectivity, Relativism, and Truth: Philosophical Papers*, vol. 1, Richard Rorty, ed. (Cambridge: Cambridge University Press, 1991), p. 203.
6. William J. Bennett, "Revolt Against God: America's Spiritual Despair," *Policy Review* (Winter 1994), p. 24.

7. Leslie McAnemy, "It Was a Very Bad Year: Belief in Hell and the Devil on the Rise," *The Gallup Poll* (January 13, 1995), p. 1.

8. John Dewey, *Theory of the Moral Life* (New York: Holt, Rinehart and Winston, 1960 [1908]).

9. Dewey, *Theory of the Moral Life*, p., 3.

10. "There is not simply a succession of disconnected acts but each thing done carries forward an underlying tendency and intent, *conducting*, leading up, to further acts and to a final fulfillment or consummation" (*Theory of the Moral Life*, p. 11).

11. Charles Taylor, "What Is Human Agency?" in Taylor, *Human Agency and Language* (Cambridge: Cambridge University Press, 1985), pp. 3–27.

12. Daniel M. Weinstock, "A Political Theory of Strong Evaluation," in James Tully, ed., *Philosophy in an Age of Pluralism: The Philosophy of Charles Taylor in Question* (Cambridge: Cambridge University Press, 1994), p. 173. Weinstock's emphasis, it should be noted, differs from that of Adam Seligman in his chapter in the present volume.

13. Charles Taylor, *Sources of the Self* (Cambridge, Mass.: Harvard University Press, 1989), p. 523.

14. Alasdair MacIntyre, *After Virtue: A Study in Moral Theory*, second edition (Notre Dame, Ind.: University of Notre Dame Press, 1984); Jeffrey Stout, *Ethics After Babel: The Languages of Morals and Their Discontents* (Boston: Beacon, 1988).

15. George Kateb, "Exile, Alienation, and Estrangement: Introduction," in Arien Mack, ed., *Home: A Place in the World* (New York: New York University Press, 1993), pp. 135–38; Robert N. Bellah, Richard Madsen, William M. Sullivan, Ann Swidler, and Steven M. Tipton, *The Good Society* (New York: Alfred A. Knopf, 1991).

16. Wuthnow, *God and Mammon in America* (New York: The Free Press, 1994).

17. Wuthnow, *God and Mammon*.

18. John Rawls, *Political Liberalism* (New York: Columbia University Press, 1993).

19. Robert D. Putnam, "Bowling Alone: America's Declining Social Capital," *Journal of Democracy* 6 (January 1995): 65–78.

20. Michael J. Sandel, *Liberalism and the Limits of Justice* (Cambridge: Cambridge University Press, 1982).

21. Kenneth J. Gergen, *The Saturated Self: Dilemmas of Identity in Contemporary Life* (New York: Basic Books, 1991).

22. Robert N. Bellah, Richard Madsen, William M. Sullivan, Ann Swidler, and Steven M. Tipton, *Habits of the Heart: Individualism and Commitment in American Life* (Berkeley: University of California Press, 1985).

23. Thomas Jefferson, *Notes on the State of Virginia*, Query XVII, in A. A. Lipscomb and A. E. Bergh, eds., *The Writings of Thomas Jefferson*, (Washington, D.C., n.p., 1905), 2: 217.

24. Rorty, Objectivity, Relativism, and Truth, p. 193.

5

The Social Roots of Prosperity and Liberty

Brigitte Berger

For some time now scholars across the academic disciplines have been preoccupied with questions relating to the nature of modern society, its career, and its future. Today most analysts agree with Alexis de Tocqueville that the rise of the modern world is a consequence of peculiar institutional developments which found their clearest expression in the capitalist economy, political democracy, and individual liberty. In present-day analyses it is taken for granted that these institutions constitutive of modern society are "functionally" interrelated and dependent upon each other. What precisely these linkages are and the ways in which they are anchored in society, however, remains elusive and the subject of much debate.

This chapter seeks to contribute to this debate by identifying some of the key factors instrumental in the rise of the modern world that have been strangely disregarded by most analysts. Supported by a wealth of evidence, I will suggest that the institutions characteristic of modern society have common sources and, more specifically, that these common sources must be located in the inner dynamics of a type of family established in parts of Europe long before the onset of the modern era, its ethos, and the moral communities in which it was embedded.

After having made the case for the historic role of the family in the rise of the modern world, I will further argue that the institutional structures constitutive of it continue to be dependent on the same inner dynamics that propelled and structured its rise in the first place. If it can be shown that the distinguishing institutions of modern society have been set into motion by the inner dynamics peculiar to a particular family type, it stands to reason that a strong argument can be made that similar—or minimally analogous—mechanisms are needed also today for industrial liberal democracies to flourish. The exploration of the validity of this argument provides this paper with its ordering principle.

The argument will be developed along four separate, though related, lines: *First*, the parameters of the argument will be set by providing a rough sketch of the theoretical and methodological presuppositions on which this paper rests. *Second*, in view of the fact that the family in a great variety of forms stands at the core of every society—be it the family of antiquity, that of exotic groups in remote corners of the globe, or, as the case may be, in the teeming centers of contemporary Third World urban conglomerations—it will be argued that dynamics emanating from the private world of the family provides not only the rock-bottom foundation for the development of corresponding macro-level economic and political institutions *within* that society, but that family-related dynamics also set up cultural *potentials* for future economic and political developments to occur. *Third*, I will attempt to provide a summary overview of research findings from social demography and social history that allows me to argue with a good deal of confidence that the type of family in question—which for lack of a better term I shall call the nuclear, individualistic, proto-bourgeois family—was the *only* institution sufficiently dynamic to *spontaneously* engender social processes that made for both the development of a modern market economy and the rise of civil society during the eighteenth and nineteenth centuries in the northwestern part of Europe. *Fourth*, I will try to spell out in a preliminary manner why the social habits, norms and the cognitive style peculiar to this type of individualistic family system remain the core features of any social order based on the principles of individual liberty, political democracy, and a market economy. In short, despite the industrial system's numerous permutations during the past century that exacted social, political, and economic adjustments on a grand scale, the forces that stood at its cradle continue to be constitutive of it in the future as well.

Before starting the substantive analysis of this chapter, it becomes necessary to say a few words about the use of the term "individualistic, proto-bourgeois family" as used in this paper. The term encompasses the nuclear or domestic family of father, mother, and their children living and working together, tied to each other by mutual bonds of affection and obligation that can be found in a number of variations in history and across distinctive cultures. In the literature the distinctive characteristics of this family are typically associated with what at a later stage has come to be known as the "bourgeois family" and its

correlative individualistic, striving and acquisitive "bourgeois ethos."[1]
It includes the "proto-industrial" family social historians hold to have
been the precursor of the European family system under industrialism,
and in the literature the term is frequently used interchangeably with
the "Victorian family" and its "Victorian virtues."[2] In more recent decades all these terms have come to be replaced by the term "the middle-
class family" and its corresponding "middle-class life-style." While I
think it quite acceptable to use all these terms interchangeably—as long
as one knows what type of family one is precisely talking about—for
analytical purposes I prefer the use of the terms "proto-bourgeois" and
"bourgeois family." For one, both terms neither confine the phenomenon to geography or historical time, but are reflective of particular
behavior patterns and mind-sets. For another, the proposed labels side-
step an undue emphasis on the economic dimension which the term
"class" invariably carries. In contrast I think it necessary to liberate the
term "bourgeois" from its clichéd Marxist connotation which, to my
mind, profoundly misrepresents its culture and its values. Like Simon
Schama, I find it of considerable importance to broaden the economic
aspect of the term to include its civic dimensions—as the Dutch with
the term *burgerlijk* or the Germans with the term "bürgerlich" do. If
one broadens the term "bourgeois" to include its civic dimensions, more
is altered than just its linguistic form.[3] What sets the bourgeois family
apart from other family forms, including the "amoral familism" characteristic of some traditional (and modern) societies, is precisely the
novel combination of economically productive behavior patterns, a
growing civic consciousness, and an intensified respect for individuals
and their rights.

Theoretical and Methodological Considerations

Wherever one turns today one encounters the argument for the primacy of structure and structural constellations—the technology, the
economy, the law and so forth—from which everything else is alleged
to flow. In this view, the family in its form as well as in its content, is
determined by factors of the social structure, or, to put it into more
technical terms, the family is understood as a "dependent" rather than
an "independent" variable. Although economists and political theorists
differ sharply with regard to which particular structural features are the
more dominant—with those following in the footsteps of Adam Smith
attributing major power to the rationality flowing from the market, and

those working in the Hegelian tradition emphasizing the importance of the rationality flowing from shifts in ideas and cognition culminating in the progress of political freedom—most take the autonomy of systemic forces for granted. The same holds true for Marxism, that other great philosophical paradigm that has dominated philosophical thinking for the past century and a half. All these theoretical approaches are united in the postulate that the more subjective forces of the "lifeworld"—a term coined by the sociologist Alfred Schutz[4]—in which the family typically figures prominently, are overshadowed and shaped by the influence of external, objective factors. While anthropologists and some social historians are willing to grant that social life prior to the establishment of the industrial order may also have been determined by the more or less unchangeable and uncontested connections of family, kinship, religion, and community, once industrialism was ensconced, a fundamentally new reality emerged. Forces flowing from the impersonal, instrumental "rationality" of the ever-expanding industrial system, it is argued, now gained autonomy and became all-powerful. The lifeworld, or what is left of it, lost its dynamic quality and, in Juergen Habermas' terms, was subjected to a relentless "colonization" by the instrumental rationality peculiar to the expanding macro-institutions of the public sphere.[5] In this process the spontaneous, free and all-embracing forces of the private sphere which once gave succor and meaning to individual life are seen to have been increasingly stifled and subverted to a degree whereby a situation has been reached today in which modern individuals find themselves as helpless pawns of forces beyond their control. The first sentence of C.Wright Mills' celebrated *The Sociological Imagination* that starts with the lapidary statement, "Nowadays men often feel that their private lives are a series of traps," succinctly captures this pervasive assessment of the modern situation.[6] In this vision, the public sphere now reigns supreme, punctuated on occasion only by the self-seeking hedonism of alienated, anomic individuals who in their search for meaning enter into surrogate communal arrangements, fleeting and ultimately unsatisfactory.

To be sure, a plausible argument can be made for a structuralist interpretation of what makes the modern world tick. Yet this type of approach tells only one side of the story. If one looks at the history of modern social life through the prism of an approach championed by Max Weber, a very different interpretative perspective suggests itself. It is a perspective that starts with micro-level processes based on individual actions and the values they hold and traces their influence on the formation of the macro-structures that constitute the public sphere.[7] This perspective, I would propose, is a humanizing perspective. At its center stand individual actors and the meanings individuals attach to their actions. It proceeds from the "bottom up" rather than from the "top down," and it makes one cautious to speak about systems, structures, functions, and even institutions as autonomous realities. All such concepts are seen to be human artifacts or constructions which have no ontological status apart from the meaningful actions that led to their creation. It is an approach in which social institutions only exist as long as living human beings hold them up by their actions and in this sense it is possible to say that there are no free-floating institutions, there is no one here but us people. In a reversal of the Habermasean dictum, one is tempted to propose that it is the rationality of the private sphere that creates and colonizes the public sphere, rather than the other way around. What is more, this "bottom-up" direction of social processes does not only apply to the past, but, *mutatis mutandis*, to the present as well, and there are no theoretical reasons why this should not be the case in the future,

To be sure, scholars informed by Durkheimean structuralist presuppositions can argue that while social phenomena emerge on the basis of individual actions, once created, they become more than simply the sum-part of such actions and take on dynamics of their own.[8] Similarly those working within the Marxist paradigm can make good use of Marx's concept of reification in this context. Yet if one takes Max Weber's reminder seriously that it is the business of the social sciences to interpret (*verstehen*) the meaning of human actions, the analyst is bound to foresake a purely structural analysis and turn to individuals whose patterned behavior made for the rise of social structures in the first place. The researchers then will start his or her inquiry with an investigation of the conditions and forces that gave purpose *and* meaning to individual actions.

Because of the centrality of the family in the everyday life of individuals, regardless of geographical space or historical time, this line of theoretical reasoning compels the analyst to link the motivated actions of individuals with the rise and shape of social institutions. Jan Romein, the Dutch historian, has coined the term "the common human pattern" to capture the historical significance of the "natural" desire of all human beings to care for the members of their family and protect them from harm. Yet this perhaps "natural" desire does not necessarily lead to lifelong self-denial, to delay gratification, to plan, to save, to build, to accumulate capital, to care for ones neighbors and community, in short, it does not lead to behavior patterns customarily associated with the market economy and civil society. In ignoring the Weberian insight that for behavior to become purposive it must be motivated, successive generations of economic historians and structuralist analysts have left out the most important questions of human existence. The theoretical design of this essay then is to take a first stab at demonstrating how public institutions are linked to private virtues.

Following theoretical presuppositions the German sociological theorist Hansfried Kellner elaborated in a different context,[9] this essay works on the premise that the lifeworld of the individual and the systemic sphere of macro-institutions are interconnected in a variety of ways and neither is able to function without the other. Each sphere is distinguished by separate, though overlapping relevance structures, and each is defined by a sphere-appropriate rationality that provides purpose and meaning to their actions. On the one hand, individuals motivated by their very personal needs, interests and searches for meanings, operate within the private sphere of their familial and communal life on the basis of culturally conditioned knowledge that is available to them. Factors of the system, or the public sphere, enter into their field of action only insofar as they are relevant for what appears to them to be rational for their very personal pursuits. On the other hand, in selecting particular aspects from the objectively available resources provided by the system, individuals become carriers of the system, thereby contributing to its maintenance. Although the rational requirements of the system frequently appear to be overpowering and autonomous, if not even indifferent to the constitutive elements of their lifeworld, the system itself largely continues to depend upon the very same elements of the lifeworld that stood at its cradle. In putting these theoretical considerations into the context of the essay before us, we may conclude our argument with the almost banal observation that system and family are just two sides of the same coin. With shifts in the one sphere affecting the function of the other, both are by definition dependent upon each other.

It would, of course, be foolish to deny that external factors of technology and production as well as those of law and politics have no influence on the rise of prosperity and liberty. In their masterful *The Rise of the Western World: A New Economic History* , Douglas North and Robert Thomas, among others, have detailed many of these external factors.[10] Yet this is only half of the story. The other half has not received sufficient consideration to date.

The Family and Culture

Let me start my argument with the straightforward proposition that the family is *the* culture-creating institution par excellence. All over the world wherever one turns, today as in the past, an incontestable argument can be made that the family, and not the individual of the economist's paradigm, is the most basic building block on which all other social forms rest. The family itself is the product of the most elementary and virulent emotions of human nature—love, hate, sex, hunger, sacrifice, loneliness, punishment, yearnings for transcendence, and others. It is also the basic locale in which human production and reproduction takes place, becomes routinized, habituated, and ultimately institutionalized. The patterns or ways in which these properties of human nature and human existence interact and reinforce each other over time lead to the formation of very particularistic family systems which, in turn, provide the foundations from which vastly different cultures and civilizations arise. In other words, it may be argued, that distinctive family cultures shaped and activated in a complicated interactive process by the "enabling force" of an ethos anchored in religion, not only provide the rock-bottom foundation for the development of corresponding political and economic structures, they also set up cultural potentials for future economic and political developments.[11] As will be argued presently, we know today with a fair degree of certainty that the emergence of the capitalist market in the northwestern part of Europe was only possible on the basis of preexisting family-based cultural tendencies that antedated the industrial revolution by centuries. A wealth of materials derived from detailed social-demographic and social-historical studies permit us to glean those factors productive of a modern manner of life that in one way or another can be linked to the region's highly dynamic and adaptable family system existing at the time. In the case of China, on the other hand, we also know that one of the major factors preventing this venerable and highly sophisticated civilization from unleashing the potential for the spontaneous development of a modern market economy must be sought in the apparent immutability of its all-pervasive kinship structure. Only today, when stifling controls by the state have been muted and the "sib fetters" of Chinese culture have grown thin in the overseas Chinese communities of Hong Kong, Singapore, and Taiwan has the Chinese family been able to develop an "entrepreneurial familism" productive of the capitalist market that is awesome to behold.[12] It is, however, a question of considerable debate whether the newly created capitalist market economy will lead also to the creation of democracy and civic consciousness.

A similar argument can be made with regard to the emergence of liberal democracy, one of Western civilization's great achievements. As pointed out earlier, history shows that the "common human pattern" that has ruled human history for millennia is characterized by a familism that is preoccupied with the well-being and advancement of the members of one's immediate family. This type of familism is still alive in many parts of the world today just as it continues to exist alongside civil-society traditions in parts of the highly advanced industrial societies of the West. The old Arab proverb that says "Me and my brother against my cousins, me and my cousins against the world" still dominates the politics of many contemporary nations, and not only in the Arab world at that. To think politically in ways that transcend the interests of the immediate family, to act in ways that allow for the emergence of a civil society capable of incorporating nonfamily members—regardless of race, ethnicity, religion, and social origin—into new political and economic networks, may appear to be "unnatural" from the point of view of the common human pattern that has ruled the world for millenia. Yet the acceptance of such "unnatural" ways as the only legitimate way to conduct politics is precisely what happened in the rising democratic societies in the West. If one wants to uncover the reasons that motivated people to behave in such "unnatural" ways, I would propose, one is compelled to look at the inner dynamics peculiar to the rising bourgeois or middle-class family.

By the same token, it is also important to keep in mind that deeply ingrained cultural traditions can serve to subvert the family's dynamic potentials. A case in point are the polygamous societies of the sub-Saharan African continent, whose cultures remain profoundly antithetical to the emergence of a genuinely modern market economy. Here all aspects of life are determined by factors of kinship, the family has failed to emerge as a modern economic unit, and politics to this day remains largely determined by family and tribal factors. To be sure, the recent migration of large number of people to the sprawling cities of the sub-Saharan continent has weakened the control of powerful traditions. Yet to this date there exists little evidence for the formation of a family system conducive to economic development and that is strong enough to withstand the dual pressures of dislocation and modernization. Marriage in the urban centers of Africa is an extremely fragile bond, with men, women, and children forever on the move, making and remaking in a single lifetime domestic forms which logically cannot be called either a household or a family.[13] Small wonder then, that the eyes of the world are turned today on South Africa's Nelson Mandela who alone among African leaders appears to have found a magic formula to overcome Africa's tribal captivity.

When one makes generalizations as broad as these, one has to take great care *not* to assume that some civilizations are predestined to advance while others, like the just cited polygamous societies of the African continent, are condemned to lag eternally behind. Under propitious circumstances cultures have not only the *capacity* to change, they actually *do change*. But for such change to occur—as the insights of this paper strongly suggest—it must include changes at the lived reality of family and communal life, and cannot merely be dictated from the planning boards of distant agencies and governments.

An example may illustrate what is at issue here. When one looks through the prism of the family at a growing set of data that traces the social consequences of the mass migration of often desperately poor people to the teeming cities of Latin America—in Brazil, Chile, and Peru, for instance—it does not take long to discover that traditional behavior patterns that for long had subverted the emergence of a modern market economy are in the process of being transformed by the migratory process. Here in the favelas and barrios of Latin American cities, at the bottom of society, unaided by their governments and largely unnoticed by researchers, a new manner of life is about to crystallize around new family-centered values and behavior patterns.[14] In his pathbreaking book *Tongues of Fire*, David Martin records how under the influence of Pentecostalism a new manner of life is emerging in Rio de Janeiro.[15] Since Martin, like other observers of this revolutionary phenomenon, is preoccupied with the description and analysis of the religious dimensions of conversion, he, like others, does not sufficiently recognize that sentiments of family are equally important factors in the conversion process. It is women, incidentally, who are playing a pivotal role here. Exhausted by their lonely, neverending struggle for survival for themselves and their numerous children, women are turning to Pentecostalism for comfort and sustenance. Yet Pentecostalism's stark commands also served to instill new behavior patterns just as it served to "domesticate" the macho, irresponsible, philandering, and boozing males of the Brazilian slum to a life of work, thrift, and abstinence. In sum, this particular religious ethos was instrumental in fusing men and women together into a family-centered way of life that provides deep preparations for future larger-scaled changes to occur. The example also shows how a new manner of life is created almost spontaneously at the intersection between family, work, and religious yearnings and practices that holds revolutionary potential for a whole continent. In the process of adapting to the demands of industrial urban life, old behavior patterns are weakened and—under propitious circumstances—new patterns conducive the formation of civil society and economic progress emerge almost spontaneously.

By the same token, it is equally important to recognize that already highly industrialized liberal democracies like England and Japan which may be said to have been "modern from the beginning," could loose their comparative cultural advantages *if* their distinctive familistic ethos should loose its dynamic power. Economic stagnation and political transformation are sure to follow. At a recent workshop in Cambridge, British social scientists were in rare agreement when voicing their apprehensions about the future of England. They blamed the weakening of the British family for the British worker's loss of resilience and adaptability, a change in style of life which they were convinced could endanger Britain's future.[16]

The Bourgeois Family and the Creation
of Democratic Capitalism

A formidable body of research available today definitively documents that what social demographers call the "proto-industrial" family served as the link between the feudal and the modern industrial world.[17] Its existence long antedated the rise of the industrial order and, if the Cambridge social demographers around Peter Laslett and Alan MacFarlane are right, it was the proto-industrial family that set the stage for industrialization as far back as the thirteenth century.[18] In the course of a few centuries, but not later than the middle of the nineteenth century, the proto-industrial family household—now reinforced and given meaning by what MacFarlane calls the "enabling" force of the Protestant ethic—had solidified into an ethos and "new manner of life" that to this day remains constitutive of industrial capitalism writ large.

What made the proto-industrial—or in the language of this paper, the "proto-bourgeois"—family so special? Among its outstanding structural features three in particular deserve to be mentioned: the sanctity of private property and an inheritance system based on primogeniture; a marriage system dependent upon individual choice; and the requirement to establish and provide for one's own conjugal household. These characteristics, taken together, made for late marriage and responsible procreation just as they encouraged individual responsibility, hard work, attention to training, parsimony, and the necessity to save, for without the wherewithal it was impossible to establish one's own conjugal household.[19] These habits and norms were galvanized by new forms of work that became available in the latter part of the eighteenth century in the "putting out" cottage work system typically connected to the emergent textile industry and the myriad of household-based small artisan enterprises that produced a great variety of objects for everyday use.

Detailed studies—such as the one by the Swiss social demographer Rudolf Braun—show that the new ways to earn an independent living provided for the first time in history opportunities to large numbers of individuals to become autonomous, to marry and to establish their own independent households.[20] All that was needed was a good measure of self-reliance, persistence, planning, frugality, prudence and the willingness to take rationally calculated risks. Since the creation of one's own "little world" was the desired way of life for most, and since the new patterns of behavior and work rendered tangible results fairly quickly, the new manner of life was emulated by many. Such family-engendered patterns of behavior that emphasized responsibility, individualism and rationality were to be of far-reaching consequences.

On the *economic level*, family sentiments played a pivotal role in the expansion of capitalist production as they not only unleashed new productive work patterns, but also created demands for consumer goods on a large scale. As Neil McKendrick recently put it:

> Who bought the cottons, woolens, linens and silks of the burgeoning British textile industries? Who consumed the massive increases in beer production? Who bought the crockery which poured from the Staffordshire potteries? Who bought the buckles, the buttons, the pins and all the minor metal-products on which Birmingham fortunes were built? Who bought-the Sheffield cutlery...etc.[21]

In passing it may be worth noting that the widespread desire to build a home of one's own provides grist for the mills of those who argue that the market is driven just as much by factors of consumption as it is by those of production. It also lends added strength to the "bottom-up" perspective that informs the analysis presented here.

On the *political* level the egalitarian, individualistic, and achievement-oriented behavioral rules that governed the inner life of the proto-bourgeois family were externalized to provide nineteenth-century

liberalism with its lasting political creed. Together with affections revolving around trust and confidence—all developed in the privacy of
family life—they came to provide the stable foundations for what we
call "civil society" today. The equality of individuals before the law,
equal treatment by the state, and the notion of individual freedom—all
those guiding principles of liberalism, can be shown to have their origin here. Parentage, religious background and, in subsequent periods,
also factors of race and gender, decreased in importance and ultimately
made for the breakdown of traditional economic and political barriers.
Contrary to Karl Marx's theory of class conflict that holds that capitalism would lead to the economic immiseration and political enslave-
ment of the industrial worker the expanding industrial capitalist system
and the concomitant rise of political liberalism offered unmatched economic opportunities to the poor and set them politically free.

It cannot be emphasized enough that sentiments revolving around
family and home propelled ever larger numbers of people mired in the
subsistence economy to adapt to the rigors of industrial life. (These
surely did not come easily and when they did then they came at a considerable price!) A new culture of domesticity spread like wildfire from
one end of Victorian England to the other, engulfing even the child of
the slums into its folds. As Edward Shorter put it:

> Home however poor, was the focus of all his love and interests, a sure fortress
> against a hostile world. Songs about its beauties were ever on people's lips. "Home
> Sweet Home" first heard in the 1870s , had become almost a national anthem by
> the turn of the century.[22]

In passing, permit me to comment, however briefly, on the perception common among contemporary intellectuals that by the end of the
nineteenth century the "cult of domesticity" promoted by the bourgeois
family heralded in not only the separation of social life into two separate spheres, the private and the public, but also promoted their increasing isolation and encapsulation. The names of Edward Shorter
and Christopher Lash come to mind in this connection, whose books
gained much public attention and continue to influence public perception to this day.[23] Despite considerable differences between the many
contributors to this perception, most agree that there occurred a withdrawal of the family into the "emotional fortress" of the bourgeois home
not because the home become warmer and more attractive in the course
of the nineteenth century, but because the outside world came to be
seen as more forbidding and alien. This, I think, is a gross misunder-

standing of the bourgeois family ethos. On the basis of a wealth of diaries and memoirs, a much better argument can be made that by the end of the nineteenth century the bourgeois family saw itself as the launching pad for its individual members for participation in the changing world of work. Far from individuals retreating into a shrinking private world, we may observe that the private world had extended itself into that of the public, creating ever more structures in its progress. By the end of that century the intermesh between these two spheres was successfully completed.

Nowhere does the degree of the interlock between these two spheres become more clearly evident than in the growth of education. As the century progressed it became ever more apparent that middle-class family and the schools are but two sides of the same coin. The rising bourgeois family not only inculcated the bourgeois virtues at home, it expected, nay even demanded, that schools do the same. Until a few decades ago, the two institutions, the bourgeois family and the bourgeois conception of education—for better or for worse—set together the standards for socialization and education that were binding for all members of society. Although with the development of technology formal education gained in importance in the preparation of children for participation in the modern economy and the complexities of a democratic polity, family influences became no less, and, in some respects, even more important than in the past. It was precisely the lack of access to bourgeois socialization practices and the behavioral norms it promoted that put the children of the lower classes at a disadvantage. What is more, to this day this lag of behavioral patterns and aspirations in growing segments of the population that remains one of the key dilemmas plaguing the educational system today. Instead of continuing to promote long-tested patterns of behavior and learning that have led to success in the past, contemporary society has taken the easy way out to define socialization and education "down," rather than "up." A wealth of studies demonstrates that the cardinal virtues of civil society and a well-functioning market society are of family origin. The school's function is to hone and refine them further.

Space does not permit a review of the many misperceptions swirling around the bourgeois family today. The literature almost completely ignores the new freedoms the type of family provides to its members, such as freedom from the stifling controls of tradition for men, women and children, the new appreciation of individualism, equality, and personal responsibility. What has to be emphasized for our purposes, how-

ever, is that the type of analysis proposed in this chapter is able to
connect the inner life of a particular type of family to the creation and
the maintenance of liberal democracy and a market economy. It is
equally important to realize that the "new manner of life," that to this
day is the manner of life constitutive of modern civil society and capitalist production, is in large measure a spontaneous product of the rising middle classes, frequently, though not only, recruited from the
flotsam and jetsam of the period. Far from being simply imitators of an
older bourgeoisie of the eighteenth century, as Jean-Francois Bergier
has shown, it is this "petite" bourgeoisie of small producers, artisans,
and merchants who managed to merge family values with ideas of private property and civil liberty most effectively. Together with their de-
scendants the "petite bourgeoisie" prepared the cultural soil from which
both a capitalist economy and civil society could rise.[24] Their cher-
ished virtues of hard work, frugality, prudence, reliability, punctuality,
and responsibility coupled with overarching principles of Christianity
propelled them to expand their horizons and have become a part of the
air we breath today. This ethos committed them to a world beyond that
of the family and even beyond that of the nation. In sum, this type of
family produced a culture that stands for the value of the individual,
regardless of race, social background, or physical endowment. Closely
related to this is the belief that every individual has the right to freedom
from constraints to which he or she has not assented, and this right
includes the freedom of beliefs. Implied in this is the acceptance of a
pluralism of beliefs and the democratic assumption that freedom is the
right of every individual and that this right must be institutionalized.

The Western Family Today

When one turns one's attention to the situation of the Western family today one is compelled to observe that recent history has not been
kind to the bourgeois family. The confluence of distinct sets of powerful social forces—demographic, economic, sociocultural, and moral—
served to undermine both its structure as well as its legitimacy that has
been taken for granted for long. This is not the place to trace the history
of these forces, nor is it the place to enter into a debate about the consequences of three decades of public efforts to shore up—and, at times,
even to replace—a family system many argued to be no longer viable
nor desirable. Suffice it to note that both bourgeois family and its correlative bourgeois ethos were heavily attacked during the 1960s cul-

ture revolution and have come into disrepute since then. Looking back at the war against the family one cannot help but note that many, though not all, of the public efforts to supplement or to replace the functions of what came to be called the "traditional" family (a misnomer, if there ever was one) have not achieved a whole lot. A mass of depressing statistics attests to their failure to stem the rising tide of delinquency, crime, drug use, teenage pregnancy, and a growing welfare dependency. With the exception of Japan and, to a somewhat lesser degree, Korea and the overseas Chinese communities of Taiwan, Hong Kong, and Singapore, the rise in social ills has been fairly consistent in all industrial societies, with the United States and the countries of Northern Europe outdistancing, by a wide margin, countries such as France, Italy, Germany and the Czech Republic.[25] A growing body of research reveals that public efforts frequently turned out to be not only wasteful of large sums of public moneys, but destructive of human lives as well. All too often they encouraged individuals to turn their backs on the traditional path of self-sufficiency and upward mobility that relies on the dynamic potential of families and the moral communities in which they are embedded—the churches, neighborhoods, self-help groups, and the many voluntary organizations that provide civil society with its dynamics and compass. If one views the politics of the past decades through the prism of the family, one cannot help but conclude that in turning away from the normative order of the middle-class family all those costly public efforts combined to undermine the social fabric of Western civilization. Although of late we can witness a public rediscovery of the salutary role of the nuclear family of father, mother, and their children living together and caring for their individual and collective progress, policy elites appear neither to have fully understood that public life lies at the mercy of private life, nor to have apprehended the degree to which the bourgeois virtues and bourgeois ethos continue to be indispensable for the maintenance of both the market economy and civil society.

It may be difficult to entertain the hypothesis that events as long ago as the early modern period could still have profound effects upon the highly technologized industrial societies of today. During the past century the industrial system has undergone numerous economic permutations that exacted social adjustments in the ways we work, where we live, how we live and what and how we consume. On the political level we have witnessed the radicalization of the rational individualism and rational cognitive style distinctive of democratic capitalism. Under the banner of individual self-realization and a bewildering number of newly discovered rights the contours of this unique system has been transformed, almost beyond recognition, in the short span of a few decades. And yet the modern world with its awesome technological capacities and its sophisticated organizational structures depends upon a large reservoir of people psychologically well-adjusted, educationally prepared, and socially competent to execute the kind of performances necessary to acquire and operate the instruments of the postindustrial system. Civil society, particularly in view of its ever-expanding desire to incorporate a new and untested democratic pluralism, is in equal measure dependent upon autonomous individuals who have the capacity to reason rationally and act responsibly, and perhaps also passionately, on the basis of principles of individual freedom, equality, and justice. Whatever the future will bring, one thing is for sure, it will be a system of life in which the principal unit of action is based on the motivation, the performance, and the responsibility of autonomous individuals. Where such self-reliant, highly motivated, and ethically responsible individuals are to come from is then a question that poses itself with great urgency today.

Considerations of this kind bring once more into focus the earlier claim that there exists a peculiar "cognitive fit" between the requirements of liberal democracy organized around the economy of the market and the much-maligned bourgeois family. It is a cognitive fit that fosters habits and sentiments which still today are conducive to economic progress, which promotes a commitment to civic responsibility, and which has the capacity to instill in its individual members a "rational cognitive restlessness" without which the future of the postindustrial world looks dim.

The empirical evidence for the beneficence of the necessary linkage between the macro-world of public institutions and the microworld of a particular kind of family is massive. It reveals itself most clearly in the area of socialization and education. For quite some time now social psychologists have demonstrated that there exists a great deal of evidence for the existence of continuity between childhood experiences and attitudes and adult attitudes and actions.[26] The process is understood to proceed in a circular pattern whereby the values of the adult society are transmitted through child-rearing and other teaching practices to children, who, when they become adults, reinforce and help to maintain the culture in which they live. The social science literature comprising theorists as diverse as George Herbert Mead, Jean Piaget,

Erik Erikson, Robert Sears, Shmuel Eisenstadt, and Jerome Bruner—and with them the legions of researchers who make use of their distinctive approaches—have established this, by now almost clichéd linkage. Small wonder then that a wealth of data has accumulated over the past thirty years that indicates beyond the question of a doubt that a nuclear family of father, mother, and children, living together, mindful of each other and actively involved with each other, is still today a child's best guarantee for success in school and life beyond. The same data also show that an individual's progress in all walks of life depends largely upon the traditional virtues and practices of the bourgeois family which critics have taken great joy to deride.[27] The old adage that it does not so much matter what cards life has dealt you, but how you play them, is still as true today as it was a hundred years ago. What is more, contrary to fashionable arguments, the evidence is in that the prudent use of traditional socialization practices may still be the best service parents can render their children, and the often contested commitment of the middle-class family to mold character traits of perseverance, self-reliance, effort, and trustworthiness still remain the very mechanisms best suited to fortify children against the odds of life ahead.[28] By the same token, the massive data collected during the past thirty years also show that the absence of such family resources makes it much harder for a child to achieve, compete, and progress. Equally important, there exist some data as well that lead us to believe that the two parent family is important for the development of a sense of civic responsibility in the growing child.[29] Children raised in single-parent households showed a higher level of authoritarianism, were less politically interested, and less politically efficacious than their peers growing up in nuclear families.

When one turns to the life of adults, large sets of data document as well that the institution of marriage, despite all its problems and tedium, is still the best thing around. Both men and women are healthier, happier, more productive, and live longer when married. The bad news is, that many are not aware of this linkage and there exists a widespread suspicion among all too many that the grass is greener on the other side of the fence. Yet considerable apprehensions aside, marriage appears to continue to enjoy considerable popularity, and although middle-class couples have fewer children than before, they *do* have children nonetheless. Within the analytical paradigm proposed in this paper there are no reasons to doubt that this will not also continue in the future. What is more, the much ridiculed "Victorian" desire for an exclusive sexual relationship is as strong, if not stronger, today as it was a hundred years ago and judging by reports from far-flung corners of the world such as Japan, China, and Africa, this desire appears to be spreading. If we are to trust the three researchers of the recent *The Social Construction of Sexuality*, there is much less philandering going on than sensationalist media reports have led us to believe.[30]

As pointed out earlier, the nuclear-bourgeois family has experienced considerable shifts in its structure and its function since it first entered the historical arena. Within the context of the argument developed here, however, it is of considerable importance to appreciate that the bourgeois family is a state of mind rather than a particular kind of structure and cannot merely be structurally defined as statisticians of the census are prone to do. What distinguishes it from other types of families still today is its ethos that regardless of structure places a premium on individual initiative and responsibility. No substitute to this type of family has emerged as the depressing record of the commune movement of the 1960s and 1970s and the growing number of single-headed households during the past three decades so blatantly shows.

More generally, there is the question of the moral foundation of any human society, and especially of a democratic polity. Emile Durkheim, close to a hundred years ago, argued that at its core every human society is a moral community; conversely, he tried to show that in the absence of shared moral values, a society must begin to disintegrate. This general sociological truth is doubly valid when a society organizes itself politically as a democracy. The reason for this is simple: in the absence of moral consensus, coercion remains the only instrument for the maintenance of even minimal social integration. Such coercion, however, cannot coexist with democracy. Although social thinkers since John Dewey strongly argued that education could perform this role, the recent record shows that the school as an institution appears to be quite ineffective in instilling basic moral values—*unless* they serve to reinforce values already instilled in the individual by his homelife. Very much the same is true for the churches as well as the law. The family, today as always, remains the institution in which the very great majority of individuals learn whatever they will ever learn about morality. It is in this sense that the family has a political function of the greatest importance. This is especially true in a democracy where there exists an ongoing need for achieving a balance between the rights of individuals and the needs of society. The balancing act of democracy, in this sense, is the balancing act of the bourgeois family. Regardless of future permutations this linkage is likely to remain.

In concluding it has to be observed that while these findings imply that the bourgeois family is essential for the formation as well as the survival of democratic capitalism, it is also important to understand that this family and its peculiar ethos is not the exclusive property of the countries of the West. Regardless of origin and history, *any* family system—be it Chinese, Japanese, German, Indian, Islamic, or African in origin—can meet the challenges of the future, *as long as* it contains the core features constitutive of the family system that was instrumental in the creation of the modern world. A year or so ago, Samuel Huntington caused a considerable stir with his proposition that world politics is moving into a period of "civilizational clash" in which the primary identification of people around the world will not be ideological, as during the Cold War, but rather cultural.[31] Now that Western-style capitalism and democracy have remained triumphant, Huntington argued that conflict will arise not between fascism, socialism, and democracy, but between the world's major cultural groups, Western, Islamic, Confucian, Hindu, and so on. While only time will tell whether and to what degree Huntington's predictions are accurate, his essay performs the crucial service of bringing into focus the role factors of culture play in the affairs of nations. In contrast to Huntington, however, the findings of this essay propel us to emphasize the singular importance of the family in the formation of civilizations. And this observation takes me back to the beginning of the essay. If such "a clash of civilization" should occur some time in the future, then this clash, at its roots, will be one between different family systems and the ways in which they are able to integrate the properties of human nature and human existence with the requirements of the post-modern world rushing towards us today. Any society that disregards this fundamental reality does so at its own peril.

Notes

1. William J. Goode, *World Revolution and Family Patterns* (New York: The Free Press, 1963).
2. Gertrude Himmelfarb, *The Democratization of Society: From Victorian Virtues to Modern Values* (New York: Alfred A. Knopf, 1991).
3. Simon Schama, *An Embarrassment of Riches* (New York: Cambridge University Press), 1979.
4. Alfred Schutz, *Collected Papers*, vol.I (The Hague: Nijhoff, 1962).
5. Jurgen Habermas, *Theory and Practice*, John Viertel, trans. (Boston: Beacon Press, 1973).
6. C. Wright Mills, *The Sociological Imagination* (New York: Oxford University Press, 1959).
7. Max Weber, *The Methodology of the Social Sciences*, Edward A. Shils and Henry A. Finch, trans. (New York: The Free Press, 1949).

8. Emile Durkheim, *The Rules of Sociological Method* (Glencoe, Ill.: The Free Press, 1938).

9. Hansfried Kellner, 1995, "Die *zwei* Rationalitäten aus phenomenologischer Sicht: Beitrag zu Max Webers Begriff der Rationalität," unpublished manuscript (Frankfurt: Department of Sociology, Universität Frankfurt).

10. Douglas C. North and Robert Thomas, *The Rise of the Western World : A New Economic History* (Cambridge: Cambridge University Press, 1973).

11. The term "enabling force" is borrowed from Alan Macfarlane, *The Culture of Capitalism* (Cambridge and Oxford: Basil Blackwell, 1987).

12. See Gilbert (Sin-Lun) Wong, "The Chinese Family Firm: A Model," *The British Journal of Sociology*, 36 (1985): 58–72.

13. See William Bascom, "The Urban African and His World" in Sylvia S. Fava, ed., *Urbanization in World Perspective* (New York: Thomas Y. Cromwell, 1968), pp. 36–51; A.L. Epstein, "Urbanization and Social Change in Africa," in Gerald Breese, ed.,*The City in Newly Developing Countries* (Englewood Cliffs, N.J.: Prentice-Hall), pp. 117–34; and T. Dunbar Moodie, *Going for the Gold* (Berkeley: University of California Press, 1994).

14. See Bernard Rosen, *The Industrial Connection* (New York: Aldine Press, 1982).

15. David Martin, *Tongues of Fire: The Explosion of Protestantism in Latin America* (Cambridge: Basil Blackwell, 1990).

16. See David Green's "Forword" to Jon Davis, ed., *The Family: Is It Just Another Lifestyle Choice?*, (London: Institute of Economic Affairs, Health and Welfare Unit, Occasional Papers # 15, 1991).

17. Hans Medick, "The proto-industrial family economy: the structural function of household and family during the transition from peasant society to industrial capitalism," In Charles Tilly, ed., *The Formation of National States in Western Europe*, pp. 211–37 (Princeton, N.J.: Princeton University Press, 1975).

18. See Peter Laslett, *The World We Have Lost: England Before the Industrial Revolution* (New York: Charles Scribner & Sons, 1965); see also Peter Laslett, "The European Family and Early Industrialization" in Jean Baechler, John A. Hall, and Michael Mann, *Europe and the Rise of Capitalism* (Cambridge: Basil Blackwell), 1988; and, perhaps most importantly, see Alan Mac Farlane, *The Culture of Capitalism* (Cambridge: Basil Blackwell, 1987).

19. See Peter Laslett, *The World We Have Lost.*

20. Rudolf Braun, "The Demographic Transition of the Canton of Zurich in the early 19th Century" in Charles Tilly, ed., *The Formation of National States in Europe*, pp. 171–97.

21. Neil McKendrick, "Home Demand and Economic Growth: A New View of the Role of Women and Children in the Industrial Revolution" in Neil McKendrick, ed., *Historical Perspective: Studies in English Thought and Society in Honour of J. H. Plumb* (London: Europa Publication, 1974), pp.152 ff.

22. Edward Shorter, *The Making of the Modern Family* (New York: Basic Books, 1975).

23. Edward Shorter, ibid.; Christopher Lash, *Haven in a Heartless World* (New York: Basic Books, 1977).

24. Jean-Francois Bergier, *The Industrial Bourgeoisie and the Rise of the Working Class, 1700–1914* (Cambridge: Cambridge University Press, 1971); see also Rudolf Braun, "The Demographic Transition in the Canton of Zuerich in the 18th and 19th Century" in Charles Tilly, ed., *Historical Studies of Changing Fertility* (Princeton, N.J.: Princeton University Press, 1978); as well as Edward Shorter, *The Making of the Modern Family*, p. 231.

25. See Special Report of the Population Council, New York, 1995

26. For a fine summary see Patricia Morgan, *Who Needs Parents?* (London: Institute of Economic Affairs, Health & Welfare Unit, no. 31, 1991).
27. See Brigitte and Peter Berger, *The War Over the Family* (New York, Doubleday & Co, 1983).
28. See Travis Hirschi, *Delinquency and Family Life* (New York: Basic Books, 1986).
29. Recent studies appear to reconfirm earlier findings that children raised in single-mother households seem to be less politically interested, less politically efficacious, and display inclinations that are not conducive to the maintenance of liberal democracy.
30. Eduard Lauman, John Gagnon, and Gina Kolata, *The Social Construction of Sexuality* (New York: Basic Books, 1994).
31. Samuel Huntington, "The Clash of Civilizations?" In *Foreign Affairs*, 72 (1993): 22–49.

6

Civil Society, Pillarization, and the Welfare State

Anton C. Zijderveld

There is an important sociological difference between horizontal and vertical social structures. A society is horizontally structured if there is a variety of associations and institutions in which individual citizens group together in order to pursue their collective interests, and to realize their shared communal plans and motives in civic engagement. The presence of voluntary associations comes to mind, if one tries to conceptualize such a horizontally structured society. But societal horizontalism consists also of religious, educational, and leisure institutions (sports, the arts, etc.)—generally the rich field of nongovernmental organizations—which are autonomous vis-à-vis the state, and manage to transcend individualism and particularism by binding people together in various collective activities of civic engagement. In fact, horizontalism is the major condition for the existence of a civic spirit and culture.

The metaphor of horizontalism is used in order to emphasize the fact that power and authority are not exerted in a top-down manner from an overarching state down to particular groups and to individual citizens. These groups and individuals, on the contrary, exert their own power and authority within their relatively autonomous associations and institutions. In a horizontally structured society and a civic culture, the role and functions of the state are decentralized and, in a sense, residual and secondary: it does what these autonomous associations and institutions are unable to do, that is, to set and guard the general rules of the game (laid down in laws, above all the constitution), to guarantee safety and security, to advocate internationally the political and collective interests of the nation, to develop and maintain the nation's infrastructure. Beyond these crucial functions of the state, the associations and institutions in society are free to design and exert their own patterns of power and authority.

In the European Union this is called today the *subsidiarity principle*— a relatively old concept that stems from Catholic social philosophy. In The Netherlands there exists the even more radical, Calvinist concept of *sovereignty within one's own circle*. The difference is significant. Catholic social philosophy argues in terms of the state: what the state is unable to do efficiently and effectively should be left to the autonomous associations and institutions. The Catholic idea of subsidiarity is, of course, a corporatist conception. The Calvinist notion of institutional sovereignty argues the other way round and is, in a sense, much more republican: there are a few things that autonomous associations and institutions cannot do in an effective and efficient manner; these should be taken care of by the state. In any case, institutional subsidiarity, associational sovereignty, and a residual state are the essence of horizontalism.

A society is vertically structured when individual citizens and their associations and institutions are ruled in a top-down manner by an overarching state, be it a tyrannical, an absolute-monarchical, or a welfare spending state. In a sense, in these societies, each of them in their own way ruled by a centralized state, societal associations and institutions function in actual fact as the extension pieces of the state. It has been proven historically that, as a result of such a centralization of power, the civic spirit and culture will decline in stamina and lose its impact on human minds, emotions, and actions. The forces of coercion and control are conducted top-down through the associations and institution of society, and thus affect the positive and negative liberty of citizens in a detrimental manner.[1]

Naturally there are considerable qualitative and quantitative differences as to the top-down coercion of a tyranny or dictatorship, an absolute monarchy, and a welfare state. Yet, as to the mutual relationships of state, society, and individuals they have verticalism in common. It is the verticalism of state-regulated associations and institutions that socially and politically typifies these admittedly very different kinds of society and polity. The associations and institutions of individual citizens function, even if they possess a high degree of legal autonomy, as in the case of the welfare state, in the final analysis as the lubricants of the power and authority of the centralized state. Needless to add that verticalism tends to cripple civic engagement and participation, as it is detrimental to the civic spirit and culture. Particularly in the case of the welfare state, legal and bureaucratic rules and formalities penetrate deeply into the lives and privacy of individuals through the very associations and institutions of society. Formally and legally they may be independent and autonomous, materially and socially they are not.

However, as to verticalism the role of the overarching state should not be over-emphasized. There are and have been verticalist contexts in which the state has not played such a predominant role. In his celebrated book on the making of Italy's democracy Robert Putnam, for example, focused on the social structure of southern Italy, where not a centralized state but an informal patron-client system, historically inherited from the feudal past, managed to maintain a rather ancient, top-down verticalism.[2] The Dutch anthropologist Anton Blok made a similar point much earlier in his study of the Sicilian mafia. In fact, he argued that the top-down patron-client system of the mafia functioned as a substitute for a weak or even absent centralized government.[3] Where the state is weak or even absent, organized crime and gangs with warlords step in to fill up the void. This can be witnessed today as well in Russia and former Yugoslavia, not to speak of Somalia and similar African nations.

According to Putnam, the recent history of Italy has demonstrated once more that there is an inverse relationship between verticalism and economic development. This inverse relationship has been demonstrated clearly also by communist societies, such as the former Soviet Union and Cuba. Italy, however, is a particularly interesting case since it demonstrates as in a laboratory setting that the decentralization which began as a conscious policy in the beginning of the 1970s, yielded political and social fruits in the north, but not in the south. This led to a spectacular difference in economic performance. The north decentralized and next fortified its horizontal civil society with an increased civic consciousness and engagement. This appeared to be the fertile context for a spectacular economic performance. Decentralization in the south, on the contrary, ran up against a traditional and tenacious patron-client system which perpetuated social verticalism with a demonstrable lack of civic engagement and social connectedness. As a result, Putnam argues, the economic performance of the south lagged behind the development of its northern counterpart.

As I shall argue later, Dutch pillarization prior to the 1960s is another and quite different example of a verticalist patron-client system without a strong, overarching state. Yet, unlike southern Italy this verticalist system managed to maintain a pluralist kind of civil society, while its stern traditionalism and authoritarianism bolstered the economy which was in ruins at the conclusion of World War II. It was not until the spectacular rise of a centralized, intensive, and extensive welfare state that verticalism began to exert its adverse effects upon the civil society and the market. I shall return to this later.

American Democracy and Social Decapitalization

It stands to reason to conclude that there is an elective affinity between democracy and horizontalism, that, as it was phrased in Putnam's study of the fate of democracy in Italy, democracy cannot be made to work properly in a verticalist context. Tocqueville, as we all know, emphasized the horizontalism of early American democracy. This was repeated by Max Weber and, incidentally, somewhat later also by Johan Huizinga.[4] Weber and Huizinga viewed the horizontal voluntary associations of America as vital societal structures which mediated between the strongly individualized American citizens and the rather decentralized American state. Also these associations and institutions managed to bind the individualized citizens of America together, forging them, as it were, into a coherent civil society and a vital civic culture that transcended the potential for disintegration through particularist interests. It was the fertile soil for civic engagement and social connectedness.

Civic engagement and social connectedness, Putnam argued, have produced a better society—"better schools, faster economic development, lower crime, and more effective government."[5] He added the by now well-known concept of *social capital*. In analogy to such concepts as physical and human capital, social capital refers to networks of interaction, to shared norms and values which foster mutual social trust. Networks, norms, and trust facilitate cooperation and coordination.[6] Social capital is the lubricant of democracy. It is also, as Fukuyama recently argued, the fertile soil for a successful economy.[7] Or, in Durkheimian terms, social capital consists of structures and processes which ward off the forces of disintegrating anomie. Where social capital declines, that is, where a downward trend of social decapitalization sets in, anomie is bound to rise.

There is in America for roughly two decades, according to Putnam and others, a growing empirical evidence of a steady decline of civic engagement and social trust, and thus of increasing social decapitalization. During the past two decades, Putnam claims, organizational membership among Americans has declined steadily. The churches, the labor unions, the parent-teacher associations, fraternal organizations, and the voluntarist mainline civic organizations have witnessed significant drops in membership and in membership engagement as well. As to the latter, he gives the telling example of bowling in organized leagues. Between 1980 and 1993 the number of bowlers increased by 10 percent but league bowling decreased by 40 percent. This individualization is indicative for scores of leisure activities and testifies to an increasing social decapitalization.[8]

Putnam tries to explain this hazardous trend which is bound to affect the quality of American democracy and eventually the health of the American economy. He suggests that the rather massive entrance of women into the labor force, the residential instability of an increased mobility, the demographic transformation of the family and the individualization of leisure due to technological inventions and developments account for this dramatic transformation of American civil society. They contributed each in their own way to the decline, if not destruction, of social networks and norms, to civic engagement and social trust.

Yet, he cautions against romanticizing middle-class American civic life of the 1950s. But he is also unable to come up with viable alternatives. He is not a proponent of a neoconservative restoration of traditional values and institutions, the family first of all. He also fails to mention the ideas and ideologies of communitarianism.[9]

At the end of his essay Putnam suggests a more systematic inquiry into the possible impact of public policy. The state, he surmises, often impinges on both the creation and the destruction of social capital. As to the latter, in the 1950s and 1960s slum-clearing policies may well have contributed to the renovation of physical capital but did so at a rather high cost to existing social capital. This is an important remark, since *the role of the state* and the effects of its inherent verticalism on civil society deserve attention in a discussion of social decapitalization. At the very end of his essay Putnam places high on the scholarly agenda "the question whether a comparable erosion of social capital may be under way in other advanced democracies, perhaps in different institutional and behavioral guises."[10] Such comparative insights may, he suggest, help to reverse the adverse trends in civic engagement and civic trust in present-day America. It is with this in mind that I shall focus now on Dutch society which after the last war changed rapidly from a decentralized-vertical system based upon pillarization, characterized by a compartmentalized civic engagement and trust, to a centralized-vertical welfare state in which a massive social decapitalization has occurred. It is since the 1980s that a gradual restoration of social capital, called "social renewal," takes place as an important part of the public policy of urban conglomerates.

Pillarized Verticalism, Strong Social Capital

Pillarization, or columnization, is the process by which society is divided vertically in terms of different religious and secular worldviews, facilitating the emergence of a plural society. The organizations in the fields of education, health care, mass media, labor relations, leisure, politics, and the market (in particular agriculture and medium-sized and small businesses) are mutually differentiated in a pillarized society according to worldview.

In The Netherlands one distinguishes usually among the following pillars: Roman Catholic, orthodox Protestant, liberal Protestant, and humanist organizations. As to the latter, a social-democratic and a liberal variant can be distinguished. However, pillarization, as we shall see instantly, began as a process of predominantly religious organization. It was due to their resistance to religiously pillarized organizations that social-democratic and liberal humanists organized themselves and thus developed inadvertently their own pillars. Incidentally, despite this pillarization Dutch society has always maintained the constitutional separation of church and state: pillarized organizations, one should bear in mind, are *social* and *not ecclesiastical* organizations. The Roman Catholic Church in particular kept Catholic organizations and institutions under close surveillance, but they remained legally autonomous foundations with boards and governors recruited from the top layers of society.

These organizational pillars were vertical in a double sense. Culturally, since they were ruled in an authoritarian, top-down, elitist, and patriarchical manner; structurally, since they cut through the horizontal layers of classes and status groups. As a result, solidarity was dependent on one's belonging to a pillar first, to a class second. Labor unions were pillarized, and even today there is a "neutral" next to a Protestant labor union. As a result, it was exceedingly difficult to organize general strikes. There was, in other words, within these pillars a very strong social capital. Since the pillars were ruled top-down in an authoritarian and elitist manner, and since the elites of these pillars entertained strong mutual networks in which they made political deals as to the economy of the nation, pillarization contributed strongly to the general pacification of the nation. This, of course, enabled the economy to recover rapidly after World War II. That is, unlike the vertical patron-client system of southern Italy the verticalism of pillarization which in its own way was a patron-client system as well, did not bar but on the contrary, reinforced and fortified the economic revival of The Netherlands.

Historically, pillarization began at the end of the last century as a process of emancipation on the part of the Roman Catholic and orthodox Protestant minorities. Traditionally, the country was being ruled from Holland by the traditionally liberal-minded patriciate in the larger cities. The Roman Catholics in the southern provinces and the Calvinist lower middle classes in the northern provinces were generally kept powerless by this ruling patriciate. In the second half of the nineteenth century these two minorities set their theological disputes aside and formed a political coalition in order to acquire state subsidies for their schools and universities equal to the subsidies which nonconfessional, "neutral" schools and universities received from the state. In response the social democrats and liberals set their political disputes aside and forged a politial coalition against such an equal state subsidizing of the confessional educational institutions. This has been called the *schoolstrijd*, the school struggle which was won by the confessional parties in 1917. Since this so-called Pacification religious institutions in all the various branches of society receive state subsidies equal to the ones nonreligious institutions obtain. Pillarization was by now a solid political and sociological fact. The Netherlands in a way consisted from then on of "four/five nations": a Roman Catholic, an orthodox Protestant, a liberal Protestant, and a humanist nation, the latter divided politically in a social-democratic and a liberal branch.

The Dutch-American political scientist Arend Lijphart has argued that the vertical, top-down, rather authoritarian, and elitist rule of these pillars may have contributed to a rather undemocratic culture but it simultaneously was the cause of a remarkable social and political pacification.[11] These gentlemen at the top of the pillars set the political agenda, forged the coalition governments (due to pillarization there has never been a majority government in The Netherlands), and abstained from theological debates. They agreed to disagree and ruled in a no-nonsense manner according to a nonideological *raison d'état* which, incidentally, was not difficult because there was not much state to speak of. The state bureaucracies were small, and the parliament was not very influential since the agenda was set and its solutions preempted by the pillarized elites. There certainly was not the overproduction of laws and policies, rules and regulations which became so characteristic of the welfare state in the 1960s and 1970s.

The cultural dimensions of pillarization deserve special attention. To begin with, Dutch society, one should bear in mind, was deeply divided ideologically, yet at all times consensus, norms, and even trust prevailed. Or in other words, despite all the ideological divisiveness between the pillars, social capital was kept unimpaired. The ingrained authoritarianism of the system contributed much to this. People might have distrusted their neighbors who belonged to another pillar, but they fully trusted the consociates and in particular the leaders of their own pillar. These patrons of their own pillar, however, trusted their colleague-patrons of the other pillars with whom they often entertained friendly and at all times politically fruitful relations. They made political deals amongst each other in rather friendly ambiences which took the lid off potentially grave social and political conflicts.

In addition, historically the predominant culture of the Dutch nation has always been the merchant culture of the big cities of Holland: merchants compete on the market, but do not fight in the streets or in parliament; merchants want governments they can trust and count on, no matter what their ideological bent may be. As a result Dutch culture is very bourgeois, very moderate, and, as a result, at times very boring. This, of course, is the right climate for tolerance—a tolerance which endured in pillarization: "I do not like you, in fact I strongly disagree with your ideological point of view, but I tolerate you because intolerance is dysfunctional for all of us." In other words, in this system of pillarization mutual trust and tolerance were a matter of rational choice.

A third cultural characteristic was the obvious fact that the common people, subjected to rather authoritarian and elitist rule, were locked in, boxed in within their respective pillars. This was a system of inclusion and exclusion which was particularly felt in everyday social life. An inter-pillar marriage, for instance, could be the cause of familial dramas, and even the labor market was compartmentalized according to pillar-differences.

Needless to add that the system was a solidly collectivist one, and its ethos was predominantly moralistic. In particular priests and protestant ministers exerted a pervasive control and moral coercion through the solidly pillarized mass media. The work ethic and the ethic of reponsibility were solidly ingrained in the Dutch social capital.

All this, however, began to change dramatically roughly after 1960. However, before we have a closer look at this transformation, we should realize that until this very day this change has been more a cultural than a structural one. The crucial sectors of Dutch society, notably education, health care, and the media, are still pillarized structurally today. It is their ideologies that have changed: the pillarized worldviews have modernized, which is to say that they became more generalized and abstract. There are still Roman Catholic schools, universities, and hospitals; there is a Protestant labor union and an orthodox Protestant university. Yet, their ideological contents have been eroded during the 1960s and 1970s. People in these pillarized structures today no longer firmly (fundamentally!) believe in their worldviews. As a result, their commitment and engagement to their pillars have eroded drastically.

Yet, the pillars still stand, at least structurally. In fact, the humanists opened their own university in the late 1980s in counterpoint to the Roman Catholic and Protestant divinity schools. Increasingly also, Turkish and Moroccan Muslims erect their own Muslim schools and organizations, requesting the state subsidies to which they are constitutionally entitled as "confessional" institutions. In a sense, this pristine form of Islamic pillarization is a healthy sign of their integration into Dutch society, adding to the Dutch variant of multiculturalism which is not based on ethnicity but on worldview.[12]

The question poses itself, of course, why and how these pillars remain intact, while their ideological contact has, apart from the Muslim variant, eroded? The main answer is that, apart from the Muslim organizations, today's pillarization is based more upon material interests and reasons of power than on ideological principles and religious convictions. This also suggests that the social capital that was so typical of pillarization has lost much of its stamina and vigor. This is indeed the case. Social decapitalization, however, has been exacerbated in particular by the rise of the welfare state during the 1960s and 1970s.

Welfare State Verticalism, Weak Social Capital

If social capital still had strength and stamina in the verticalist system of pillarization, it grew weak during the spectacular rise of the welfare state in Dutch society after 1960. As in other Northwestern European nations the Dutch began to develop their welfare state after the war. Yet, although the foundations of the welfare state were laid in the period between 1945 and 1960, the pillars retarded the rise of this centralized system of state-provided welfare. As we saw, in the pillarized patron-client system there was not much room for a centralized and elaborate state. However, at the end of the 1950s and during the 1960s the above-mentioned ideological depillarization gained momentum which contributed to the expansion of the welfare state.

The main factors of this ideological depillarization are briefly summarized as follows. First, due to the spectacular resurgence of the economy, the nation's wealth and potential affluence had reached by 1960 a level never before attained. Workers who up till then had accepted wages which compared to neighboring nations were rather low, began to demand sizable wage increases. Dutch society witnessed the first postwar strikes.

Second, as was said before, pillarization began as a process of emancipation and integration of the Roman Catholic and orthodox Protestant minorities. At the end of the 1950s this basic objective of pillarization had been achieved, since these minorities were entrenched solidly in the political arena and integrated into the economy and into societal organizations and institutions. There was in fact no need anymore to safeguard one's own, specific, cultural identity behind the walls of one's very own pillar. Pillarization had done its job, and could from now on be loosened ideologically and organizationally. Or, in other words, there was actually no need anymore to cling to one's pillarized ideology with grim tenacity. It was a process of "defundamentalization."

Third, in the 1960s the notorious baby-boom generation entered its adolescence. Being better educated than their parents, without personal knowledge of the economic crisis of 1929 and the bitter years of the war, in fact having been spoiled by their parents and the relatively affluent circumstances, of the postwar era, these young men and women were no longer prepared to accept the authoritarianism of the pillarized patron-client system. In a facetious manner of speech, the young critics of pillarization often spoke of the "Catholic mafia" and of the "mafiosos" of the pillarized establishment, as if to emphasize the undemocratic nature of the system. They grew into critical citizens for whom democratization meant deliverance from the restrictions and coercion of the pillarized organizations. The New Left movement in the Netherlands was more a movement against pillarization than against capitalism. However, it remained rather ironic that, while the confessional pillars began to erode ideologically, the social democratic pillar began to fortify its ideology, often by means of a rather hollow and trite Marxist phraseology.

Fourth, the media, in particular television, showed images of other worlds and other societies which contributed to the opening up of the parochial cages of pillarization. Similarly, the improved geographical mobility due to the car which gradually pushed the typically Dutch bicycle aside, enabled these young men and women to move away from their traditional social environments.

Fifth, all this contributed to a rather rapid decline of church memberships in the 1960s and 1970s. Although, as was said before, pillarization was in a strict sense not a church affair, this "dechurching" of Dutch society contributed nevertheless to the rapid erosion of the ideological contents of the religious (Catholic and Protestant) pillars.

In sum, all these developments contributed to a rather rapid decline of the pillarized cohesiveness of Dutch society, and a concomitant rise of typically modern individualization. It also entailed, though unwittingly, a rapid decline of the social capital that was an inherent part of the pillarized system. In a sense, these transformations and their social decapitalization were part of a belated modernization of Dutch society, and facilitated the spectacular rise of the centralized welfare state. In fact, the verticalism of the pillars and the erosion of their ideological content enabled the intensification and the extension of the centralized welfare state. The ideologically "empty" pillars functioned as the conductors of the welfare spending and regulating state. It should be borne in mind that this rise of the welfare state meant a proportional decline of social capital.

There were in particular two factors that contributed to the rapid emergence of a strong, centralized state after 1960. First, there was the gradual and steep increase of state subsidies. It was an inheritance of the system of pillarization that the state provided subsidies for activities in fields as varied as education, health care, and social security, among others. These activities were, and to a certain extent still are today, executed by autonomous, pillarized organizations. However, after 1960 these organizations began to turn rather massively to the state as the guarantor of ever more subsidies. Naturally, scores of bureaucratic rules and regulations were attached to these state handouts. Thus, the rise of the centralized state was not the result of a socialist plot, as is often thought and said by conservatives, but the consequence of the subsidizing system of pillarization.

Second, the main areas of care and welfare began to professionalize after 1960. During the heyday of the pillar system, education, health care, and social security provisions were predominantly in the hands of

---

well-intentioned pillar volunteers and nonprofessionals. During the 1950s, and then rapidly during the 1960s and 1970s this system of care and welfare was professionalized. The associated professionals subsequently looked up to the welfare spending state and its bureaucrats as their main employers and benefactors, and no longer to the boards and trustees of their pillarized organizations. This professionalization of care and welfare contributed greatly to the intensification and extension of the centralized and bureaucratized welfare state.

Not surprisingly, the traditional, patriarchical, pillarized elites began to lose political clout rapidly. The plurality of power was replaced by the centralization of power in The Hague, where the rapidly expanding state ministries were located. The former elites were in fact replaced by the professionals of the organizations and the bureaucrats of the expanding state ministries. As to the common citizens, they changed from collectivist subjects of pillars into ever more individualized citizens of the welfare state and consumers of welfare state provisions. In fact, assisted by the professionals of their societal organizations these consumers of welfare state provisions raised their demands ever higher. As a result, the welfare state became a prime example of the adverse effects of a system of rising expectations. Commitment, engagement and trust declined, dissatisfaction and the call for ever more subsidies and state provisions grew louder and louder. The German sociologist and philosopher Arnold Gehlen could have had Dutch society of the 1960s and 1970s in mind, when he once remarked wryly that in the welfare state Leviathan has assumed more and more the traits of a milk cow.[13]

Yet, during the 1970s, in particular during the two oil crises, it became ever more apparent that this system of an extensive and intensive welfare state was no longer viable and sustainable. Politically, the ever-expanding bureaucratization became unmanageable, and led to an overproduction of policies with countless rules and regulations that caused an inflation of public policy. Economically, the incessant interventions by the state in the mechanisms of the market, the growing national debts due to public overspending, and the cancerous growth of the nonproductive quarternary service sector contributed further to the crisis. Socially, rising expectations led only to further social decapitalization and reliance on the state. Culturally, the gradual rise of consumerism and decline of engagement and commitment on the part of the citizens was paired to a technocratic instrumentalism on the part of bureaucrats and state officials. In short, it was not just physical and economic capital that was in decline, but social capital too.

At the start of the 1980s it became abundantly clear that this adverse political, economic, social, and cultural constellation had to be changed drastically. This has indeed been the conscious policy on the part of political parties, coalition governments, and public and private organizations. As elsewhere in Europe the centralized and bureaucratic power of the state has been reduced, a process that lasted during the 1980's and will continue to develop further in the 1990's. The process can be briefly summarized in the following way:

- decentralization of power towards lower echelons of public policy, notably the metropolitan areas, and within these towards burroughs and districts;
- deregulation of the public and the private sector, but also of the organizations and institutions of the public sector in order to revitalize the market and the civil society;
- privatization of scores of governmental services that had been socialized in the welfare state regime;
- coalescence of the public and the private sector through scores of public-private partnerships;
- a renewed search for meaning, for viable values and norms, strengthening the corporate culture of organizations and the urban culture of large and small cities;
- in line herewith a combined effort on the part of urban governments and informal groups of citizens to revitalize the social capital of streets and neighborhoods in order to establish what has become to be called "social renewal."

Thus, the verticalism with a strong social capital as established in the pillarized society was succeeded by the verticalism of the welfare state with a weakening of social capital. Under the welfare state regime the civil society of autonomous associations and institutions was subjected to the bureaucratic and technocratic rules and regulations of the ever-more centralized state. In fact, during the 1970s it became obvious that this deepening "statism" was detrimental to the market economy, and also detrimental to social capital. Yet, roughly after 1980 the processes of decentralization, deregulation, privatization, and urban social renewal began to contribute to a gradual horizontalization of society and a concomitant strengthening of the social capital.

The Democratic Triangle

In this latest transformation which will certainly last beyond the start of the next millennium, it will be of the utmost importance to establish some sort of balance between the state, the market, and society. In a democracy, the Netherlands example suggests, there ought to be a balance between these three institutional spheres of democratic life, with each performing its own functions. Thus, the state's core business is the production and maintenance of *political capital*. That is to say, the state ought to guarantee the safety and security of its citizens, to defend and represent as a constitutional state (*Rechtsstaat*) the interests of the powerless and defenseless, to preserve and guarantee within limits the rule of law and social order, and to defend and represent the collective interests of the nation in terms of international affairs. The market's core business is to produce and maintain *economic capital*, that is, wealth and profits as the basic components of the material foundation of the nation, contributing to the general material welfare of its citizens. The core business of civil society is to create and maintain *social capital*—meaningful interactions, norms and trust, through associations and institutions in which citizens realize their potential of commitment and engagement. Social capital functions as the immaterial and moral foundation of the nation.

These three institutional spheres of democracy have each of them their own medium of exchange, or "currency": power, profit, and trust. The three are interdependent in a systemic manner: if one of them is weakened the other two suffer the consequences. Thus, if the centralized state loosens its ties with the market and with civil society, its power runs the risk of suffocating them, as has happened bluntly in communist regimes and less forcefully but still significantly in overdeveloped versions of the welfare state. It is also possible that society claims primacy over the state and the market, as happened in the heydays of Dutch pillarization in which the pillarized trust of an authoritarian patron-client system kept the state small and the market inflexible. Finally, if, as in classic-liberal laissez-faire capitalism, the market and its restless search for profit demands primacy at the cost of the state and society, we may witness a rapid social decapitalization in society and a decline of the basic functions of the state.

In the anti-welfare state discourse of the 1980s, the liberation of the market from state control and societal inhibitions was advocated by Reaganites and Thatcherites. Mrs. Thatcher, for instance, is once said even to have remarked in her inimitably crisp manner, "Society does not exist." For her, the only relevant social realities were the state, the market, and individual citizens. After the heyday of the centralized welfare state that suffocated the market and kept society under bureaucratic tutelage, Thatcherism, like Reagonomics, managed to establish a necessary political and economic turnaround. Yet, at the end of the 1980s the main problem of this turnaround appeared to emerge precisely in that part of the democratic triangle they had treated with a rather unbenign neglect—civil society. The social decapitalization inherent to the welfare state was unintentionally continued by the policies of Reagonomics and Thatcherism, both of which called for decentralizatrion, deregulation, and privatization, but actually contributed to an unheard-of increase of state power.

The 1990s, as could have been expected, became the decade of the resurgence of civil society and its primary currency—trust. Social renewal, social capital, and civil society became the concepts of the hour. Communatarianism and neo-institutionalism emerged and called for a renewed moral engagement and commitment based upon meaningful interactions, values, and, above all, mutual trust. The central ideas are that civil society must be kept strong and social capital functions as the precondition for the working of democracy and for the working of the market.

Apart from all their differences—which cannot be discussed in this this essay—these intellectual debates on the nature and merits of civil society and social capital generally make two assumptions that stand in need of a critical discussion. First, it is assumed that verticalism tends to minimize, if not destroy, social capital, and therefore tends to inhibit the working of democracy and to frustrate the working of the market. Civil society is thus envisaged as an essentially horizontalist system. Second, it is assumed that if civil society is to be a vital factor in democracy, the state and its power ought to be reduced drastically.

As to the first assumption, the example of Dutch pillarization—a vertical patron-client system—seems to suggest that the effects of verticalism need not always be so negative. There is a superficial similarity between the Netherlands system and the patron-clientage of southern Italy as described by Banfield,[14] Blok, and Putnam. Yet the difference as to the strength of social capital is immense. Unlike Italian patron-clientage, the Dutch pillar system was characterized by a high measure of trust. Admittedly, this trust was of a rather traditional and authoritarian sort. Due to ideological differences betweem the pillars, it was also a pluralistic or multiple trust, guaranteed by the pacts struck among the pillar elites. Pillarization did allow for the nurturance of strong social capital couched in consensus; and this social capital contributed to the swift and remarkable resurgence of the Dutch economy. However, as an inherently authoritarian system, pillarization was rather weak when it came to to enhancing the working of democracy. Formally, the Dutch nation was a multiparty, constitutional state and thus a democracy. However, until 1960, it was culturally traditional, authoritarian, and undemocratic. Both negative liberty and positive liberty were restricted and kept under tutelage by the ruling elites of the various pillars. However, in the fifteen years of the post-bellum period in which the economy had to be rebuilt the undemocratic authoritarianism of the pillars kept wage demands low and the work ethic high. It contributed to the revitalization of the market.

Civil Society and the State

In sociological postmodernism the argument has been made that we are living these days in a postinstitutional era. Contemporary citizens, the argument goes, are radically individualized persons who have lost trust in the basic institutions of society—the family, the church, the neighborhood, the university, and the state. Instead, their social connections and commitments occur within *networks* which lack the stability, the durability, and the coercive control of the traditional institutions. Facilitated by the electronic revolution of the 1970s and 1980s, these networks are said to be flexible and interchangeable, and leave more room for negative liberty than the traditional institutions. Trust is not based upon tradition, is not couched in the control and coercion of institutions, but is individualized, highly subjective, and flexible. In fact, someone traditional will hesitate to call the calculated mutual exchange of networks a matter of trust at all. It is rather a matter of individualized rational choice and calculus.

This postinstitutional vision of society is a radically horizontal one. Patron-client systems are, of course, rejected as premodern and feudal, and the notion of a nation-state is scorned as the fossilized survival of an Enlightenment modernism which has lost all legitimacy in our postmodern age. For example, the French politician and philosopher Jean-Marie Guéhenno has argued forcefully that the state as we know it is an outdated institution.[15] Invented by Enlightenment modernism it has run its intellectual and political course. Like other outdated institutions, such as the church and the family, the state can no longer function properly in a civil society which is characterized not so much by institutions and institutional norms and relationships, but by flexible, transnational and highly individualized networks.

It is significant that Guéhenno gave his lucid essay the telling title "the end of democracy." The antistate animus that infuses his argument, we see, is thus no longer an anarchistic or ultra-right-wing affair. It gains respectability within neoliberal, postmodernist circles. There is an alarming naiveté in this anti-state vision of civil society. In fact, behind all the loose talk about the end of the nation-state and of democracy, there seems to lurk a rather disquieting vision of the future society. It is a society of individualized networks, based more on rational choice and the pursuit of narrow interests than on trust and common or general interests. The society is, in addition, guided electronically beyond physical and moral boundaries. However, in all probability, the electronic highways of this postinstitutional and postmodern society will not be egalitarian and horizontal, but vulnerable to control by strong men, who exert their own kind of power over the powerless and vulnerable. Their power will, of course, not be of a physical nature. It will consist of expert knowledge—the knowledge of how to manipulate the means of electronic information and communication.

Electronic sophisticates, these postinstitutional and postmodern "Aideeds" will call for the radical decentralization of power. These are, needless to say, not the premodern members of the American Rifle Association who defend their right to bear arms. Their antistate animus is very antiquated and naive. The "bandits" of the postinstitutional age of networks are the electronic highwaymen who declare the death of the modern nation-state and its controls, in order to enlarge their individualized negative liberty and, through it, their personal power. If they have any awareness of positive liberty, they will in all probability not use it for the enlargement and strengthening of the common interests and the common wealth. It is their very own particularized and individualized interests and wealth that they are after in their "flexible and transnational" networks. Their morality is not one of trust but of rational choice and calculus—a thin morality indeed. They forget that the democratic state is, and must be, a constitutional state—a *Rechtsstaat*. It stands to reason that this neoliberal and postmodern antistate animus will only contribute further to social and moral decapitalization.

But there is still another danger in this anti-state animus of the 1990s. The basic idea of a modern *democratic* state is that it possesses through the rule of law a monopoly over the use of force. That is, in a civilized and democratic society the use of force is strictly regulated by the law and exerted in extreme cases by the state only. This doctrine and practice is, of course, of great importance to the vulnerable, weak, and powerless in society. Now, one step beyond the call for a radical decentralization of state power is the call for the *privatization* of this power. The Dutch-Israeli military historian Martin van Creveld recently expressed in a Dutch interview his passionate hatred of the state, as we have come to know it in the past centuries.[16] The state is in his view the originator of all the major miseries in the world, including the worldwide slaughters of men, women, and children in two world wars. He will soon publish a book on the rise and fall of the state in which he predicts the radical demise of the state and the radical *privatization* of its power. The state, he prophesizes, has run its gruesome course and will soon be completely passé. This is already visible today: there are scores of chaotic wars and genocidal conflicts, as in Rwanda and the former Yugoslavia, and the traditional nation-states are no longer able to intervene. They have lost their credibility. The privatization of the power of the state is, of course, the privatization of its monopoly of the use of force and violence. We already witness this in the increase of corruption, organized crime, and urban terrorism within our own societies. We will, according to Van Creveld, witness more of this, and he applauds it, even if it means chaos. In his interview, he says that he accepts a few Oklahoma's in exchange for the privatization of the state's power and its monopoly of the use of force and violence. It is obvious, that trust and social capital are not part of this rather cynical and paranoid view of state and society. Indeed, his vision would be the end of democracy and entail an ironic return to the medieval world of feudalism and banditism.

In conclusion, what we need in the present debates on civil society and social capital is a well-balanced conception of the democratic triangle, consisting of the state and its political capital, the market and its economic capital, and civil society and its social capital. We need in addition to develop a new theory of institutions in the style of Putnam's neo-institutionalism[17]—a theory which focuses on the basic anthropological fact that actions and interactions, norms and values, trust and rational choice can only bear fruit if they are embedded in a social framework that transcends narrow individual interests and calculi. With the family, the church, the law, the university, and other institutions of civil society, the state and the market will remain vital to democracy and contribute to a life of liberty and safety.

Notes

1. Isaiah Berlin, "Two Concepts of Liberty," in Berlin, *Four Essays on Liberty* (Oxford: Oxford University Press, 1991), pp. 118–73.

2. Robert Putnam, *Making Democracy Work: Civic Traditions in Modern Italy* (Princeton, N.J.: Princeton University Press, 1993).

3. Anton Blok, *The Mafia of a Sicilian Village, 1860–1960. A Study of Violent Peasant Entrepreneurs* (New York: Harper Torchbooks, 1975).

4. Max Weber, "The Protestant Sects and the Spirit of Capitalism," 1906, translated by H. Gerth and C.W. Mills, in *From Max Weber. Essays in Sociology* (New York: Galaxy Books, 1958), pp. 302–23; Johan Huizinga, *Mensch en Menigte in Amerika*, (Man and Crowd in America), in: Johan Huizinga, *Verzamelde Werken*, (Collected Works), vol. V (Haarlem: Tjeenk Willink, 1950), pp. 249–418.

5. Putnam, *Making Democracy Work*, p. 66f.

6. Putnam, *Making Democracy Work*, pp. 167–71.

7. Francis Fukuyama, *Trust: The Social Virtues and the Creation of Prosperity* (New York: The Free Press, 1995).

8. Putnam, *Making Democracy Work*, pp. 67–70.

9. Philip Selznick, *The Moral Commonwealth: Social Theory and the Promise of Community* (Berkeley: University of California Press, 1992).

10. Robert Putnam, "Bowling Alone: America's Declining Social Capital," *Journal of Democracy*, 6:7 (January 1995): 65–79.

11. Arent Lijphart, *Verzuiling, Pacificatie en Kentering in de Nederlandse Politiek*, (Pillarization, Pacification and Turn-around in Dutch Politics) (Amsterdam: J.H. de Bussy, 1968).

12. I defended this controversial position in a short essay "Islamitische Verzuiling" (Islamic Pillarization), in Anton C. Zijderveld, *De Paradox van het Alledaagse Leven*, (The Paradox of Everyday Life) (Kampen: Kok Agora, 1995), pp. 158–64.

13. Arnold Gehlen, *Moral und Hypermoral: Eine Pluralistische Ethik*, (Morality and Hyper-Morality. A Pluralistic Ethic) (Frankfurt am Main: Athenäum Verlag, 1969), p. 110.

14. Edward Banfield, *The Moral Basis of a Backward Society*, 1958 (New York: The Free Press, 1965).

15. Jean-Marie Guéhenno, *La Fin de la Démocratie* (Paris: Editions Flammarion, 1994).

16. Caroline de Gruyter, "De Militairen Verliezen hun Zelfrespect," (Soldiers Lose their Self-Esteem), in *NRC Handelsblad*, Saturday September 9, 1995, p. 4.

17. Putnam, *Making Democracy Work*, pp. 7–10, 181–85.

Part 2

Comparative Possibilities

7

Is Civil Society Enough?
Comparing Romania and
the American South

Daniel Chirot

The current debate about the relationship between various forms of community, civic democracy, and the growth of capitalism take us back to classical nineteenth- and early twentieth-century theories.[1] Not only Alexis de Tocqueville, but many others were interested in the connection between different types of social solidarity and the evolution of distinct political and economic systems throughout the world. After about the middle of the nineteenth century, the problem took the form of asking how capitalist, industrial systems arose in the West, and how they might be tamed. This became the central sociological issue, so much so that as late as 1970 Alvin Gouldner could devote an entire book to explaining why it was time to go beyond this old question.[2] But in fact, we have never fully answered the questions raised by the classical debates. Now, with the obvious uncertainties raised by the collapse of communism, the continuing decline of community in the West, and the rise of new industrial powers in East Asia that have seemed to succeed precisely because they are less committed to individualistic democracy than the West, we find out that we should go back to the classics to see if we can provide more definitive answers than did our intellectual ancestors.

It is not necessary to decide whether or not we have made theoretical progress since, say, the death of Max Weber to admit that we know a lot more than he did simply because almost eight decades of social change have taken place since then. Furthermore, thousands of researchers have worked throughout the world to extend our knowledge, so that even our historical base is far sounder than what was available to him. One of the greatest advantages we possess is that we can pick examples from a far greater universe of cases, and some of them are particularly interesting to those of us addressing fundamental, classical theoretical issues.

One such case is Romania,[3] a country that has never been cited as much of an example of anything, but that has managed to experience many of the most typical experiences of non-Western societies over the past 150 years. During that time it developed a colonial type of plantation economy in which peasants were virtually bound to the land to produce cereals for export. This eventually provoked a major peasant uprising in 1907. Romania also experienced a late form of nationalism, filled with jealous admiration and resentment of Western Europe. As a result, after World War I its intellectuals increasingly turned to anti-capitalist, antidemocratic fascism. After World War II Romania had forced upon it a typical communist developmental state that industrialized the economy, but inefficiently and at a very high cost. In the end, this also degenerated into a type of xenophobic, nationalist autarkic autocracy typical of other late Stalinist tyrannies. And it is now searching for an appropriate model to adopt in order to recover from the catastrophe of communism.[4]

Modern Romanian history has been one of periodic near-successes followed by catastrophic failures. Its cereal export economy created great wealth for a small upper and middle class, but also social strains that were not resolved peacefully. Its industrial growth that began even before World War II increased the size of the middle class and allowed a cultural flowering unmatched before or since, but it did not produce sufficient prosperity or greater liberalism and tolerance. Romanian nationalism spread throughout much of the population, and after 1918 the country was given vast new territories, but this neither democratized the society nor assuaged the frustrations of its educated classes. After 1948 its communism urbanized the society and gave it a modern infrastructure, but it failed to make Romania either an egalitarian or a prosperous modern society. Its postcommunist democratization and privatization have been incomplete and, compared to changes in Hungary, Slovenia, the Czech Republic, or Poland, pathetically incomplete.

Despite its Romance language, Romanian social history is much more like that of Russia, with a tradition of late serfdom, *ressentiment* against the West, authoritarianism, and communism, than like that of France, with which Romanian intellectuals have long, almost comically identified. In many ways, Russia has had similar experiences, but Russia is a big power that has had a centralized autocracy for a long time.[5] Romania, aside from being a small power, never had a centralized, autocratic, Russian type of state until it became communist.

If there is any Romance-speaking society which it resembles, Romania is most like a kind of southern Italy. Yet it is even poorer and less successful than southern Italy, and it is entirely on its own, unable to count on a rich northern Romania to bail it out.

Today, the tension between Romania's large Hungarian minority from Transylvania and Romanian nationalism remains a potential source of internal and international conflict. Romanian corruption and dishonesty are legendary throughout the Balkans. Its old tradition of vicious anti-Semitism, which matched that of the worst cases in Europe, has been partially revived as a new form of militant nationalism, and the far right, though relatively small, plays a crucial swing role in the Romanian parliament.[6]

Surely, then, we should be able to go into Romania and find all the classical symptoms of what makes societies dysfunctional and unprogressive in the modern world: weak associations, no democratic tradition, and so on. In a sense, it is easy to find these things. But by stepping back a bit, and asking how Romania came to be as it is, considerable light can be shed on theoretical issues that transcend this particular, seemingly exotic, sad little Balkan case.

Did the Peasants Lack Defensive and Autonomous Associations?

One of the more curious aspects of Romanian history is that in the Old Kingdom (about two-thirds of contemporary Romania, and all of it until 1918, when it annexed Hungarian-ruled Transylvania) most of the peasant communities until the nineteenth century possessed formidable associational structures. The villages were mostly free, but even if they "belonged" to lords, they largely regulated their own affairs, organized to preserve their rights, and adhered to very ancient rules for the control of land. In the mountainous areas of the Old Kingdom where the majority of the population lived until the plains were heavily settled and cultivated in the nineteenth century, strong village communities survived well into the twentieth century. When overcrowding forced them to divide their communal lands among their families, they used surveying techniques that created characteristic very long, thin private strips easily identified from aerial observation.[7] In the spring of 1995, flying over Romania, I was able to see that these patterns, which had virtually disappeared during communist collectivization, were beginning to reappear in a few parts of the country, suggesting that even today the old communal traditions of self-rule and land management have not been entirely forgotten! (Needless to say, it is not in the flat parts of the country that contained the giant estates of the late nineteenth century, or the most modernized state and collective farms of the communist period that one sees such reversions to tradition.)[8]

Knowing about this resolves many of the paradoxes of Romanian history. There is ample documentary evidence of serfdom, but also repeated regulations freeing serfs. Until the early modern period the population density was low, and serfdom was far looser in practice than according to law. Most villagers engaged in semi-itinerant sheep herding as well as in agriculture. Young men would wander over substantial distances and be away from home for long periods of time in search of pastures, and also to drive flocks to various distant urban markets. The rules of serfdom were artificial constructs often translated literally from medieval Byzantine law by a largely foreign, Greek-speaking court aristocracy, and they corresponded only weakly to existing realities. Yet, most Romanian historians in the late nineteenth and twentieth centuries have ignored these realities because they have relied too heavily on written documents, and not enough on the observation of village traditions and, before collectivization, on patterns of landholding in the mountains and hills.[9]

Why did these strong communal traditions, which were very much alive at the time of the formation of the modern Romanian state in the mid-nineteenth century, have virtually no effect on the subsequent political life of the country? In the twentieth century one of the elements of Romanian nationalism was the heavy-handed romanticization of peasant life. The peasants were said to be noble of heart, unsullied by superficial Westernization, and of pure Dacian (the ancient Thracian tribe that dominated the region before it was conquered by Trajan's legions in the early second century) and Roman blood. This nonsense, best exemplified by romantic poets from Mihai Eminescu to Lucian Blaga was at the heart of both fascist prewar ideology and of Ceausescu's ardent nationalism. The same poets were idolized and the same idiotic legends about blood purity were current in the 1980s as in the 1930s. But in fact, none of this peasant worship extended so far as an examination of actual peasant life, much less a study of why genuine peasant tradition had played so insignificant a role in creating modern Romania.[10]

The ability of the peasants to govern and defend themselves was fatally undermined by the fact that the state that emerged in the nineteenth century was dominated by lords who managed to seize the land in the plains and force migrants to work for them to grow wheat for the growing export economy. But these landowners were not a class rooted in the countryside. Rather, as in Russia, they were more of a court aristocracy that used its political power to take land, but had no independent standing of its own or much of a local base on which to rely.

Landed interests dominated the government, with the sons of the lesser lords (as in neighboring Hungary) providing many of the nationalist, revolutionary youth in the mid-nineteenth century who set the ideological tone for the future. Taking as their model what they understood to be Western, that is French and German notions of nationalism, they idealized their common peasant tradition without ever paying the slightest attention to what it was. The peasants, progressively weakened by the growth of large estates and by their inability to deal as equals with the ever more Westernized political elite, were not a voice until the bloody rebellion of 1907 sowed the seeds for a land reform in the 1920s. By then, it was somewhat late. The land was overcrowded and the peasants struggled with the common legacy of such social changes throughout the world: tiny plots of land, lack of access to capital or technology, and weak national organization.[11]

This is not an unusual story. Such decay of communal village institutions took place elsewhere, too. The existence of such communities, even when they were substantially free and self-governing, has very rarely been translated into modern democratic institutions because of the discontinuity between premodern, agrarian states and modern political forms. This has been particularly true where the market and modern state formations were established quickly, in response to the sudden intrusion of the Western world, as happened in Romania in the nineteenth century. The elites who were well placed to take charge of political and economic modernization were not the village leaders, and population growth, the development of powerful markets for crops and land, and the imposition of central state institutions were entirely inimical to the survival of village institutions. Finally, of course, where communism was installed, whatever rural associational independence still survived was obliterated by collectivization from above.

Yet, it must be recognized that as far as cultural legacies are concerned, many non-Western societies did indeed possess rural traditions that might have predisposed them to more democratic outcomes.

Were there other forms of social solidarity that might have helped create more local independence, and therefore, a greater bias in favor of democracy in Romania, and were they any more effective than the rural tradition?

The Bypassed Urban Bourgeoisie

We know that towns have the reputation of having fostered a greater spirit of capitalism than the countryside, and that an urban middle class is especially valuable as a source of independent, self-ruling political sentiment. According to the theory, non-Western societies with low levels of urbanization and small middle classes had less of a chance to develop democratic institutions, and were less likely to experience successful transitions to capitalist industrialization than Western Europe or the United States because of this absence. Furthermore, following Max Weber, we can identify the independent bourgeoisie of late medieval and early modern Europe as a class particularly prone to think of the world in a rational, experimental way. This was vital for the flowering of Protestantism, and subsequently modern science as well. It is even possible to connect the triumph of a rational, ultimately secularized, and intellectually open bourgeois culture with the rise of democracy as well as capitalism, though in England and especially North America, such a culture also flourished among the rural gentry and to a certain extent among independent "yeomen" farmers as well.[12]

As far as Romania goes, the lack of independent towns, of a Protestant urban bourgeoisie, and the small size of the middle class would seem to confirm that in this case, at least, the Weberian theory is right. Yet, once again, the historical reality is not quite so simple.

By the early twentieth century, Romania did have an urban life and a substantial, growing middle class. In one part of Romania, Transylvania, which was annexed after 1918, there were well-established old cities that had possessed substantial independence since the Middle Ages. And Transylvania had even been one of Central Europe's centers of the Protestant reformation. Did this have no effect on Romanian political and economic culture in the twentieth century?

The trouble was that the independent merchant cities of Transylvania were German speaking, and the Protestant reformation was a German and Hungarian affair. Romanian nationalism which developed in Transylvania in the nineteenth century identified with its linguistic brethren across the border in the Old Kingdom, and rejected as alien those aspects of Transylvanian culture which were most rational, Protestant, and bourgeois.[13] In the Old Kingdom itself, particularly in the towns of Moldova, but also in the primate city of Bucharest itself, a large proportion of the urban middle class that grew in the nineteenth and twentieth centuries was Jewish, composed mostly of Ashkenazi immigrants from Galicia and the Ukraine. There were also smaller entrepreneurial Greek and Armenian minorities.[14] And as the twentieth century advanced, these "foreign" urbanites proved to be disproportionately capable of absorbing Western European professional educations and moving into the medical and legal professions. Government service, however, was largely reserved for "native" Romanians, and the Romanian-speaking, urban middle class was largely (though of course not entirely) in the civil service, including the teaching corps, the army, or in related political and administrative positions.[15]

As might be expected from our knowledge of similar situations elsewhere in the world, say in Southeast Asia or East Africa, this predisposed the growing Romanian administrative middle class to view business activity and the "foreigners" who dominated it with suspicion. Also, and perhaps even more telling, the early ranks of the administrative elite were filled with young men from the lower nobility, or from the families of Orthodox priests. Their cultural ethic was quite different from that of the urban merchants and they tended to despise "money" at the same time as they idealized the grand romantic gesture and the supposed rural roots of "genuine" Romanians.[16]

The Orthodox Church was another major source of nationalism, especially in Transylvania where it was the first institution to promote Romanian cultural self-consciousness. But this meant that nationalism was associated with a bias against Western European Christianity, and particularly with a traditional theological horror of the Jews as unreconstructed Christ killers. The walls of the medieval monasteries of Bukovina are still adorned with paintings of Jews, Muslims, and heretics as well as adulterers, murderers, and other heinous sinners being roasted on spits and undergoing agonizing tortures in hell. This old anti-Semitism, however, was joined to something much newer.

The rise of an export cereal economy and the growth of large estates in some parts of Romania, particularly Moldova, depended on the presence of Jewish entrepreneurs who leased lands from the landlords and managed them by squeezing the peasants as hard as possible. The Jews had the financing and knowledge of the grain and capital markets to manage this, something which the big landlords did not, by and large, care to do. The peasants, who were largely illiterate and who lacked outside connections, were mostly unable to take up these roles. This did nothing to lessen the anti-Semitic predisposition of Romania's nationalists, or for that matter, of its peasants, either.[17]

For all these reasons the Romanian nationalism that grew in the nineteenth century was deeply anti-Semitic and antimercantile. This was one of the main issues at the Congress of Berlin that decided on the political future of the Balkans in 1878. The West Europeans, including Otto von Bismarck, supported by the liberal French and Italians, demanded that Romania grant its Jewish minority full citizenship rights. Fortunately for the Romanian nationalists, who were united on this issue, and perhaps unfortunately for Romania, The Congress of Berlin marked a high point in West European liberalism on the Jewish question. In the 1880s a powerful anti-Semitic reaction against the consequences of economic modernization, the corruption of traditional life, the influence of high finance, and the supposed decay of old communal solidarities became strong and set the tone for the growth of the far right in Western and Central Europe in the early twentieth century. So in the end Romania was not forced to abandon its anti-Semitic citizenship laws until after World War I. Then, for a few brief years, Wilsonian liberalism brought about legal changes that only increased the resentment of the nationalists.[18]

Identification of Romania as fundamentally antiforeign made its nationalism antibourgeois and profoundly hostile to the entire Enlightenment tradition as well. The bourgeoisie was too foreign, liberalism was too philo-Semitic, and capitalism was too dirty and unfair to appeal to the nationalist intellectuals, much less to those young peasants who managed to receive some education and move into low level administrative positions. Nor did this improve after World War I. Then the frustrations of young Romanian nationalist intellectuals only grew, even though Romania obtained reunification with most of the previously claimed Austro-Hungarian and Russian provinces that had possessed large Romanian speaking populations. The unification into a "Great Romania" (*Romania Mare*) did not bring as many jobs or the universal prosperity that had been hoped for. In much of Transylvania, the Banat, and Bukovina Germans, Hungarians, and Jews continued to hold a disproportionate number of the middle-class positions. Even in backward, formerly Russian Bessarabia (today called the independent Republic of Moldova), Jews and Russians maintained their positions. This produced a growing call to solve Romania's problems by cleansing it of foreign, and mostly Jewish influences.[19]

In short, whatever positive effects Romania's urban, bourgeois tradition might have contributed to the country's democratization, these were entirely negated by its perceived "foreign" nature. Western democracy, liberalism, and virtually the whole of the Enlightenment tradition were thrown out as well by the extreme nationalists who chose instead to emphasize the "spontaneity," and "authenticity" of what they rather falsely thought they saw in the native peasant culture. But in so doing, they destroyed a second major source of genuine democratic, autonomous civil society in Romania.

The Orthodox Church and Its Turn to the Radical Right

There is no question that the Romanian Orthodox Church was for most Romanian-speaking peasants the only link to a higher, literate culture for many centuries. (The Uniate, that is, Eastern rite Catholic church filled a similar function for parts of Transylvania as well.) As such, the Orthodox Church played a major role in creating modern Romanian nationalism.

Orthodox churches have long been compared unfavorably to both Catholic and Protestant ones for being "state" churches subservient to the authorities since the early Middle Ages. Without going over the entire history of church-state relations in Western Europe, the Byzantine Empire, and Russia, and without trying to discuss the theological and philosophical issues this raises, it should be said that Romanian Orthodoxy has not always been entirely passive. In nineteenth-century Transylvania it became an important organizational base for Romanian political action, and in the twentieth century a significant number of Orthodox priests, particularly younger ones, took part in ultranationalist movements.[20] This has been the case, and in fact continues to this day in Serbia and Greece as well. There has been considerable variation in the degree of church activism in politics from period to period and from place to place, just as there has been among Eastern and Central European Catholics. (For example, even if the Polish Catholic church became a center for the creation and maintenance of a strong civil society in communist Poland, this was not the case with the Czech or Hungarian Catholic churches.)[21]

The problem in Romania is that the independent political activism of Orthodox priests in the 1920s and especially the 1930s led young nationalist priests into the arms of the anti-Semitic, rabidly xenophobic Iron Guard, perhaps the most religiously inclined and also the most successful and popular fascist movement in all of Eastern Europe during the 1930s. The problem, then, was not that Orthodoxy somehow discouraged independent political participation outside of state institutions, but that its activists picked a movement and ideology that was radically antidemocratic, antiliberal, and anticapitalist.

This gets us to the heart of the Romanian tragedy. There were traditional sources of independent civil society. But the peasants were bypassed by economic changes and a class structure that marginalized them. The nonstate bourgeoisie was deemed too foreign and became politically irrelevant, except as scapegoat for Romania's many problems. On the other hand, the nationalist intellectuals, including Orthodox priests, were converted to an ideology that was antithetical to both democracy and the survival of any civil society. Instead, they focused their goal on seizing the state and creating a unified, communal, aggressive entity that would propel Romania to greatness while cleansing it of foreign influence. Of course not all political forces or intellectuals agreed, but the liberal opposition, such as it was, had no ideological or strong class base on which to rely.

Before going on to the communist period and its aftermath, it is worth noting that despite the nature of its nationalism, Romania did begin to develop a modern industrial economy, and it was not entirely bereft of democratic influences before World War II.

Cultural and Economic Growth with Political Failure

Before 1940 Romania was in no sense a totalitarian society. It had a weak state and some independent political, social, and religious organizations. The Hungarians, Jews, Germans, and other minorities who were disliked by the nationalists (though Germans were never viewed as being particularly threatening, unlike Hungarians and Jews) retained their property and their political rights. They organized into their own ethnic parties, or otherwise took part in the confusing, multiparty political life of Romania. Elections were partly fixed, but also substantially honest, and at least partly representative, so that the many political groups had a chance to express their views. As late as 1937 Romania held its freest ever parliamentary elections.[22]

Nor was there an absence of organization at every level. The growth of the school system and rural literacy, though slower than might have been wished, enabled the peasants to become more active in politics and to defend their interests for the first time in the modern state. A significant minority, perhaps as many as 5% of the peasants and artisans in villages and small towns converted to various fundamentalist Protestant sects. In the cities labor unions developed, and occasionally conducted successful strikes. There were many independent associations, from student groups, to literary societies, the YMCA, and chambers of commerce.[23]

At no time before or since the 1920s and 1930s has Romanian cultural life been as rich and diversified. Music, theater, literature, the natural and social sciences, and political commentary flourished, as did the number of publications.

Though the Romanian economy was disrupted by World War I and the subsequent boundary changes, and again by the Great Depression in the early 1930s, by the late 1930s there were signs of substantial economic development. From 1925 to 1937 industrial production more than doubled. Even though the land reform allowed the peasants to keep much more of their production, and thus sharply reduced cereal exports, the level of nutrition improved, and the production of food crops grew during the 1920s and 1930s at a rate considerably above the rate of population growth. This helps to explain decreases in death rates. In other words, Romania in the late 1930s was in many ways better off than it had ever been before.

Compared to other European countries, Romania remained a backward, agrarian society. Nevertheless, by the 1930s it was in the process of developing quite quickly. But along with the rest of Eastern Europe, Romania's perception of stagnation and poverty in the in 1930s was a function of the fact that its intellectuals compared themselves with Western Europe, not with the rest of the world, and that the early 1930s had been a time of temporary regression.[24]

Had Romanian nationalists been content to treat their most enterprising minorities as equals, had there not been a general drift toward the far right throughout Central and Eastern Europe, and had there been no Second World War, Romania might well have been an the road to sustained modernization. Those are very big ifs, and the last two were beyond the control of local forces. But the first of these conditions was not met, either, and this contributed very significantly to the disaster the befell Romania in the 1940s.

The elections of 1937 showed an alarming rise in the electoral strength of the Iron Guard which gained significant strength among Romanian workers in Transylvanian cities (where bosses were overwhelming non-Romanian), among the most prosperous and independent peasants, and among intellectuals in the cities, particularly the university youth. This translated into an increasingly violent political atmosphere which prompted the king of Romania, Carol II, to seize direct control of the political process and try to preempt extreme nationalism. Ultimately, he failed, and when Nazi Germany forced Romania to surrender some of its territory to Hungary in 1940, King Carol was overthrown by the Iron Guard. They, in turn, were replaced by an authoritarian military regime that led Romania into World War II on the side of Germany in 1941.[25]

The German intervention in Balkan affairs should not obscure the fact that by 1939 Romania was already drifting to the far right on its own, preparing the way for a rightist, nationalist regime that would have seriously curbed political, intellectual, and social pluralism and strengthened the central state apparatus even had there been no Nazi aggression. In that sense, Romanian events were part of a long-term ideological shift in all of Central and Eastern Europe.

The essence of the shift was a philosophical and ideological current that came to dominate European thought in the 1930s. It viewed the world in the following way:

1. History consists of antagonistic nations competing with others, and especially their neighbors for survival. Thus Mircea Eliade, one of the brightest of the young Iron Guardist intellectuals in the 1930s, and later a distinguished professor at the University of Chicago from whom a whole generation of American undergraduates would learn the beauties of mystical religion, could write in the 1930s that the Hungarians and Bulgarians were the two most idiotic peoples on earth. The essence of such an ideological view is that our nation, in this case the Romanians, possesses superior traits that give it a right to use any means in this competition. To lose would mean eventual extermination, and therefore, the most extreme forms of conflict are not only justified but required.[26]

2. Our has been a uniquely wronged nation. As we are a superior people, if we are not as strong as the dominant nations of the time, the English, the French, the Germans, the Russians—whomever—it is because we have been betrayed, or infiltrated by traitors. We have also been spurned by the great powers who should recognize that we are a great people, unlike our perfidious local enemies who are an inferior, lot, mongrelized lot. It is only historical justice if we are compensated for having been wronged, and those who refuse to see this are our enemies, too.[27]

3. Our strength lies in our communal solidarity, which has been undermined by modern markets and corrupting liberalism. Therefore any

elements within our borders who are not part of the original community, are a menace because they weaken and divide it.[28]

4. Finally, our unique characteristics are carried in our blood. Outsiders cannot hope to achieve the grandeur and purity which makes us great.[29]

How this mixture of social Darwinism, self-pity, racial animosity, sentimental worship of communal solidarity, and exaggerated sense of greatness became so common in Central and Eastern Europe (and elsewhere, too) is a long story that is well known, though perhaps not yet well enough understood. In Romania, it was partly the influence of European, and after World War I particularly German thinking that established this worldview among the intellectuals. But even before they had read Oswald Spengler, their antiforeign, anti-Semitic form of nationalism predisposed them toward accepting such a ideology. And their frustrations with their own weakness, continuing poverty, and inability to turn their nationalist ardor into the purity and greatness they sought only accentuated these tendencies. In other words, Romanian nationalism as felt by most of the intelligentsia predisposed it to accept these currents of European thought, and even to contribute to their development. Mihail Manoilescu's theories about corporatism, for example, were widely translated and influenced thinking as far away as Brazil and Argentina. Romanian nationalist intellectuals, in other words, were not merely passive recipients of rightist thought, but active contributors. Their anti-Semitism in particular had been even more pronounced than that of Germany's in the late nineteenth century, so that what happened in Germany in the 1930s only confirmed the sentiments that were already widespread in Romania.[30]

As the nationalist intellectuals dominated universities and the school system, as they prevailed in the administration and military, and as there was no class basis for opposing ideologies, those who objected were marginalized.

The peasants could not be counted on to oppose this trend because their old independent institutions had failed to protect them from capitalism. As literacy spread in rural areas, and some young peasants went to school and joined the ranks of the lower intelligentsia and administration, they became nationalists as well. They were not all Iron Guardists, to be sure, and the more liberal Peasant Party remained strong. But the leaders of the Peasant Party were quite willing to cooperate with a somewhat milder form of nationalist military dictatorship even when they feared the extremism of the Iron Guard. And workers were not drawn in large numbers to socialism or communism because of the national issue, namely, because control of private capital was so disproportionately in the hands of those identified as aliens.

By the late 1930s, the only serious opposition to the far right was among more moderate nationalists like Nicolae Iorga, and the Peasant Liberal Party. But their popular support was so weak that they relied on King Carol, who was a personally corrupt and autocratic individual, to support their efforts at moderation. When Carol was overthrown, what was left of the moderates turned to a right-wing general, Antonescu, to save them from the worst excesses of fascism.

In the end, Romania's drift toward the far right was a matter of elite ideology, and its success among a people with few viable alternatives. This was hardly unique. The drift toward intransigent Croatian and Serbian nationalism in Yugoslavia during the 1920s and 1930s was quite similar, and had led, by the start of World War II to a situation in which the communists were the only major political group that still believed in a liberal, civic conception of Yugoslav nationhood.[31] It was similar to what happened in Germany where, by 1932, two thirds to three quarters (depending on which election) of the voting population that was neither with the traditional Catholic Party nor with one of the two leftist parties opted for the Nazis.[32] In Romania, the left was very weak, and the Orthodox Church was edging toward the far right. In time, even without German aggression, the far right would have come to dominate local affairs entirely, and established a more centralized, autocratic state. The right would also have systematically weakened the "foreign" entrepreneurial class and reigned in market forces in favor of a more state-oriented economy. In fact, that is what happened during World War II, thus easing the way for further anticapitalist state centralization under communism.[33]

What I am suggesting is that the ideology of the elite is a vital determinant of whether or not democracy succeeds in a modern society, and that this is based on the class interests of this elite and on the international philosophical climate in which it exists. The first point remains the most valuable contribution of Barrington Moore's classical argument about the economic role of elites in the major modernizing societies, and the second is a matter of old fashioned, conventional intellectual history. Neither has much to do with the prior existence of a "civil" society. It is true that liberally inclined elites further the growth of civic institutions that promote further liberalism, as happened in England and most of the United States in the eighteenth and nineteenth centuries, or in the more commercially developed parts of Western

Europe with independent bourgeoisies. But reversing the sequence of causality misses the essence of such changes.

We can understand why the Romanian nationalists were hostile to what they perceived to be foreign domination of bourgeois life in their country, and why, therefore, they became increasingly hostile to the liberal, rational worldview that they considered a noxious product of Western bourgeois thought. We can, further, see that the associational life of the peasants which might have provided some hope for democratic developments was deemed irrelevant, and on the whole not even understood by the intelligentsia. And finally, we can appreciate how the social Darwinism and growing anti-Semitism of Europe in the late nineteenth century, and then again in the 1920s and 1930s, only fueled these most adverse ideological tendencies in Romania. Whatever civic traditions may have existed in Romania in the nineteenth and early twentieth centuries never had a chance to shape its political future, though they were not fully killed off until the totalitarian 1940s.

This does not, of course, answer the question of why the United States, or England, or the Netherlands, or Sweden, or a few other places were so different. But it does remind us to look for the obvious, class interest and ideology, if we want to explain democracy.

Before going on to Romania in the late twentieth century, a brief mention of an American example will clarify this contention.

A Confederate Parenthesis

For those who celebrate all those civic virtues that have made the United States democratic and produced a dynamic capitalist economy, the American South has always been an embarrassment best left to specialists of that region.[34] Yet, it is not a small part of America, and its history suggests that it takes much more than the correct tradition of English civic virtue, Protestantism, and the American revolutionary tradition to produce a healthy democracy. Because of its geography, the profitability of slavery, and the way in which a landholding elite developed, the South turned into something quite different from the North.[35]

The South created a neofeudal society, complete with powerful, independent local lords, bound peasant labor, a weak central government, and an ethical system which justified hereditary inequality that was supposed to be alleviated by patrimonial *noblesse oblige*. (It hardly matters that the reality was not quite like the ideal, because it never is.) That this was accomplished in a capitalist setting and was viable in a world market economy was all the more remarkable, but there is now no question that it was economically profitable and was only partially dismantled by the South's defeat during the Civil War.[36]

Historians of the American South, most notably Eugene Genovese, but also careful students of American political thought such as Louis Hartz, have noted that the South produced the only seriously antiliberal, antiindividualistic, and anticapitalist ideological movement in American history to justify slavery and rule by an elite.[37] A later, twentieth-century version of this reactionary strand of political and social thought manifested itself in the "agrarian" literary movement whose manifesto, *I'll Take My Stand* was "a determined reassertion of the validity of the legend of the Old South."[38] In more recent years the South has become the chief base of the serious American right. Its politics are now characterized by a kind of aggressive, xenophobic nationalism that is implicitly based on notions of blood and race and that loudly rejects the Enlightenment project of rational learning in favor of fundamentalist religiosity. That this political style has recently been spreading throughout the country, along with the anarchical tendency to violence long characteristic of Southern society should alert us to the fact that perhaps the South did not, in the long run, suffer total defeat during the Civil War.[39]

Aside from the fact that Southern reaction never developed much of a totalitarian, fascist strain, its ideology has some resemblance to that of Romanian nationalism. It was, in the first instance, the ideology of a landholding elite that kept not only black slaves but also the majority of poor whites outside the political process. But in adapting to the spread of democracy imposed on it after the Civil War, to the extension of literacy, urbanization, and industry, it produced a kind of popular self-pitying, nostalgic, and romantic nationalism quite different from that which prevailed elsewhere in the United States.[40] This combination of racial antagonism, suspicion of the North, antiurbanism, and distrust of modernity remains a contradiction of what American ideology is supposed to epitomize.[41]

This suggests that the class basis and ideology of an elite is crucial in determining the future of democratic institutions in any society. That the American South could develop in so undemocratic a direction, and retain deeply antiliberal sentiments so long after the end of the Civil War, and despite the two efforts of the North to bring it into line with the rest of the country (the Reconstruction after the Civil War, and the forced racial integration of the 1960s and 1970s), suggests that antidemocratic elite ideologies, once they are deeply rooted, may spread to the larger population and maintain themselves long after the disappearance of the original elite. The relative decentralization of American society and politics, its social civility, and all those traditions of Lockean liberalism and Enlightenment rationality present in the South were largely overcome by the interests and ideology of the planter elite and their successors after the Civil War.[42]

Today Southern antiliberalism is a genuinely mass phenomenon that has no connection, except a historical one, with the old slave-owning elite that originally produced it; but its roots still lie in that past. Because it is a growing rather than a declining force in general American politics, it might help Americans understand their own society better if they were able to recognize that contemporary antiliberalism is not a function of the decline or absence of civil society, but an ideological rejection of Enlightenment values and modernism.

Similarly, in Romania, populist nationalism was growing in the 1930s, even though it came originally from a small, elite class that was also eventually stripped of its original economic base. For a society that feels itself marginalized, backward, and unjustly persecuted (as the South did compared to the North after the Civil War, or as Romania did compared to the rest of Europe), extreme nationalism can become an appealing solution. If it is antiforeign, antibourgeois, and if it romanticizes a largely mythical agrarian past, it will also be hostile to large parts of Enlightenment rationality. It will also, inevitably, be strongly antidemocratic.

By looking quickly at Romania under communism and since its liberation in December, 1989, we can judge whether or not contemporary Romania has much chance of escaping its antidemocratic tradition.

Fascism and Communism in Romania

The Antonescu dictatorship during World War II accelerated the centralization of state and industry, and was based on an exclusive, blood definition of who was Romanian. Toward the end of communist rule, in the 1980s, and even more since the fall of communism there have been attempts to rehabilitate the Antonescu regime by pointing out that it was not as genocidal as the Nazis, that it protected its Jews somewhat, and most of all, that it was patriotic and tried to promote Romanian independence and grandeur.[43]

Actually, most of the autonomous right-wing nationalists who came to power in Central and Eastern Europe were not nearly as vicious as the Nazis, with the possible exception of the Croatian Ustasha and the certain exception of the Hungarian Arrow Cross that was put into power by the Germans only in the last months of 1944. In that sense, it is quite true that Antonescu's regime was milder than Hitler's, though it certainly deported many Jews and Gypsies in abominable conditions to Bessarabia. And of course Antonescu did not persecute Hungarians, who were also Germany's allies, much less his own favored German minority.

But the attempt to find redeeming humanitarian qualities in the Antonescu regime is actually something more important; it is a manifestation of the enduring strength of the same kind of nationalism in Romania as the type that prevailed in the 1930s. In that sense, the rehabilitation of the wartime regime is genuine because Antonescu was a legitimate representative of that nationalism. He was not a mere Nazi puppet by any means, any more than the right-wing nationalist regimes in Hungary before 1944, or in Slovakia and Bulgaria. For that matter, the collaborationist regimes in other parts of Europe, including especially the Vichy state in France, were also genuine representatives of the nationalist right in those societies. The difference is that this right would not have come to power in France, Norway, Belgium, or the Netherlands without a German occupation, whereas in Romania it was on the road to power well before World War II. German influence in 1941 actually helped Antonescu curb the more radical Iron Guard that would have initiated an immediate mass slaughter of the Jews on the spot. (Hitler decided that the Iron Guard would disrupt the Romanian economy too much, and so allowed it to be crushed by Antonescu.) But the military regime that ruled form 1941 to mid-1944 was truly a fair representative of what all but the most radical Romanian nationalists wanted to see in power.[44] Those who have tried to rehabilitate him, therefore, have a good point, though any liberal observer cannot escape alarm at how valid a point it is![45]

Communism would never have come to power in Romania without the occupation by the Soviet Army in 1944. Unlike in Czechoslovakia, there was no strong communist party. Unlike in Bulgaria or Germany, there never had been one. Unlike in Yugoslavia, Albania, Greece, Italy, France, or Poland, there were no communist Partisans fighting against the Germans during the War. Romania and Hungary had by far the weakest possible base for communism in Eastern Europe, but as former Axis powers, there was not much sympathy for them among the Western allies.[46]

Nevertheless, after years of seeming subservience to Soviet interests, from the late 1940s to the early 1960s, the Romanian Communist Party began to assert its own national interests. Under Nicolae Ceausescu, who came to power in 1964, Romania struck out on its own, independent Stalinist road of heavy, autarkic industrialization at any cost. This appeared to the West as a form of liberalization, because it was occasionally anti-Soviet, but it was nothing of the sort. Instead, it was pure socialist nationalism, and already in the 1970s the cultural symbols of the ultranationalist 1930s were fully rehabilitated. In the 1970s, the very same type of nationalism prevailed as had in the late 1930s and early 1940s, and in fact the very structure of the society built by the communists corresponded closely to the corporatist blueprint set out by Manoilescu and others in the 1920s and 1930s.[47]

Ceausescu's regime tried in this way to gain legitimation for itself, and it succeeded. In the 1970s much of the intelligentsia accepted Ceausescu as a genuine nationalist, and the rapidly growing cities and working class learned in school and through nationalist propaganda that his regime was the descendant of a long series of Romanian heroes who had been struggling for national purity and greatness for two thousand years. Only in the 1980s, as the economy collapsed, did the regime lose its standing.[48]

What, we might ask, does this portend for the future of Romanian democracy?

Prospects for the Future

The Ceausescu regime was overthrown after a public demonstration against the dictator in Bucharest on December 22, 1989. Nicolae and Elena Ceausescu were summarily shot at an army base on Christmas day. But aside from Albania, Romania's was the last communist regime to fall in Eastern Europe, and the only one in which there were more than a handful of deaths. (In the confused struggle that lasted a few days after Ceausescu's fall, and in the Timisoara demonstrations that preceded this event, almost a thousand people were killed.) The delay in change in Romania was due to the fact that the Ceausescu regime had more effectively suppressed nongovernmental organizations than any of the other East European communist regimes, again with the exception of Albania. This may have been, as some said, because Romania had a lesser tradition of an independent civil society, or it may simply have been that the combination of repression and economic decline had left less room for dissent and independence in Romania than elsewhere. Albania, of course, was even more repressive, and far poorer.

Within a few months of the end of communism, however, new parties, newspapers, nongovernmental organizations, private businesses, and schools, including universities, had been established. Though it took a bit longer to see which ones of these would survive, within two years there were somewhat stabilized opposition parties, an active free press, and a considerable number of private organizations active in civic, cultural, and business life. A revived civil society was flourishing. By 1993 the Ministry of Education was trying to handle some 200 private universities clamoring for certification, even though some of them existed more on paper than in reality.[49]

Also by 1992 and 1993 there were human rights organizations issuing bulletins and providing defense lawyers in cases where there seemed to have been police or judicial abuse. The Hungarians had become a major political force in parliament. Groups to defend the rights of Gypsies, especially in the countryside and small towns, where they are a despised and often persecuted minority, were becoming active. Student groups were proliferating in the universities, some explicitly political, others concentrating on various topics of interest such as computers and communications, and others based on ethnic affiliation, particularly among Hungarians in Transylvania or Gypsies in Bucharest. There were several competing Orthodox Christian organizations, at least one of which was publishing theological books not officially approved by the main Church hierarchy. Missionaries from abroad were catering to the renewed demand for help from Protestant fundamentalist converts.

In the business world privatization of the huge industrial firms left from communist days moved slowly. But by 1994 the multiplication of small shops, small and medium-sized joint enterprises with foreigners (many of them unheralded, unregistered, and sometimes not quite legal), and the increasing involvement by larger foreign multinational firms were changing the face of Romania daily life. Even in small towns consumer goods were far more available than they had been in the best days of communism. By mid-1995 about 40 percent of the land had been privatized, and as a result the food supply was excellent. To be sure, as in other communist countries, all these goods were expensive, but their availability in small provincial towns suggested that someone, not just a few rich tourists and Bucharest gangsters, was buying the frozen fish, fresh vegetables, imported Chinese textiles, and computers for sale in the shops.

To be sure, many of the NGOs working at the edge of political life, including the main human rights groups, some of the better political newspapers, and various groups promoting political pluralism and ethnic tolerance were being financed by Western aid groups from the United States, the Netherlands, Germany, the United Kingdom, France, and Scandinavia. But they were being tolerated by the government, and significant numbers of Romanians were being exposed to their various activities.

All this contributed to the sweeping victory of the liberal forces in the elections of 1996.

Does this mean that Romania is now on the way to becoming a normal capitalist democratic society? The American Embassy and the American aid organizations in Romania certainly think so, and believe that the way to further promote such a trend is to continue to finance NGOs and encourage the Government of Romania to decentralize and practice multiculturalism. That is, of course, the mandate of all American embassies throughout the world, because the theory that a proliferation of secondary, independent organizations will create a democratic civil society, has been fully accepted. And it is assumed that democracy and capitalism will flourish together.

I would be foolish to try to predict the future of democratization and capitalism in Romania. Partly, this will depend on the international atmosphere in the Balkans and Central Europe, and in Russia. An unexpected peace in the Balkans, democratization and economic stabilization in Russia and Ukraine, and a continuing presence in the area by a liberal Germany would do much to help Romania. But as for internal Romanian developments, the emphasis on creating a civil society misses the crucial influence of elite ideology and the nature of nationalism in Romania.

Reading through contemporary Romanian publications, whether of the far right, moderate right, or center (there are hardly any serious leftist publications these days), it quickly becomes evident that even those who praise democracy are highly nationalistic and resentful of their neighbors and of the West for not helping them more. The Romanians, even the supposedly most liberal of the major newspapers such as *Romania Libera*, verge constantly on being offensively anti-Hungarian. The Hungarian political organizations, on the other hand, clearly express the wish that their people did not have to live in Romania, though they recognize that the option of secession and joining Hungary is not realistic. The self-pitying, romantic appeal to past greatness and peasant purity is alive among the intellectuals, and especially within the Orthodox Church. This accounts for the considerable sympathy most aware Romanians have with the Serbian cause in the Yugoslav War. And though practical politicians in both Romania and the independent Republic of Moldova (which is now officially Romanian speaking) are not eager to unite these two states, there are a host of cultural organizations that trumpet their common roots and "Latinity."

One of the issues not addressed by the American aid organizations, especially the American Embassy, is the actual content of ideological discussions among Romanian intellectuals and within universities. Nor is the popular perception of nationalism well understood. There is widespread poverty, and there will be for many years. Who is being blamed, now that the memory of communism is beginning to fade? Are foreigners at fault? Private businesses?

It would be astonishing, in fact virtually unprecedented if the Romanian intelligentsia had changed its attitudes toward nationalism since the overthrow of communism. After all, there was much continuity between the ideology of the precommunist and of the communist years, and there was never a forced examination of the past as in postwar Germany. Now, with the overthrow of communism, there is virtually no recognition within any political group that one of the greatest excesses of the Ceausescu regime was its xenophobia and fascination with blood purity and the eternal virtues of the Romanian people. In fact, the very intellectuals who best served Ceausescu's hypernationalism are now writing anti-Semitic, antiliberal, anti-Western propaganda as if they were living in the 1930s. Communism is ascribed to another foreign imposition, and Ceausescu is dismissed as a purely corrupt petty politician who lacked a domestic base. It is therefore easy to forge a sentimental tie with the immediate precommunist past and return to the rabid nationalism of that time.

In the end, it is the intelligentsia that will provide the leading political figures, educators, and administrators of the new Romania. It is the frustrated masses, taught nationalist doctrines throughout their stay in school, who will provide the electoral base for the parties in power if Romania continues to have reasonably free elections. All the little NGOs and private universities will be unable to resist concerted central power if the those in charge of the government assert their will. For that matter, there is not even much indication that many of those in charge of these NGOs have much understanding of the pitfalls of the nationalism they also espouse.

Thus, if we want to know how democracy is faring in Romania, let us not get carried away too much with counting the sprouts of civil society.[50] As many of the articles in this book suggest, particularly the one on Islamic organizations in Turkey by Resat Kasaba, let us not forget to look at what types of ideology are current among those heading and inspiring these groups, and what their followers except from them. Let us look at what economic classes are gaining ground, and try to understand their ideology. In other words, rather than believing in the magic of civil society, let us try to understand how those with power and those who oppose them are thinking. This is a conclusion that is worth keeping in mind wherever in the world we want to forecast the future.

Notes

1. See Jean L. Cohen and Andrew Arato, *Civil Society and Political Theory* (Cambridge, Mass.: MIT Press, 1992); John A. Hall, *Coercion and Consent* (Cambridge: Polity Press, 1994) and Hall, ed., *Civil Society, Theory and Comparison* (Cambridge: Polity Press, 1995); Adam B. Seligman, *The Idea of Civil Society* (New York: The Free Press, 1992). But there are many others as well, and for a more complete list see the chapters by these authors.
2. Alvin Gouldner, *The Coming Crisis of Western Sociology* (New York: Basic Books, 1970).
3. "Romania" is now usually spelled with an "o" because that is the way the Romanians themselves spell it. It used to be spelled "Rumania" in English, and sometimes appeared as "Roumania," following the French spelling "Roumanie."
4. Unfortunately much of the standard historical material available on Romania in English simply repeats the standard nationalist claims made by Romanian intellectuals themselves. In particular, Keith Hitchins' recent history, *Romania, 1866–1947* (Oxford: Clarendon Press, 1994), despite its impressive erudition, is seriously flawed because of this. But there are more specialized works that are excellent, notably: Henry L. Roberts, *Rumania: The Political Problems of an Agrarian State* (New Haven, Conn.: Yale University Press, 1951); Eugen Weber, "Romania," in Hans Rogger and Eugen Weber, eds., *The European Right* (Berkeley: University of California Press, 1966); Kenneth Jowitt, ed., *Social Change in Romania, 1860–1940: A Debate on Development in a European Nation* (Berkeley: Institute of International Studies of the University of California, 1978); Michael Shafir, *Romania: Politics, Economy, and Society* (Boulder, Colo.: Lynne Rienner, 1985); Katherine Verdery, *National Ideology Under Socialism: Identity and Cultural Politics in Ceausescu's Romania* (Berkeley: University of California Press, 1991).
5. On Russia, see the magnificent recent book by Tim McDaniel, *The Agony of the Russian Idea* (Princeton, N.J.: Princeton University Press, 1996). For Romania, Eugen Weber, "Romania," pp. 504–8 summarizes the situation.
6. On Romania's tradition of anti-Semitism and anti-Westernism, Leon Volovici's *Nationalist Ideology and Anti-Semitism: The Case of Romanian Intellectuals in*

the 1930s (Oxford: Pergamon Press, 1991) is worth reading. A nice summary of his argument, and an interesting, though brief discussion of the issues raised by the anti-Enlightenment ideology that Romania's best precommunist intellectuals adhered to at a time, in the 1930s, when Romanian high culture reached its freest and most developed stage, is found in Vladimir Tismaneanu's "Romania's Mystical Revolutionaries," *Partisan Review* (Fall 1994), pp. 600–9.

7. The history of Romania's peasant communities is told by Henri H. Stahl in *Traditional Romanian Village Communities* (Cambridge: Cambridge University Press, 1980).

8. This observation, and some that follow about the current situation in Romania, are based on research I conducted there while evaluating programs funded by an American Foundation that promotes the development of civil society throughout the world, the National Endowment for Democracy. The report I filed is entitled "An evaluation of the work done by the Institute for Democracy in Eastern Europe with grants funded by the National Endowment for Democracy" (Washington, D.C.: National Endowment for Democracy, 1995).

9. Stahl in *Traditional Romanian Village Communities* is the notable exception, largely because he followed Marc Bloch's suggestion that to understand the agrarian past you have to begin looking at the situation in the present and work backward. Stahl spent the 1920s and 1930s exploring Romanian villages in detail.

10. Lucian Blaga, revered by both the Romanian right and by the nationalist communists under Ceausescu, popularized a romantic, entirely subjective view of the peasant that continues to be far more appreciated in Romania than Henri Stahl's historically and sociologically objective view. The two argued in print in the 1930s, and as a very old man (he lived from 1901 to 1991) Stahl published a new critique of the romantic view of the peasant, and particularly of Blaga, in *Eseuri Critice Despre Cultural Populara Romaneasca* (Bucharest: Minerva, 1983). Though this book slipped by the censor, it raised such an outcry among nationalist intellectuals, who were at that time pro-Ceausescu, but are now among the most rabidly right-wing xenophobes in Romania, that Stahl was prohibited from publishing anything else during the communist period. See, also, Verdery, *National Ideology*, pp. 66–67.

11. Roberts, *Rumania*; Daniel Chirot, *Social Change in a Peripheral Society: The Creation of a Balkan Colony* (New York: Academic Press, 1976), chapters 6–8.

12. This is, of course, one of the most written about aspects of the rise of the West, of modernity, of capitalism, and of modern democracy. My own view, and some of the relevant bibliography, including appropriate citations from Max Weber, is summarized in Chirot, "The Rise of the West," *American Sociological Review* 50: 2 (1985): 181–95.

13. It should come as no surprise that few Romanian scholars show much interest in the German and Protestant tradition of Transylvania. One has to go to German publications for that. There were a spate of German scholarly books on this subject during World War II, but they were tainted by the association with the Nazi glorification of the *Volksdeutsch* or ethnic Germans spread throughout Eastern Europe. More recently, there have been good monographs published by the Siebenbürgisches Archiv (Böhlau Verlag, Cologne and Vienna). The Romanian scholarship on the Hungarians of Transylvania is more ample, but almost singlemindedly devoted to proving that the Romanians were always much more numerous than the Hungarians in this province. Hungarian scholarship tends to be better, but also suffers from the opposite obsession, to prove that the province was originally majority Hungarian. For anyone interested in these disputes, Laszlo Peter, ed., *Historians and the History of Transylvania* (Boulder, Colo.:

East European Monographs and Columbia University, 1992), offers some thoughtful commentary.

14. Chirot, *Social Change*, pp. 107–9.
15. This is one of the main themes in Irina Livezeanu's examination of how Romanian intellectuals moved toward an extreme form of fascism in the 1920s and early 1930s, *Cultural Politics in Greater Romania* (Ithaca, N.Y.: Cornell University Press, 1995).
16. Romanian nationalism was born in the mid-nineteenth anti-Semitic and xenophobic for these reasons. Romania's "national poet," Mihai Eminescu, was anti-Greek and anti-Semitic. This was part of a larger resentment against the more advanced West, and accompanied the celebration of the virtues of Romania's supposedly pre-Roman roots. Eugen Weber, "Romania," 502–3; Verdery, *National Ideology*, pp. 36–40; William Oldson, *A Providential Anti-Semitism: Nationalism and Polity in Nineteenth-Century Romania* (Philadelphia, Pa.: American Philosophical Society, 1991).
17. Thus, one of Romania's finest analysts of the condition of peasants in the late nineteenth century and early twentieth, Radu Rosetti, also wrote a detailed and in some sense scholarly, though vindictive, paranoid, and highly prejudiced attack on Jews. He published this under the pseudonym "Verax": *La Roumanie et les Juifs* (Bucharest: Socecu, 1903).
18. Oldson, *A Providential Anti-Semitism*, pp. 13–45.
19. Livezeanu, *Cultural Politics*, covers the conflicts of the post-World War I period province by province.
20. On the association between the Orthodox Church and Romanian nationalism in Transylvania, see Keith Hitchins, *The Rumanian National Movement in Transylvania, 1780–1849* (Cambridge, Mass.: Harvard University Press, 1969) and *Orthodoxy and Nationality: Andreiu Saguna and the Rumanians of Transylvania, 1846–1873* (Cambridge, Mass.: Harvard University Press, 1977). On the role of Orthodoxy in the twentieth century, see Livezeanu, *Cultural Politics*, 305, 309–10.
21. Mary Jane Osa's comparison of the Hungarian and Polish Catholic churches during the communist period should warn us against facile generalizations from just one example, namely, the link between Solidarity and the Church in Poland: "Resistance, Persistence and Change: The Transformation of the Catholic Church in Poland," *Eastern European Politics and Societies* 3: 2 (1989): 268–99. Furthermore, even in Poland, recent events make one suspect that the liberalizing influence of the Catholic Church was the result of a coincidental union of secular civil society and the Church against communism. See Ewa Morawska, "The Polish Roman Catholic Church Unbound: Change of Face or of Context," in Stephen E. Hanson and Willfried Spohn, eds., *Can Europe Work?* (Seattle: University of Washington Press, 1995).
22. Roberts, *Rumania* is the best source on this. See also Mattei Dogan, "L'origine sociale du personnel parlementaire d'un pays essentiellement agraire, la Roumanie," Revue de l'Institut de Sociologie 2–3 (Brussels, 1953), pp. 165–208. Of particular interest is the analysis of the election of 1937, Romania's last free one until the 1990s, published in 1937 by Romania's leading sociology journal, *Sociologia Romaneasca* (vol. II, nos. 11–12, 1937). It was reprinted for the first time in 1991 in Petre Datculescu and Klaus Liepelt, eds., *Renasterea Unei Democratii* (Bucharest: IRSOP, 1991), pp. 145–75.
23. I was able to interview many of the survivors who had been involved in these institutions before World War II while doing research in Romania in 1970. Many of their leaders suffered particularly badly at the hands of the communists after

1948, as every effort was made by the Stalinist regime of that time to crush any independent organization. But it would be misleading to believe that before 1948 Romania's civil society had been nonexistent. Quite the contrary was true. The two leading social science journals of the inter-war period, *Arhiva pentru stiinta si reforma sociala,* and in the late 1930s, *Sociologia Romaneasca* contain many articles about a variety of nonstate organizations, and also many very open, contentious, and revealing debates among leading Romanian intellectuals about the nature of their society. This was in no sense either a closed or uniformly statist society.

24. On the state of the economy, see Chirot, "Ideology, Reality, and Competing Models of Development in Eastern Europe Between the Two World Wars," *Eastern European Politics and Societies* 3: 3 (1989): 378–411.

25. C. Enescu, "Semnificatia alegerilor din decembrie 1937," *Sociologia Romaneasca* 2: 11–12 (1937); Eugen Weber, "Rumania," pp. 554–67. A somewhat romanticized, but essentially correct journalistic version of the events of this time in Bucharest can be found in R. G. Waldeck, *Athene Palace* (Garden City, N.Y.: Blue Ribbon Books, 1942).

26. Norman Manea, "Happy Guilt: Mircea Eliade, Fascism, and the Unhappy Fate of Romania," *The New Republic* (August 8, 1991), pp. 27–36.

27. This is a central theme in the nationalism of "ressentiment" that Liah Greenfeld has discussed in *Nationalism: Five Roads to Modernity* (Cambridge, Mass.: Harvard University Press, 1992). For its application to Romania, see Chirot, *Modern Tyrants: The Power and Prevalence of Evil in Our Age* (Princeton, N.J.: Princeton University Press, 1996), pp. 231–65.

28. Chirot, *Modern Tyrants* and, particularly on the dangers of communal ideologies, "Modernism Without Liberalism: The Ideological Roots of Modern Tyranny," *Contention* 5:1 (1995): 141–66.

29. This could be expressed in the form of Blaga's celebration of Romanians' "exuberance" and "vitality" that supposedly came from the "Slavic and Thracian blood seeth[ing] in our veins." (Verdery, *National Ideology,* p. 49). Or it could be more subtly stated, as in Mircea Eliade's fondness for Jungian mysticism and his highly elliptical allusions to the virtues of Romanian ultranationalism in his very popular *Images and Symbols: Studies in Religious Symbolism* (originally published in French in 1952) (New York: Sheed and Ward, 1969). The national soul, in either case, was carried by heredity, and foreigners, namely Jews and Hungarians, were excluded from consideration as part of the nation.

30. Chirot, *Modern Tyrants,* 25–119 on the consequences of this kind of thought for Europe, and particularly for Germany and Russia.

31. Aleksa Djilas, *The Contested Country: Yugoslav Unity and Communist Revolution, 1919–1953* (Cambridge, Mass.: Harvard University Press, 1991), shows that by the 1930s the only major political force in Yugoslavia that advocated ethnic reconciliation and tolerance was the Communist Party. And so it remained during the period of communist rule as well.

32. Richard F. Hamilton, *Who Voted for Hitler?* (Princeton, N.J.: Princeton University Press, 1982).

33. One of the major theorists of state-centered corporatism in Europe and Latin America, in fact, was the Romanian economist and diplomat Mihail Manoilescu whose work was, in its time, very influential and widely translated. It was his ideology which dominated in Romania during World War II, and in a strange way, came back as the blueprint for national communism under Nicolae Ceausescu. See Philippe C. Schmitter, "Still the Century of Corporatism?" *Review of Politics* (January 1974): 85–131; and Chirot, "The corporatist model

and socialism: notes on Romanian development," *Theory and Society* 9 (1980): 363–81.

34. As the following remarks will show, I do not claim to be an expert on the American South. I want to address the comparison because it has struck me over many years that those who celebrate America's civil society and democratic virtues tend to avoid the subject of the South, and those who, on the contrary, are specialists of that region or who address its problems tend to have a rather bleaker view of American civic virtue than their Lockean counterparts.

35. Alexis de Tocqueville's famous remarks about the difference between the free and slaveholding parts of the country show that he considered them virtually different civilizations. ("Upon the left bank of the Ohio labor is confounded with the idea of slavery, while upon the right bank it is identified with that of prosperity and improvement; on the one side it is degraded, on the other it is honored.") *Democracy in America*, volume 1, Henry Reeve Text, revised by Francis Bowen, and edited by Philips Bradley (New York: Vintage, 1954), p. 377, and more generally pp. 370–97. This, ultimately, is also Barrington Moore's explanation of the causes of the American Civil War: the North and South had developed fundamentally incompatible political cultures and societies. Barrington Moore, Jr., *Social Origins of Dictatorship and Democracy* (Boston: Beacon, 1966), chapter 3. This is also the central theme in the more recent book by Gary Wills, *Lincoln at Gettysburg: The Words That Remade America* (New York: Simon & Schuster/Touchstone, 1992), especially chapters 3 and 4.

36. Moore, *Social Origins*, pp. 143–49. The now classic, though still controversial work of Robert W. Fogel and Stanley L. Engerman, *Time on the Cross: The Economics of American Negro Slavery* (Boston: Little, Brown and Co., 1974), suggests how much of a going economic concern the slave plantation system actually was up to 1860.

37. Eugene D. Genovese, *The World the Slaveholders Made* (New York: Pantheon, 1969); Louis Hartz, *The Liberal Tradition in America* (New York: Harcourt, Brace and World, 1955), pp. 145–77. It can be somewhat of a shock to someone versed in European anti-Enlightenment, antimodern thought to see how similar were the ideas of the South's great ideologue, George Fitzhugh in *Cannibals All! Or Slaves Without Masters*, edited by C. Vann Woodward (Cambridge, Mass.: Harvard University Press, 1960).

38. W.J. Cash, *The Mind of the South* (New York: Vintage, 1969 [1941]).

39. Some of the best analysis of Southern politics and culture and its influence is found in John S. Reed, *Southerners: The Social Psychology of Sectionalism* (Chapel Hill: University of North Carolina Press, 1983) and *My Tears Spoiled My Aim and Other Reflections on Southern Culture* (Columbia: University of Missouri Press, 1993).

40. Reed, *Southerners*, chapter 5 ("'Not Forgotten,' Southern Grievances, Southern History, and Symbolic Sectionalism"). See also the essays in Edgar T. Thompson, *Plantation Societies, Race Relations, and the South* (Durham, N.C.: Duke University Press, 1975); and especially C. Vann Woodward, *The Burden of Southern History* (Baton Rouge: Louisiana State University Press, 1960).

41. The fact, emphasized by C. Vann Woodward in *The Strange Case of Jim Crow*, third revised edition (New York: Oxford University Press, 1974), pp. 17–21, that the North was in a sense as racist as the South, and that segregation developed there before the Civil War, should alert us to the fact that it is not prejudice as such that is the essence of the reactionary ideology being discussed here. Whatever prejudice Southern or Northern American whites have felt toward blacks, or Romanians toward Jews was indeed widespread and not limited to

those hostile to modernism and Western classical liberalism. On the other hand, there have always been examples of reactionary Southerners, and ultranationalist Romanians who were not personally hostile to individual blacks or Jews. The point is that in a fundamentally liberal society continuing industrialization and urbanization result in decreasing legal prejudice against minorities, and their acceptance as individuals within the society. But when the prevailing ideology rejects individualism and classical liberalism as alienating and artificial modern constructs that destroy communal solidarities, any minority that seems to benefit from modernization and liberal tolerance is associated with and blamed for the unwelcome changes that occur. This is probably the single most difficult aspect of either American racism or European anti-Semitism to understand. Pure prejudice without any ideological basis may be morally objectionable, but it is not as dangerous as antimodernism and formally forcing individual into hereditary communal categories from which they cannot legally exit. The failure to make this distinction is not limited to the general public, but remains the rule rather the exception in most scholarly analysis of both anti-Semitism and American race relations.

42. The way in which integrationist and progressive sentiment were split apart in the late nineteenth-century South is explored by Carl N. Degler, *The Other South: Southern Dissenters in the Nineteenth Century* (New York: Harper and Row, 1974). On Southern politics before the 1960s civil rights movements, see Valdimer O. Key, Jr., *Southern Politics in State and Nation* (New York: Alfred A. Knopf, 1949).

43. An American who has accepted this line of reasoning and become associated with the ultra-nationalists in Romania is Larry L. Watts, in his *Romanian Cassandra: Ion Antonescu and the Struggle for Reform, 1916–1941* (Boulder, Colo.: East European Monographs and Columbia University, 1993).

44. Weber, "Romania," pp. 562–67.

45. These issues are often debated in the contemporary Romanian political press. The leading ultra-rightist, nationalist, and outspokenly anti-Semitic viewpoint appears in the pages of the weekly *Romania Mare*. The weekly *22* expresses the liberal viewpoint on these issues, as does the satirical weekly *Academia Catavencu*.

46. Ghita Ionescu, *Communism in Romania, 1944–1962* (London: Oxford University Press, 1964).

47. George Schöpflin, "Rumanian Nationalism," *Survey* 4 (Autumn 1974): 77–104; Chirot, "Romania," *Social Forces* 57: 2 (1978): 457–99.

48. Chirot, "Romania: Ceausescu's Last Folly," *Dissent* (Summer, 1988): 271–75.

49. These observations and those that follow about contemporary Romanian civil society are based on research trips I took to Romania in 1993 for the United States Information Agency and in 1995 for the National Endowment for Democracy. The report, cited above in note 8, "An Evaluation," for N.E.D. contains an analysis of the situation.

50. This means that the enormously influential book by Robert D. Putnam, *Making Democracy Work: Civic Tradition in Modern Italy* (Princeton, N.J.: Princeton University Press, 1993) and his now-famous article, "Bowling Alone: America's Declining Social Capital," *Journal of Democracy* 6: 1 (1995): 65–78, have to be used cautiously, even when they are applied to Italy and the United States. When exported to other societies, even greater circumspection is called for.

8

Between Nation and Civil Society: Ethnolinguistic and Religious Pluralism in Independent Ukraine

José Casanova

Caveat

Most recent discussions of civil society begin by pointing to the widespread and overinflated usage of the category by both analysts and social and political actors throughout the world. This statement of fact is usually followed by a critical reconstruction of the analytical, normative, and practical- programmatic ambiguities, if not outright confusions, that are built into the contemporary usages of the concept of civil society. Moreover, the call for analytical clarity is often accompanied by a cautious and sobering, if not outright pessimistic, reassesment of the prospects for the actual emergence and institutionalization of civil societies beyond the real existing civil societies of the civilized West.[1]

The simultaneous emergence or rediscovery of the category in various settings—East and West, North and South—and its nearly global diffusion proves, in my view, the relevance of the concept for an understanding of some of the most remarkable and distinguishable characteristics of "the third wave of democratization."[2] It is precisely because the category is so intrinsically connected with the phenomenological and reflexive self-understanding of contemporary actors and observers alike that the concept of civil society can be simultaneously so illuminating of the historical present and so equivocal in its contradictory meanings. It should be the task of social analysts, of course, to disentangle the empirical-analytical and normative-ideational components of the concept. But empirical realism and analytical precision need not be bought at the price of either reducing the phenomenological complexity or blunting the normative-teleological dimension and global resonance of "the dream of civil society."

Civil Society in Ukraine?

Given the widespread skepticism one finds among "experts" concerning the very viability of Ukraine as an independent nation-state, and the dire warnings about the dangers of Ukrainian nationalism, and the interjected references to Bosnia and nuclear disaster when discussing the Crimea question, given all that, to pose the question of the chances of success of the institutionalization of civil society in Ukraine would seem a provocative, almost futile exercise.[3] My aim, however, is to inject some cautious optimism into the discussion. Indeed, if a civil society can emerge in such an unexpected setting as Ukraine, it could possibly emerge in many other unlikely places. Put provocatively, Ukraine is a place located on the margins of Eastern Europe, beset by a long and tragic history of uncivil ethnoreligious conflicts, civilizational clashes, imperial rule and great power struggles, and seemingly bereft of the social capital, self-organizational resources, and elementary institutional structures required to sustain a civil society. Nevertheless, there are compelling signs indicating that the solid foundations for the building of civil society are being established today in post-Soviet Ukraine.

It is often asserted that the further east one goes the more insoluble appear the dilemmas of the transitions facing postcommunist societies. Alas! Besides the double transition from an authoritarian to a democratic regime and from a command to a market economy, Ukraine is faced with the additional double transition of basic postcolonial nation building and postimperial state making.[4] The historical task appears even more daunting if one takes into account the inherent weakness of the administrative elites inherited by the newly independent republic. In a carefully stated argument that puts into question many common assumptions, Alexander Motyl has shown convincingly that given such constraints in order to be successful the transformation in Ukraine would have to be "piecemeal and slow" and most importantly "sequential."[5] State making, nation building and elite formation would have to be pursued first and interrelatedly before the other transformational imperatives could be tackled. This, in any case, has been the path followed consciously and relatively successfully by policymakers in Ukraine.

By relative success I mean that even though the projects of state making and nation building may still appear insecure and very much unfinished, after four arduous years the foundations appear sound and the basic direction taken seems to be one conducive to the eventual consolidation of a democratic nation-state. This is not the place to reconstruct in detail the milestones of the Ukrainian transformation. But it is necessary to keep in mind some of the most characteristic and determinant factors of the ongoing process.[6]

The Ukrainian Transitions

Liberalization

The liberating winds of glasnost and perestroika and of the Eastern European revolutions also reached finally Ukraine in the fall of 1989 when massive public pressure forced the resignation of V. Shcherbytsky, Ukraine's party leader since 1972 and the last holdover of the Brezhnev era in the Politburo. The following spring, Rukh, the national-democratic movement of civil society against the authoritarian and imperial state, modeled after Polish Solidarity and the Popular Fronts of the Baltic Republics, was successfully launched.[7] Yet, the independence of Ukraine did not come as a result of the national liberation struggle, but rather as a marvelous gift from the failed coup of August 1991 in Moscow. The miraculousness of the process was prefigured, so at least believers think, in the words of the Ukrainian national anthem, "Our enemies will vanish like dew under sunshine," so often sang with much élan and a certain incredulity by Ukrainian patriots. A more accurate anticipation of the actual course of events that led to the disintegration of the Soviet Union can be found in an appeal to Russian national-democrats by Ivan Drach, the leader of Rukh, published in the Moscow *Literaturnaia Gazeta* (April 11, 1990) stating that "A free Ukraine is impossible without a free Russia.... The responsibility of Russia is to secede first from the Union and help others...." (p. 112). Yeltsin's Russia's recognition of Ukraine's declaration of independence two days after the coup, at a time when most Western powers were rather hesitant, sealed the fate of the Union.[8]

Independence and Elite Formation

The Declaration of Ukraine's Independence by the unreformed Ukrainian Communist Supreme Council came once it became evident that the coup had failed. The ruling faction of the Ukrainian Communist Party under the leadership of Kravchuk coopted the platform of the national-democratic opposition in order to maintain itself in power. The tacit coalition between ex-communists and national democrats in support of national independence and state sovereignty became the fundamental factor in Ukrainian politics during the Kravchuk administration. Other urgent tasks such as economic reform would simply have to wait. The overwhelming response in favor of the ratification of the Declaration of Independence in the December 1991 referendum throughout Ukraine, including the ethnically and linguistically Russified eastern oblasts still under rigid communist control, gave the aura of democratic legitimacy to an intra-elite agreement that now became the basic national consensus within which the struggles for power, the negotiations of the basic rules of the game, and the policy compromises could be regulated and contained.

The dissolution of Rukh and the decision not to become an opposition party, the demobilization of civil society, the slow institutionalization of a political society restricted to elites with a very weak party base, the deadlocks and self-restraints in intra-elite power struggles, the apathy, lack of voice and loss of confidence in the political elites on the part of the citizenry, combined with patient stoicism, fundamental system loyalty, and surprising civility, all were interrelated pieces of the Ukrainian political puzzle. One must be surely concerned about the absence of a genuine party system in Ukraine and the demobilization of civil society from the public sphere. But this can also be viewed as the price to be paid for a successful process of political and administrative elite formation in postimperial Ukraine, without which the tasks of state making and nation building could not be confronted with any chance of success. Nor could any serious economic reform be entertained before those other processes had already be set on the right track.[9]

The basic issues in the tug of war between central and regional administrative elites, between president and parliament, between the reform and antireform factions within parliament were not much different in Ukraine than in Russia. The deadlock and the impossibiliy to adopt or carry through any meaningful reform measures were also similar in both places. Yet the civility with which Ukrainian elites carried their disputes and power struggles in comparison to the incivility of the Russian process points to some fundamental differences in the emergence of intraelite trust, of basic elite consensus, and even of a democratic elite culture. Motyl has argued perceptively that government deadlock in Ukraine actually facilitated the process of learning the rules of the democratic political game, both sides coming to recognize the indispensability of each other to the very act of playing the game: "The inertia of the political process created an elite *esprit de corps*, a perhaps unconsciously and unwillfully developed tolerance, and a sense of moderation that facilitate the formation of a genuine Ukrainian elite. The parliamentary and presidential elections of 1994, and the smooth transfer of power from Kravchuk to Kuchma, testified to the growth of real institutions within the Ukrainian state."[10]

Moreover, the same public opinion surveys which register a profound lack of confidence in political leaders, in the political class, in all political parties and all political institutions also indicate clearly that the majority of the population do not want to change the rules of the game. A December 1994 survey in the city of Kiev registered the following alarming rates of negative confidence, in ascending order: President Kuchma (53 percent little or no confidence vs. 39 percent some or absolute confidence), army (55 percent vs. 37 percent), new independent trade unions (60 percent vs. 16 percent), Chair of Parliament O. Moroz (67 percent vs. 18 percent), private entrepreneurs (68 percent vs. 19 percent), City Mayor L. Kosakivsky (68 percent vs. 14 percent), political parties (72 percent vs. 7 percent), directors of large state entreprises (75 percent vs. 13 percent), old trade unions (76 percent vs. 10 percent), city council (77 percent vs. 6 percent), parliament (79 percent vs. 12 percent). The highest expression of negative confidence was reserved for the government (82 percent vs. 8 percent).

Yet, when asked whether they favored "an authoritarian administration for a restricted period of time in order to come out of the crisis," the answer was: 52 percent opposed, 25 percent in favor, 23 percent don't know. Moreover, although evidently fed up with government deadlock, most people did not want to change the checks and balances built into the democratic political game. When asked their opinion about "the kind of division of power most needed for the reform period," the choice of answers was: "power should be divided constitutionally between the President, the legislature, the executive, and the judiciary, each of them fulfilling their functions in accordance with constitutional rules" (40 percent), "the President should assume absolute power and rule by decree" (21 percent), "the most important decisions should be approved by Parliament and executed by the President and the Cabinet of Ministers (7 percent), no interest in the question (22 percent), don't know (10 percent).[11] The picture that emerges from this and many other surveys throughout Ukraine is that of profound political apathy and disenchantment with the political process, as well as loss of confidence in the ability of the political elites to solve Ukraine's economic problems, but within a frame of basic loyalty to the system.

State-Making

When analyzing the process of state-making in Ukraine it is crucial to keep in mind that, as Roman Szporluk has pointed out, "the independent Ukraine proclaimed in August 1991 did not define itself as an ethnic state. It was a jurisdiction, a territorial and legal entity, in fact, a successor of the Ukrainian SSSR. Its citizens were of different ethnic backgrounds and spoke Ukrainian and Russian to varying degrees, but also other languages. The new state declared that all power in it derives from "the people of Ukraine."[12] The category, "the people of Ukraine," included all inhabitants of Ukraine irrespective of nationality, ethnicity, language, religious confession, or any other ascriptive marker. In other words, the *polis*, that is, the political community of the Ukrainian state was being explicitly differentiated from the Ukrainian *demos*, that is, from the ethnic imagined community of the historical Ukrainian nation. The two ambiguously overlapping identities of the Ukrainian *narod* as "the people of Ukraine" and as "the Ukrainian nation" were now open to individual and collective reflexive dissociations, contestations, and rearreagements.

The conscious adoption of a policy of inclusive state making in Ukraine was as much a carryover of Soviet constitutional discourse and practices by a Ukrainian *nomenklatura* turned nationalist overnight, as the reflexive contribution of the national democratic oppposition. From its inception Rukh had incorporated explicitly such an inclusive policy in its platform. In a polemical reply to the slanderous anti-Rukh campaign in the official press, then under the direction of Party Secretary of Ideology L. Kravchuk, Drach wrote: "Rukh has often stated that it stands on the following positions: Russians are to live better in Ukraine than in Moscow, Leningrad, New York. Jews living in Ukraine are to live and feel better than in Moscow, Leningrad, New York, Tel Aviv, Jerusalem. Then it will be possible for Ukrainians to demand the kind of system which will enable them to live better than the Ukrainians in the U.S. and Canada. Such is the 'nationalism' of Rukh."[13]

The publication of such a text in Moscow's *Literaturnaia Gazeta* shows the strategic considerations that led the Ukrainian nationalist elites to adopt such a policy. Given Ukraine's geopolitical conditions, if the project of Ukrainian independence was to have any realistic chance of success, Ukraine could ill afford either to alienate its large Russian minority (21 percent of the population) or to provoke any kind of inter-ethnic Russian-Ukrainian conflict. The fact that a majority of Russians in Ukraine voted for Ukraine's independence in the December 1991 referendum and the absence of major incidents of interethnic conflict in Ukraine in the last four years, leaving aside here the more complex issue of Crimea, are evidence of the success of the policy.

The reference to "Jews living in Ukraine," a numerically much smaller minority (less than 1 percent of the population) but with great symbolic and international relevance, shows similar strategic consid-erations but points to deeper normative concerns of special significance in any discussion of civil society. It points to the adoption by the dissi-dent Ukrainian national movement of the 1960s and 1970s of modern principles of individual, universal human rights, as well as to the pro-cess of an open dialogue between Jewish and Ukrainian dissidents that took place in the Soviet Gulag and led to a mutual recognition of the respective claims and grievances and to a reflexive reconsideration of the long and tragic history of anti-Semitism and Jewish-Ukrainian con-flicts in Ukraine. The absence of major incidents of anti-Semitism in Ukraine today is not a mere fortunate coincidence, but it is the result of a process of reflexive collective learning from the negative experiences of the past on the part of Ukrainian nationalist elites and of the prin-cipled adoption on the part of the Ukrainian state of the appropriate policies.

Surveys of privately expressed public opinion in Ukraine still regis-ter rates of latent anti-Semitism almost as high as those in Russia.[14] The fundamental difference is the conscious decision on the part of all prominent political elites in Ukraine not to "play the ethnic card" and to banish from Ukrainian public discourse anti-Semitic and other xe-nophobic expressions. There is, no doubt, also an extreme nationalist right in Ukraine that advocates "Ukraine for Ukrainians only." But it is no more radical and numerically and electorally less significant than the extreme nationalist right in most Western European democracies with supposedly normally working civil societies.[15] Public opinion sur-veys from independence to the present show that there is a basic na-tional consensus shared by the overwhelming majority of the population in nationalist Western Ukraine as much as in Russified Eastern Ukraine around the principle of "equality before the law" and the project of a state bound by the rule of law to protect the universal, individual, equal rights of all its citizens irrespective of their ethnic origin or allegiance.[16]

Nation-Building

Issues of the type and direction of the process of nation building taking place today in Ukraine are more complex, ambiguous, and debatable. The question whether Ukraine has already succumbed to the temptation of the "nationalizing state" is not easily answerable in so far as the very category of a nationalizing state is and must perforce be ambiguous and imprecise.[17] At the one extreme pole would be the paradigmatic model of a fascist totalitarian state using aggressively its resources to construct a pure homogeneous national community "cleansed" from any foreign heterogeneous element. That such a model is incompatible with "modern" democracy, with the rule of law, and with civil society goes without saying. That the Ukrainian state does not in any way approximate the model is also obvious.

At the other extreme pole would be the libertarian utopian model of a minimal, noninterventionist, laissez-faire state that would have no national policy whatsoever, cultural, linguistic, educational, or otherwise, and no symbolic or semiotic representation of the collectivity. Whether such a state is at all possible is questionable. What is sure is that such a model would be incompatible with the project of a democratic state based on some kind of political community of its citizens, with some basic solidarity, and some form of symbolic collective representation. In any case the Ukrainian state, if it is to survive as a state, cannot avoid the task of nation building in the sense of constructing some kind of Ukrainian political community.

The empirically and normatively relevant question of course is, which type of community or which type of political integration? Here Juan Linz's systematic conceptualization of the categories of polis and demos and the extent of their congruence, as well as the conceptual differentiation between "nation-states" and "state-nations" seems more useful for an analysis of nation building in Ukraine than the lately fashionable category of the "nationalizing state."[18] Ukraine is not and cannot become a nation-state in the strict sense of the term of absolute congruence of its polis (community of citizens) and its demos (national community). So far, the process of state making in Ukraine has taken the form of state-nation rather than nation-state formation.[19] But what complicates the dilemmas of nation building in Ukraine is the fact that the very criteria of national inclusion and exclusion are not, and under modern democratic conditions are unlikely to ever become, unambiguous.

Ethnicity, language, and religion, have been historically and continue to be today the three main symbolic bricks customarily used either singly or in various combinations for the construction of national identities, that is, of collective memories of the common past, of collective symbolic representations of the common present, and of collective shared projects of the future. Even in those ever more rare cases in which the three markers happen to coincide, so that the criteria of national inclusion may seem unambiguous, the contents of the collective representations of that identity are likely to be open to various contested interpretations and to diverse individual appropriations and reconstructions. When, as it happens in Ukraine, ethnicity, language and religion do not coincide but rather overlap in different directions, national identity becomes more ambiguous and the task of nation building much more complex.

Ethnolinguistic Pluralism

In Ukraine, the category of ethnicity is relatively unproblematic only insofar as the Soviet system ascribed to each of its "citizen-subjects" one single ethnic identity.[20] Thus, according to the 1989 census, the population of Ukraine was made up of over 37 million Ukrainians (appx. 75 percent of the population), over 11 million Russians (21 percent), half a million Jews and some additional significant numbers from neighboring nationalities: Belarussians (440,000), Moldovians (324,500), Bulgarians (234,000), Poles (219,000), Hungarians (163,000), Romanians (135,000), and so on.[21]

The dilemmas of Ukraine's nation building would be relatively straightforward, though politically more dangerous due to the greater risk of Ukrainian-Russian polarization, if the main problem would be simply how to accommodate, that is, include or exclude the large Russian minority into the Ukrainian demos. The inherent risk derives from the fact that the Russians in Ukraine are a relatively privileged "imperial minority" which can respond to the real or perceived threat of Ukrainization with the counterthreat of secession.[22] Yet what really complicates matters for the task of Ukrainian nation building is the fact that ethnic Ukrainians are linguistically split between Ukrainophones and Russophones in such a way that there are three clearly distinct "ethnolinguistic groups" in Ukraine, though of course even those boundaries are rather porous and labile: Ukrainophone Ukrainians (40 percent), Russophone Ukrainians (33–34 percent), and Russophone Russians (20–21 percent). The fourth possible ethnolinguistic combination, Ukrainophone Russians, is numerically insignificant (1–2 percent).[23]

The figures show conclusively the asymmetrical consequences of imperial hegemony. The Russian language is unquestionably the hegemonic language in Ukraine. Russians in Ukraine have felt no need whatsoever to assimilate and adopt the Ukrainian language. In fact, they have felt no need or desire to even learn it. Despite the similarities between the two languages, Russians remain functionally monolingual. All Ukrainophone Ukrainians by contrast are fully bilingual having been functionally compelled to learn the language of the empire. Indeed the pressures of linguistic Russification were such that almost half of the Ukrainian population felt the compulsion or the need to adopt the imperial language as their own.

Not surprisingly, the Ukrainophone population is concentrated in Western Ukraine forming an overwhelming majority there, while the two Russophone groups are concentrated in Eastern Ukraine. The central oblasts and the central capital, Kyiv, represent "middle" Ukraine literally and figuratively, holding the center together, mediating and reducing the polarization between East and West, and mirroring the overall Ukrainian ethnic and linguistic distribution. Paradoxically, Russophone Ukrainians hold the key to the politics of nation building in Ukraine, being free to privilege either the ethnic or the linguistic component of their identity and thus to form majority coalitions with their fellow Ukrainians on certain issues or majority coalitions with their Russophone fellows on other issues. Their national identity being more a matter of choice than is the case with the other two groups, their identity will also tend to be more ambiguous and labile. Insofar as they do not renounce their equivocal identity by assimilating into any of the other two groups, they can also help to build the bridges of trust between the otherwise polarized groups.

In this respect, Rusophone Ukranians hold the key to the emergence of a genuinely pluralistic and not just plural civil society in Ukraine, a society that not only accepts diversity as the perhaps unfortunate but inevitable fact of the imperial legacy, but actually accepts cultural diversity and flexible individual identities as a value in itself.[24] Being in the middle, they serve as a structural condition for the survival of Ukraine's independence. They can literally hold Ukraine together in a way in which no of the other two poles can. Without them, both temptations, the nationalizing one on the part of aggrieved Ukrainian nationalists and the colonial one on the part of alarmed Russian *pieds noirs*, and the concomitant danger of Russian-Ukrainian communal violence in Ukraine, which could easily spill over into an international confrontation between Russia and Ukraine, would be much greater. In this respect, Russophone Ukrainians can simultaneously protect Ukrainian nationalism from its natural impulse to attempt to form a more homogeneous national community and free the Russian imperial minority from its impulse to secede and thus to provoke a Russian-Ukranian conflagration that would end most likely in a reincorporation of Ukraine to the Russian empire.[25]

Linguistic Policies and Politics

Given the long history of discrimination and outright persecution suffered by the Ukrainian language in Ukraine, having been either banned from the public sphere by colonial state power or banished by the power of imperial cultural hegemony to the place of a second-rate dialect proper of peasants but improper of urban, educated and cultured individuals, and given also the de facto hegemony of the Russian language in Ukraine, it is rather disingenuous to focus on the decision of the Ukrainian government to elevate the Ukrainian language to the symbolic status of official state language as an act of reverse discrimination, that supposedly infringes upon the linguistic rights of the Rusophone majority.[26] Social scientific "experts" are basing their characterization of the Ukrainian state as a "nationalizing" one on this language policy.[27]

It is true that the decision touched a raw nerve in Russophone eastern and southern Ukraine and contributed further to the polarization between eastern and western Ukraine that became so evident in the 1994 presidential elections.[28] In almost exact reversal of the results of the first presidential elections, President Kravchuck received 70.8 percent of the votes in Western Ukraine but only 26.3 percent in the East, while the victorious candidate, Russophone Kuchma (who apparently learned Ukrainian for his inauguration speech), received 73.1 percent of the vote in the East but only 24.3 percent in the West. The fact that the Russophone majority was likely to perceive the elevation of Ukrainian to official state language as a threat to its de facto privileged status and that they were likely to mobilize against the decision could have been expected. What is more surprising is the way in which Western social scientific "experts" have focused on these facts to spin a whole literature characterizing the Ukrainian state as a "nationalizing" one. In so doing they are in fact intervening in the Ukrainian debate on linguistic policies on the side of the Russophone majority in defense of the linguistic status quo. They seem to forget that the hegemony of the Russian language in Ukraine is not simply a matter of fact but also a matter of inequity that resulted from the deliberate imperialist policies carried out by the Russian empire and its successor state, the Soviet Union. On this occasion, I do not pretend to be a neutral scientific analyst. I am consciously and intentionally siding with the colonized underdog.

Whether the government decision, which certainly had a high symbolic value but carried few significant material effects, actually infringed upon the legally protected civil or political rights of the Russophone majority is of course a question that the Ukrainian courts can decide. In democratic states, such as Ukraine formally is, linguistic or any other cultural policy issues are usually contested agonically and discursively in the public sphere of civil society and/or through electoral mobilization, lobbying, and parliamentary debates. The Russophone majority in Ukraine certainly has free and equal access to legal, political, and civil processes and institutions plus the advantages in resources that hegemonic privileged majorities usually have. They certainly can and will take care of their own interests. The idea that the Ukrainian state has been hijacked by Galician nationalists is not a very credible one when it is obvious that the leading members of the ruling *nomenklatura*, now better known as "the party of power," are predominantly Russophones. Publicly, in their activities as representatives of the Ukrainian state administration, they may be constrained to speak Ukrainian, but when they are out of the limelight at home, among themselves, and at work in the exercise of their normally secretive administrative functions they revert to Russian.

On this issue Russophone Ukrainians possess also the key resource that can either swing the balance of forces in any of the two centrifugal directions or hold the middle ground and serve as centripetal nation-building force. But they can only fulfill the latter function if they themselves become truly bilingual, that is, if they not only learn the Ukrainian language but also learn to hold it in at least equal esteem to Russian. Ukraine, in any case, is structurally destined to remain for generations to come a bilingual society. The question is whether at least parity and greater symmetry between the Russian and Ukrainian languages can be achieved and whether linguistic diversity is to be accepted not only as a fact but actually as a value. From the historical answer to this two questions will actually depend to some considerable extent the equally open question as to how pluralistic, civilized, and solidaristic Ukrainian civil society is likely to be.

Religious Pluralism in Ukraine

The ideal type of a highly pluralistic, open and free linguistic market is certainly conceivable but the sociological reality principle tells one that it can hardly be practicable. A multicultural society could plausibly have hundreds of languages as the viable means of communication in as many private lifeworlds. But if that society is to be a civil one and if its *polis* is to be a democratic one, it will require that a very reduced number of languages serve as public ones, that is, that they serve the function of open lingua franca that guarantees universal equal access to the public sphere to all the members. Of course, the actual linguistic competencies and even the desire to use them are likely to be distributed unequally and equal access is not likely to produce therefore automatically equal results. But this is a different matter. A modern civil society, in any case, requires the normative principle of free universal access and this in turn sets realistic limits to linguistic pluralism in the public sphere, unless that sphere is to turn into Babel.

The model of a free, and highly pluralistic indeed almost boundless religious market is, by contrast, conceivable and viable. In fact, the American religious market comes close to an actualization of the ideal type. The argument I would like to present in the following section is that of all European societies, Ukraine is the one most likely to approximate the American model. Indeed, Ukraine has already gone through the first incipient stages of religious denominationalism to an extent unusual in Europe. This in my view augurs very well for the success of civil society in Ukraine.

The dual clause of the First Amendment to the Constitution of the United States of America, "free exercise of religion" and "no establishment thereof" serves as the constitutional regulative principle of the American religious market.[29] That America had invented something historically novel was obvious to the group of Catholic priests which in a letter to Rome in 1783 wrote with enthusiastic approval: "in these United States, our Religious system has undergone a revolution, if possible, more extraordinary, than our political one."[30] Yet, it would take

Rome almost two centuries to recognize the legitimacy of the invention, to accept the modern principle of religious freedom and to abandon its ideal of church establishment.

The American constitutional formula challenged the taken-for-granted notion, shared by religionists and secularists alike, that the state or the political community of citizens needed a religion, ecclesiastical or civil, as the base of its normative integration and that, moreover, it was the business of the sovereign to regulate the religious sphere. The First Amendment drew not only a "wall of separation" between church and state, but actually established a principle of differentiation between the political community of citizens and any and all religious communities. Eventually, all religions in America, churches as well as sects, irrespective of their origins, doctrinal claims and ecclesiastical identities, would turn into denominations, formally equal under the constitution and competing in a relatively free, pluralistic, and voluntaristic religious market. As the organizational form and principle of such a religious system, denominationalism constitutes the great American religious invention.

The reason for this felicitous invention, as in so many other social inventions, was a combination of facilitating structural conditions, the peculiar dispositions of a few key actors, and some firmly held normative principles. The particular conjuncture in the American case has been called "the Jeffersonian moment." After independence of the American colonies, the establishment of any particular church at the federal national level was probably precluded by the territorial distribution and the relative equal strength of the three colonial churches at the time of Independence: Congregational, Presbyterian, and Anglican. But either multiple establishment or the establishment of a generalized Christian (i.e., Protestant) religion could have been a likely outcome had it not been for the active coalition of Jefferson, Madison, and dissenting Baptists in Virginia.[31]

The Jeffersonian moment brought together the enlightened republican deism of Jefferson, the democratic principles of Madison which recognize equal rights for error and truth and for minorities as well as majorities, and the radical sectarian antiestablishmentarian principles of Baptists such as John Leland. It is interesting that from very different premises, Thomas Jefferson and John Leland reached almost identical formulations of the dual principles of no establishment and free exercise of religion. From the utilitarian-secularist perspective of somebody who cannot take religion very seriously, Jefferson argued that "it does me no injury for my neighbour to say there are twenty gods, or no god. It neither picks my pocket nor breaks my leg." From the religious-sectarian perspective of somebody used to defending courageously his God-given right to religious freedom and to attacking the evil of the state meddling into sacred affairs best left to the individual conscience, Leland argued that the First Amendment permitted every man to speak freely without fear, maintaining the principles that he believes, and to worship according to his own faith either one god, three gods or no god or twenty gods, and let government protect him in doing so.[32]

One should notice here that as a dissenting Baptist, Leland under-stood very well that one needs a state to protect the freedom of reli-gious minorities against the majority. Indeed, even in the United States it took some considerable time before a free religious market open to all religions could become a reality. A pluralistic denominational mar-ket had to be created first within hegemonic Protestantism before it could be extended to other religions. In fact the Jeffersonian moment was brief and fragile. Soon the established ministry of the New En-gland Standing Order began its nativist attacks against deism, infidel-ity, and foreign revolution, setting the pattern and the tone for the anti-Catholic nativist movements of the nineteenth century.

Nevertheless the brief coalition of republican deism and radical-pi-etist sectarian Protestantism in Virginia was able to create a revolution-ary constitutional reality which, thanks to the progressive sacralization of the Constitution, was able to withstand the wide gap between the *pays constitutionel* and the *pays real*, as well as the repeated Protestant crusades to put God or Christ in the Constitution, to define America as a Christian nation, or to protect Christianity as the common law of the land.[33] In fact, the secularization of the state did not bring in its wake either the decline or the privatization of religion. On the contrary, as it is widely recognized today, the constitutional protection of "free exer-cise" of religion created the structural framework for the emergence and the unprecedented expansion of "the crazy quilt of Protestant de-nominationalism." At a time when continental European Christianity was mostly retreating, unable to withstand the waves of industrial, po-litical, and cultural revolution, American Christianity was "awash in a sea of faith." The Evangelical revivalism that grew out of the Second Great Awakening became the organizational principle and the common denominator of all the religious groups competing in the Protestant denominational religious system. By the 1830s, evangelical Protestant-ism had become established de facto as the American civil religion, that is, as the public religion of American civil society. The homogenization of the main Protestant denominations made possible the launching of a transdenominational evangelical crusade to "Christianize" the people, the social order and the republic.[34]

The democratization of the aristocratic republic and the democratization of Christianity went hand and hand and had simmilar effects upon political and religious culture.[35] Through the public school, the common school and the Sunday school movements, it encompassed the entire public realm of education and religious instruction, and it extended to the mass media and to societies and movements for moral and social reform. Indeed, evangelical societies established the framework for all forms of American voluntary societies and evangelical revivalism became the cradle of American social movements. Tocqueville, who saw very clearly this relation between religious, civil, and political associationism, would observe that "religion in America takes no direct part in the government of society, but it must be regarded as the first of their political institutions."[36]

In Europe, by contrast, we find two different patterns of separation. Some states, notably England and the Scandinavian Lutheran countries, also attained a high level of toleration of sectarian religions but would nevertheless maintain one religion as the established official church. In other countries, France being the paradigmatic model, the disestablishment of religion from the state became an issue of heated political contestation and when it took place it did so usually under secularist premises of suspicion if not open hostility toward religion. Here, the state not only failed to protect the free exercise of religion in society, but actually developed a secularist republican ideology which functioned as a civil religion in competition with ecclesiastical religion.

Everywhere in Europe, moreover, the model has remained either that of one single national church which claims to be coextensive with the nation or that of two (usually Catholic and Protestant) competing but territorially based national churches along with an indefinite number of religious minorities which have assumed the structural position of sects vis-a-vis the officially established church or churches. Eventually, the process of secularization in Europe has entailed not only the constitutional separation of church and state, but also the privatization of religion and the dramatic decline of religious beliefs and practices, particularly among those churches which have maintained some kind of formal or informal quasi-establishment. The particular historical arrangements tend to oscillate between three patterns: that of the formal establishment of the Church of England, that of the formal disestablishment of the Catholic Church in France which maintains, nonetheless, an informal status as the national church, and that of formal constituional separation along with informal multichurch establishment of Germany or corporatist-consociational arrangements such as pillarization in Holland.[37]

It is not necessary to emphasize in this context that a proper resolution of the problem of religious freedom and religious pluralism is crucial for the development of civil society, both in its historical emergence in early modern Europe as much as today. What John A. Hall has called "the drive to politico-religious unification" continues to be today as the experience in Bosnia shows the main obstacle to the institutionalization of civil society. What is important about the situation in Ukraine today is not only that such a drive is very weak, but more importantly that the structural conditions in Ukraine do not permit it to gain more strength.

Incipient Religious Denominationalism in Ukraine

One can observe today in Ukraine the rather striking phenomenon of the emergence of four Eastern rite churches, all competing with one another, all claiming to be the legitimate heir of the Kievan-Rus Church and therefore claiming also to be the legitimate church of the entire Ukrainian territory. These churches are: the Ukrainian Orthodox Church-Moscow Patriarchate (UOC-MP), the Ukrainian Orthodox Church-Kiev Patriarchate (UOC-KP), the Ukrainian Autocephalous Orthodox Church (UAOC), and the Ukrainian Catholic Church.

The first two emerged as the result of a recent schism within the Russian Orthodox Church in Ukraine, as the latter was trying to develop a strategy to counter the legalization and explosive reemergence of the other two churches. The existence of the Ukrainian Greek Catholic or Uniate Church, which is Eastern in rite and spiritual doctrines but accepts Roman canonical and administrative jurisdiction, goes back to the 1596 Union of Brest, when the Ruthenian church of the Ukrainian lands in the Polish-Lithuanian Commonwealth agreed after much Polish political pressure and Jesuit maneuvres to "reunite" itself with Rome. In nineteenth-century Galicia, under Hapsburg rule, there took place the fusion of a revitalized Greek Catholic Church and Galician-Ukrainian nationalism which has remained the fundamental factor in Western Ukrainian politics until today. In 1945, following the incorporation of Galicia into the Soviet Union, the Church ceased legally to exist wheen it was forcibly reunited back into the Russian Orthodox Church. Proscribed and severely persecuted, the Uniate Church maintained its identity both underground as well as latently within the Orthodox Church. The moment glasnost reached Ukraine in the fall of 1989, massive mobilizations for the legalization of the proscribed Ukrainian Catholic or Uniate Church took place throughout Galicia. As the process of legalization promised by the Moscow authorities was too slow in coming, the parishioners took affairs in their own hands and reclaimed forcefully their churches for the Uniate Church.[38]

The Ukrainian Autocephalous Orthodox Church (UAOC) was established in Kiev in 1922, in the aftermath of the Russian Revolution, Civil War, and the failed attempt to establish an independent Ukraine. Because of its populist national (*narodnik*) orientation, and its conciliar, antihierarchical ecclesiastical structure, the Soviets at first supported its growth in order to use it in their struggles against the Russian Orthodox Church. The UAOC was able to gain a significant stronghold in Soviet Ukraine, but it was not able to gain recognition either from the patriarch of Constantinople or other Orthodox churches. In the 1930s the UAOC was liquidated by Stalin along with every manifestation of Ukrainian nationalism. It reemerged briefly during World War II under German occupation, to be suppressed again by the Soviets. It survived in the Ukrainian diaspora in U.S. and Canada, under the leadership of Patriarch Mstyslav, who returned to Kiev in 1992 and reclaimed the title of Patriarch of Kiev and All Rus.[39] A situation of incipient religious denominationalism is emerging which is closer to the American than to the European models. The structural conditions are similar to those in the United States after independence. No particular denomination could possible become the established religion of the new Ukrainian state or, for that matter, the disestablished but quasi-official national religion.

Though only halfheartedly, Rome continues to support the autonomy of the Uniate Church while trying to contain it within its historical territories and simultaneously pursuing an aggressive policy of Roman Catholic expansion in Ukraine and throughout the former Soviet Union. In any case, the stubborn resistance of Ukrainian Catholics and the reemergence of the Ukrainian Autocephalus Orthodox Church have frustrated the various attempts of the Moscow patriarchate to establish an oligopolistic bargain between Rome and Moscow which would have forced Ukrainian believers to choose between Roman Catholicism and Russian Orthodoxy. Moreover, in addition to the revival of Protestant sects and churches with historical roots in Ukraine, countless branches of American evangelical Protestantism are pursuing zealously their own missionary efforts, comfortably ignorant of local language, culture, and religious traditions but eager to bring the Gospel of Jesus Christ to the natives. The reemergence of Jewish and Muslim (Crimean Tatars) religious identities adds complexity and pluralism to the emerging denominational pattern. Furthermore, Ukraine is also emerging as a flourishing center for new religions, exotic cults, and spiritual movements of all kinds, such as Mormons, Roon Virists trying to revive pre-Christian pagan traditions, Hare Krishnas and other Eastern religious movements, or the more bizarre and apocalyptic White Brotherhood which captured the international news in the fall of 1993 when it announced that it would stage in Kiev the crucifixion and resurrection of its messianic leader, Maria Devi Khristos. In sort, Ukraine's independence and the partial institutionalization of religious freedom have created the conditions for the most pluralistic and competitive denominational religious market in all of Eastern Europe.[40]

From the perspective of Christian ecumenism, the Byzantine denominational schisms may be viewed as unfortunate and unfraternal divisions. From the perspective of Ukrainian nationalism, religious pluralism can be viewed as an impediment to the establishment of a single national church which could be used instrumentally in the efforts to build a homogeneous nation under an independent Ukrainian state. Yet the absence of religious unity may turn out to be a blessing in disguise in so far as it may be conducive to the formation of a culturally pluralistic, religiously tolerant, and democratic Ukraine.

Although it goes against the religious and nationalist traditions so ingrained in the region, the wall of separation between church and state and the differentiation of the religious and the political community which it creates, is crucial not only for the well-being of all religions, but also for the establishment of democratic states and for a long-term resolution of ethnic-religious and nationalist conflicts. Churches, at least those which doctrinally are part of transnational religious bodies and maintain universalistic religious claims, may cease viewing themselves as community cults of the nation-state and become voluntary religious communities anchored in civil society rather than in the nation. Such a move would facilitate the organization of democratic states and political society through the individualist principle of citizenship rather than through ascriptive ethnic principles.

The dissociation of the religious and political communities is per se no guarantee that serious interdenominational religious conflicts may not be the order of the day.[41] But once religion is disestablished from the state and differentiated from political society, litigations over ecclesiastical property rights could be resolved in the courts and religious conflicts could be routinized into the normal institutional competition between religious firms competing on a more or less free and open religious market. Although it may take some time before it becomes generalized throughout Europe, it is becoming increasingly clear that the American model of disestablishment and free exercise of religion, voluntary denominationalism and religious pluralism, is, despite its historically "exceptional" character, the one most congruent with the differentiated structures of modernity.

While the benefits of religious pluralism for a democratic political culture may be evident, one should not overlook the fact that the American experience also indicates that denominational competition and a free religious market may also be beneficial to religion. At the time of American independence, as in Ukraine today, a majority of the population in the thirteen colonies were also unchurched. The Christianization of the American people only took place afterwords through recurrent religious revivals and awakenings once the denominational system took hold. Baptists and Methodists, tiny religious minorities at the time of independence, had become by the 1830s following the Second Great Awakening the largest Protestant denominations. Only the Presbyterian Church was able to expand and hold its ground by adopting the principle of voluntaristic religious affiliation and the evangelical and revivalist techniques pioneered by the newcomers. Meanwhile, the Congregational and Episcopal churches were languishing and losing ground dramatically despite their official status in some of the states in which they had been historically based. Thanks to immigration the Catholic Church had become by the late 1840s and would remain thereafter the largest American denomination. Despite Protestant nativist harassment, Catholicism and most other immigrant churches would flourish in the new world while they were languishing in the old European countries despite official state protection.

The lesson for the historical churches in Ukraine should be apparent. If they want to hold their ground and prosper under the new denominational conditions, they will have to accept the modern principle of religious freedom and voluntaristic affiliation and adopt the evangelical pastoral attitude required to survive in a free religious market. Only under such premises can one envision the possibility of a religious revival and the re-Christianization of the Ukrainian people.

Barring the unlikely unification of the various Ukrainian denominations, Catholic and Orthodox, under a single Ukrainian national church, religious denominationalism in Ukraine could also be beneficial to Ukrainian-Russian relations. Despite the frequent calls by Ukrainian nationalist elites to this effect, the emergence of a single Ukrainian national church confronting the imperial claims of the Moscow patriarchate in Ukraine could only serve to exacerbate Ukrainian-Russian conflicts and to jeopardize not only democratic politics in Ukraine but even the national independence which those elites are pursuing with such exclusive obstinacy. The pitiful clashes over the proper burial of Patriarch Wolodymyr in August 1995 and the attempt to involve the Ukrainian state in a conflict with the Moscow patriarchate over the rights of inheritance of religious shrines in Ukraine could serve as illustration.

Obviously, the process of decolonization taking place in Ukraine carries with it the difficult task of finding negotiated solutions to the problems of allocating equitably all kinds of contested resources, military, financial and ecclesiastical. But the challenge of allocating the ecclesiastical resources of Ukraine among the various denominations should not be in principle more intractable than the problem of allocating the resources of the Black Sea Fleet between the Ukrainian and Russian navies. As desirable as it may seem from a Ukrainian national perspective, it may be unrealistic to expect that the Orthodox Church-Moscow patriarchate in Ukraine will cut its institutional links with its mother church in Moscow, as the Episcopal Church in America did with its mother Anglican Church after independence. After all, the Ukrainian faithful who want to maintain their allegiance to the Moscow patriarchate should have the same religious rights, no more or less, than any other religious group in Ukraine. But one should expect and demand that the Moscow patriarchate accepts the principles of a free religious market in Ukraine.

As in so many other issues, the solution to religious conflicts in Ukraine will depend as much from developments in Moscow, particularly from the direction taken by the complex relations between the Russian state, Russian nationalism, and the Russian Orthodox Church, as from developments in Ukraine itself. Ultimately, the more the Russian Orthodox Church accepts the modern principle of religious freedom and learns to free itself from its historical caesaro-papist dependence and to become a free autonomous institution of civil society, the greater the chances that the incipient religious denominationalism in Ukraine may become institutionalized.[42] If Russian nationalism learns to come to terms with the "loss" of Ukraine, if Rome and Moscow refrain from their tendency to view Ukraine as a battleground for their millenary religious conflict, if the calls for national religious unity uttered by political elites continue to fall on deaf ears, then there is a real chance for the emergence of a democratic Ukraine where the principles of religious affiliation, ethnic-national identity, and political citizenship would be clearly differentiated.

Perhaps, instead of viewing the denominational conflicts as ominous signs of the kind of future civilizational clashes which, according to Samuel Huntington and other political observers, are bound to replace the international conflicts of the age of nation-states and of the Cold War era, one may also view them as positive signs, indeed as harbingers of a general European process of open religious pluralism and genuinely voluntary religious denominationalism which could contribute to more open and pluralistic cultural and political structures by dissociating the religious communities from their traditional associations with states and nations. To become a reality, however, this second vision requires that the new Ukrainian constitution establishes a wall of separation between church and state, while legally also protecting the free exercise of all religions.

Notes

1. Cf. the discussions by Hall and Seligman in this volume.
2. Samuel Huntington, *The Third Wave: Democratization in the Late Twentieth Century* (Norman: University of Oklahoma Press, 1991).
3. Cf., "Ukraine: The Birth and Possible Death of a Country," *The Economist*, May 7, 1994; and Eugene B. Rumer, "Will Ukraine Return to Russia?," *Foreign Policy* 96 (Fall 1994):129–144.
4. For pessimistic views of the viability of the double or "triple" transition see, Adam Przeworski,*Democracy and the Market: Political and Economic Reforms in Eastern Europe and Latin America* (New York: Cambridge University Press, 1991); and Claus Offe, "Capitalism by Democratic Design? Democratic Theory Facing the Triple Transition in East Central Europe," *Social Research* 58: 4 (Winter 1991), p. 872. I have countered these views in José Casanova, "Las enseñanzas de la transición democrática en España," *Ayer*, no. 15 (1994).
5. See, Alexander J. Motyl, "Structural Constraints and Starting Points: Postimperial States and Nations in Ukraine and Russia," p. 5. Paper presented at the conference on "Post-Communism and Ethnic Mobilization," Cornell University, April 21–23, 1995; and *Dilemmas of Independence: Ukraine after Totalitarianism* (New York: Council on Foreign Relations, 1993).
6. Cf., Taras Kuzio and Andrew Wilson, *Ukraine: Perestroika to Independence* (New York: St. Martin's Press, 1994); and Bohdan Krawchenko, "Ukraine: The Politics of Independence," in Ian Bremmer and Ray Taras, eds., *Nation and*

Politics in the Soviet Successor States (Cambridge: Cambridge University Press, 1993), pp. 75–98.

7. Mykola Ryabchuk, "Civil Society and National Emancipation: The Ukrainian Case," in Zbigniew Rau, eds., *The Remergence of Civil Society in Eastern Europe and the Soviet Union* (Boulder, Colo.: Westview Press, 1991).

8. Cf. John B. Dunlop, *The Rise of Russia and the Fall of the Soviet Empire* (Princeton, N.J.: Princeton University Press, 1993), and Gail W. Lapidus, Victor Zaslavsky, and Philip Goldman, eds., *From Union to Commonwealth: Nationalism and Separatism in the Soviet Republics* (Cambridge: Cambridge University Press, 1992).

9. The need to solve first the fundamental political problems of the trnasition before issues of economic reform can be tackled succesfully has been argued persuasively by Juan Linz. See Juan Linz and Alfred Stepan, "Political Crafting of Democratic Consolidation or Destruction: European and South American Comparisons," in Robert A. Pastor, ed., *Democracy in the Americas: Stopping the Pendulum* (New York: Holmes & Meier, 1989), pp. 41–61.

10. Motyl, "Structural Constrainsts and Starting Points," p. 10.

11. Iryna Bekeshkina, "Hromadska Dumka Kyian: Hryden 1994, Sichen 1995," *Politychnyi Portret Ukraiine* 11, 1995, pp. 18–20; as well as the periodical bulletins, *Politychnyi Portret Ukraiine*, nos. 1–13, of the Democratic Initiatives Polling Network.

12. Roman Szporluk, "Reflections on Ukraine After 1994: The Dilemmas of Nationhood," *The Harriman Review* 7: 7–9 (March-May 1994), p. 1.

13. Ryabchuk, "Civil Society and National Emancipation," p. 112.

14. Papers presented in a session on "Russian Jews,"at the ASR Meeting in Washington, August 19, 1995.

15. Oksana Khomchuk, "The Far Right in Russia and Ukraine," *The Harriman Review* (July 1995): 40–44.

16. Cf., Evhen I. Golovakha and Nataliya V. Panina, "The Development of a Democratic Political Identity in Contemporary Ukrainian Political Culture," in Russell F. Farnen, ed., *Nationalism, Ethnicity, and Identity: Cross National and Comparative Perspectives* (New Brunswick, N.J.: Transaction Publishers, 1994), pp. 403–25; and *A Political Portrait of Ukraine: The Results of Four Polls Conducted during the 1994 Election Campaign in Ukraine* (Kiev: Democratic Initiatives Research and Educational Center, 1994).

17. It was this question, whether the Ukrainian state or some of its policies can be characterized as "nationalizing" in the sense of the term first used by Rogers Brubaker, that provoked the most lively debates in the Conference on "Peoples, Nations, Identities: the Russian-Ukrainian Encounter," at the Harriman Institute, Columbia University, 21–23 September 1995. For a discussion of the concept see, Rogers Brubaker, "National Minorities, Nationalizing States, and External National Homelands in the New Europe," *Daedalus* 124: 2 (Spring 1995): 107–32. On its applicabitly to Ukraine see Dominique Arel, "Ukraine: The Temptation of the Nationalizing State," in Vladimir Tismaneanu, ed., *Political Culture and Civil Society in the Former Soviet Union* (Armonk, N.Y.: Sharpe, 1995), and the papers presented at the above mentioned conference: Andrew Wilson, "Ukraine as a Nationalising State. Will the 'Russians' Rebel"; and Ian Bremmer, "How Russians the Russians? New Minorities in the Post-Soviet Regions."

18. Juan J. Linz, "Plurinazionalismo e Democrazia," *Revista Italiana di Scienza Politica* 25: 1 (April 1995): 21–50.

19. For an analytical differentiation of these processes see, Juan J. Linz,

"Staatsbildung, Nationbildung und Demokratie," *Transit*, Heft 7 (Frühjahr 1994), pp. 43–62.

20. That the simple and not uncommon fact of mixed marriages brings complexity into the neat scheme should be obvious. That individuals and groups can change their ethnic identity either voluntarily or involuntarily is the most elementary fact of Ukrainian history. That ethnic identities do not need to be exclusionary and that individuals and groups might have simultaneously or sequentially multiethnic identities, is also obvious. In any case, that ethnicity is not a matter of nature, birth, or blood but rather a matter of culture, nurture, and soul should be perfectly clear, despite the many disastrous attemps of modern nationalist ideologies to hide the fact.

21. Volodymyr Evtoukh, "Ethnische Minderheiten der Ukraine: Zwischen Realitaeten und Politik," paper presented at the Harriman Institute Conference, "Peoples, Nations, Identities."

22. Yuri I. Shevchuk, "Dual Citizenship in Old and New States," unpublished manuscript (New York: Political Science Department, New School for Social Research).

23. Valery Khmelko and Dominique Arel, "Russian Factor and Territorial Polarization in Ukraine," p. 7. Paper presented at the Conference on "Peoples, Nations, Identities: the Russian-Ukrainian Encounter," at the Harriman Institute, Columbia University, 21–23 September 1995.

24. On the difference between a plural and a pluralistic society see, Linz, "Plurinazionalismo e democrazia."

25. On Russian-Ukrainian relations see Roman Solchanyk, "Russia, Ukraine, and the Imperial Legacy," *Post-Soviet Affairs*, 9: 4 (October-December 1993): 337–65; John-Paul Himka, "Ukrainians, Russians, and Alexander Solzhenitsyn," *Cross Currents: A Yearbook of Central European Culture*, 11 (1992): 193–205; and John Morrison, "Pereslayav and After: The Russian-Ukrainian Relationship," *International Affairs*, 69: 4 (1993): 677–703.

26. Roman Solchanyk, "The Politics of Language in Ukraine," *RFE\RL Research Report* 2: 5 (5 March, 1993): 1–4.

27. See for instance Andrew Wilson's paper, "Ukraine as a Nationalising State," which recognizes from the outset that Ukraine grants universal and equal citizenship and voting rights to all its residents, that it has liberal laws on association and party formation which allow a level playing field for groups of any nationality, and can find no evidence for incidents of national or ethnic discrimination, yet still argues that "the model of the 'nationalising state' is a plausible description of contemporary Ukrainian politics." The author explains that, "in the Ukrainian context a nationalising state is one which promotes Ukrainisation policies, particularly in the spheres of language use (education, state bureaucracy) and state semiotics." (p. 1). One should add here that the status of official state language remains mainly symbolic and that there is very little evidence of Ukrainianization of education or state bureucracy. The author points out that several politicians in the city of Donetsk expressed hostility to the opening of the one and only Ukrainian-language secondary school in the city, even though there is a sizable Ukrainophone minority there (20 percent). The similar in size Russophone minority in the nationalist city of Lviv has a greater choice of Russian language schools.

28. David P. Marples, "Ukraine after the Presidential Election," *RFE\RL Research Report* 3: 26 (12 August 1994): 7–10.

29. For a more detailed and systematic elaboration of these issues see José Casanova, *Public Religions in the Modern World* (Chicago: University of Chicago Press, 1994).

30. In James Hennesey, S.J. *American Catholics: A History of the Roman Catholic Community in the United States* (New York: Oxford University Press, 1981), p. 68.

31. On the "Jeffersonian moment" see, Henry F. May, "The Jeffersonian Moment," in *The Divided Heart: Essays on Protestantism and the Enlightenment in America* (New York: Oxford University Press, 1991), pp. 27–97, and *The Enlightenment in America* (New York: Oxford University Press, 1976). On the disestablishment of religion in America cf., Thomas J. Curry, *The First Freedoms: Church and State in America to the Passage of the First Amendment* (New York: Oxford University Press, 1986); William Lee Miller, *The First Liberty: Religion and the American Republic* (New York: Alfred A. Knopf, 1985); and Leonard Levy, *The Establishment Clause: Religion and the First Amendment* (New York: Macmillan, 1986).

32. Both quotations in Martin E. Marty, *The Righteous Empire: The Protestant Experience in America* (New York: Dial Press, 1970) pp. 42–43.

33. Some New England states maintained their established Congregational churches for several decades and, despite Article 6, Section 3 of the Constitution, most state constitutions maintained for even longer periods of time clauses disqualifying non-Protestants, non-Christians or atheists from public office. On the protracted struggle to approximate reality to constitutional principles see, Morton Borden, *Jews, Turks, and Infidels* (Chapel Hill: The University of North Carolina Press, 1984).

34. Among the immense literature on this issue cf., Sidney E. Ahlstrom, *A Religious History of the American People* (New Haven, Conn.: Yale University Press, 1972); Sidney Mead, *The Lively Experiment: The Shaping of Christianity in America* (New York: Harper and Row, 1963); Winthrop S. Hudson, *The Great Tradition of the American Churches* (New York: Harper, 1953); Jon Butler, *Awash in a Sea of Faith: Christianizing the American People* (Cambridge: Harvard University Press, 1990); Robert T. Handy, *A Christian America: Protestant Hopes and Historical Realities*, second edition (New York: Oxford University Press, 1984); Martin E. Marty, *The Righteous Empire: The Protestant Experience in America* (New York: The Dial Press, 1970); and Charles I. Foster, *An Errand of Mercy: The Evangelical United Front, 1790–1837* (Chapel Hill: University of North Carolina Press, 1960).

35. Cf. Nathan O. Hatch, *The Democratization of American Christianity* (New Haven, Conn.: Yale University Press, 1989); and Joseph Forcinelli, *The Democratization of Religion in America* (Lewiston, N.Y.: Edwin Mellen Press, 1990).

36. Alexis de Tocqueville, *Democracy in America* (New York: Vintage, 1990), vol. 1, p. 305.

37. The most comprehensive comparative-historical analysis of processes of secularization in Europe is to be found in David Martin, *A General Theory of Secularization* (New York: Harper & Row, 1978).

38. On the Uniate Church and its relation to Ukrainian nationalism from the Union of Brest to the present cf. Oscar Halecky, *From Florence to Brest, 1439–1596* (Rome: Sacrum Poloniac Millennium, 1959); John-Paul Himka, "The Greek Catholic Church and Nation-Building in Galicia, 1772–1918," *Harvard Ukrainian Studies* 8:3–4 (December 1984), pp.426–52; Paul R. Magocsi, ed., *Morality and Religion: The Life and Times of Andrei Sheptyts'kyi* (Edmonton: Canadian Institute of Ukrainian Studies, 1989); Vasyl Markus, "Religion and Nationality: The Uniates of the Ukraine," in Bohdan Bociurkiw and John Strong, eds., *Religion and Atheism in the U.S.S.R. and Eastern Europe* (London: Macmillan, 1975), pp.101–22, and "Religion and Nationalism in Ukraine," in Pedro Ramet, ed., *Religion and Nationalism in Soviet and East European Poli-*

tics (Durham, N.C.: Duke University Press, 1984), pp. 172–89; M. Labunka and L. Rudnytzky, eds., *The Ukrainian Catholic Church 1945–1975* Philadelphia, Pa.: St. Sophia Religious Association, 1976); and Bohdan Bociurkiw, "The Ukrainian Catholic Church in the USSR Under Gorbachev," *Problems of Communism* 39:6 (November-December 1990): 1–19, and "The Ukrainian Greek Catholic Church in the Contemporary USSR," in *Nationalities Papers* (Special Issue on Religious Consciousness in the Glasnost Era) 20:1 (Spring 1992): 16–28.

39. On the Ukrainian Orthodox Church, see Ivan Wlasovsky, *Outline History of the Ukrainian Orthodox Church*, 2 vols. (New York: Ukrainian Orthodox Church of USA, 1974–1979); Bohdan Bociurkiw, "The Ukrainian Autocephalous Orthodox Church, 1920–1930: A Case Study in Religious Modernization," in Dennis Dunn, ed., *Religion and Modernization in the Soviet Union* (Boulder, Colo.: Westview Press, 1977), pp. 310–47, and *Ukrainian Churches under Soviet Rule: Two Case Studies* (Cambridge, Mass.: Harvard Ukrainian Studies Fund, 1984).

40. Jaroslav Martyniuk, "Religious Preferences in Five Urban Areas of Ukraine," *RFE/RL Research Report* 2: 15 (9 April 1993), pp. 17–28; and "The State of the Orthodox Church in Ukraine," *RFE/RL Research Report,* vol.3, no.7, 18 February, 1994, pp. 34–41.

41. David Little, *Ukraine: The Legacy of Intolerence* (Washington, D.C.: United States Institute of Peace Press, 1991).

42. Cf., Geoffrey A. Hosking, ed., *Church, Nation and State in Russia and Ukraine* (New York: St. Martin's Press, 1991); and C. Niels, Jr., ed., *Christianity After Communism: Social, Political and Cultural Struggle in Russia* (Boulder, Colo.: Westview Press, 1994).

9

Horizontal Ties and Civil Institutions in Chinese Societies

Robert P. Weller

The events of 1989 in China and Eastern Europe caused a minor stampede of Western China scholars looking to identify the "sprouts" of civil society in Chinese tradition, or to blame the failure of the student movement on the lack of such traditions.[1] Far less attention was devoted to the end of martial law and the beginning of genuine two-party political competition in Taiwan at about the same time. I will relate both processes here, especially as they bear on developing market economies, on contact with Western ideas, and on earlier Chinese cultural resources that affect ideas about civil society.

Much of our understanding of civil society—where horizontal civil institutions offer a vital arena that both respects and mediates between the conflicting realms of state and individual—draws on specifically European philosophical and historical roots.[2] We can hardly expect to find the same formulations elsewhere before extensive contact with Europeans, and I will argue that the concept of "civil society" is not very useful for China before the twentieth century. Yet there certainly were broad-based horizontal institutions, and it makes sense to ask what implications they held for the new conditions of the present.

The literature on China has already split on this issue, with one faction arguing that a Habermasian public sphere existed (even if it was not quite a civil society), and the other seeing the Chinese stuck with a hopelessly authoritarian political culture. While I take these cultural roots very seriously, it is worth remembering that culture is not immobile. It lives in a dialogue with social life, through which it is both reproduced and transformed. Whatever one concludes about the cultural potentials for civil society in late imperial China, it will be important to take a close look at the enormous transformations of the last century.

Especially in the twentieth century, we have to face two further broad influences on the possibilities of civil association. One is direct influence from the West through contacts that include colonialism, the education system, foreign aid, and the acceptance of foreign institutions from churches to the Rotary Club and Greenpeace. The other is the influence of ecnomic change toward increasingly market-based systems, whose ties to the development of civil society in the West are historically clear.[3]

Until fairly recently, various lines of general theory about capitalism and culture led us to expect a global cultural homogenization accompanying economic development. The modernization theory that thrived in the 1960s, for example, tried to generalize Weber's argument about the Protestant ethic to all societies, looking for the creation of a functional equivalent to the rationalizing work ethic as a precondition for capitalist development, and for the simultaneous development of civil institutions and ideas. Thus, in a spectacularly unsuccessful prediction, many expected Chinese East Asia to be a developmental disappointment. The "enchanted garden" of Chinese religion was thought to discourage ascetic secular rationalization, while family-centered particularism impeded effective economic decisions and broader ties of trust.[4] Culture, in these views, was monolithic and powerful. If countries were to develop successfully, however, all would eventually have to recreate similar fundamental features—a single culture of capitalism that was secular, rationalizing, and civil. No one can any longer argue that Chinese culture has prevented economic development, but many still argue about whether it may prevent the creation of civil society.

One line of modernization theory expected each country, eventually, to follow the English path of development, or at least to play variations on a common theme.[5] By the 1970s, however, critics began to point out that developing countries in the twentieth century faced a fundamentally different world than had Europe in earlier times. Dependency and world systems theory argued that the economic integration of the world in the sixteenth century created a single global division of labor.[6] New relations between the core and periphery fundamentally altered developmental chances in the third world. There was, in essence, only a single case of capitalism after that, and one could not argue for the independent recapitulation of European change in culture or economy.

While these ideas in general have also been empirically weak as explanations of East and Southeast Asian development, they carry important implications for the problem of global culture. World systems theorists in general gave short shrift to the idea of culture, but the approach did make clear that indigenous cultural responses to economic change could not possibly recreate European experience. The real-world cultural system of the twentieth century has established very powerful cultural pressures from the West that simply did not exist as the West itself was developing.[7]

These approaches differ from each other quite fundamentally, but both lead us to expect the world to develop a shared ideological core, including the implication that Western civil society will have to arise in every successful case of development. This could stem independently from the shared pressures of successful modernization, or from a hegemony growing out of the structural dominance of the core.[8] Neither approach, however, initially took seriously the inherent tensions in culture, its potentials for change or the resulting possibilities in other cultural adaptations to markets.

Culture was musclebound for many modernization theorists, propping up societies to the point where they can no longer bend and change.[9] Local interpretations were too often sacrificed to the search for functional equivalents to the Protestant ethic, or whole societies were written off as being in the thrall of an all-encompassing "traditional" culture. World systems discussions have instead often made culture irrelevant. The expansion of capitalism has appeared as an unstoppable force, driven by the structure of the system itself, and swallowing everything in its way. Wallerstein has recently expanded this analysis to culture, arguing that a contradictory but mutually necessary pair of ideas—racism/sexism and universalism—spreads along with the system and helps to paper over its inherent contradictions.[10] Typically for this kind of analysis, however, culture appears as both just a functionalist prop for the economic system and a reflex of the core toward which the periphery has no significant input. This essay thus attempts to build on earlier theories—looking at internal market dynamics and external cultural and political pressures—but within the context of an adaptable, varying, relatively disorganized culture, a culture as it is really lived.

Social Capital in the Late Qing Dynasty

The China field currently hosts a lively debate on whether China had a growing public sphere during the Ming and Qing dynasties. William Rowe, for example, points to the founding of public charitable institutions run by the local elite (including granaries and religious welfare organizations), the emergence of popular print media, the growth of a merchant class, and popularizing texts on "etiquette" (*li*).[11] Mary Rankin similarly points to weakening ties between local elites and the state, especially in the nineteenth century.[12] Both authors speak of a growing public sphere, although both also back away from the term "civil society." On the other hand, Frederic Wakeman has offered a very different interpretation of the same material.[13] He emphasizes how local elites consistently sought state sponsorship for their activities, and often were state bureaucrats (or would-be bureaucrats) themselves. He also challenges the idea that merchants, even in the nineteenth century, had much independence from the local political system.

I am no expert in this period, but tend to agree with the Wakeman position primarily because late imperial China did not conceive of state/society relations in ways that left much room for a civil society, or even a public sphere. Perhaps it would be better to say that they did not conceive of state/society relations at all, or certainly not in those terms. The neo-Confucian ideology that had dominated for most of a millennium left no room to distinguish state from society, except in the way that fathers can be distinguished from sons. Those fundamental Confucian relationships were the model of family and politics both at once. Ruler or father or local elite led (in principle) by upright example, by maintaining proper relations of hierarchy, and by careful attention to ritual/ceremony/etiquette (*li*).

The Board of Rites (Li Bu) was thus one of the major administrative departments under the Emperor, responsible for administering the civil service exams (which tested knowledge of li as proper behavior, an understanding of the forms of social life that would allow humanity to thrive), for receiving tribute from foreign lands, and for guaranteeing the execution of the annual cycle of imperial and official rituals, without which the world would lose its proper ordering.[14] There is no inherent conflict between state and society as entities with different interests here, but instead a harmonious reverberation of microcosm and macrocosm, between the hierarchies of mutual responsibility from within the family to the Emperor himself, and within the systems of ritual behavior that emanated from the Emperor down to the householder through widely publicized neo-Confucian ritual texts.[15] Local elites, even when they acted on their own, would have had great difficulty thinking of themselves as anything other than an aspect of this overarching sociopolitical unity.

This quick discussion runs grave risks of brushing over the very real and lively internal arguments about the proper nature of Chinese statecraft that also characterized this period. Yet the differences from the West in the conception of the state itself seem clear throughout. There was no plausible translation of "civil society" into Chinese in the nineteenth century. Li is clearly very different, as I have discussed. *Gong* (public) was important in political discourse (as Rankin discusses), but also often served to point up the contrast with *si* (private), a word usually used to condemn personalistic interests that ran counter to the state-society. *Gong* thus need not imply any public apart from the state, although it could refer to privately funded granaries for emergency relief, and other such institutions. Yet these represent local elites acting in consort with the state/society, and do not promote elite interests to (or against) the state.

Another possibility that later becomes important is *wen*, which literally means writing. It is used, for instance, in the terms *wenming* (civilized, literally lettered and bright), *wenhua* (culture or to enculturate), and *wenya* (elegant). *Wen* also refers to civil authorities, as opposed to the military (*wu*). China expressed its own self-image through such terms, seeing culture or civilization defined in part as Chinese literacy, and thus as a clear marker between classes of people and between China and other nations. The various combinations of *wen* thus overlap with various uses of civil-based words (civilized, civil authority, civility, civilian) in English, but the ties to literacy, class and specifically Chinese identity leave it rather different from "civil society."

Even today, Chinese has no clear term to translate the Western idea of civil society. Instead it hosts an argument of awkward neologisms including *wenming shehui* (civilized society), *gongmin shehui* (society of citizens), *shimin shehui* (bourgeois, in the sense of urban, society), or *minjian shehui* (popular society). None of them easily capture the connotations of the English term, and for good reason—"civil society" was until very recently a very exotic concept for nearly all Chinese.

None of this, however, implies that China lacked the kinds of social capital that form the armature of Western civil society, particularly networks of horizontal ties that extended beyond the immediate family but were not themselves political. In fact, China had many kinds of such resources, in spite of the lack of a *political* culture of civil society. The elite united locally around philanthropic institutions like relief granaries or temples.[16] They also got together to enjoy their gardens or to discuss their book collections.[17] Their wives often went together on pilgrimages to distant sacred sites; these were organized through standing "temple committees" of various sorts.[18]

Local and sometimes national communities could also be invoked through all kinds of *tong* ("same") ties—*tong xiang* (same native place), *tong xue* (same study, usually having had the same teacher or having passed the exams in the same year), *tong xing* (same surname, usually with no traceable kinship), and so on. These ties helped people find trustworthy partners all across China. Sojourners in late imperial cities frequently organized by common native place and common surname, a practice later repeated by migrants moving to new lands beyond China. These ties continue to be important today, with the growth of surname associations in cities, or the flourishing of classmate ties to create business connections.

Confucianism itself helped justify such horizontal ties. Society for Confucius grew out of five crucial kinds of ties, each with an appropriate attitude: affection between father and son, righteousness between ruler and minister, attention to appropriate roles between husband and wife, proper hierarchy between older and younger, and faithfulness between friends. Friendship (*you*) is the only nonhierarchical tie in the set. Quick summaries of Confucianism (both pro and con) tend to emphasize only the hierarchy (although all involve reciprocity), but Confucius himself clearly left room for horizontal ties in this most basic of his teachings, known to anyone in China with even the barest knowledge of Confucian philosophy.

Other kinds of ties united people at more local levels. Religion and ritual in particular brought people together to worship community gods, appease wandering ghosts, celebrate marriages and mourn deaths. This kind of religion was based in temples without priests; community committees ran them. Although local elites in fact controlled most of these committees, membership was decided by divination, and thus theoretically open to all men. Large rituals would explicitly mark out local territory by parading the god over his area, and small ones like funerals did the same by marching through village streets. The actual community functions of these temples showed most clearly when they took on political functions—temples were among the focal organizers of resistance to the Japanese takeover of Taiwan in 1895, for example. Religion also provided the language of sworn brotherhood that formalized friendship ties; sworn brotherhoods usually occurred under the auspices of a deity.

Religious ties were mostly strictly local, however, with the partial exception of Buddhism. Neither community temples nor local religious experts tied into broader levels of hierarchy.[19] Lineages similarly could be major actors at the local level, but rarely achieved a broader stage unless they had produced an extraordinary number of degree holders. Like religious institutions, lineages varied widely across China. They existed everywhere, but only sometimes grew large and numerically powerful. Where they did, they formed a kind of tie that went far beyond family, uniting thousands of people, even though it remained rooted in kinship.

Rotating credit associations were (and are) another common tie that could cut across local divisions of family and lineage. These were small groups of men or women who made monthly contributions to a common pot, generally taken by the highest bidder each month. Much as in other parts of the world where they are equally common, such organizations in essence provide loans at interest for people who have no other sources of credit beyond usurious moneylenders. More important for our purposes, they provide a kind of map of networks of community trust. Such associations always left open the possibility that someone would take the money and leave town without making the rest of their payments. Rotating credit associations could not function without high levels of horizontal trust.

Finally, it is worth recalling the informal ties that often united village wives, few of whom were village natives. As Margery Wolf has documented, these women often interacted daily in places like the part of the creek where they washed their clothes.[20] They also got together more formally at occasions like weddings. Such groups tend to remain almost invisible in the background, but could effectively apply public pressure (through their husbands) and were sometimes actively mobilized (as on occasion during the Revolution).

While this set of community ties was strictly local, its principles could easily be extended to new and wider arenas. Emigrant and sojourner communities, for instance, quickly widened the net of lineage into common surname associations. Religion burst its local bounds in China's long tradition of secret societies and closely related popularizing Buddhist sects. Many of these organizations (based on master/disciple relations in some cases, and sworn brotherhoods in others) travelled up and down China's communication routes with the rivermen (and later railroad workers) who plied them. Such groups contained an inherent potential to rebel against the state (like the White Lotus rebellion), or to evolve into gangster organizations (as in the tongs and Triads infamous in Chinese emigrant communities). Yet they were primarily voluntary pietistic associations, membership in which implied that same kinds of trust that Weber attributed to Protestant sect membership.[21]

It would thus be an error to dismiss these things as hopelessly particularistic. This was the mistake, after all, of the literature that saw little hope for economic development in Chinese societies because of the overwhelming strength of family and local loyalties. It is being repeated in some of the claims about the impossibility of civil society in Chinese nations. While this range of ties certainly did not constitute a civil society of people united in their interests as citizens, neither was it just a collection of isolated and self-serving families, united only through ties of patron and client. Various forms of extra-familial trust existed in Chinese society, and have remained as an undeveloped possibility through all kinds of regimes.

Authoritarian Control

The last dynasty fell in 1911, and brought an era of political disorder interspersed with the modernist authoritarian rule of Chiang Kai-shek. There was nothing civil about this society, in spite of a few trappings of democracy. The Nationalist (KMT) regime had been powerfully (if tacitly) influenced by Leninist political and military organization ever since the first United Front with the Communists, although Chiang later also used Nazi military models. The regime is generally recognized as having been largely corrupt, brutal, and ineffective. Voices outside the central authorities were channeled through corporatist institutions at best, and crushed at worst. The warlords who ruled where Chiang did not were still worse.

Nevertheless, "civility" and "civilization" played important roles in various ideological campaigns for authoritarian order under Chiang and the KMT, and would be revived later under the communists. This peaked under Chiang in the 1930s, with the New Life Movement, a broad campaign for personal hygiene and polite behavior. The goals sound trivial, but the stakes were high. The campaign certainly drew in part on Western ideas of civility and citizenship—harnessing the image of a "civil" society to a not-so-civil state. It also harked back to Confucian values, including *li*, interpreted in the most authoritarian sense as externally exposed discipline. The goal, ultimately, was an extended state control by letting the state dominate the micro-practices of daily life.[22] The campaign intended to remake identity in ways that would be both modern and malleable to the will of the government.

Civility here becomes a kind of ethical cage, serving to promote obedience and stifle any antagonism toward the regime.[23] Talk of civility, at least, offers little progress toward a civil society, and may promote just the contrary. The campaign was generally unsuccessful, in part because the KMT had little ability to carry out most of its mass campaigns, but also in part because an uncivil state is in a weak position to promote civility.

Campaigns in the People's Republic of China during the 1980s and 1990s have been disconcertingly similar. The key term in these modern campaigns has been *wenming shehui*, civilized society. The rubric has included campaigns to line up, to stop spitting, and to say "thank you." The general tone is of a patronizing father lecturing an ill-mannered child. Anagnost discusses in detail how this constitutes a state attempt to expand control over the smallest details of life, even as government planners lose control over larger areas of the economy.[24] As in the New Life campaign, this is done in the name of both (socialist) modernity and Chinese tradition, in contrast to the corruption of the capitalist West.

The revival of Cultural Revolution socialist heroes like Lei Feng in the last few years is another example of the attempt to create a socialist citizen, or perhaps to read everyone as parts of the single totalitarian body.[25] Lei Feng was a young soldier who kept a detailed diary of his love for Chairman Mao, and of the many good and generous deeds he performed as a result. He achieved socialist beatification after his accidental death, and was heavily promoted as a role model, especially to young students. He embodies a particular image of the "selfless self," living (and dying) for the greater good of the nation alone. As with the earlier New Life campaign, successes have been difficult to identify.

Taiwan for a long time continued the tradition of the New Life campaign (and New Life Rd. is a major Taipei thoroughfare). When I first lived there in the 1970s, the police frequently picked up young men to give them involuntary haircuts, dancing parties were illegal, and there were still more campaigns to line up for busses and not to spit. Singapore's infamous ban on chewing gum fits right in. Like the others, these campaigns promote a patronizing civility, hoping to mold an internal loyalty to the state by enforcing the outward behaviors of a polite child. The most significant difference in Singapore is that its microscopic scale has allowed it some success in these campaigns; the streets really are clean in Singapore. All three of these cases make a dual argument for modernity and Chinese tradition (increasingly seen as Confucian even in the People's Republic). In each case "civility" has been borrowed to promote a docile populace and not to guarantee an independent one, to enhance the scope of the state and not to support a distinct civil society.

None of these projects fully succeeded, and none are likely to. I have argued elsewhere that authoritarian (and particularly socialist) control can never fully control meaning for people, in part because the attempt to control social life itself creates ties beyond control.[26] I do not have space to reproduce my earlier argument, but the inevitable existence of a second economy is one example, and so is the necessity for personal connections in such societies. Every move to control the image of the body through politeness campaigns or through extolling the selfless self via Lei Feng is met with a disorganized alternative, like the qigong exercise craze, which delineates a very different bodily and moral universe. The kinds of horizontal connections that permeated late imperial society continue unabated, if somewhat transformed. Families and sometimes lineages remain strong in all these regimes, but so do surname ties, classmate ties, place of origin ties, and religious ties. In some ways, both market and socialist economies have promoted horizontal ties—they are crucial for raising capital in Taiwan, for finding overseas partners and markets in Singapore, and for all those things plus manipulating the remaining socialist system on the mainland.

Authoritarian control has thus never been fully successful. Such regimes can, however, be powerfully effective in preventing any large-scale civil organizations from forming. Thus the Chinese crushed all signs of incipient independent labor unions after 4 June 1989, even though labor had played only a marginal role. The leadership was struck by the events in Poland just as much as Western scholars of civil society were, and had no intention of allowing any Chinese Solidarity to develop. Mass organizations exist in great numbers, of course, but only when organized through the state and under the control of the Communist Party. No other nonstate organizations are allowed to reach a large scale.

Yet the economic reforms of the last fifteen years, by necessity, are creating new forms of formal and informal associations, from chambers of commerce to restaurants like Beijing's Heping Fandian, which tries to cater only to big businessmen.[27] The need to raise capital, find markets, identify business partners and enforce contracts is fostering a new range of nonstate ties. As the government has gradually let go of the economy, it has also allowed much more room for private activity. Dissent is still not tolerated, but nonpolitical organizations are beginning to thrive for the first time in decades. The general loosening of control, for example, has opened the door for an enormous religious revival/re-creation, especially in rural areas. The number of community temples has expanded enormously in the last decade, with every village building new temples in parts of China.

Do these gaps in control or these new kinds of organization constitute incipient civil society? The answer is largely that they do not, at least not now. The main reason for this is that much of the new business organization remains tightly linked to the state. It is simply impossible to do business on a large scale in China without intimate ties to officials. Indeed state units run their own businesses to make money (schools run factories instead of sponsoring bake sales; the army was running nightclubs), officials often moonlight in business, and many businessmen are ex-officials. In the absence of a full market economy, the state still controls key resources and contracts; and in the absence of an independent legal system, connections (to the state, to the underworld, or both) are the only guarantors. Children of high cadres have been gobbled up by large firms, including foreign firms, hoping to cement their connections. Thus even where large businesses have no direct and obvious ties to the state, they thrive only by having close and cooperative contacts with officials.

Wank found that large businessmen in the booming southern port of Xiamen did not particularly complain about corruption in 1989, even though it was the driving issue behind that year's demonstrations.[28] Instead, they simply saw gifts and other financial cultivation of connections as part of the cost of business. The people truly upset about corruption were the most petty entrepreneurs, whose fruit stalls and shoe repair shops could not hope to compete for lucrative connections. Their basic strategy toward the state was avoidance, not cultivation. The most organized and powerful groups are thus no more independent from the state than those philanthropic elites in the Qing Dynasty.[29] The petty capitalists, while potentially more of an independent lobby, do not have the power to change society, and will become powerful only by establishing close ties to the state.

Taiwan Transformed

While Taiwan's government often indulged in repressive tactics and campaigned for control of body and mind, it left the economy much less tied to the state than in the People's Republic. Certain kinds of civil association familiar in the West thus arose fairly early in Taiwan, partly through contact with the West. Rotary Clubs, Lions Clubs, and other standard forms of informal business association have a long history there. If such associations thrived in Taiwan, it is only partially an emulation of the West. They also reinforce the older kinds of connections (kinship, common place of origin, classmate), whose role in Taiwan's business success has now been clearly documented.[30] Such groups have increasingly played an important role in promoting political change in Taiwan, especially concerning relations with the mainland in the last few years. The lifting of martial law in 1987 allowed big business to exert new leverage on the state, and businessmen are coming to dominate elected bodies the way lawyers do in the United States.[31]

In general, however, it would have been difficult to characterize Taiwan as having a civil society before 1987. As on the mainland, the government would not tolerate any institutionalization of public opinion outside of its control. Just like the mainland, all kinds of horizontal ties in fact existed (religion, fictive and real kinship, rotating credit associations), but they had no chance to grow. One could have argued in the early 1980s, as Singapore argues now, that Chinese political culture simply left no room for civil society.[32] This would have been supported at the time by comments from many people about how there is too much freedom in the West, leading to social disorder.[33]

That is why the lifting of martial law on 15 July 1987 offers such an important lesson. Within months, Taiwan had a nationally organized environmental movement, women's movement, and labor movement.[34] Each of these movements has continued to thrive and grow. Taiwan's newspapers, for example, documented just ten cases of environmental demonstrations in 1981, but there were 278 a decade later.[35] Many of these involved island-wide environmental organizations, which continue to thrive. Within the next few years, Taipei also developed new institutions of public gathering, from discos (and now KTV parlors) to beer halls to revived tea houses.

Nationally organized religious sects also suddenly blossomed. Pietistic sects came out of the closet, having become legal at last. Like the Buddhist orders to which many of them trace roots, these sects worship universal deities, quite unlike the community base to most popular religion. They often focus around spirit writing sessions, and emphasize both curing and commentaries on traditional texts.[36] The general tenor of their meetings is one of moral renewal through Chinese tradition (although their cousins in earlier periods had occasionally turned rebellious). They urge filial piety, patriotism, sobriety, and other quite standard values.

Their universalizing deities and commentaries on Confucian philosophy are matched by an individualism that popular religion also does not emphasize. Followers join these sects voluntarily, and take personal responsibility for their own salvation.[37] They join as individuals, and not as the family or community representatives they play in most local ritual. They are thus in a sense classic intermediate institutions of the kind important to civil society—recognizing both individual and society, but giving in to neither.

The most important of these sects has been the Way of Unity (Yiguan Dao), which controls most of the vegetarian restaurants in Taiwan, and also boasts the active membership of Zhang Rongfa, one of the island's wealthiest businessmen. It claims over a million followers (almost 5 percent of the island's population), and suggests that its members enjoy disproportionate business success. These claims have not been proven, but the social organization of the sects certainly recalls Weber's analysis of Protestant sects as a way of substituting a self-selected group of trustworthy (and thus credit worthy) comrades for the potential problems of more particularistic ties.[38]

More standard Buddhist organization has also thrived in this period. Most striking by far is the Compassion Merit Society (Ciji Gongdehui), which organizes philanthropic work.[39] It claims over 3 million members (perhaps 15 percent of the population), and gives away more than U.S.$ 20 million each year. It runs a major hospital in Taiwan, and has recently opened a free clinic in Los Angeles. A charismatic Buddhist nun named Zhengyan runs the organization. She founded it in the 1960s on Taiwan's poor eastern coast. Her handful of lay followers contributed daily pin money and sold handicrafts to fund charity for the ill.

The organization really boomed, however, with the economic growth and political loosening of the 1980s. Many members contribute as much as a million N.T. dollars (about U.S.$ 40,000) annually, and undergo long waiting lists to volunteer at the hospital. Local chapters organize members to make charitable visits to the poor, the sick, and the aged. They also have regular meetings featuring testimonials from members about how their lives have improved, and live or videotaped speeches by Zhengyan.

Buddhist they may be, but strictly religious content can be hard to find in their meetings and texts. There are few commentaries on Buddhist sutras, not much sutra chanting or reciting the Buddha's name or even burning incense. The emphasis, quite unlike most Buddhism, is firmly on action in this world, and religious texts generally come in only in defense of that simple concept: do good works.

It is thus possible to mobilize a genuine civil society on Chinese cultural resources. Some of this clearly grows out of direct contact with the West. The currency of the very idea of "civil society," which is as important now in Taiwan as in Eastern Europe, is a twentieth-century borrowing, as are many of its institutions, from the Rotary Club to Taiwan Greenpeace. International pressures also had some influence on Taiwan's democratization, of course. The fall of Marcos and the large-scale unrest in South Korea in the mid-1980s offered examples of the dangers of staying the course.[40] Taiwan must also have understood the political capital it would gain in the West from its reforms (as has in fact occurred).

On the other hand, neither international pressure nor direct borrowing from the West explain why the reforms have taken such root internally—why, for example, so many kinds of horizontal associations flowered in the months immediately after martial law was lifted, or why new kinds of large-scale association like Ciji currently thrive. While some forms of association have been borrowed, the social ties on which they rest have clear Taiwanese and generally Chinese roots. The religious movements build directly on indigenous tradition, and grass-roots environmental action also depends on local social capital, especially organized through religion, kinship, and political factions. These ties may not have had any earlier links to a concept of civil society or to a democratic political culture, but they can be mobilized, just as they have been mobilized in the construction of Taiwan's economic boom.

Conclusion

I have tried to make four points from the Chinese and Taiwanese cases. The first is that we cannot sensibly speak of civil society in China before the twentieth century, in part because state and society themselves were conceptualized so differently from the Western discourse. The Western dichotomy between individual and state on which the idea rests had no strong parallel in China. "Civility" (as *li*) had long been important, but never a political culture of democracy or civil society. Nevertheless, there were many kinds of horizontal linkages, whose important potential for the present is clear from their role in the rapid economic development of all Chinese societies in recent years.

Second, the idea of civility/civilization is no guarantee of civil society, in spite of their long association in the West. Civil society may indeed require some degree of civility—the ability to accept the "otherness" of others, at least within mutually expected boundaries. John Hall argues this quite strongly elsewhere in this volume. Yet the reverse is clearly not necessary: civility can play a central role and not offer an iota of pressure toward building a civil society. The primary use of "civility" in this century (under both Republican and communist rule) has been as a prop for authoritarian rule. The communists in particular tried to colonize the entire society from the state, and campaigns for polite behavior are a small part of that larger effort.

Third, the long history of gaps and openings in political/personal control in the People's Republic suggests the impossibility of the totalitarian project in practice. It does succeed, at least in China, at preventing the growth of alternative civil institutions, and both the existence of gaps and the lack of alternative institutions have important implications for the future. The gaps mean that various forms of horizontal association continue to exist, as they always have in China. They thus offer a kind of seed for possible future political changes (as they also do in Singapore). More broadly, they suggest that a diversity of opinion and organization, within culturally accepted limits, provides a crucial resource for any society facing major social changes.[41] Yet the effective repression of any institutional realization of these ties means that a rapid political transition will be both dangerous and difficult without organizations prepared to take over political responsibilities, as the Russians have shown.

Finally, there is the important example of Taiwan. A civil society does exist there now—and this is a statement that neither I nor nearly any other observer would have predicted two decades ago. This transformation speaks to the possibilities of Chinese culture, at least in a particular social context. China may never have had a democratic political culture, but it did have the kinds of intermediate institutions outside politics that could evolve to support one. The Taiwan case requires a revision of the most pessimistic arguments about the PRC, and provides a challenge to Singapore's claim to speak for the naturalness of Chinese authoritarian culture.

This essay thus echoes a conclusion implied by others in this volume (especially Chirot, Hall, and Hefner)—that neither social capital in the form of horizontal associations nor a moral consensus around the idea of civility suffices to create a civil society. China has a long history of horizontal associations and of a strong moral emphasis on civility/civilization. Taiwan shows us these can aid the development of a genuine civil society even though they were rather different from the

Western tradition. Yet for most of Chinese history, and most current Chinese societies outside of Taiwan, no civil society has developed. Two critical differences stand out from the Taiwanese experience: the success of the market economy and the eventual decision of the political elite to step back from attempts at total social control. The People's Republic of China has increasingly opened to market forces, but the political elite so far shows no interest in the diversity of a civil society. The next decade should help give us an idea of whether the pressures of running a market economy alone are enough to force the political hand of the elite.

Notes

1. I borrow the sprouts image from the extensive debate over whether China was growing its own "sprouts of capitalism" before extensive contact with the West uprooted them to plant its own version instead. This literature predates the civil society debates and has some of its major champions inside China.
2. For a history of the concept of civil society in the West, see Adam B. Seligman, *The Idea of Civil Society* (New York: The Free Press, 1992). See also Hall's contribution to this volume for the importance of accepting both state and individual autonomy, as well as organizing between the two levels.
3. The ties between civil society and market economies are widely recognized, but the causation remains open to argument. While most argue that the market sets the stage for civil society, Robert D. Putnam, in *Making Democracy Work: Civic Traditions in Modern Italy* (Princeton, N.J.: Princeton University Press, 1993), has recently made a case that a long tradition of horizontal association in northern Italy fostered economic development there.
4. See Max Weber, *The Religion of China: Confucianism and Taoism*, edited and translated by Hans H. Gerth (New York: The Free Press, 1951), and Robert N. Bellah, "Epilogue: Religion and Progress in Modern Asia," in Robert N. Bellah, ed., *Religion and Progress in Modern Asia* (New York: The Free Press, 1965), pp. 168–229 on religion. See Marion J. Levy, *The Family Revolution in Modern China* (Cambridge, Mass.: Harvard University Press, 1949), pp. 354–59, on the family.
5. See, for example, Walter W. Rostow, *The Stages of Economic Growth: A Non-Communist Manifesto* (Cambridge: Cambridge University Press, 1960).
6. The key work was Immanuel Wallerstein, *The Modern World-System: Capitalist Agriculture and the Origins of the European World-Economy in the Sixteenth Century* (New York: Academic Press, 1974).
7. For further discussion of modernization and world systems theory as they have been applied specifically to Taiwan, see Hsin-Huang Michael Hsiao, "Explaining the Taiwan Development Model: Lessons to Be Learned," in Dalchoong Kim, Ku-Hyun Jung, and Kap-Young Jeong, eds., *The Role of Market and State: Economic and Social Reforms in East Asia and East Central Europe* (Yonsei, Korea: Institute of East West Studies, 1991), pp. 127–47.
8. Note that for world systems theorists, civil society need not develop where countries remain in the periphery.
9. I am thinking here of seminal works by Parsons, Shils, and, to a certain extent, the early Geertz. Geertz, however, always showed a greater sensitivity to the

roles of culture. Quite another strain of modernization theory simply dismissed culture as unimportant.

10. See Immanuel Wallerstein, "Culture as the Ideological Battleground of the Modern World-System," *Theory, Culture & Society* 7 (1990): 31–55.

11. See Willliam T. Rowe, "The Problem of `Civil Society' in Late Imperial China," *Modern China* 19: 2 (1993): 139–57. The term li is equally well glossed as "ritual," which creates more awkward ties to European civility than "etiquette." I discuss this important term more below.

12. Mary Backus Rankin, "Some Observations on a Chinese Public Sphere," *Modern China* 19: 2 (1993): 158–82.

13. Frederic Wakeman, "The Civil Society and Public Sphere Debate: Western Reflections on Chinese Political Culture," *Modern China* 19: 2 (1993): 108–38.

14. There were only six Boards, thus making Rites parallel with others like Revenue and Punishment.

15. Legalists of more than two millennia ago did attack Confucianism's failure to realize potential conflicts of interest between state and family—if all sons were so filial, where would the soldiers come from? Yet that view was largely silenced after the Han adoption of Confucianism. On neo-Confucian ritual texts, see Patricia Buckley Ebrey, *Confucianism and Family Rituals in Imperial China: A Social History of Writing About Rites* (Princeton, N.J.: Princeton University Press, 1991).

16. Robert Hymes, "Way and Byway," unpublished manuscript, 1996, argues that local elite sponsorship of temples greatly increased in the Southern Song dynasty, as part of a general strengthening of local society and weakening of the central state. If this finding can be generalized, it implies a general strengthening of horizontal ties among the elite when the state is weak—less in opposition to the state than to take over its functions.

17. On gardens, see Joanna F. Handlin Smith, "Gardens in Ch'i Pao-chia's Social World: Wealth and Values in Late-Ming Kiangnan," *Journal of Asian Studies* 51: 1 (1992): 55–81.

18. See Glen Dudbridge, "Women Pilgrims to T'ai Shan: Some Pages from a Seventeenth-century Novel," in Susan Naquin and Chün-fang Yü, eds., *Sacred Sites in China* (Berkeley: University of California Press, 1992), pp. 39–64, and Susan Naquin, "The Peking Pilgrimage to Miao-feng Shan: Religious Organizations and Sacred Sites," in Susan Naquin and Chün-fang Yü, eds., *Pilgrims and Sacred Sites in China* (Berkeley: University of California Press, 1992), pp. 333–77 on women and pilgrimage in imperial China.

19. There is some argument about whether the village or the market town and its hinterland is the proper level of analysis. See, for example, Philip C. C. Huang, *The Peasant Family and Rural Development in the Yangzi Delta, 1350–1988* (Stanford, Cal.: Stanford University Press, 1990). Either way, such ties are essentially local. Local government could sometimes control temple administrations (see James Wilkerson, "Productive Consumption and Consumptive Production in Human Relatedness in the P'enghu Islands," paper presented to the annual meeting of the American Anthropological Association, Altanta, 1994), but this was often not the case.

20. Margery Wolf, *Women and the Family in Rural Taiwan* (Stanford, Cal.: Stanford University Press, 1972).

21. See Robert P. Weller, "Ideology, Organization and Rebellion in Chinese Sectarian Religion," in Janos M. Bak and Gerhard Benecke, eds., *Religion and Rural Revolt* (Manchester: Manchester University Press, 1984), pp. 390–406, and Max Weber, "The Protestant Sects and the Spirit of Capitalism," in H. H. Gerth and

C. Wright Mills, eds., *From Max Weber: Essays in Sociology* (New York: Oxford University Press, 1946), pp. 302–22.

22. See Arif Dirlik, "The Ideological Foundations of the New Life Movement: A Study in Counterrevolution," *Journal of Asian Studies* 34: 4 (1975): 945–80.

23. I take the idea of an ethical cage from discussion with John Hall at the conference that led to this volume. In partial contrast to his emphasis on the importance of a morality of civility, however, I see the Chinese material as showing that not any "civility" will do.

24. Ann S. Anagnost, *National Past-times: Narrative, Writing, and History in Modern China* (Durham, N.C.: Duke University Press, in press).

25. See Claude Lefort, *The Political Forms of Modern Society: Bureaucracy, Democracy, Totalitarianism*, edited by John B. Thompson (Cambridge, Mass.: MIT Press, 1986), p. 299, and Robert P. Weller, *Resistance, Chaos and Control in China: Taiping Rebels, Taiwanese Ghosts and Tiananmen* (London: Macmillan, 1994), p. 214.

26. Weller, *Resistance*.

27. See David L. Wank, "Private Business, Bureaucracy, and Political Alliance in a Chinese City," *Australian Journal of Chinese Affairs* 33 (1995): 55–71, on chambers of commerce.

28. Wank, "Private Business."

29. This is the area Philip C. C. Huang, "Between Informal Mediation and Formal Adjudication: The Third Realm of Qing Civil Justice," *Modern China* 19: 3 (1993): 251–98 describes as the third realm, including both this kind of colluding business and the booming collective sector in the countryside.

30. See Ichiro Numazaki "The Role of Personal Networks in the Making of Taiwan's Guanxiqiye (`Related Enterprises')," in Gary G. Hamilton, ed., *Business Networks and Economic Development in East and Southeast Asia* (Hong Kong: Centre of Asian Studies, University of Hong Kong, 1991), pp. 78–97, and Joseph Bosco, "Family Factories in Taiwan: The Use and Abuse of the Family Metaphor," paper presented at the annual meeting of the American Anthropological Association, Atlanta, 1994.

31. See Hsin-Huang Michael Hsiao, "The Political Economy of State-Business Relations in Taiwan: Formation and Transformation," paper presented at the Second East Asian and East-Central European Conference, Budapest, 1992.

32. See Heath B. Chamberlain, "On the Search for Civil Society in China," *Modern China* 19: 2 (1993): 199–215, for a similar argument about civil society in the People's Republic.

33. Ironically, this is exactly how Singapore now characterizes Taiwan.

34. See Zhang Maogui, *Shehui Yundong yu Zhengzhi Zhuanhua* (Social Movements and Political Change) (Taipei: Guojia Zhengce Yanjiu Ziliao Zhongxin, 1990).

35. This is based on research conducted jointly with Hsin-Huang Michael Hsiao. See also Hsin-Huang Michael Hsiao, *Qishi Niandai Fan Wuran Zili Jiuji de Jiegou yu Guocheng Fenxi* (Analysis of the Structure and Process of Anti-pollution Self-help Movements in the 1980s; Taipei: Xingzheng Yuan Huanjing Baohu, 1988), on the earlier period.

36. See David K. Jordan and Daniel L. Overmyer, *The Flying Phoenix: Aspects of Chinese Sectarianism in Taiwan* (Princeton, N.J.: Princeton University Press, 1986).

37. See Joseph Bosco, *"Yiguan Dao:* 'Heterodoxy' and Popular Religion in Taiwan," in Murray R. Rubenstein, ed., *Taiwan, 1945–1991: Responses to Directed Political and Socio-economic Change* (Armonk, N.Y.: M. E. Sharpe, 1992), pp. 117–36.

38. See Weber, "The Protestant Sects."
39. See Lu Hwei-syin, "Women's Self-Growth Groups and Empowerment of the 'Uterine Family' in Taiwan," *Bulletin of the Institute of Ethnology, Academia Sinica* 71 (1991): 29–62.
40. Chiang Ching-kuo's apparent change of heart about how Taiwan should be run in the last years of his life—unexpected by most observers and still not fully explained—also set the stage for the reforms.
41. Similar ideas appear in the essays by Casanova on multiple religious traditions in the Ukraine and Wuthnow on "multiphrenic spirituality" elsewhere in this volume.

10

The Function of Business-Related Reciprocity in Chinese Non-Civil Societies

S. Gordon Redding

Two conversations in particular prompt this tentative exploration of the complex topic of trust and its place in Chinese economic life. One was with Thomas Gold after a workshop at the American Academy of Arts and Sciences where we both concluded that the Western-rooted notion of civil society was misplaced in application to China, and that some functional equivalent had traditionally operated there via Confucian familism, a point echoed elsewhere in this volume by Robert Weller. The second more recently was with Orjan Sjoberg of the Stockholm School of Economics who described his study of the workings of rural industry in the PRC in the early 1990's. In a follow-up personal letter he confirmed the following:

> [U]nder the conditions of uncertainty that prevail throughout much of China's economy we would identify current forms of networking and enterprise-local government relations as substitutes, however imperfect, for the trust that is not present.

A large number of questions stem from such thoughts: Did traditional Chinese social norms create a social form equivalent to civil society and, if so, how? How must the concept of trust be disaggregated in order to understand its workings in the Chinese context? Do the circumscribed forms of Chinese trust act as a barrier to modernization and intensive growth? Is institutional borrowing now going on and having any effect? What consequences of change may be estimated?

This chapter will not follow the sequence of such questions but will attempt to illuminate them by working through the following, related conceptual issues: the nature of transactions required to operate smoothly in a modern economy, the nature of the societal context which facilitates such smoothness and also facilitates societal progress, traditional Chinese responses to such needs, the nature of Chinese trust in the context of trust more generally seen, changes now occurring in the field of Chinese business.

Transactions Required in a Modern Economy

By a modern economy, I mean in simple terms one which can sustain the move from extensive to intensive growth. In even simpler economic terms I am referring to a transition that increases per capita income from below U.S. $2,000 to upwards of U.S. $20,000. As E.L. Jones has noted, the real question about China is why the Sung economic achievement has not been repeated. It was moving towards intensive growth then, but halted and has never recovered the initiative. As he observes crisply, "Premodern China perhaps illustrates the costs of running heavily on rules and lightly on laws."[1]

The key point of the transition from extensive to intensive growth is what D.C. North has termed "credible commitment," entailing impersonal exchange across time and space on the basis of credible agreements between anonymous parties.[2] This is a key component in any economic take-off. But we need to understand two aspects of it more clearly: what is included in such exchanges and in what circumstances this sort of exchange brings about broader economic progress.

A definition of the core activities which give rise to transaction costs has been provided by Eggertsson.[3] He sees the principal components as, first, the search for information about the distribution of price and quality of commodities and labor inputs; second, the search for potential buyers and sellers and for relevant information about their behavior and circumstances; third, the bargaining that is needed to find the true position of buyers and sellers when prices are endogenous; fourth, the making of contracts; fifth, the monitoring of contractual partners to see whether they abide by the terms of the contract; sixth, the enforcement of a contract and the collection of damages when partners fail to observe their contractual obligations; and, seventh, the protection of property rights against third-party encroachment.

The last four items in this list, if they are to be managed efficiently, would prima facie benefit from the existence of an independent and impartial legal system, accessible to all those involved in the economic exchange. Such legal systems are typically put in place by responsible

states. In the case of China, this has not, perhaps arguably never, occurred. Instead, the burden of protecting economic transactions has been
carried by cooperative moral standards promulgated and enforced by
three structures: internal loyalties within kinship networks; friendship-
and reciprocity-ethics that bind familistic units in ties of mutual dependence, but remain nevertheless of specific nature only; and, lastly, norms
of cooperative association based on common denominators such as
trades, native-place identities, or charitable interests. The key question
in the Chinese cast is not so much whether there have been effective
substitutes for law, but whether these nonlegal structures will be sufficient in the future for sustained and competitive growth.

The issues of market understanding and bargaining call into question other aspects of Chinese commercial life, for example in the domain of information. As Boisot argues, the lack of codification and
diffusion of information in the PRC creates a business context in which
it is particularly difficult to comprehend market structures. As he notes,
the recent response in the PRC has been the growth of network capitalism and the *repersonalization* of exchange. "Uncertainty is *absorbed*
through the gradual build-up of trust relationships rather than *reduced*
through the writing of contracts."[4] The end result is the growth of entrepreneurial capitalism to regulate intrafirm relationships and network
capitalism to regulate interfirm relationships. These issues will be examined in more detail later in this paper, but some preliminary indication of their significance is evident in much higher rates of current
growth in China's private sector compared to other sectors.

Facilitators of Development

China is not consciously attempting a move to a capitalist system.
The official goal remains "Socialism with Chinese characteristics." Nor,
I suspect, will China be a fertile context for the replication of Western
patterns of modernization, as the extreme nature of its totalitarianism
and centralization present great obstacles to a repeat of European experiences. Even so, official state doctrine speaks of achieving a condition
of modernity by the middle of next century, and there are clearly moves
to adopt many capitalist-style institutions in the economic if not yet the
political sphere.[5]

The rapid growth of network capitalism accounts for much of China's
recent economic success, and it is anticipated that by the year 2000 the
economy will be as much as 75 percent dependent on two sectors which

behave in a capitalist manner: town and village enterprise and the private sector. Nor must one forget in this scenario the enormous influence of Hong Kong and Taiwan as providers of evidence and example.

In these strangely mixed circumstances of a buoyant if unofficial capitalism implanted within totalitarian socialism, it may nevertheless be useful to take note of the conditions under which capitalism has flourished historically elsewhere, a recent summary account of which is provided by Innes.[6] Capitalism, we must first remember, is capable of assuming a variety of social forms. Nonetheless, the divide between capitalist and noncapitalist remains clear and founded on the existence in the former of three sets of conditions. In the economic sphere, there is commonly free labor and a private property system which allows land, labor, and productive resources to be commoditized. A market orientation, including surplus production, is induced via free trading towns and the division of labor. Facilitating institutions include commercial credit, negotiable instruments, double-entry bookkeeping, and rationalized savings and reinvestment. Discipline is often introduced by production for international markets at standardized prices.

In the societal sphere, the institutions of a viable civil society have tended to include a unified nation state, the rule of law, constitutional controls on government, popular sovereignty, and government with high infrastructural capacity and low despotic power (see John Hall's essay in this volume). Local, municipally based polities foster decentralization. The weakness of craft guilds prevents conservations. State granted monopolies should not be strong and the state elite should be autonomous from social class.

In the cultural sphere, values should sponsor a link between individual and collective well-being, as well as a positive attitude towards wealth, time and work discipline, and deferred gratification. Individual autonomy should be related to responsibility. Rationality and activism should enhance the view of wealth as productive capital. Literacy and numeracy are clearly also contributors.

Innes also notes certain parallel and reinforcing conditions which were arguably contributors to the Western development process: the parallel nature of free economic choice and free democratic choice; the connection between Calvinist individualism and contract-based commerce; the relationship between Judeo-Christian monotheism and individual freedom.

He also argues that the importance of civil society lies in its curbing of the destructive consequences of capitalist development. This idea of civil society as constraint on exploitation is an important one and is often given insufficient attention. Yet in light of Peter Berger's observation, it is of critical importance to political and economic civility:

> Capitalism has an intrinsic incapacity to generate legitimations, and it is particularly deprived of mythic potency; consequently it depends upon the legitimating effects of its sheer facticity or upon association with other legitimating symbols.[7]

In treating East Asian capitalism as a second case rather than a replica of the Western pattern,[8] Berger takes special note of the social pecularities of the Asian variant: its high levels of state intervention, the fact that wealth does always seem to create pressures towards democracy, the somewhat late emergence of trends towards individuation, and the significance of influences from the international capitalist system centered in the West. He also notes, however, that many of the cognitive traits associated with Western bourgeois culture *do* seem relevant in the East Asian case—including activism, rational innovativeness, and self-discipline.

Having noted some of the universal and variable features of capitalist development in East Asia, let me now consider these same cultural and institutional conditions in light of the three primary forms of Chinese capitalism: traditional small-scale family business especially in Hong Kong and Taiwan but now emerging fast in China, new hybrid enterprises mixing traditional and modern management at large scale, especially visible in Hong Kong and Taiwan but also investing heavily in China; and forms of proto-capitalism still under state influence in China. The essential questions with which I am concerned are how do forms of Chinese capitalism respond to the requirements of modernization, and what kind of society—civil or otherwise—do such business forms help to shape?

Chinese Capitalist Responses to Modernization

Traditional Chinese culture placed the merchant at the bottom of a four-tier social structure beneath the literati, the peasant, and the artisan. Articulating a culture for such a subgroup would have been thus a somewhat fruitless pursuit and instead success tended to lead them towards echoing the culture of the literati.[9] In doing so they evolved as a group with a combination of values which included (a) traditional Chinese universals such as familism, thrift, honesty, loyalty and industriousness; (b) more specific attitudes of profit seeking, risk taking, and networking; and (c) a philosophy of philanthropy which served to hold together and legitimize merchant interest groups such as trade coalitions. It is in this philanthropic work that some elements of civil society can be traced, although the issue remains a matter of contention.[10]

It is possible to use the term guild to represent Chinese merchant associations but necessary at the same time to distinguish the type from its European equivalent. Features common to both were protection and exclusion but an important difference occurs in their functioning. In Europe guilds formed a component of municipal government. In China they did not. In Europe guilds operated in a fairly dependable legal order. In China they did not.[11]

Most Chinese guilds began as gatherings of fellow provincials posted for trade purposes to a city outside their province, who found it advantageous to bargain collectively with local brokers appointed by government to manage local trade, and with other local government officials. It was not until the early nineteenth century that emphasis shifted from common place of origin to common trade, craft, or service. This new form then expanded substantially in the period after 1840. During the nineteenth century the functions of guilds expanded so that they might include various means of standardizing aspects of commerce, such as weights and measures, training and membership, payment methods, dispute resolution, and pricing.

It is clear that the protection, mutual aid, and trade facilitation practiced by merchants for most of Chinese history were highly circumscribed or "segmentary" (to cite the term introduced in this volume's introduction). They helped a specific trade but could not be extended into society more generally. Excluded were the interests of producers and consumers as opposed to merchants. Excluded also was foreign business. As Liu also notes, "from the eleventh through the nineteenth centuries, there was no development of merchant—controlled municipal government."[12]

Given the different nature of the Chinese state from that of the prototypical Western state, and given a different conception of citizenship, it is inappropriate to look for traces of Western-style civil society there until much more recent times when the possible effects of borrowing might be visible. At the same time however it is necessary to note that within the overpowering constraints of the totalitarian bureaucracy, a certain amount of order initiated from the base did emerge. It was restricted to trades and was essentially about commerce as opposed to industry, but the scene is not entirely barren of autonomous institutions trying to regularize exchange processes and improve the credibility of commitment.

Industrialization in more recent years has tended to extend the lessons learned over centuries in the commercial realm to the networking of cooperation for production processes. Relations in the environment, of extensive networking, relational contracting, interlocking directorships, and strategic alliances are arguably responses to environments of high uncertainty, lack of regulation, unclear and largely unavailable information, and policy volatility, but their form is mediated by the cultural matrix in which they are embedded.

That such adaptations are now common in China where the public and private domains are mixed together is evident from a study of rural industries by Zhang and Sjoberg.[13] This concludes that the disorder in the business environment plus the necessary political cooptation can only efficiently be coped with by *guanxi* networking and traditional forms of trust bonding.

It is now appropriate to focus more closely on the cement which holds such exchange processes together. After that some attention will be given to the injection from outside of new institutional structures to assist with the reliability of exchange. We will then be in a position to consider implications.

Trust and Chinese Trust

The literature on trust is extensive and has been concerned with trust at many levels of analysis—individual, interpersonal, in economic exchange, and in societal systems. Treatments of trust in society have tended to lie on a continuum between the transaction cost economists' position based on individual calculated rationalities, and the "embeddedness" position, represented most cogently by Granovetter's now well-known analysis.[14] The latter sees trust as social and normative, rather than individual and calculative, and requires the prior existence of a social fabric.

A more detailed treatment of this latter position by Zucker disaggregated the process of achieving trust into three components: *process-based*, in which the experience of reliable past behavior is extrapolated to underwrite commitments now and in the future; *person-based*, in which trust is formed within a group whose similarities (ethnicity, location of origin etc.) provide some basis for reliable reciprocity; and *institution-based*, in which formal structures such as professionalism, legal contract, and third-party insurance supply under-pinning guarantees.[15]

The workings of all of these processes might also be argued to depend on perceived connections to wider societal benefits. Hence Hosmer proposes a definition of trust which includes the notion of societal ethics as a framework

> Trust is the expectation by one person, group or firm, of ethically justifiable behaviour—that is, morally correct decisions and actions based upon ethical principles of analysis—on the part of the other person, group, or firm in a joint endeavour or economic exchange.[16]

Chinese forms of trust would appear to rely heavily on personal reciprocities, to a lesser degree on process, and hardly at all on institutional support structures. The United States' disposition would be balanced much more towards reliance on institutional bases as primary. The Hong Kong position would arguably be a half-way combination of both tendencies.

This argument begins with the assumption that although societal ethics vary enormously in their modes of expression, the ultimate intention of achieving a cooperative society is constant. The United States' attempt, for instance to foster cooperation via flourishing civil society, and the related attempts to achieve fairness and equity in distribution of benefits, are no more strong or ethical than Chinese traditional prescriptions for stable social order combined with "human-heartedness," or even the mythic appeals of Marxism about communal sharing in conditions of equality. It is not in the wider social philosophies that we should search for an understanding of how trust works differently. It is in the practical applications on the ground, themselves historical artifacts of social evolution.

The significance of personalism in Chinese economic exchange is well attested to empirically,[17] and also in the widespread acknowledgment of the critical factor of *guanxi* in coping with transactions in China today. The explanation of it is usually based on the absence of institutional fabric whereby society could provide guarantees of reliable exchange. There is also the added feature of actual threat from an interfering and volatile system of administration which is inclined to undermine the stability of agreements made, by changes of policy and the alteration of rules. A little acknowledged feature in discussions of personalism in Chinese economic exchange is the need to use guanxi networks to find critical information in otherwise very puzzling and confusing environments.

It is also possible to argue that the insecurity engendered by such environments (none of the features of which are really new to the Chinese context), when combined with the powerful drive to secure enough wealth for family security, lead to a highly developed tendency towards entrepreneurship and opportunity seeking. This latter especially requires the seeking out of information about opportunities and the likelihood of sharing in the exploitation of them.

The trust-bonding process which is required to make such exchange work has been studied in detail by Menkhoff for Singaporean Chinese traders operating internationally with other ethnic Chinese.[18] Although not based in China, this work reveals such strong influence of Chinese cultural norms that its relevance may be at least provisionally assumed. Certainly the findings accord with earlier work in Hong Kong and Taiwan by Silin.[19] Also it is arguable that the business environments of Indonesia, Thailand, and the Philippines to which Menkhoff's work relates, are as unstructured and uncertain as those of China, at least in terms of the past few decades in which appropriate responses would need to be shaped.

Menkhoff's study of trusting behaviour among Chinese merchants led to his describing the meaning of their core concept, *xinyong*, as follows:

> [I]t was not so much the faith in another's good character (in terms of blind trust) that was perceived as *xinyong*, but the relative evidence that long-standing trading relations enlarge reciprocal (sometimes affectionately *ganqing*) relations and that they can rely…on different sanctions and on efficient information networks to decide whether or not (potential) business partners can be trusted.[20]

Closely connected with this is the sensitivity to not losing face. An important component of face is *lien* or moral character and the fear of losing it thus provides a moral underpinning in face transactions and in turn, trust transactions.[21] The workings of face are also embedded in Chinese norms for the exercise of civility, a feature which in the West led to an ability to absorb differences of opinion, as Hall points out elsewhere in this volume. It is less sure however, as Robert Weller would argue, that Chinese civility or *li* works to the same end, and as Adam Seligman observes civility can be related to structures of domination and the democratization of prestige.

Philanthropy is another powerful tradition in the Chinese business world and helps to achieve for an individual what Menkhoff terms "diffuse trustworthiness."[22] This becomes especially relevant when a person needs help under pressure.

Trustworthiness is thus achieved and ascribed by personality, background, social structure, and participation in society. A vivid Chinese metaphor distinguishing those whom a particular person might trust from those outside the circle is to see them as either "cooked" as "raw." The latter may eventually become the former but the process may be long.

Pragmatically the transition to being "cooked" is a matter of assessing a person's background, local business reputation, reliability in transactions, and promptness in payment. Clearly in such a context length of relationship becomes especially important. A way of speeding up the process is the use of a go-between who informally stands as guarantor of each party to the other. In the end however what counts is performance in the ensuing exchanges.

It is possible to conclude from this account that although personal- and process-based sources of trust are analytically separate, they are closely interconnected in everyday exchange. The reason for assuming a higher relevance for the personal in the PRC context is because of the salience of individual position-power in the Chinese state structure. There is less opportunity than in a normal market economy to test the relationship over years of transaction processes. Instead exchange comes to rely a great deal on connections into the power structure. These are personal attributes in the context of the PRC and form the basis for much alliance seeking and bonding.

In the case of Hong Kong processes can flow more freely and manifestly do. There the availability of institutional structures such as reliable accounting systems and effective commercial law reduces somewhat the need to rely on particularism. However they do not eliminate it and it is so deeply rooted that it remains dominant as a combined personal-process form of trust-bonding.

The Western case, in this simple typology, is seen as one where trust based on institutional support structures, particularly the law of contract, but also systems of dense, reliable information, has come to be the prime source of reliability in exchange and credibility of commitment.

Change and Chinese Business Environments

Any further consideration of Chinese exchange processes in several Asian settings must take account of a little acknowledged feature of the scene. It is that Chinese capitalism has proved to be an extremely successful form. The lateness of China's opening and the immense difficulties of its current transformation have tended to take attention away from the achievements of this distinct business system in related environments among overseas Chinese.

In contrast with the kind of state-influenced industrial capitalism which followed the Meiji restoration in Japan, it can be argued that a vibrant form of capitalism developed in among Chinese based on small, societally based, network organizations. These two main Asian trajectories for capitalist development—the Japanese and the Chinese—have over the last century led to quite significant differences of enterprise, industry, products, and competitive strength. The lack of large "glamorous" organizations and international brand names in the Chinese case, and the personalistic nature of much of the system's coordinative processes, have led to its being described as "ersatz capitalism."[23] So too the lack of a single national boundary within which to measure its scale has also hindered our recognition of the Chinese system as a respectable economic system. However, it is possible to argue that—with the foreign reserves of Taiwan, Hong Kong, and Singapore now standing at U.S. $230 billion, with incomes per capita comfortably in the Western league table (a recent World Economic Forum report putting Hong Kong in third place worldwide), and with China's extraordinary growth rates driven by this same type of economic organization— we now see a maturing system of efficient capitalism based on distinctly Chinese norms for vertical and horizontal relationships.

Why has the system proved so dynamic? Its power comes in the main from three features, one of which is unique and, I would argue, holds the key to China's future. The three features are as follows:

1. *Decision quality* (speed, clarity and knowledge). Typically one person in a a business makes the crucial strategic decisions and does so on the basis of having accumulated deep knowledge about a particular industry. The depth of that knowledge cannot be matched in many other business cultures where people move around to a far greater degree.

2. *Strategic partnerships.* Business partnerships rest on very specific trust bonds and are essentially interpersonal. They operate internationally as well as locally and are particularly strong in connecting the economies surrounding the South China Sea. These alliances have several distinct features. First, they are initially made informally and without benefit of consultants or lawyers. Second, they are ways of enhancing mutual obligation. The relationship is a perpetual motion machine in search of opportunity. Third, it creates a flow of capital towards opportunity. Fourth and last, it works at very high speed because the individuals doing the deals together have real power to com-

mit resources without relying on anyone else's approval. It is this capacity of the system to gear up on the acumen of individuals that produces the extraordinary wealth. There are reasons why few other cultures have similar arrangements to this degree. An obsession with control means that the retention of dominance within the firm by its paterfamilias is deeply culturally rooted. This, I believe, is the product of centuries of insecurity in the culture, and it is supported by societal norms about authority. The horizontal ties between owners cutting each other in on deals are very specific and based on the ethics of trust mentioned earlier.

I should add here that in identifying this morally supported and societally derived form of networking as a key contributor to development, I am not claiming it is a perfect system. It is an elegant and efficient response to uncertainty and to the need for collaborative opportunity-hunting. It includes the acknowledgment that local political support has to be coopted and that one of the players will make this his contribution.

Criticism of this system would be that it remains essentially biased towards private rather than public interest. It has a voracious appetite for state-granted monopoly. In that, it is highly rational. Over time it may be reigned in and made more societally accountable. But for that to happen requires the growth of social pluralism and the emergence of societal consciousness of a much higher order than currently obtains in either Hong Kong or China.

3. *Managerial intensity.* The third source of the system's efficiency is that the key units of the economy are managed by people who own them. The vast majority of Hong Kong companies are small, with the total number of employees averaging but nineteen. Businesses counteract the problems of small scale by networking to produce goods. The arrangement is similar to having a large Western corporation in which every department is managed by someone whose personal wealth and livelihood were invested in that department. That would soon put a stop to the tea breaks, the long lunches, the carpets, the new furniture and the executive washroom.

Hong Kong is a hybrid society, and particularly now, needs to be seen for what it is. It is a combination of a Western infrastructure providing order—the existence of which permits the Chinese business sector to get on peacefully with its own activities undisturbed—and a Chinese system which needs such order to flourish. A relatively new feature of this system has been the emergence of a new and more experimental organizational hybrid, most notably in the fields of finance and management. In finance the access to stock market capital introduces an important new element into local business culture. In management, the growth of Chinese family business is increasingly dependent on professionalism, hired in part in response to the effects of competition and economic internationalization. However, the hybrid organizations now growing out of the family businesses still retain their essential Chineseness, most visibly in the retention of strategic decision-making by the owner-operator family.

How, finally, will Hong Kong's business culture affect the transformation of China? The role of culture in the transformation of any society is not a matter of simple mechanical cause and effect. Confucianism, familism, and Chinese traditions of trust and identity will not directly lead to economic growth. If they had been alone sufficient to promote such growth they would have done so already. Instead, the role of cultural tradition will largely be to legitimize or provide a moral basis for the emergence of new institutions.

As these changes unfold, the *real* question will be how the tension will be resolved between the totalitarian state's obsession with control and the need for freedom on the part of the entrepreneur. This tension is exacerbated, of course, by the absence in Chinese political experience of any genuine decentralization of power, an absence that stands in sharp contrast with the administrative history of both Japan and the West.

While market forces and more widespread wealth may bring with them democratic pressures, as have been seen in Korea and Taiwan, we cannot ignore the fact that the sheer size of the Chinese state means that such examples may not be applicable. Nor must we ignore the lessons of history. In reviewing the history of economic systems, Innes wrote that "what does need to be underscored…is that the great divide between economic systems occurred more than two centuries *before* the Industrial Revolution."[24] In other words the successful and stable dismantling of totalitarianism takes centuries not decades.

I would conclude therefore that we should not be misled by the past sixteen years of economic progress in China. Changes during that period represent the easy part of the developmental task, taking up the organizational slack. There may still be a huge amount of slack left, especially in light of the availability of low-cost labor and land. These factors could provide momentum for a long time yet. By themselves, however, they are not sufficient to move China from premodern totalitarianism to modern pluralism. Until that transition occurs, growth will remain extensive not intensive.

Such transitions are of course messy, unclear, partial, and un-measurable. During the transition process Hong Kong will, with a little luck, make three positive contributions. First, the Chinese family business—well adapted to conditions of uncertainty, political cooptation, unstructured markets, and unregulated environments—may well repeat in other areas of China the remarkable performance achieved to date in East Asia as a whole. In doing so, family businesses will create a bourgeoisie and a growing intolerance of totalitarianism. Second, the supporting institutions hybridized in Hong Kong, and the structures of civil society built there to increase the density of trust in society and transactions, will be extended into China itself. Third, the business culture of Hong Kong will serve to provide the norms and values needed to legitimize the transformation of China's institutional fabric. Its role will be to make manifest the virtues, both moral and practical, of Chinese capitalism. If these transitions do not occur China's future is dismal. However, if they do occur, the future will see a very different China. Such difference can only be achieved by internal change. Societies are not really changed from outside. This is to say that the real significance of the 1997 transfer of Hong Kong is that serious internal change in China as a whole may yet become possible.

Notes

1. E.L. Jones "The real question about China: Why was the Song economic achievement not repeated?" *Australian Economic History Review* 30: 2 (1990): 20.
2. D.C. North "The evolution of efficient markets in history," in J.A. James and M. Thomas, eds., *Capitalism in Context* (Chicago, University of Chicago Press, 1994), p. 259.
3. T. Eggertsson, *Economic Behaviour and Institutions* (Cambridge: Cambridge University Press, 1990), p. 15.
4. M.H. Boisot, *Information Space* (London: Routledge, 1995), p. 419.
5. S.G. Redding, "Capitalism and Civil Society in China and the Role of Hong Kong," in S.H. Ng, I. Nish, and S.G. Redding, eds., *Work and Society: Labour and Human Resources in East Asia* (Hong Kong: University of Hong Kong Press, 1995), pp. 119–34.
6. S. Innes, "Puritanism and capitalism in early Massachusetts," in J.A. Jones and M. Thomas eds., *Capitalism in Context* (Chicago, University of Chicago Press, 1994), p. 91.
7. P.L. Berger, *The Capitalist Revolution* (New York: Basic Books, 1986), p. 215.
8. See also R.D. Whitley, *Business Systems in East Asia* (London: Sage, 1992).
9. Gungwu Wang, "The Culture of Chinese Merchants" (Toronto: Working Paper No. 57, University of Toronto-York University Joint Centre for Asia Pacific Studies, 1990).
10. See Deng Zhenglai and Jing Yuejin (1994), "Constructing Chinese Civil Society" (Beijing: Chinese Social Sciences Yearbook, 1994), pp. 61–76; F. Wakeman

(1992), "Did China ever enjoy a civil society?" (Hong Kong: Public lecture, Department of History, University of Hong Kong, 10 June 1992); and Robert Weller's essay in this volume.

11. Liu Kwang Ching, "Chinese Merchants Guilds: An Historical Enquiry" (Davis: Working Paper 13, Program in East Asian Culture and Development Research, University of California-Davis, 1987).
12. Liu, "Chinese Merchant Guilds," p. 11.
13. Zhang Gang and O. Sjoberg, "Institutions and Managerial Strategies in China: A Transaction Costs Approach to the Study of Rural Industries" (Stockholm: Research Report No. 13, Economic Research Institute, Stockholm School of Economics, 1992).
14. M. Granovetter, "Economic Action and Social Structure: The Problem of Embeddedness," *American Journal of Sociology* 91 (1985): 481–510.
15. L.G. Zucker, "Production of Trust: Institutional Sources of Economic Structure, 1840–1920," in B.M. Staw and L.L. Cummings eds., *Research in Organizational Behaviour*, 8 (1986): 53–111 (Greenwich, Conn.: JAI Press).
16. L.T. Hosmer, "Trust: The Connecting Link between Organizational Theory and Philosophical Ethics," *Academy of Management Review* 20: 2 (1995), p. 399.
17. S.G. Redding, *The Spirit of Chinese Capitalism* (New York: de Gruyter, 1990).
18. T. Menkhoff, "Trade Routes, Trust and Trading Networks: Chinese Family-Based Trading Firms in Singapore and Their External Economic Dealings." Unpublished doctoral dissertation. Bielefeld, Germany: Department of Sociology, University of Bielefeld.
19. R. H. Silin, "Marketing and Credit in a Hong Kong Wholesale Market," in W.E. Willmott, ed., *Economic Organization in Chinese Society* (Stanford, Cal.: Stanford University Press, 1972), pp. 121–35; R.H. Silin, *Leadership and Values* (Cambridge, Mass.: Harvard University Press, 1976).
20. Menkhoff, "Trade Routes," p. 192.
21. S.G. Redding and M. Ng, "The Role of 'Face' in the Organizational Perceptions of Chinese Managers," *Organization Studies* 3: 3 (1982): 201–19.
22. Menkhoff, "Trade Routes," p. 199. K. Yoshihara, *The Rise of Ersatz Capitalism in South-East Asia* (Singapore: Oxford University Press, 1988). Innes, "Puritanism," p. 109.

11

Cohabitation?
Islamist and Secular Groups
in Modern Turkey[1]

Resat Kasaba

> *"But a true revival of a religious faith on the level of modern thought and life is within the bounds of possibility. The Turkish people, by the exercise of their practical common sense and powers of improvisation, may yet find a workable compromise between Islam and modernism that will enable them, without conflict, to follow both their fathers' path to freedom and progress and their grandfathers' path to God."*
>
> —Bernard Lewis[2]

On December 24, 1995, the pro-Islamic Refah Party added another impressive victory to its recent string of gains in Turkish politics. The general elections that were held on that day showed that Refah had become the largest and most popular party in Turkey. Since 1991 Refah had increased its share of votes from 16.5 to 21.4 percent; holding a 158-seat plurality in the 550-member parliament. The December 24 elections came on the heels of the local elections of 1994 when Refah captured 28 of the 76 open provincial mayorships nationwide including the two most prominent cities in the country, Istanbul and Ankara. With these showings Refah was poised to play a decisive role in both the local and national politics in Turkey. Indeed, after the failure of a series of attempts at keeping the Islamists out of power, the Refah became the senior partner in a coalition government and its leader became prime minister on July 8, 1996.

These developments appear to have caught many observers of the Turkish scene by surprise. For some time, the consensus in the West had been that the secularists had won the battle in Turkey, and that the Turks were not likely to abandon the tenets of secularism and reembrace Islam in the way the Ottomans had in previous centuries. For example, we find Daniel Lerner confidently stating in the late 1950s that the "production of 'New Turks' can now be halted, in all probability only by the countervailance of some stochastic factor of cataclysmic proportions—such as the atomic war."[3] Could it be true that these prophecies were now proven wrong and that as we approach the closing years of the millennium, Turks were turning their backs to the modern world? What did it mean that Islam was returning not as a result of a war or a violent revolution but through democratic procedures? What was the relationship between the electoral success of the Islamist movement in Turkey and the constituents of civil society such as civic culture, tolerance, individuation, and political engagement? In the years that led up to the latest Refah achievements and since then, policymakers, scholars, and others who are interested in Turkey have been discussing these questions in many different forums both in and out of the country. These questions also inform the central focus of this chapter, not only because they are intrinsically valuable for studying the Turkish case, but also because they are likely to shed light on the more general discussions of civil society and its relationship to economic relations, civic values, and political movements.

In most popular and even some scholarly writings one still finds a general acceptance of the view that Islam is essentially and fundamentally opposed to the West and to Western modernity. In this perspective, elections in Turkey are studied not as bona fide political events but as a part of the age-old struggle between traditionalism and modernity. But in the 1980s, with the growing success of Islamist politics, came a wider awareness of the diverse views which the Muslim intellectuals, activists, and professionals hold in the modern Middle East and in Southeast Asia.[4] For example in Turkey, there is a large Independent Businessmen's Association dominated by Islamist industrialists and manufacturers; Islamists are very active in local chambers of commerce and other professional associations, and in universities some of the most rigorous technical disciplines have been attracting a large and growing number of Islamist students. As is evident from the periodic purges of Islamist militants from its ranks, even the military, that bastion and guardian of Turkish secularism, seems to contain some Islamist officers and servicemen.[5] In recent years, the spread and diversity of the Islamist opinion has contributed to a lively atmosphere of debate and discussion in the media, especially on television and radio, both of which are now partially privatized. In addition to participating in various programs and forums, the Islamists have set up their own media outlets where they debate various issues among themselves. According to one count, as of early 1996, nationwide, there are close to 500 daily newspapers, 350 radio stations, 4 TV channels, and over 8,000 published titles in Turkey that are characterized as being "Islamist."[6] Not all these groups practice or preach the same brand of Islamism, neither do they all vote for Refah. This background of diversity undermines the credibility of the monolithic portrayals of Islamist points of view as "backward," "traditional," or even "anti-enlightenment."

But the presence of different and sometimes moderating views among the Islamists does not diminish the historical significance of recent Refah victories in Turkey. It is indeed remarkable that in the capital city of a country where people were hanged in 1925 for refusing to wear a Western-style hat, there is now a prime minister with a very long record of antisecular pronouncements and a well-known antipathy toward the West. More importantly, the 1994 local and the 1995 general elections clearly represent the common aspiration of a sizable and growing plurality in Turkey. Rather than being an accident that can be reversed by tinkering with the voting procedures these votes signal nothing less than a thorough realignment of the Turkish electorate. For example, compared with the 4.4 percent which Refah captured only ten years ago in local elections, their recent gains represent an almost 500 percent increase in their share of votes.[7] As for the status and prospects of the other parties, only between 1991 and 1994, the share of the largest party on the left, the Republican People's Party declined from 20.8 percent to 13.4 percent; and that of the governing right-of-center True Path Party from 27 to 21.9 percent. Refah's share in the same time period rose from 16 to 21 percent. If we take yet a longer perspective and compare, for example, over 40 percent which the Republican People's Party had received in the 1977 with its current 10.8 percent, the magnitude of this shift becomes even clearer.

Not all the explanations of this startling turn in Turkish politics are locked into the older perspectives where the lines are drawn starkly between the forces of darkness and the forces of enlightenment. There are other, more nuanced analyses of Refah's success where the emphasis is placed not on a cultural or civilizational competition or clash but on the economic difficulties and transformations which Turkey has been experiencing since the 1970s.[8] According to this, the rise of Islamist politics in Turkey and other poor countries in the Middle East results from the general breakdown of the state-centered policies of economic development that had been installed in the earlier part of the twentieth century. Far from generating economic independence, public wealth and social equality, these policies produced little more than bloated bureaucracies that were highly inefficient, corrupt, and generally incompetent to manage their affairs or to deliver on their grand promises. These regimes have tried to cover their failures and stay in power by relying on external help from the United States or the Soviet Union while repressing internal opposition. This has led to a general depreciation in their legitimacy and popularity in the eyes of their citizens. Islam, according to this explanation, has emerged as the only alternative that seems to promise something different especially to the fast-growing and overwhelmingly young population in these countries.[9]

It is hard to exaggerate the difficulties which the Turkish economy has been experiencing since the mid 1970s. While the increases in oil prices left Turkey with a growing import bill, the recession in European countries restricted outlets for its commodity exports and also put a complete stop to the migration of Turkish workers. In other words, the Turkish economy was squeezed from both ends; it was being forced to close a growing deficit in its current account with diminishing sources of foreign exchange. In the 1980s, successive attempts at restructuring the Turkish economy have met with deep resistance from a variety of entrenched groups who had vested interests in some aspect of the status quo. The result has been one of an incomplete transformation where a limited number of new institutions and practices have been grafted on the old. This has created an uncertain economic environment that inspires little confidence in those who might be interested in investing or trading in Turkey. Over the two decades since the mid-1970s, the average annual rate of inflation in Turkey has been around 80 percent and the value of the Turkish Lira has declined from about TL. 25 to the dollar in 1976 to about TL. 126,000 to the dollar in 1997. During the same time period the country's external debt has grown from negligible amounts to close to $100 billion.

The most immediate and visible effect of these deteriorating economic conditions has been on the distribution of income in Turkey. For example, only between 1992 and 1994 the index of real wages have declined from a base of 100 to 74.4.[10] Today, the average price of a single-family home in Istanbul hovers around U.S. $250,000 where the minimum wage corresponds to no more than $1.00 per hour. According to one calculation in 1990, the wealthiest 20 percent of Istanbul's population was receiving 57.4 percent of the income generated in the city whereas the share of the poorest 20 percent was 4.6 percent.[11] Poverty is spreading fast among a part of the population that includes not only the unemployed and underemployed youth but also the pensioners and others with fixed incomes. The built-in indexation of government salaries and pensions has provided a cushion for the latter group and helped protect social peace but this very policy has also made the implementation of a true structural reform difficult. Any attempt by the government to put a ceiling on wage increases has been met with widespread resistance and strikes. For example in 1995 when the coalition government that included the Social Democratic Republican People's Party was forced to resign when it resisted the pressures to raise the minimum wage. In the meantime, the more fortunate part of the population pretend to insulate themselves from most of this unpleasantness. They work in postmodern office buildings, live in gated housing complexes, and spend a large part of their year abroad for work or pleasure. It would not be an exaggeration to say that their connections to other parts of the world are much more intense and "real" than their contacts with the poor neighborhoods that surround cities like Istanbul.

That Refah took full advantage of this situation of economic uncertainty and polarization is beyond question. In the 1980s they set up a widespread network of party workers and quickly assumed the role of the interlocutors for the downtrodden and excluded. In the election campaign, rather than relying solely on the mass media, Refah took its message directly to the people through a program called Operation Worry Beads.[12] A string of activists were linked with each other through interpersonal connections and this network extended the party's influence down to the neighborhoods, streets, and even the apartment buildings and households in poor quarters of the cities. Refah put women in charge of organizing women, workers to work with workers, and students with students. Refah's approach proved to be much more effective and real than the more conventional methods of campaign that relied on the rapidly expanding media outlets. For example, to prove that they were responsive to the needs of their constituency, Refah workers delivered pots pans, and groceries to needy families; and on the day of the election they transported voters to voting booths in "laptop equipped Jeep Cherokees."[13] While Refah was reaching out to poor neighborhoods in such a concerted manner, a mayoral candidate from the Social Democratic Party was passing out carnations in parades that were held on the main streets of Istanbul.

Even though the economic difficulties of the 1980s provided an important stimulus to the spread of Islamists' appeal in the Middle East, we should remember some key differences between Turkey and some of the other states in the region before giving too much weight to economic factors in explaining Refah's popularity. After close to a half a century of independence, the states like Egypt, Sudan, or Algeria don't have much to offer as a substitute for their shallow ideologies that created bankrupt economies and huge and dysfunctional bureaucracies. These conditions have generated widespread desperation and rage, especially among the youth, and this anger is an important factor in the thrust behind the Islamist resurgence in these countries. It is not as easy to label the entire period of state-centered economic developmentalism in Turkey as a total failure. Even on a superficial level, a comparison of several economic and social indicators suggest that Turkey has moved far beyond the tenuous Republic which it was seventy-five years ago. For example, in 1948 per capita income was about $128, in 1993 this number had gone up to $2970. For comparative purposes it is helpful to note that the Egyptian per capita income grew from $100 to only $660 in the same years. In 1953, only ten out of the 40,000 villages in Turkey had electricity whereas today, virtually all of them are linked to electric power. In 1923, agriculture accounted for 43 percent of the GNP and the industrial sector for 10.6 percent. In 1990 the share of agriculture had dropped to 17.9 percent and that of industry had risen to 29.2 percent. In the latter year over 80 percent of Turkey's exports consisted of manufactured goods. Also in the 1980s geographical distribution of the population reversed its centuries-old characteristic so that now more than half of the Turkish population is living in urban centers.[14] More significantly, of those who support the Islamist movement, a large segment have come out not as hopeless losers but as successful competitors from the recent economic travails of the country. One such example is the Ihlas Holding, the highly successful company among whose ventures is an overnight courier system that moves cargo in and out of Turkey. Politically too there are some crucial differences between Turkey and her Middle Eastern neighbors. Compared with the authoritarian Arab states who have never relaxed their tight grip over their citizens, Turkey has been living under a system of multiparty democracy with popularly elected governments since 1946. Even the oft-mentioned coups of 1960, 1971, and 1980 did not alter this picture significantly because each one of these interventions unfolded in a pattern that showed not the weakness but the strength of democratic consciousness in the country.[15] It is by no means insignificant that the Refah and its predecessors have been very careful to abide by the democratic procedures in their quest for power in Turkey. Hence, we should consider the possibility that in addition to registering their unhappiness with their economic positions and with the policies of the secular state, 5.9 million people who voted for Refah in 1995 were also casting their ballots *for* something as well. *What* they were voting for, however, requires a closer look.

The Refah program consisted of a series of general statements about poverty, unemployment, inflation, and corruption that were caused by a "slave order that is established and run by imperialism and Zionism." This corrupt system, according to the program, could be alleviated by the establishment of a "just order" that would include a planned economic system. Being based not on profits but on "usefulness," this system would guarantee everybody's welfare.[16] What makes Refah's program attractive cannot just be these platitudes which, after all, are not that different from what the leftist parties have been promising for years without much success. Refah owes most of its popularity not to this or any other particular economic plan or promise but to a clearly stated conviction that a "Just System" can be established in this world if "believers" are put in charge because their covenant with God would give the true believers no option but to work for the good of the community. Such persons would never cheat, steal, or charge compound interest. For example in a survey conducted in one of the districts in Istanbul in 1994, 46.9 percent of the respondents said that they voted for Refah because its mayoral candidate was "honest." In answer to another question in the same survey, the largest plurality of the respondents (32 percent) said that adopting Islamic ideology would be the most important qualification they would look for in a politician.[17] Refah's pronouncements about the importance of recruiting and electing believers resonate perfectly with its constituents' belief that the personal, political, and moral aspects of an individual's life can be woven into a coherent whole and that believing in an ideology and acting accordingly can be a panacea for the problems that an individual faces in the modern world.

The idealist bond between the party and its supporters is the most important factor that contributed to the success of Refah in the last ten years in Turkey. Also through this bond we can see the gradual closing of what had remained as an insurmountable gap between the Turkish state and society.[18] This gap originated with the fundamentally illiberal and undemocratic path of reform which the Ottoman/Turkish elite chose in the last century. The modern Turkish state which originated from this reorganization had three defining and "inalienable" features. One of these was defined as *laicism* which amounted to a radical separation of religious practices and institutions from public life and their subordination to an all powerful secular state. The second was Turkish nationalism which, after a beginning that had some civic pretensions, moved increasingly closer to an ethnic definition of Turkishness. This ideology ended up excluding from its project of modernity all non-Muslims as well as others such as the Kurds who did not agree to be identified as "Turks." The third feature of the new state would be its economic nationalism that evolved into a full-fledged plan of development and industrialization in the third decade of the twentieth century. In the entire reform process, any link between the political elite who envisioned this project and the broader society which was its object, was conceived solely in terms of the former acting upon the latter. This unidirectional vision comes across very clearly in the "Six Arrows" which the single party of the early republic adopted as a symbol where the arrows represented the main planks of the nationalist project; namely, republicanism, secularism, nationalism, populism, statism, and revolutionism. There was no room in this construct for any initiative from below that could contribute to the defining of the parameters, contents, or the nature of the reform or of the new national community. Integration within the society and, more importantly, the articulation between the new state and the society was to be achieved only through the top-bottom initiatives that would originate from the state and extend across the country to the various levels and segments of the society.

Previously, the only other time when the barriers between the republican state and Turkish society seemed to be coming down was in the 1950s when an extraordinarily close tie had developed between Adnan Menderes who was the leader of the Democratic Party and a vast majority of the electorate. In those years better means of communication and transportation, rising rates of literacy, and the beginnings of vast waves of migration into cities were all factors that contributed to the creation of a society that was better integrated, both materially and culturally. The adoption and practice of multiparty system of elections after 1946 provided a participatory political framework to this process of change which had been largely absent from its nineteenth and early twentieth-century predecessors. On the one hand, as of the end of the 1950s it seemed that the modernization script which authors like Lerner had prescribed was in fact being realized. Western-oriented, fast-paced economic and social changes were indeed generating a more open and democratic society. It was against this background that Lerner expressed his confidence about the future of Turkey which I cited earlier in this chapter. On the other hand, the opening of this new political space allowed people to reassert their religious convictions with a newly charged vigor even though these were the very sentiments that were supposed to lose their hold in a modern and open society. It was partly on the pretext of the dangers that this development caused to the secular republic that the political elites intervened in 1960 with a military coup and interrupted the political evolution of the country.

From this historical perspective, Refah appears not as a threat but as the embodiment of the aspirations of large segments of the population who had been excluded and alienated from the Republican policies of modernization.[19] As such its success can be seen not as a return to the dark ages but as a positive step in the broadening of democratic politics in Turkey, a process that had been interrupted by the 1960 coup. But to many, Refah appears more as an enigma than a clearly identifiable step in Turkey's political evolution. In particular, there are two areas where doubts persist concerning the place of Refah and the Islamist movement in the development of civil society in Turkey. One of these has to do with the degree to which Refah and its supporters are open to ideas of democracy, tolerance, and coexistence with other groups. Many analysts continue to detect considerable equivocation in the party's professed willingness to "cohabit" in the same political space with un- or anti-Islamic political parties and movements. Civic credentials of the Islamist movement are questioned also because the Muslim activists put so much emphasis on the importance of various collectivities (families, neighborhoods, tarikats) as opposed to individuals and their rights as the building blocks of not only their political movement but also the society to which they aspire.

In the first area the discussion is no longer purely hypothetical since a large number of important municipalities have been under Refah rule for three years and the central government has been dominated by them since July 1996. In the immediate aftermath of the municipal elections in 1994, the public discourse of Refah was such that many people felt justified in worrying about whether any cohabitation would be pos-

sible under the new leaders. Especially the victories in Istanbul and
Ankara were of great symbolic importance both for Refah and its detractors. The election, according to the party's propaganda, was the
first step in the "reconquest" of this city which would be achieved by
freeing her from the immoral and corrupt influences of the west.[20] The
Refah candidates promised to destroy the Byzantine Walls, close down
the Orthodox Patriarchate, reconvert the Hagia Sophia Church/Museum
into a mosque, and even ban *al-fresco* dining in order to "take back our
city."[21] The outcome of the elections further deepened the wedge that
had already separated the supporters of Refah from the urban elite who
saw themselves as the vanguard of the secular regime. They were fear-
ful that even the slightest deviation from Atatürk's militant secularism
would spell the beginning of the end for the modern republic. In 1994,
as soon as the results of the local elections became known, a flood of
fax messages poured out of Turkey calling on the followers of Atatürk
to take up his mantle and declare a second war of liberation, this time
against not the Greeks but the "reactionary Islamists" who were threatening the republic.

Symbolically at least, the new Islamist mayors started off by trying
to alter the overall image of their cities according to their ideological
tenets. A big mosque complex was planned for Taksim Square in Istanbul
to overwhelm the five-star hotels and the Atatürk Cultural Center that
now dominate the area. In Ankara, the municipality adopted a new "Islamic" logo to replace the old Hittite sun which was deemed a pagan
idol. In both of these big cities and in other centers dominated by Refah,
the municipalities stopped serving alcohol in the restaurants and cafes
which they owned and ran. They also changed the Friday work hours
so that people could attend public prayers on that day. Dress codes that
were adopted during Atatürk's time were relaxed and women were permitted to come to work wearing Islamic dress. Some of the Refah policies were also tinted with a heavy dose of populism. For example, the
walls of one of the local municipality were torn down and replaced
with glass windows in order to create a "transparent administration"
and some of the mayors instituted open-house sessions on Fridays where
they personally listened and attempted to solve the problems of suppli-
cants. Refah municipalities also tried to bypass the market and started
to sell subsidized bread directly to urban population attempting to further
strengthen the special bond they had established with their electorate.[22]

As visible as some of these steps were, they certainly did not amount
to a "reconquest" of Istanbul, neither did they redefine the characteris-

tics of urban life in Turkey. In part, this was because of the limited autonomy cities have in public administration in Turkey. In order to realize some of the bigger projects they had promised, the Refah municipalities would have to obtain the cooperation of the national government, which was not forthcoming in the first two years when Refah was not part of the government. But more importantly, as soon as they assumed their posts, the new mayors were faced with the practical problems of running bureaucracies that had become enormous under previous administrations. The budgets of Istanbul and Ankara had big deficits that needed to be covered and large debts that had to be repaid. In one locality in Istanbul, the new mayor discovered that his administration had inherited TL. 100 million in the bank and TL. 40 billion in overdue debts.[23] Hence as their first tangible measures, some of the Refah mayors fired large numbers of workers, streamlined the cities' bureaucracies, and devised ways of bringing private capital into municipal services. The irony of this situation did not escape the cynicism of the local press which ran headlines about the "Injustices of the Refah's Just Order."

In this respect, the evolution of Istanbul's metropolitan mayor, Tayyip Erdogan is particularly telling. Erdogan had run on a platform that explicitly embraced the shantytowns and emphasized his own roots in one of these areas. In his campaign he had promised a major redistribution of the city's resources towards the newly settled outlying zones and had deliberately avoided any mention of Istanbul's status as a European city or its pretensions in that direction. But once in power, Erdogan was confronted with the practical problems of serving a city that grows by half a million every year and now exceeds 10 million in population. After a brief hesitation, he dropped his plans for reorienting the city's priorities and continued the projects that were designed to improve the modern infrastructure of Istanbul and enhance its status in the regional and global division of labor. A little over one year after he took over, Istanbul's new mayor had to face widespread protests and demonstrations over his decision to dump the city's garbage in a landfill right outside the city; an area that was still technically zoned for this purpose but in reality had long been settled by immigrants from other parts of the country. On August 26–27, 1995 Erdogan ordered the gendarmerie and municipal security to use force in order to break the sit-in that was organized by the inhabitants of a shantytown and proceed with his plans.[24] So radical was Erdogan's conversion that in 1995, at a conference in New York he even endorsed the idea of instituting a head tax in order to curb the growing population in shanty towns.

Refah's experience in national government has already produced a similar turnaround. A foreign trip that included visits to countries like Iran, Sudan, and Libya was carried out with much fanfare by the new prime minister, Necmettin Erbakan, in the fall of 1996 shortly after he assumed his new position. He also promised instituting a new Islamic currency, abolishing interest, and creating new alliances with Islamic states to rival the European Union and other Western associations. However, what actually took place was the reaffirmation and expansion of defense treaties with Israel, continuation of negotiations with the IMF, and a new and concerted push toward privatization. In recent months, the Independent Businessmen's Association which is dominated by Islamist entrepreneurs has emerged as one of the most vocal advocates of selling off of government-owned industries and forming cooperative ventures with European and especially American companies to buy some of these. In February 1997, after some foot-dragging, Erbakan has also signed on to a formal declaration that was drafted by the military and included some uncompromising language concerning the importance of the secular nature of the Turkish state.

Hence both on the local and more recently on the national level, Refah and its supporting associations seem to have developed a modicum of understanding with other parties and groups that allows them to cohabit the same political space. But necessary as it may be this is not sufficient for improving the chances for *civic* coexistence in Turkey. After all, more than anything else, it is the economic necessities and the consequences of Turkey's close ties with regional and global networks that are behind the apparent accommodation between Refah and others. For us to talk about civil society in the true sense of the word, men and women who are members of the Refah, other political parties and their constituent organizations should be allowed to participate in the political realm not only as parts of a group but also as independently thinking separate individuals. And in this area, both the discourse and the record of some of the groups within the Islamist movement continue to be somewhat ambiguous.[25]

Islamists derive some of their strongest support from big cities where ties that hold large families, clans, tribes, and religious orders tend to be less effective. In this sense, it should be plausible to argue that a certain degree of modern individuation underlies the growing power of Refah. For example, in the declining influence of the Sufi tarikats in the Refah hierarchy we can see the expansion of a space where individuals exist not just as cogs in a machinery or as simple objects of a plan but as democratic subjects, able and willing to affect their collective future.[26] Nevertheless, Refah as a party and various components of its constituency still have considerable limitations in these areas.

For one thing, there is a strong countermovement generated by economic insecurity and social uncertainty that keeps individuals in small, segregated groups even in large cities and even if these are physically close to each other. Some of these groups look like the revival or even the extension of the older rural-based networks, or the re-creation of the Sufi communities, but in their modern context they assume new functions that have little relationship with their previous incarnation. For example, new immigrants tend to gravitate toward networks based on places of origin, ethnicity, or religious beliefs partly to maintain their ties with their villages but more importantly as a means of integration into the city because it is through these enclaves that they find information about jobs, share resources, and attain a degree of protection in the big city. By maintaining their ties with their native places the immigrants can also move back and forth depending on their fortunes and supplement their urban income with their rural resources, which in turn makes it possible for them to live and work for very low wages.[27] In Istanbul, there are Alawite neighborhoods, and Kurdish districts and different parts of the city are well known as places of concentration for people coming from specific regions of Anatolia. Over time, instead of disappearing and melting into the urban cauldron, such areas have become increasingly better established and organized and have continued to expand in tandem with the continuing flow of migrants into the city.

In addition to the space-bound formations, people have also sought a degree of familiarity and protection in religious orders some of which have proven remarkably adaptive to the changing conditions in Turkey. Over their long history before and during the single-party era, some of these orders had evolved and developed means of not only surviving under restrictive conditions but also of broadening their horizons in reaching out to other groups. To the extent they are voluntary, perform civic functions, and serve as means of political participation, religious orders and other networks can be seen as constituents of civil society in Turkey.[28] However, one should also point out that some of these formations function not to encourage but to stunt the effective growth of men and women as free-thinking subjects of history which was key to the development of civil society in the West. One prominent writer among Islamic intellectuals clearly sees this orientation of the religious orders as one of their assets. He writes, "the most degenerate mental disease that passed onto us from the modern bourgeois civilization is the belief that within certain limits we are free to determine our own future."[29] In some of these orders, the Shaikh's authority can be so absolute that even speaking in his presence can be seen as an offense, let alone asking questions or challenging his position. In the Ismail Aga Order in Istanbul which is a branch of the *Naqshis* the disciples are permitted to enter the Shaikh's presence only on their knees and wait like that until they are noticed, which may take hours.[30]

Potentially, the restrictive and authoritarian character of these orders is likely to play a particularly significant role in shaping the general disposition of a large segment of the urban youth especially the university students a significant part of whom come from Anatolian provinces. Typically the representatives of these orders try to meet the new students as they arrive in Istanbul or Ankara. They are usually taken to a hostel that is maintained by the order and may even be identified by the name of the students' home province. There the student finds himself in a friendly environment that has close ties with the familiar networks that had surrounded him at his home province. Over time, in addition to the material benefits of cheap lodging and food, a fear of failure strengthens the ties among these students, other immigrants, and the religious order. Failure, here, however, refers not to "not making it" in the city but to the possibility of being corrupted by this juggernaut while trying to be successful. In this sense, the primary function of many of these communities may become not necessarily to integrate but to isolate the newly arriving individuals from modern society and, to the extent that it is possible, keep to a minimum their interactions with city life.

The low status assigned to women constitutes another division that makes the development of integrative communities very difficult in those parts of Turkish society that are dominated by certain variants of Islamist ideology. There is some irony here because women are very active in many aspects of the organization and activities of both the Refah Party and some of the other formations and orders.[31] As such it is misleading to think of them as undifferentiated objects who are manipulated at will by sinister patriarchal elements. Nevertheless there is no denying that women are considered not only the second but intrinsically the lesser sex both in Islamist thought and Islamic politics in Turkey and elsewhere. For example, even though Refah utilized a large number of female activists in the election campaign, not one woman was put forth as a candidate for any of the posts that were contested in March 1994 or in 1995. When the latter caused widespread demonstrations and even resignations from the party, Refah leaders defended themselves by arguing that the culture of the Turkish National Assembly was such that it would never permit female parliamentarians from Refah to sit in session in their Islamic dress. Rather than causing them embarrassment, they claimed, it was better not to nominate any women! Hence, the formidable barriers which they place in the way of individual growth, their strictly hierarchical and rigid organization, their function in insulating large numbers of people from modern society, and the low status they ascribe to their women members provide cautionary notes against looking for building blocks of civil society among religious orders or among other associations that resemble the older extended families in Turkey. While these groupings may be a conduit for political participation they may also hinder the two other elements that play an important role in the constitution of civil society as provided by John Hall in this volume, namely, cooperation *and* individuation.[32]

With an essentially illiberal state ideology that has proven remarkably enduring and a society that seems to be fragmenting and closing on itself, we are not left with much to be optimistic about the future of civil society and civic morality in Turkey. Writing in the late 1950s, Bernard Lewis cautioned against the possibility that Turkey might "slide back into darkness,"[33] and in 1996, Thomas Friedman admonished the West for "losing" Turkey. Yet it is still possible to describe these prophecies as unduly pessimistic and the obituaries somewhat premature. There are some links and channels of communication both among the seemingly insular groups within the society and between this amalgam and the Turkish state that seem to counteract the corrosive effects of economic crisis, social fragmentation, and political uncertainty. The first and foremost among these is the more or less uninterrupted practice of democratic politics in Turkey during the past fifty years which has provided some avenue for orderly expression of civil and political discontent. Even though many state policies and practices make mockery of notions of individual, human, and civil rights, this is one area where Turkey is still in a much better position than most of the other states in the Middle East. The very fact that the Islamist Refah Party is able to organize, run in elections, is governing a plurality of major cities, and is the senior partner in a coalition government provides the most powerful check against extremism in Turkey. As long as the rules of the game are not altered and the different parties continue to find a common space to compete, communicate, and cooperate with each other there is hope that the fractures in society and the deep distrust between the secularists and the Islamists can be mended and a space for civic organization can be protected.[34]

Secondly, massive urbanization that has carried more than half of Turkey's population into cities in the last four decades, has generated new hybrid cultural forms that help bridge some of the gaps that separate the various segments of the society. Popular culture is especially dominated by amalgams that freely borrow elements from distinct geographical, ethnic, religious, and social loci and combine them in new syntheses. The fast spread of private television in the last ten years has facilitated the development and dissemination of these forms across the country at a very quick pace.[35] People who take part in the creation and consumption of such products create a very strong basis for the development of broader types of cooperation on the societal level.

Finally, there are influential new groups among the Islamists who maintain some distance from the established parties and organizations but have developed an increasingly powerful and accommodating discourse about Turkish politics and history.[36] Among these the older but very dynamic Nurcus and the newer Fethullah Gülen Group (named after a religious scholar and intellectual) have become particularly prominent in recent years. Both of these groups are explicitly critical of the mystical orders in Anatolia for their overindulgence in spiritual concerns and their neglect of the practical and political requirements of living in the modern world. Yet they also criticize the "slavish Westernization" of the mid-nineteenth-century Ottoman governments which they interpret as involving a breach of the social pact that had existed between the Ottoman subjects and the Imperial State. Their criticism of the early reformers leads them to support simultaneously both an idealized version of the classical Ottoman state and the antiimperialism of the Young Turks and early Kemalism. The founder of the Nurcu Order, Said-i Nursi took active part in the Young Turk Revolution and aided Mustafa Kemal's forces during the Turco-Greek War.[37] But following the 1925 purges he spent long years in prison and became an ardent supporter of the democratic regime in the 1950s. The disciples (students) of the Nur order engage in spreading the writings and teachings of Said-i Nursi which comprises hundreds of tracks that include commentaries on politics, Islam, modernity as well as advocating a more open, flexible and tolerant practice of Islam. Nurcus put a lot of emphasis on the verbal transmission of this message which makes them an important factor of dialogue across the various strata in Turkish society.

Over the last twenty years, Fethullah Gülen has built a strong following for himself that extends into religious groups, secular schools, and most importantly the military. Gülen sees Turks as having played a very important role as the most effective defenders of Islam in history. Accordingly he emphasizes the specificity of Turkish Islam and his teachings strongly identify with Turkish history, including not only the Ottoman and pre-Ottoman parts but also the republican years. Gülen advocates that Turkey should establish closer ties with the new republics in central Asia and support the creation of a new community of Muslim Turks.[38] To help forge these ties and help spread his brand of national Islam, Gülen has established foundations and schools in Turkey, Germany, Belgium, Denmark, and Central Asian countries.[39] The curriculum of Gülen's Milky Way Schools combines religious training with a variety of courses in hard sciences, as well as study of Mustafa Kemal's achievements. Gülen explains his mission as one of bringing the *medrese* (the religious school) and the *mektep* (secular school) together. He sees the former as indispensable for the gaining of the moral rectitude which then will form a strong foundation for the adoption and practice of modern forms of life and economy. Gülen says, "it is important that we protect our essence and identity but we need to be able to interact with other states in a globalizing world…and be open to changes in science and technology…. We can't just say that everybody will cook their favorite dishes in their homes and we will somehow end up with a complete menu…. Being an enemy of the west cannot but push us outside of our age."[40] He argues that, Islam holds the spiritual and physical aspects of an individual's identity in a delicate balance and that neglecting either one of these will lead us to dogmatism "either of religion or secularism."[41]

Today, Gülen represents a more tolerant and flexible voice of Islam that tries to repair the ties among the fractured communities and groups in Turkey. He has become very prominent among the political elite as well as among Islamist intellectuals and education circles. Some secular politicians including President Demirel and the former Prime Minister Ciller court him as a check against the growing popularity of Refah. In the writings, actions, and interventions of groups such as the Nurcus and Fethullah Gülen, one recognizes a tacit acceptance of a shared sense of identity and an agreement over the rough boundaries of the political unit within which they are functioning and coexisting with their rivals and detractors. For this reason, the growing prominence of Gülen and other influential writers and community-based organizations that are not closely affiliated with tarikats or with established political parties portends a more hopeful future for the building of an effective civil society and a stronger democracy in Turkey. In the fast-changing society that Turkey has become, it is hard to imagine that any one monolithic definition of this society (secular, Islamic, Turkish, Kurdish...) will prevail over all the others and will become the exclusive characteristic of this society. Neither is there any chance that any one of these components will disappear any time soon to leave the field to the others. The challenge is to nurture simultaneously all of the many forces that make up the Turkish society in relationship to each other and especially make sure that the context which makes possible their cohabitation is protected. This, of course, is a challenge that should be shouldered by all those who are party to this debate and engagement.

Notes

1. Research for this essay was supported by a grant from the Royalty Research Fund of the University of Washington.
2. Bernard Lewis, *The Emergence of Modern Turkey* (London: Oxford University Press, 1961), p. 424.
3. Daniel Lerner, *The Passing of Traditional Society* (New York: The Free Press, 1964), p. 128.
4. Dale Eickleman and James Piscatori, *Muslim Politics* (Princeton, N.J.: Princeton University Press, 1996).
5. For example, just two weeks before the election on December 10, 1995, the High Council of the Armed Forces purged forty-three "extreme Islamist" officers form the army. *Hürriyet*, 11 December 1995.
6. *Nokta*, 14–20 January 1996, p. 26.
7. For results of elections, see *The Economist*, 2 April 1994, "Turkey"; *Foreign Broadcast Information Service*, 10 May 1994, p. 73; Rusen Cakir, *Ne Seriat Ne Demokrasi* (Istanbul: Metis, 1994), p. 218.
8. For a representative collection of views on this issue, see *Türkiye Günlüğü*, 27, March-April 1994. This argument is popular especially among what Serif Mardin calls the Marxisant writers who had developed a materialist interpretation of Turkish history in the 1970s. See Serif Mardin, "Projects as Methodology: Some Thoughts on Modern Turkish Social Science,"in S. Bozdogan and R. Kasaba, eds., *Rethinking Modernity and National Identity in Turkey* (Seattle: University of Washington Press, 1997), pp. 112–37.
9. For an early and clear summary of this perspective see, Philip Khoury, "Islamic Revivalism and the Crisis of the Secular State in the Arab World"; I. Ibrahim, ed., *Arab Resources* (London: Croom Helm, 1983), pp. 213–36. For a recent application to Turkey, see Haldun Gülalp, "Islamist Party Poised for National

Power in Turkey," *Middle East Report*, 194/5, May-June/July/August, pp. 54–46.

10. *Yeni Yüzyil* 17 August 1995, p. 11.
11. Mustafa Sönmez, *Istanbul'un Iki Yüzü* (Anakara: Arkadas, 1996), p. 135.
12. Rusen Cakir, *Ne Seriat Ne Demokrasi*, p. 51.
13. *The Wall Street Journal*, September 12, 1994. Also see, Cakir, *Ne Seriat*, pp. 51–52; and Jenny White, "Islam and Democracy: The Turkish Experience," *Current History*, January, 1995, pp. 7–12.
14. See, inter alia, International Bank for Reconstruction and Development, *The Economy of Turkey* (Baltimore, Md.: Johns Hopkins University Press, 1951), p. 25; Eric Zürcher, *Turkey: A Modern History* (London: I.B.Tauris, 1993), p. 215; The World Bank, *World Development Report 1995, Workers in an Integrating World* (New York: Oxford University Press, 1995), pp. 162–63; Ziya Onis, "Turkey in the Post-Cold War Era: In search of Identity," *Middle East Journal*, 48: 1 (Winter 1995): 48–68.
15. None of these interventions lasted for more than three years, and each period of military rule ended with elections where the results were diametrically opposed to what the military had in mind and tried to bring about when they intervened. See Resat Kasaba, "Populism and Democracy in Turkey, 1946–1961," in E. Goldberg, R. Kasaba, J. Migdal, eds., *Rules and Rights in the Middle East* (Seattle: University of Washington Press, 1993), pp. 43–68.
16. Rusen Cakir, *Ne SeriatNe Seriat*, pp. 131–45.
17. *Pendik Belediyesi Kamuoyu Arastirmasi*, 1994.
18. On this see Serif Mardin, "Just and Unjust," *Daedalus*, 120:3 (Summer 1991): 117–19.
19. The most eloquent writers among this group are Serif Mardin and Nilüfer Göle. See for example, Serif Mardin, *Religion and Social Change in Modern Turkey* (Albany: SUNY Press, 1989); Nilüfer Göle, *The Forbidden Modern* (Ann Arbor: University of Michigan Press, 1996). See also Hakan Yavuz, "Political Islam and the Welfare (Refah) Party in Turkey," *Comparative Politics* (forthcoming).
20. Tanil Bora, "Fatih'in Istanbul'u," *Birikim*, 76 (August 1995): 44–53.
21. It is ironic that most of the symbols Refah was targeting predate the Ottomans, some by as much as 1,000 years.
22. Rusen Cakir, *Ne Seriat*, pp. 175–79.
23. Ibid., pp. 181–82.
24. *Yeni Yuzyil* 26, 27 August, 1995.
25. It is highly plausible that this ambiguity does not originate exclusively from the Islamic ideology but from the illiberal state ideology that shaped most of the institutions of the modern Turkish state.
26. Indeed Refah's appeal seemed to grow significantly following the public denunciation of its leader by the *Naksibendi* sheikh, East Cosan. Cosan accused Erbakan of being a "fake and a cheat," of not knowing Arabic, and playing fast and loose with Qur'anic maxims and religious principles in order to establish a hold over the "community of believers." Cited in Rusen Cakir, *Ayet ve Slogan* (Istanbul: Metis, 1990), p. 52. See Robert Hefner in this volume for a similar argument about the role the Islamist movement in contemporary Indonesia.
27. For a description of these networks, see Korkut Boratav, *Istanbul ve Anadolu'dan Sinif Portreleri* (Istanbul: Tarih Vakfi, 1994).
28. See Augustus Richard Norton, *Civil Society in the Middle East*, vols. I, II (Leiden: E. J. Brill, 1993, 1994); and Ellis Goldberg, Resat Kasaba, and Joel S. Migdal, "Introduction," in *Rules and Rights in the Middle East*, pp. 3–14. See also the exchange between Ellis Goldberg and Michael Hudson in *Contention*, forthcoming.

29. Ismet Özel, *Irtica Elden Gidiyor* (Istanbul: Iklim Yayinlari, 1988), p. 142.
30. Rusen Cakir, *Ayet ve Slogan*, p. 61.
31. See Nilüfer Göle, *Modern Mahrem*. For an excellent discussion of the status of women in Islamist movement in Egypt, see Elizabeth McLeod, *Accommodating Protest* (New York: Columbia University Press, 1991).
32. John Hall, "Genealogies of Civility," in this volume.
33. Bernard Lewis, *The Emergence of Modern Turkey*, p. 424.
34. It should be added that the mindless violence of Islamist militants in Algeria and the complete destruction the Iranian economy suffered under the mullahs serve as additional incentives for people in Turkey to seek civil solutions for their problems.
35. See Meral Özbek, *Orhan Gencebay* (Istanbul: Iletisim, 1993); Martin Stokes, *Arabesk* (London: Oxford University Press, 1993); Can Kozanoglu, *Cilali Imaj Devri* (Istanbul: Iletisim, 1993).
36. Similar developments in Ukraine and Indonesia make José Casanova and Robert Hefner cautiously optimistic about the prospects of civil society in Ukraine and Indonesia respectively. See Casanova and Hefner essays, this volume.
37. On Said-i Nursi see Serif Mardin, *Religion and Social Change in Modern Turkey*.
38. For a recent presentation of Gülen's views, see the series of interviews published in the newspaper *Zaman*, July, August, 1995.
39. In Kazakhstan alone there are twenty-nine schools established by Gülen's foundation. *Turkish Daily News*, 16 August 1995.
40. *Turkish Daily News*, 16 August 1995.
41. *Zaman*, 15 Agustos 1995.

12

A Muslim Civil Society?
Indonesian Reflections on the
Conditions of Its Possibility[1]

Robert W. Hefner

The global reemergence of the idea of civil society surely ranks as one of the more curious events in recent history. How are we to explain this unexpected reappearance of an idea that had, afterall, become but a footnote in academic political theory? Some might suggest, as Ernest Gellner did several years ago,[2] that there is nothing unusual about this development. The peoples of Eastern Europe most responsible for the initial revival of the concept were not trained political theorists, Gellner points out, but they understood all too well what they lacked. They yearned not just for material prosperity but for tolerance of dissenting viewpoints, limits on state power, and the freedom to express their views and choose their own way of life. Somehow they felt that all of these concerns were captured in this mysterious phrase, civil society.

Even assuming for the moment that Gellner's explanation is correct, the more serious question that follows concerns just what civil society involves, and whether its cultural terms and social organizations are generalizable beyond the irony-rich landscapes of Eastern Europe. Are civil ideals meaningful or institutionally realizable outside the West? Or are efforts to disseminate their values to non-Western societies but an update on a long and recurring story of Western cultural imperialism? In a recent article on Islam and civil society, the Turkish sociologist Serif Mardin offers a brilliantly insightful but wryly inconclusive answer to these questions. "Civil society is a Western dream, a historical aspiration," he first reminds us. The dream is based on values that reach back to Greek times, entailing notions of moral autonomy and practical self-creation. Given its culturally specific genealogy, Mardin implies, the ideal of civil society will be of limited generalizability beyond Western contexts, not least of all because the ideas of personhood and agency that lie at its heart are vastly different from those of most non-Western societies.[3]

As he proceeds further into his essay, however, Mardin's argument becomes more subtly complex, moving from his initial culturalist analysis to a more dialectical genealogy of practice and meaning. Drawing on the extensive literature on the development of Western European cities, law, and parliaments, for example, he comments that civil society in the West was not merely an ideological fantasy but product of a constellation of social and political forces. The power of the Church and its separation from the state, the early appearance of legal institutions, the independent nature of towns, the rivalry between kings and feudal lords, and the eventual rise of an influential bourgeoisie—all of these things served to disperse influence and counterbalance state power, creating a pluralistic political order which John Hall, in another context, has aptly referred to as "multipolar."[4] Intriguingly, Mardin goes on to observe that in recent years "bits and pieces" of this dispersive political organization have begun to appear even in non-Western contexts, including portions of the Muslim world.[5] He cautions, however, that we should not rush to conclude that civil society is about to emerge in all such places. Though "many modern Muslim states are beginning to acquire a skeleton of institutions similar to those" established earlier in the West, "the dream of Western societies has not become the dream of Muslim societies." It has not yet done so, Mardin suggests, because Muslim societies are heir to a "collective memory of a total culture which once provided a 'civilized' life of a tone different from that of the West." The core values of that culture were not agentic individualism and self-creation, but faithful adherence to an awesome and all-encompassing idea of revelation.[6]

One might ask whether Mardin's portrayal of Muslim civilization is not too totalizing or unitary; the Muslim social imagination may well contain diverse memories and political visions (see below). But Mardin's broader analysis presents a problem that must be at the heart of any investigation of the cross-cultural prospects for this thing we know as civil society. Without always being aware of their relationship, social analyses of civil society have typically focused their attention on the two phenomena that Mardin has: on one hand, a pattern of *structural* or *institutional organization* characterized by a rich and self-regulating associational life, a countervailing balance of power, and a host of other arrangements that serve to disperse power out of the state and into society; and on the other, a set of *normative* ideals concerned with freedom, the dignity of the individual, rights of collective self-determination, and regulative procedures for coordinating interaction among groups and individuals in a fair and democratic manner. Some studies of civil society emphasize one of these two sets of variables as opposed to another. In other words, some adopt a strongly culturalist approach, as if problems of democracy and civility were primarily matters of getting cultural discourse right. By contrast, other studies emphasize structural and organizational variables, as if civility and democracy were the natural product of a certain kind of organization. However, the really critical problem for an understanding of civil society concerns not one but both of these variables, and not in isolation but in "sociogenetic" or dialectical interaction. In other words, the problem of civil society concerns the question of how social structures and cultural discourses can work in synergy, so that public organization nurtures civic ideals among a citizenry, and these ideals in turn work to strengthen civic values and practice in state and society.

Some recent literature on the relationship between civil structures and civic norms takes its cues from Tocqueville's famous observations on the associational bases of American democracy. These writings assume that the relationship between associations and civil democratic culture is relatively straightforward. "In democratic countries," Tocqueville wrote, "knowledge of how to combine is the mother of all other forms of knowledge; on its progress depends that of all others." [7] Where that knowledge gives rise to a rich associational life, the Tocquevillian argument goes, civic values and democratic politics will naturally flourish. In a recent work, Robert D. Putnam has applied this Tocquevillian perspective to civic associations in Italy, concluding that civic association is the key to both successful democracy and effective market performance.[8]

There is little doubt that there can be such a mutually reinforcing relationship between associational life, civic ideals, and political-economic development. But Mardin's Turkish example reminds us that the relationship is not always so straightforward. Even where societies share "bits and pieces" of civil organization, they may hold to profoundly different political ideals. If Mardin is right, then the relationship between associational life and civic norms may be more structurally underdetermined than many observers have thought. To evaluate the prospects for civil-democratic society in a particular setting, then, we may have to explore a more complex web of influences than civil associations alone, paying greater attention to the variety of organizations identified as "civic," and examining the social habits and discourses they sustain.

It is against this background that I want to explore the structural precedents and moral possibilities for civil society–or, more precisely, (following from my discussion in the introduction to this book) *civil democratic* integration—in the majority-Muslim nation of Indonesia. The Muslim world has the curious distinction of being among the examples most consistently cited by political theorists as least likely to develop a civil-democratic society. In his recent book on civil society and its rivals, for example, Ernest Gellner identifies political Islam as an inveterate enemy of civil pluralism and liberty. Political Islam, Gellner argues, fails to sanction the existence of countervailing associations. Its insistence on the primacy of divine law in human affairs creates a situation in which, "the state can be called to account for violation of the divinely ordained Law, or for the failure to implement it, but not for some additional requirements imposed by the popular as opposed to the divine will."[9] Under these circumstances, there are few sanctions for social and intellectual pluralism, and any sort of freedom-enhancing moral accountability (which Gellner insists must be liberal individualistic) becomes well-nigh impossible.[10]

Though many people take a less pessimistic perspective on the prospects for civil society in the Muslim world,[11] questions remain as to the cultural and organizational circumstances that might nurture its development. It is this question that I want to explore in the context of the Southeast Asian nation of Indonesia. Though far removed from the centers of Middle Eastern tradition conventionally associated in Western and some Muslims' minds with Islam, Indonesia is the largest majority-Muslim country in the world. It also offers an unusually interesting terrain in which to examine the interaction of structures and cultural ideals at the heart of civil politics. Indonesia has enjoyed a high rate of economic growth (averaging 6 percent p.a.) over the past twenty-five years. Its rapid development has catapulted it from the ranks of the world's poorest countries (in 1965, equivalent in per-capita terms to Ethiopia) to the lower tier of middle-income developing societies. Equally important, Indonesian Islam has experienced an unprecedented revival over the past fifteen of those twenty-five years.

What makes the Indonesian situation especially interesting, however, is that Muslim politics here confounds conventional portrayals of political Islam. Some of Indonesia's most ardent advocates of democratization are Muslim leaders, and some have enunciated their appeals with explicit appeals to the idea of "civil society" (Indonesian, *masyarakat sipil*). Are such statements merely political sloganeering, or do they speak to a genuine synergy of civic organization and civil-democratic ideals? To shed light on this issue, in what follows I present a summary overview of a few critical moments in the political development of Indonesian Islam. This overview is intended, first of all, to challenge stereotypes of political Islam and underscore that there are several different, indeed rival, varieties of political imagination within the Islamic tradition. The discussion is also intended to shed some light on the social circumstances that might work to amplify or "scale up" those elements within Islamic tradition that provide precedence for civil-democratic values.

Finally, and most generally, the Indonesian example also illustrates that discussions of civil democracy cannot assume that civic *norms* are somehow the inevitable or natural product of a particular pattern of societal or associational *organization*. Observers since Ferguson and Tocqueville onward have insisted, quite correctly, that there is an affinity between civil-democratic norms and associational life. At times, however, enthusiasts of this idea have assumed that civic organizations are themselves all that is needed to bring about a civil polity and society. Civil society in such views is primarily a matter of "getting associations right." Such a reduction of the problem of democratic civility to a single associational variable is misleading for a number of reasons, but one stands above the rest: However much some theorists might hope otherwise, the character of civil life is never independent of the state, but deeply shaped by its policies and powers. Inasmuch as this is the case, our effort to understand the conditions of the possibility of civil society cannot end with the analysis of associations, but must look at their interaction with the state. Just how much this point relativizes the cross-cultural utility of the concept of civil society is an issue to which I return at this chapter's end.

History and Plurality in Muslim Polity

Towards the end of his study of the idea of civil society, Adam Seligman observes that, having originated in the philosophies of Western Enlightenment, the ideals of civil society were disseminated and transformed in the late nineteenth century through their association with the modernist projects of nationhood and citizenship. Seligman implies that this association often altered the practice of civil society in a manner contrary to earlier Western ideals. In Central and Eastern Europe, for example, the absence of an independent judiciary, free cities, or an adequate separation of church and state created obstacles to the differentiation of civic selfhood from religious, ethnic, and racial solidarities: "What characterized East-Central European development was thus the lack of precisely those autonomous and plural spheres in society which in the different models of West European development were seen to be at the heart of its particular developmental path."[12] Given the weak state of civil society, ascriptive ties of ethnicity and religion continued to play a greater role in Eastern and Central Europe than in Western Europe. This impeded the development of a universal citizenship and the culture of moral individualism on which, Seligman argues, it depends. Not surprisingly, then, politics in this region often assumed a distinctly uncivil, ethnonationalist form.

If this characterization is at all applicable to Eastern and Central Europe, one would expect it to to be true in spades of a society as multiethnic and multiconfessional as Indonesia. More specifically, one would expect extant social organizations to wreak havoc with efforts to implement any version of civic citizenship. Indonesia, after all, is a nation patched together from some six thousand inhabited islands, three hundred ethnic groups, and some four hundred languages. Its small (3 percent of the total population) Chinese population is seen by non-Chinese as distinct from the "indigenous" (*pribumi*) majority, and is resented by many because of its disproportionate ownership of middle- and large-scale private enterprise (70–80 percent of the total).[13] In addition to its Muslim majority (88 percent of today's population), the country also boasts a substantial number of Christians, who, like the Chinese, are disproportionately represented in the ranks of the urban middle class. There are also Hindus, Buddhists, and tribal animists. Complicating matters even further, the Muslim majority is broadly Sunni in its theological orientation, but deeply divided along ethnic, regional, and ideological lines. Historically, many Muslims from the nation's largest ethnic group, the Javanese, have been of syncretic or nominal Islamic persuasion and thus resistant to the demands of Islamic orthodoxy. During the late 1950s and early 1960s, many rallied to Marxism-Leninism, creating what was before its bloody annihilation in 1965–1966 the largest communist party in the noncommunist world. All this is to say that, if ever there were nominations for nations least likely to develop civil society, many might expect Indonesia to rank near the top of the list.

A Western observer trained in classical modernization theory might speculate that such dizzying diversity is the result of traditional and bounded societies long lost in historyless slumber, and awakened only recently through the detraditionalizing impact of the West. In actual fact, however, Indonesia is a region that illustrates all too clearly the inapplicability to non-Western contexts of the Durkheimian models of bounded societies and cultural totalities that underlay modernization theory (and classical models of society in sociological and anthropological theory as a whole).[14] Modern Indonesia's social diversity is the result of a complex and decidedly unlinear encounter with globalizing forces that reshaped society and culture over a period stretching back easily as far as Europe's early modern era. European colonialism was a major influence in the latter stages of this process, but its role was considerably less progressive than conventional modernization models would imply. Indeed, in the early colonial period, European policies reinforced absolutism, reified ethnic divides, and undercut processes of political and cultural integration at work in the region prior to the European arrival.

When the Dutch sailed into the archipelago in the early seventeenth century, the region's coastal principalities were in the second century of a historically unprecedented "age of commerce," as the Australian historian Anthony Reid has described it.[15] The trade had many facets, but its most lucrative component involved the movement of Indonesian spices, cloth, rice, and gold around a circuit that linked eastern Indonesia to commercial centers in southern Sulawesi, Java, the Malay peninsula, and Sumatra. Goods in these ports were in turn shipped to China, India, and Arabia, creating a trading zone comparable in scale to that of the eastern Mediterranean in the early modern period.

From the beginning this trade influenced political and cultural development in the archipelago. In the first centuries of the common era, regional commerce catalyzed the emergence of Southeast Asia's first states, city-states thriving from the riches of the Asian trade. Shortly thereafter, this same trade facilitated the diffusion of Buddhism and Hinduism from India to court centers in the region. Though some remote islands and inaccessible interiors remained outside this circuit of people, goods, and ideas, the central portions of the archipelago developed a distinctly "Indonesian" array of religious, legal, and commercial institutions.

By the time the Europeans arrived, then, the Indonesian archipelago had enjoyed more than a thousand years of regionally based civilizational development. Moreover, island Southeast Asia at this time was in the second century of a new and intensive phase of economic development and cultural change, comparable in scale to the great commercial expansion of early modern Europe. Trading expeditions from India and, especially, southern China (after the ascent of the Ming in 1368) stimulated commercial activity, and this in turn had a far-reaching impact on regional politics and religion. The traffic in people and goods created pressures for the development of transethnic cultural institutions, even as political power remained dispersed among a host of competing states. From this political-economic perspective, Southeast Asia in the early modern era bore more than a passing resemblance to the dispersive, multipolar pattern of social organization that John Hall, Ernest Gellner, and others have identified as structural precedents for the emergence of European civil society.[16]

By way of illlustration, one can note that, at the time of the European arrival, Malay—a language originally spoken in small settlements of rice farmers and traders on the Malay peninsula and in eastern Sumatra—was well on its way to becoming an interethnic lingua franca for commerce and religion in the insular world. More dramatically, Islam was also spreading throughout coastal regions, at a pace that again invites comparison with the expansion of Protestantism in early modern Europe. The Muslim advance came not on the heels of conquering nomads or slave armies, but commerce and the multiethnic linkages it created.[17]

There had long been a Muslim presence in the archipelago. Arab and Central Asian Muslims had played an important role in southern China's trade with the region in the eighth century. More significantly, perhaps, the Indian branch of the Southeast Asian trade had fallen into Muslim hands after the great Mongol conquests of the thirteenth century.[18] With so much of the trade in India and China in Muslim hands, and with the trade itself creating pressures for moral commonality, Islam spread to all trading centers in the archipelago from the thirteenth to seventeenth centuries. For a while, the new religion found a significant following even in coastal Thailand and Cambodia. In what would later become the Philippines, Islam's advance from the south toward the northern island of Luzon was arrested only by the sixteenth-century arrival of the Spanish.

With the comparison with European Protestantism in mind, it has long been asked just how much the Islamization of insular Southeast Asia represented a significant transformation in popular ethics and, most especially, political culture. Clearly, in some places, Islam merely replaced what was, in effect, a hierarchical Hindu-Buddhism with a religio-political tradition that was almost equally, as the historian Anthony Milner has put it, "raja-centric."[19] Eventually this imperial Islam became the religion of state throughout most of the island region.[20] This variant of Islam elevated the ruler to the key role of defender-of-the-faith, subordinated religious jurists/scholars (*ulama*) to court authority, and otherwise downgraded Islam's civil potentialities. In regions like, most notably, Java and Malaya, this raja-centric Islam also helped to create an environment in which the concern with orthodoxy was relaxed and syncretic traditions played a prominent role in court and popular society.[21]

However, in a few areas of the archipelago, Islam was implemented in a far more complex manner, one conducive to town growth, social pluralism, and institutionalized limits on royal power. Indeed, when the Dutch and English first arrived in the archipelago, they "were frustrated by the difficulty of finding monarchs who could make decisions binding on their subjects."[22] In the most prosoperous trading centers of the archipelago, such as the great kingdom of Melaka (to the northwest of today's Singapore), royal authority sat lightly upon the local population, and the merchant class, especially, enjoyed an extraordinary measure of autonomy. As the Australian historian Anthony Reid has shown, there were times during which this pluralistic polity provided the basis for an independent urban class exercising strong controls on royal power. This was expressed in such institutions as Makassar's dual monarchy (where power was divided between a king and chancellor) and, perhaps most dramatically, in the councils of wealthy merchants which in some city-states advised and even appointed kings.[23]

Though such precedents for political pluralism were identified by local people as Islamic, many were as much based on indigenous political ideas as they were pan-Islamic ones. Islamic doctrines condemned the abuse of royal power, but, as Anthony Reid has noted, they were notably silent on the precise institutional instruments that might prevent its occurrence:

> [T]he Islamic treatises left the burden of responsibility on God and the King. There was no theoretical justification for limiting royal power or excluding certain areas from the king's authority, even to the extent that medieval Christianity separated ecclesiastic and civil power. The king should do right, but if he did not then it was left to God to punish him.[24]

Though Reid does not highlight it, there was one important exception to this lack of precedent for contractualist government. The exception was the model of limited kingship found in such commercial city-states as Buton in Eastern Indonesia. Organized around a system of kingship subjected to the authority of a customary (*adat*) council and as outlined in a government contract known as the *Martabat Tujuh*, this system of government was itself based upon the Sufi doctrine of the Seven Grades of Being, here deployed in such a manner as to make the sultan subject to a larger moral and material authority. So great was this authority that sixteen of some twenty-eight Butonese sultans were relieved of their positions, and one was actually executed.[25]

Subsequent developments insured that that this Islamic vision of conditional rulership would not spread to other regions. Not long after the Europeans' arrival, the struggle for power between wealth merchants and centralizing kings entered a new and critical stage. Prior to this time merchants had enjoyed considerable independence in many of the area's prosperous city-states. Their autonomy was reinforced by the ease of movement throughout the archipelago and—in a manner which again recalls the rivalries among kings in early modern Europe—the ability of merchants to take their trade elsewhere if the local ruler became unfriendly.

Though there had always been despots who sought to tilt the balance of power against merchants, the arrival of the Europeans made possible a decisive shift in favor of imperial authority. The Europeans were determined to secure a monopoly over the most lucrative items in the archipelagic trade, Indonesian spices, and they set out to do so through treaties or, where necessary, outright conquest. On their arrival in the area in 1499, the Portuguese "sank or plundered every Muslim spice ship they could."[26] When treaty arrangements proved ineffectual, the Europeans seized Melaka, a multiethnic and tolerant society referred to by Europeans as the "Venice of the East. " Over the next century the Portuguese and Dutch captured or sunk most of the large-tonnage junks used by native peoples for shipping, destroying one of the largest private fleets in the world. In seventeenth-century eastern Indonesia, the Dutch went even further, seizing control of the islands which produced the most lucrative spices, and, in several instances, enslaving or exterminating whole populations after they resisted Dutch demands for monopoly rights over the spice trade.

Thus what had once been a dynamic and multipolar civilization reversed course and, by the end of the age of commerce (the mid-seventeenth century), was heading in a thoroughly absolutist direction. Europeans contributed to the process by destroying the economic base of independent traders and supporting centralizing despots. These rulers were only too willing to collaborate with the Europeans, since this meant that they had to make fewer concessions to their merchant rivals. Of course, having eliminated their merchant rivals, it was only a matter of time before the Europeans would turn on their royal partners.

The consequences of the destruction of this indigenous bourgeoisie were seen not just in the disappearance of great ships and the centralization of state power, but in the demise of Southeast Asia's cities. In the mid-seventeenth century around 5 percent of Southeast Asia's population was urban—a greater proportion than northern Europe (though less than India and China). In highly commercialized areas such as Melaka as much as 40 percent of the population was urban.[27] In the two centuries following the arrival of the Europeans, however, the proportion of urban population declined drastically, as did the total population living in large cities.

It is of course foolish to speculate as to what Southeast Asia might have become had Europeans not colonized the region. But it is important to emphasize that Muslim politics here was highly varied, and included divergent ideological dispositions. Not surprisingly, the state-managed, imperial Islam that benefited from the European presence was hostile toward independent enterprise, conservative on matters of social hierarchy, and suspicious of the independent authority of Muslim scholars. However, as the colonial era continued, Indonesian Islam would again give voice to yearnings for autonomy from the powers-that-be.

From Colonial to National Islam

After its initial adventures, Dutch colonialism advanced in a piecemeal fashion throughout the archipelago. Some territories, such as coastal portions of the populous island of Java, were colonized over the course of the seventeenth and eighteenth century. However others, such as the staunchly Islamic sultanate of Aceh on the northwestern corner of Sumatra, were not effectively subjugated until the early twentieth century, and even then only after brutal military campaigns.[28] In general it was not until the middle decades of the nineteenth century that Dutch colonialism took aim at the whole of native society. Their effort was stimulated by their rivalry with the British, whose swift progress in nearby Malaya encouraged the Dutch to transform their piecemeal holdings into a continuous colonial expanse.

Even in this late period, however, the precise nature of Dutch colonization varied from region to region around the archipelago. The Dutch
tolerated some variation in regional administration, incorporating native
authorities into colonial rule where such arrangements were compatible
with European interests. In the longer-colonized central portions of the
colony, such as Minangkabau (on the island of Sumatra) and Java, the
Dutch drafted large portions of the native aristocracy into colonial service. Though the arrangement superficially resembled the British system
of indirect rule in nearby Malaya, the Dutch program was far more inter-
ventionist. It drastically limited native authority, reduced or eliminated
state supports for Islam (quite unlike the British in Malaya), and systematically reorganized indigenous industry and agriculture.

This policy of coopting native elites while transforming economy
and society eventually undermined the authority of the native rulers
who collaborated with the Europeans; pressed by colonial programs,
the peasantry came to see their rulers as mere lackeys of the Europeans. As indigenous rulers lost legitimacy, that of the Muslim leadership
outside of government increased. The eminent Javanese historian,
Sartono Kartodirjo, has described this crisis in Javanese society. He
notes that, while in the previous era Islamic scholars (*ulama*) had been
employed in royal service, the Dutch secularized government administration, removing religious leaders from key posts. Marginalized in
government circles, Muslim leaders nonetheless "displaced that elite
in exercising political authority over the peasantry."[29] As colonial programs intensified, Javanese society was shaken by peasant protest movements. At first these were of a regional and highly particularistic nature,
rarely invoking Islamic ideals. By the end of the nineteenth century,
however, all this had changed:

> The potential following of earlier social movements was...limited by their par-
> ticularized demands and the narrowing effect of reliance on regional cultural tra-
> ditions. At a time when increasing communication was broadening the horizons
> of the peasantry and making localized groups aware of their common sufferings,
> common aims, and common adversaries, the time had come to develop an intel-
> lectual or ideological definition of this wider community. Since a modern-style
> nationalist ideology did not exist, it was natural that Islam should fulfill this need....
> For an important period in the history of Java, then, Islam was seen not as mark-
> ing off one segment of society from the rest, but as supplying the political defini-
> tion of "national" identity and the focus of resistance toward the colonial ruler.[30]

Through these and other activities, European colonialism forever
changed the structure and development of Indonesian Islam. In several
quick strokes, it dismantled imperial Islam, undermined the authority

of native rulers, and unwittingly reinvigorated popular Islam. This new, societally based Islam was different, of course, from the raja-centric and contractualist Islamic traditions of the sixteenth and seventeenth centuries. Most basically, it was a nonstate organization rather than an alternative state structure. This shift of the Muslim leadership out of the state into society was of decisive importance for the subsequent evolution of Indonesian Islam. It imbued the Muslim community with a cautious, and largely critical attitude toward government. This situation is in significant contrast with the experience of Muslims in some of the Middle East or even nearby Malaya. In Malaya, particularly in the native states subject to indirect rule (where sultans retained a significant measure of authority), the British encouraged cooperation between state authorities and Muslim leaders. The long-term consequence of this policy is evident still today in the Malaysian Muslim community's tendency to take a more establishmentarian tack on matters of religion and state.[31]

In Indonesia, there was no such cozy relationship between the colonial administration and Muslim leaders. Instead, in places like nineteenth-century Java, there was a remarkable growth in societal Islam. This civil Islam was at first organized around a curious little institution known as the *pesantren*, a Javanese variant of the pan-Indonesian institution of the Qur'anic boarding school. As the Dutch pacified the countryside, improved roads, and introduced economic programs, there was a steady growth in Java's native population. The growing population fanned out across the countryside, opening the last of the island's frontier regions to settlement and cultivation. Muslim teachers took advantage of these same settlement opportunities, moving out from the the north coast, where historically they had been concentrated, and establishing pesantren across the interior of the island, where the influence of orthodox Islam had long been weak. These Islamic boarding schools have continued to play a central role in the religious and political life of traditionalist Islam to this day.[32]

Pesantren are typically organized around a respected Muslim scholar (*alim*; pl. *ulama*). They depend for their economic sustenance on gifts from the pious as well as the economic activities (usually agricultural) of resident students. In colonial times, these schools served as centers for the dissemination of Islamic knowledge–a function vital for the cultural life of the Muslim community given the state's lack of support for Islam. However, from a political perspective colonial-era pesantren were interesting because they provided an important and transregional network for nongovernmental leadership. In Java and Sumatra, many of the movements of prenationalist anticolonialism were led by graduates of these schools. In the national era (1945 on), these same traditionalist Islamic scholars have provided the leadership for Indonesia's largest social and political organization, the Nahdlatul Ulama (see below).[33]

For most of the nineteenth and early twentieth century it was this same pool of independent Muslims that provided the lion's share of native entrepreneurs. By contrast, native elites recruited to government service were notorious for their disdain of hard work and their lack of commercial acumen. Their preferred avenue of social mobility was government service, from which they often meddled in business affairs. Though in colonial times most large enterprise was controlled by Europeans or Chinese, pesantren Muslims nurtured an alternative ethic of hard work and social independence.[34] Indeed, the *santri* constituted a veritable counterculture in Javanese society, characterized by their own leaders, economic ethos, and moral vision.

In Search of the Civic

It is beyond the confines of this short paper to detail the role of Islam in the subsequent struggle for Indonesian independence. But one summary point should be noted about the normative tensions of Islamic politics during this period. As the above discussion illustrates, there was a powerful *organizational* precedent for extrastate, society-reinforcing, and power-dispersive associations in late colonial Indonesia. This situation was all the more impressive in light of the fact that the colonial authorities, though nominally committed to a variant of European liberalism, in practice institutionalized a system of government which was centrally controlled, committed to monopolistic state enterprises, culturally and racially chauvinistic, and determined to keep native participation in colonial politics to a minimum. Even by comparison with, say, the English in Malaya and India, Dutch commitment to native education and political participation was meager.

In such an environment, it is perhaps not surprising that Islamic society flourished by keeping its distance from state power and nurturing values of independence and self-organization. Despite this precedent of civil *association*, however, the fact remains that there was a far less unambiguous Muslim commitment to civic political *ideals*. There are a several of reasons for this. Though pesantren and Muslim social life generally were characterized by a dispersive organization, the structure of leadership within these and other traditional Islamic institutions remained charismatic and hierarchical.[35] Religious leaders exercised a near-total authority within the schools, buttressed by popular beliefs as to their sacral powers. Unlike a more thoroughly hierarchical society such as, say, India, this pattern of authority was not linked to an overarching ideology of societal hierarchy. Nonetheless, this hierarchical leadership made it unlikely that the Muslim community's civil organization might serve as the basis for a democratic rethinking of Islamic political theory and practice.

There are lessons in this example for the the study of civil society far from Indonesian shores. The example again underscores that by itself a vigorous tradition of nonstate social associations is not sufficient to generate encompassingly civil values. For such an organizational *structure* to become a precedent for civic *ideals* at least two additional conditions must be met. First, influentially placed intellectuals must look into that associational experience and derive from it principles of autonomy, mutual respect, and free association which can then be generalized to the whole public sphere. Needless to say, there is nothing natural or automatic about this process of political rationalization. As European history so vividly illustrates, there may be moral or cultural obstacles to the enunciation of some of the ideology's terms. Or, again, idea makers may choose to ignore the lessons of social association simply because they have other interests to pursue. Second, and equally important, for these principles to become major influences in public life, they must be given institutional force in the policies and laws of the state, so as to provide a political environment that reinforces civil association and its values. To say this is to emphasize once more that civil society is not opposed to the state but both depends on and complements it. At the same time, there is nothing natural or inevitable about this values-institutionalization, and the process can be cut short at any time by competing interests and uncivil conflicts.

In the case of early twentieth-century Indonesian Islam, there were few moral or structural incentives for leaders in the traditionalist Muslim community to engage in this kind of creative rethinking of their political tradition. Structures of prestige and authority within the traditionalist community were such that they rewarded mastery of Islamic skills such as memorization of the Qur'an, knowledge of the hadith, legal reasoning, and mystical knowledge. There were few incentives for traditionalist leaders to depart from this pattern, least of all in a direction that might make them vulnerable to conservative Muslim critics.

Other things reinforced this reluctance to engage in political renewal. Early on the colonial authorities concluded that the most effective policy toward mass-based Islam was noninterference in religious affairs combined with forceful repression of overt political activism.[36] Though in nineteenth century Java there were small-scale rebellions under the banner of Islam, pesantren leaders soon recognized the dangers of too-direct political involvements. Indeed, a few years after its founding in 1926, at a time when nationalist Indonesians were demanding changes in the colonial order, the organization of traditionalist Islamic scholars known as Nahdlatul Ulama issued a statement affirming the legitimacy of European rule and its consistency with Islam.[37]

In short, there was little in traditionalist Muslim society to leverage a critical reflection on Muslim experience in the late colonial period and abstract from it the religious bases for a civil politics. As we shall see, the potential for such a creative reformulation remained. However, it would be another half-century before events would inspire some leaders to use their own experiences as the basis for a reformulation of Islamic politics. By then, however, the project of Islamic renewal would face a whole host of new obstacles.

Modernists and Secularists

Before discussing recent Islamic politics, mention must be made of two other kinds of Muslims beyond the rural-based traditionalists discussed above: modernist Muslims associated with reformist ideas originally developed in the Middle East, and secular Muslims who looked not to Islamic tradition but to nationalism and socialism as their political guides.

Though the great majority of Indonesia's nineteenth-century Muslim leaders came from traditionalist backgrounds, in the course of the century Indonesian Islam began to feel the winds of reformist revitalization blowing from the Middle East.[38] The first of these influences were inspired by the Wahhabi reformers who had captured most of the Arabian peninsula in the early nineteenth century. The Wahhabis inveighed against traditionalist ritual practices, especially those associated with the veneration of Muslim saints. Such practices, the Wahhabis insisted, represented unacceptable innovations from Islamic tradition, since they were not explicitly sanctioned in the Quran or *hadith*. Wahhabi ideas influenced the Padri rebellion that swept Minangkabau, Sumatra in the early nineteenth century. Through the continuing influence of the Saudi royal family, elements of Wahhabi reform continue to influence Indonesian Islam to this day.[39] In general, Wahhabi reformists rejected Western forms of government, science, and education. In this sense they were reformist but unmodernist. With its conservative leadership and scripturalist bent, then, representatives from this faction of Indonesia's reform movement were little disposed to emphasize the creative reconstruction of Muslim political thought.

By the beginning of the twentieth century, however, there were other, more modernist reform currents developing in the archipelago. Influenced by the writings of such modernist luminaries as the Egyptian Muhammad Abduh and Sayyid Jamal al-Din al Afghani, these reformers were preoccupied with responding to the political and scientific challenge of the West.[40] In Indonesia, several modernist organizations were established in the early twentieth century, the most influential of which was the the "Followers of Muhammad" or Muhammadiyah. Founded in 1912 in Central Java by a religious leader who had worked for the Javanese courts, the Muhammadiyah eschewed organized politics and concentrated its energies on education, health, and care for the poor. In the final years of the colonial era, the organization spread rapidly to all corners of the archipelago; today it enjoys a following of some twenty million people.[41] The Muhammadiyah showed none of the traditionalists' hesitation toward Western education, technology, and science. Organizationally, too, the Muhammadiyah repudiated the traditionalists' emphasis on charismatic religious teachers, and developed organizations with rule-governed bureaucracies and open processes of election and appointment.

However innovative their policies in matters of education and association, Muslim modernists disagreed deeply over how to reform Islamic politics. Some were convinced that the Qur'an and hadith had no explicit or comprehensive blueprint for political organization, and in no way required the formation of an Islamic state. What Islam offers, these thinkers felt, is generalized principles of equality, mutual consultation, and social justice, values compatible if not identical with those of modern democracy. For want of a better term, these modernists are often identified as *liberal* modernists. The designation correctly implies that reformists of this stripe are generally comfortable with forms of modern political organization that resemble Western liberal or parliamentary democracy. Needless to say they do not typically embrace

ism. Conversely, in the Islamist community, political discourse has been deeply influenced by nationalist ideals and policies.

This peculiarity of its religious politics has not freed Indonesia from deep and at times bloodly rivalries among proponents of different ideological streams. During the 1950s and 1960s there was a severe polarization of politics along religio-ideological lines, culminating in the destruction of the Indonesia Communist Party in 1965-1966. Again, the details of this history would take us beyond the confines of this brief chapter. However, a few points should be mentioned, because they illustrate the way in which the emergence of a modern political society unleashed civil aspirations, but ultimately dissipated many of Indonesia's resources for civil democracy.

Politics Against Civility

Even before its declaration of independence on August 17, 1945, the movement for national independence in Indonesia was torn by deep ideological divides. In mid-1945 the committee charged with formulating the declaration of independence almost collapsed under the weight of disputes over whether to include a statement acknowledging the state's obligation to encourage implementation of Islamic law among the state's Muslim citizens.[45]

The four-year war for independence which began after the return of the Dutch in the fall of 1945 worsened these divides. It is important to remember that, among Southeast Asian nations, Indonesia's war for independence was second in intensity only to that of Vietnam. The conflict had a galvanizing effect on Indonesian society. In Java, south Sulawesi, and Sumatra it was accompanied not merely by anticolonial violence but by social revolution. In many regions, too, the military struggle was organized along religious and ideological lines. These would serve as key fault lines in bitter political struggles that intensified in the 1950s.

Dozens of political parties came into existence during Indonesia's brief experiment with parliamentary democracy from 1950-1957. However, the primary cleavage lay between, on one hand, a handful of Islamic parties, most of which advocated the establishment of some form of Islamic state, and a amalgam of nationalist, communist, socialist, and Christian parties committed to nonconfessional nationalism. At the time of the first parliamentary elections in 1955, Muslim parties expected to win an outright electoral majority. They hoped to use the victory as the springboard for introducing Islamic law among the Muslim majority, and eventually for creating a full-blown Islamic state. In the end, to the astonishment of almost everyone, Muslim parties secured just over 40 percent of the vote.[46] The left-leaning nationalist leader President Sukarno thus remained in power, and, for the moment, the nonsectarian basis of the state seemed secure.

Political tensions, however, only worsened. The parliamentary elections were followed by new elections in December of 1955 for a Constituent Assembly, whose primary task was to draft a new constitution. Once established, however, the Constituent Assembly proved to be as deeply divided as the national parliament. Though it reach agreement on several important issues, the Assembly was unable to resolve the question of whether Islam should be the official basis of the nation. Unhappy with the impasse in parliament, alarmed by the country's economic decline (due, in large part, to his own chaotic policies), and anxious about his Muslim and military rivals, in 1957 President Sukarno announced a plan to reorganize politics and return to an executive government, as had been outlined in the original constitution of 1945. In 1959, he put the policy into practice. He drastically curbed the legislature's power, expanded his own, and announced a wildly unrealistic program of political restructuration intended to unite nationalists, Muslims, and communists under a common "National-Religious-Communist" (NASAKOM) banner.[47]

This balancing act was doomed from the start. As the economy veered into hyperinflation in the early 1960s, Sukarno turned for support to the political party with the largest mass following and an international vision closest to his own, the Indonesian Communist Party (PKI). At the same time, in 1960 he lashed out at the largest and most effective of his Muslim rivals, the party of Muslim modernists known as Masyumi. Citing the participation of some of the party leadership in regional rebellions raging in West Java, Sumatra, and southern Sulawesi, Sukarno banned Masyumi outright. His tactical alliance with the communists only further outraged Muslim organizations. The political crisis deepened in 1963 when the Communist Party launched a vigorous campaign of "unilateral actions" intended to implement the terms of the 1960 agrarian reform laws. The campaign was poorly coordinated, and sometimes focused on landlords with ties to Muslim political parties rather than on all wealthy farmers as a whole. Moreover, in several well-known incidents, PKI cadres lost control of their followers and the campaign degenerated into clumsy attacks on pious Muslims.

Sukarno's actions proved equally antagonistic to the Indonesian armed forces, the single most powerful institution in Indonesia. Though hostile to advocates of an Islamic state, the armed forces command were even more bitterly opposed to the Communist Party. Well before the tumultuous events of late 1965, then, the military had quietly made contact with mass-based social organizations, such as, most notably, the party of Islamic traditionalists, Nahdlatul Ulama, a bitter foe of the PKI and Indonesia's largest Muslim organization.

The crisis came to the head on the night of September 30, 1965, when several left-wing officers in the capital launched what they later claimed was a preemptive coup against the senior military command, killing six generals and seizing command centers. The ill-planned coup fizzled in a matter of hours, and the military leaders who restored order blamed the communist leadership for the action. Though President Sukarno desperately tried to defend the crippled party, the army and Muslims, supported by smaller non-Muslim organizations, launched a national offensive against the PKI in the fall of 1965. Over the next six months, most of the communist leadership was captured, killed, or driven into exile, and several hundred thousand party members were rounded up and killed.[48] In March of 1966, military leaders forced President Sukarno to cede much of his authority to the commander of the forces for the restoration of social order, General S. Suharto. The New Order regime had come to power.

State Dominance, Civil Decline

Events in Indonesia during the 1950s and early 1960s raise complex theoretical questions as to what we mean by democratic civility and the political processes conducive to its consolidation. Most definitions of the related concept of civil society build on the rather simple idea that institutional and ideological pluralism in society serves to limit the power of the state. Indeed, in some minimalist approaches, civil society refers to little more than societally based institutions outside the state.

By itself this view of civil society is a useful beginning, identifying as it does certain social functions that *do* seem important to an appropriately contained, civil politics. But the view fails to resolve one of the most vexing problems in discussions of civil democracy: the theoretical location of politics, political parties, and political movements in civil society. From one perspective, of course, political parties should be solidly identified with the latter, especially inasmuch as they are not state-mandated entities but political bodies that arise to represent organized interest groups. From another perspective, however, political parties should be placed within the realm of the state, since, at least in representative government, they are designed to provide personnel who can direct and control the machinery of government.

One way to resolve these conceptual issues might be to break down the concept of civil society into finer, lower-level constituents. Jean L. Cohen and Andrew Arato have taken helpful steps in this direction, distinguishing "a *political society* of parties, political organizations, and political publics" (emphasis added), on one hand, from *economic society* with its "organizations of production and distribution," on the other. They in turn distinguish these spheres from civil society itself. Both "generally arise from civil society, share some of its forms of organization and communication, and are institutionalized through rights…continuous with the fabric of rights that secure modern civil society." But they are animated by quite different normative aims: state power on one hand, and production on the other.[49]

All this is helpful, but, as political philosophers, Cohen and Arato's primary interest is not to identify the empirical sources of civil society, least of all in a meaningfully cross-cultural sense, but to assert the merits of one vision of civil ideals against another. With this normative goal in mind, Cohen and Arato's primary intent in distinguishing political and economic society from civil society seems to be to identify the norms most appropriate for the latter. In their view, these include values of democratic association and freely unconstrained, egalitarian discussion, ideals they derive from Habermas's discourse ethics.[50]

These are worthy ideals, but ultimately normative analysis is quite different from the investigation of real-and-existing supports for civil norms and politics, especially across cultures. More particularly, discussion of civil society in normative terms often leads analysts to put the cart before the horse, so to speak, since what we want to determine is not just which civil ideals might be best, but, realistically, what version might be feasible within a particular social world. Nonetheless, Cohen and Arato's distinction points us in a helpful direction. It draws attention to a dynamic obscured in global or undifferentiated models of civil society: namely, that civil association is not a sui generis phenomenon, but one deeply affected by economic processes, state institutions, and, most basically, power. The distinction can thus serve as one more cautionery reminder that, *pace* some simplified readings of Tocqueville, association alone does not guarantee societal civility or democratic government. Both depend upon a more complex interaction of society, politics, culture, and the state.

All this of course is directly relevant to the Indonesian example. Whereas the Muslim community here had a long history of associational autonomy, the canalization of its interests into a relatively unbounded, winner-take-all politics in the 1950s not only ignored this remarkable civil precedent, but undermined it. When one speaks to moderate or democratic-minded Muslim leaders today, one is struck that there is a generalized recognition that, however necessary their involvement in politics, the form it took in the 1950s and early 1960s antagonized civil relationships and harmed the Muslim community's broader, nonpolitical interests. From a Muslim perspective the most telling index of this damage was the movement of more than two-million ethnic Javanese away from Islam into Christianity and (in lesser numbers) Hinduism in the aftermath of the 1965–66 killings. Almost all those who left Islam for these new religions came from nominally Islamic backgrounds and were motivated to convert by their repugnance at Muslim involvement in the postcoup killings.[51]

Conservative Muslim thinkers see no theoretical lesson in this experience and continue, as before, to invoke political ideals from an imagined classical era as the only appropriate basis for modern politics. However, in the early 1970s, a number of pluralist Muslim writers began to argue that Muslims must once and for all give up the idea of establishing an Islamic state, free themselves from (as one leader once put it) the "fetishism" of party politics, and dedicate their energies to economic development and the struggle for pluralist democracy. In a series of bold speeches and publications in the early 1970s, the former student leader and Muslim activist, Nurcholish Madjid, called for Muslims to "desacralize" party politics once and for all, even as they maintained their commitment to the idea that religious values must inform public discourse and provide a critical perspective on politics and society.[52] For these thinkers, whose influence has grown since the 1970s, developments since 1965–1966 only underscore the need to reformulate Islamic politics on the basis of democracy and pluralism. In a remarkable departure from the politics of the early 1960s, some of these leaders insist that the goal of their politics should be nothing less than the creation of a "civil society" (*masyarakat sipil*) premised on pluralism, associational freedom, and democratic politics.[53]

State Conquest?

During the first four years of the New Order regime, Muslim-state relations went from cordial to strained. As reward for their assistance in forcing President Sukarno from power and liquidating the Communist Party, Muslim leaders at first expected to be welcomed into government or, at the very least, allowed to play an active role in the next national elections. The impression in these circles—and apparently among many military leaders as well—was that, with the communists destroyed and the Nationalist Party discredited, the Muslim road to electoral victory would be swift.

Soon, however, the military-dominated government made apparent that it had no intention of holding early national elections or allowing Muslim organizations much organizational latitude when they finally did. Among other things, government leaders reitered their opposition to any effort to revive the so-called Jakarta Charter, the document which during draft discussions in 1945 had affirmed the state's obligation to implement Islamic law among the nation's Muslims. This was but the first of many indications that the new government had little interest in putting on the dress of Islamic governance. Government officials proceeded to deny requests for the rehabilitation of what had earlier been the largest of Islamic parties, the Masyumi, which had been a bitter foe of President Sukarno and banned in 1960. While, shortly thereafter, the government appeared to give in to Masyumi interests by allowing the formation of a new Islamic party, it quickly clarified the terms of that concession by refusing to allow Masyumi figures to play a leadership role in the party.

All this was part of a broader shift in state policy which was, in military eyes, designed to prevent any recurrence of the mass-based party politics of the 1950s. At the center of this strategy lay a plan to reorganize the whole of Indonesian society into a variety of government-controlled corporatist groups, known generically as "functional groups" (*golkar* or *golongan karya*). Though elections would be regularly conducted (in part so as not to estrange Western and Japanese donors), government strategists were determined to take whatever measures were necessary to prevent the recurrence of the factionalized politics of the 1950s and 1960s.

The idea of replacing interest-group politics with a system of functional-group representation was not a new one in Indonesia. In fact it reflected a strain of political thought that went back to the 1920s, and which had been reinvoked at various times in Indonesia's modern history. Originally formulated by a handful of prewar thinkers who viewed Western liberalism as a vehicle of colonialism,[54] this "integralist" view of state and society asserted that the values of collectivism and familism were more consistent with Indonesian civilization than rights-based individualism. Though their views were hotly contested by Muslim democrats and liberal-constitutionalists, a few integralist ideas were inserted into the 1945 constitution and later national policies. Perhaps the most lasting of these was the government's official commitment to cooperatives and cooperation rather than capitalism as the basis of Indonesian economy. Today, even after twenty five years of (state-managed) market development, the government's pronouncements remain deeply hostile to the idea of market capitalism and supportive of the belief that there is a middle road between capitalism and Marxist socialism.[55] Needless to say, for many Islamist intellectuals, though not for the government itself, that middle road is named Islamic economics.

The practical focus of the functional-group policy lay not in the economic sphere, however, but in politics and civil life. Already in the late 1950s the armed forces leadership had advocated the development of functional groups to weaken the influence of political parties. From 1971 on, an expanded version of this same policy became the platform for the entire New Order government. Over the next twenty-four years, every significant association in the fields of politics, business, labor, education, and the media was pressed into umbrella associations organized along "functional" rather than interest group or ideological lines.

A version of this same policy was applied even to political parties. After the 1971 elections, all of the Muslim parties—until then separated by fierce ideological disagreements—were forced into a single, united Muslim party known simply as the Party of Development and Unity. (The government chose the party's name and insisted it make no explicit reference to Islam). In a similar fashion, representatives of the nationalist, Christian, and secular parties—all of whom had been similarly fragmented along ideological lines—were merged into a single "Party of Indonesian Democracy" (PDI). Having fused the parties, the government then asserted the right to intervene in the selection of party leaders and the formulation of policy platforms. It asserted much the same right in everything from business to religious associations, though some of the larger Muslim groupings, such as the Nahdlatul Ulama, proved skilled at resisting state controls. With these and other restrictive measures in hand, the government has won easy victories in the national elections held every five years since 1973.

Since radical nationalists and the political left had been either eliminated or discredited during 1965–1966, the only significant organizations remaining outside state control were Muslim ones. The government did not hesitate to strike at Muslim political parties and intervene extensively in their affairs. But it hesitated to interfere too directly in large and long-established Muslim social associations such as the modernist Muhammadiyah and the traditionalist Nahdlatul Ulama. With its secure organizational base in village society, the Nahdlatul Ulama presented the most consistent and effective challenge to the government.

During the 1970s and early 1980s, the government responded to this even limited Muslim independence with a series of measures designed to redirect Muslim political aspirations once and for all. At the same time, however, it softened the blow by channelling significant revenues into Muslim activities of a nonpolitical nature, such as schools, mosque construction, programs of religious education (*dakwah*), and the annual religious tithe (*zakat*). In an effort to separate the minority of Muslims who still sought to create an Islamic state from the majority who were indifferent or opposed to the idea, the government in 1983 announced a policy obliging all social and political associations to acknowledge the state's *Pancasila* or "five principles" as the sole and everlasting ideological foundation of the nation. Associations that refused to do so would give up their right to exist after 1985.

This extraordinary intervention in associational life at first seemed to achieve its desired goal. It divided the Muslim community and effectively marginalized those who refused to abide by the government plan. However, as I have described elsewhere,[56] the government's policy also had an unanticipated result. With the issue of political Islam now set aside and government-Muslim relations improving, there was an extraordinary upsurge in Islamic piety, most notably in the ranks of middle and upper-middle classes heretofore renowned for their nominal adherence to Islam. This development was not, of course, the simple consequence of government policy. There had always been people in the middle echelons of the business and government elite who had quietly supported the idea of Muslim-government rapprochment. Many officials in the state's Department of Religion had long felt this way, and had helped to channel state funds quietly into Muslim educational and religious activities. During the 1970s, these programs had created a new and pervasive infrastructure for Islamic religious and social activities.[57]

By the late 1980s and early 1990s, the political climate had so thoroughly changed that President Suharto and his circle of associates were openly courting Muslim leaders and civil associations. In part the president did so in reaction to his growing tensions with the armed forces leadership. Up to this time, the armed forces had been the bulwark of the New Order state. But in the late 1980s some in the military leadership began to resent the growing concentration of wealth in the hands of the presidential family. However, the president's overtures to Muslims also reflected his advisors' awareness of the scale of the Islamic revival, and of the resulting need to avoid a polarization of government and Islam as had occurred in so many other Muslim countries. Government officials with whom I spoke in 1991, 1992, and 1993 made open reference to the Algerian crisis, and the need to prevent any similar development in Indonesia.

As a result of all of these events, by the early 1990s the president was openly supportive of such controversial initiatives as the establishment of Islamic banks, the expansion of Islamic legal jurisdication, legalization of school-girls' right to wear the Islamic veil (*jilbab*), sponsorship of a national Islamic festival (Festival Istiqlal), and, most decisively, the formation of a large and prestigious Association of Indonesian Islamic Intellectuals (ICMI). The establishment of this last group was bitterly opposed by many in the military, who perceived the organization, largely correctly, as a vehicle for Muslim penetration of the state.[58] However, the organization was also opposed by the leadership of the traditionalist Nahdlatul Ulama. They regarded ICMI as a vehicle of state penetration of Islam, designed to hijack the Muslim social movement just as it was beginning to press for a more substantial democratization.

The outspoken leader of the latter group, Abdurrahman Wahid, had worked for almost ten years in an effort to modernize N.U.'s leadership, liberalize its social policies, and transform it into a vehicle of grass-roots development and democratization. He and many others in the civic pluralist wing of the Muslim community were convinced that only through a decisive renunciation of Islamic politics (in its formal, party-politics sense) and a commitment to a plural, democratic, and "civil" (Ind., *sipil*) Indonesia could the nation progress. Others in the Muslim community, however, greeted the rapprochement of state and Islam warmly. Some continued to express concern about the president's motives. Having been marginalized from national politics for a quarter century, however, for most Muslim leaders the taste of influence was understandably sweet. Many figures previously identified with grassroots organizations put aside their democratic scruples in the hope that they could change the political system from within.

The late 1980s and early 1990s also saw extensive economic liberalization in Indonesia. The shift from import-substitution protectionism to export-oriented manufacture led many observers to expect moves toward a broader political liberalization as well. Over the course of 1993 and 1994, however, it became clear that there was no such continuity between the government's political and economic policies. After they raised questions about one prominent minister's financial dealings—a man who, it happened, also served as the government-designated leader of the Association of Indonesian Islamic Intellectuals—the government shocked even its own supporters by closing down three of the nation's most respected newsweeklies.[59] Then, confident that it had consolidated its support in the mainstream Muslim community, the government moved against some of its most ardent prodemocracy critics. Its most important target was none other than Abdurrahman Wahid, the reform-minded leader of Nahdlatul Ulama. In 1992 he had joined forces with other prodemocracy activists to establish a multiconfessional Democratic Forum. Among other things, the Forum was intended to serve as a nongovernmental response to the government-sponsored Association of Indonesian Muslim Intellectuals (ICMI), and underscore that the opening to the Muslim community was being conducted in a selective and antidemocratic manner. The Democratic Forum's challenge is said to have deeply angered advisors to the president. In an effort to oust Wahid from his position, progovernment intellectuals launched a campaign to discredit him and drive him from the N.U. leadership. The government also brought powerful pressure to bear on the leadership by restricting business contracts with firms linked to the Nahdlatul Ulama.

By 1995, the optimism of the early 1990s had given way to deep frustration in the ranks of Indonesia's democratic reformers. Perhaps the greatest disappointment for democratic Muslims and other prodemocracy activists was the awareness that the regime had succeeded in luring some of its most influential Muslim critics into government not with the promise of democratic reform, but through a selective, behind-the-scenes extension of privileges to a closed circle of Muslim clients. Whereas a few years earlier many had believed that the Islamic revival could serve as the basis for Indonesia's democratization, many now feared that this Muslim leadership might become but one more vested interest within the corporatist structure of state.

Conclusion: Islam and Civil Society

Its daunting specificity aside, the Indonesian example provides a number of lessons on problems of civil democracy and society in general, and in Muslim societies in particular. As regards Islam, first of all, Indonesian history illustrates that Islamic politics is far more variegated than implied in models like those of Ernest Gellner or Samuel Huntingon. In Indonesia there have been precedents for power-diffusing social associations since the arrival of Islam more than five centuries ago. In a few city-states early in that history, these organizations converged with an economic dynamism to limit royal authority, disperse social power, and support contractualist views of government. Though, as Anthony Reid has argued, these arrangements were influenced by indigenous as well as Islamic precedents, efforts were made in several states to devise Islamic supports for contractualism. The possibility that such contractualist precedents might be deepened or extended throughout the region was effectively killed, however, by an unholy alliance of absolutist monarchs and European power. European colonialism destroyed the economic basis of one of the world's most affluent and independent merchant classes. In so doing, it also destroyed Southeast Asia's multipolar civilization. The region's Muslim mercantilism never recovered.

Later, however, the secularizing policies of the Dutch unwittingly eroded the moral authority of rulers and the institutional basis of imperial Islam. In so doing, and in creating the infrastructure for a new movement of people and ideas, the Europeans also created the conditions for the emergence of a societally based popular Islam. It was this tradition, not the imperial Islam of the courts, that provided the foundation for a new vision of native politics and society in the twentieth century. In that same century, of course, Islam discovered it was no longer the sole voice of the native community, but one among a host of socialist and nationalist rivals. However, none of its rivals could match the depth and breadth of the Muslim community's associational life. Even in the well-controlled environment of the New Order, Muslims have been able to use their organization to resist state demands and nurture alternative visions of the public sphere.

Popular Islam encountered greater difficulties, however, when it attempted to reach a consensus on the lessons to be drawn from its own historical experience. Indeed, throughout the Muslim world this has proved a vexing problem in efforts to effect political reformation. In Indonesia, traditionalist and modernist Muslims alike could boast a proud history of autonomy and organizational pluralism. When it came to devising principles for government, however, many leaders tended to denigrate their own experience and fall back on idealized portrayals of Islam, often premised on a civility-corroding union of religious and political power.

There were other Muslim thinkers, however, who felt that a practical separation of religious association from governance was required to defend Islam itself. They insisted that the goal of establishing an Islamic state is not intrinsic to Islam. Rather than referring back to the model of the Islamic caliphates, they pointed to the precedent of Muhammad's years in Medinah, and that city's constitutional charter for institutional and religious pluralism.[60] More profoundly, when confronted with those who insisted on a literal application of Islamic law, these civil pluralists insisted that it is the spirit and not the letter of the law that must serve as the basis of an Islamic politics.

Unfortunately, in both the late colonial and independence periods, political developments provided few opportunities for the free and open dialogue required to transform these precedents into practical organization. Political rivalries encouraged politicians to focus on solidarity-enhancing symbols rather than dispassionate political discussion. Time and time again, the most serious obstacles to the rationalization of Muslim politics originated not in Islamic politics per se, but in a zero-sum cycle of uncivil politics.

Does the Indonesian example contain generalizable insights? Certainly, on the organizational side of things, the early strength of commerce and the multipolar nature of the archipelagan politics stands in striking contrast with the centrally controlled empires of the classical Middle East, and the authoritarian governance to which they gave rise. However, Muslim Indonesians' effort to protect people from governmental abuse is not unique in the Muslim world. As Ellis Goldberg has argued,[61] there is abundant evidence from the medieval Middle East of merchants and other private actors seeking to "shield themselves and others from the demands of an absolutist monarchy." Admittedly, the urban bourgeoisie was never as independent as that in a few regions of early modern Europe or Southeast Asia. However, there was sufficient mobility around the Muslim Mediterranean that the option of "exit" (to use Albert Hirschman's apt phrase) from oppressive rulers was regularly exercised. In a few periods and places, there was even more. Power was widely dispersed in the hands of religious scholars, merchants, and other notables. Particularly after the Abbasi caliphate, there was strong interest in contractarian or conditional views of government. The writing of this time also emphasized the value of property, and sought to validate a private life out of reach of the state. Much of the machinery of the market, including the hiring of religious scholars to rule on commercial matters, was supported not by the state but by the merchant class. Unfortunately, over the long run the imbalance of power between merchants, towns, and rulers insured that, rather than pushing for the development of representative institutions, merchants and other notables had to settle for merely carving out private spheres apart from the state.[62]

Though the scale of its religious revival may distinguish the Muslim world from the West, the problem of civil polity in the two regions is similar. In both, patterns of extrastate association may provide a precedent for civil ideals but they are not alone sufficient to create a culture of civility or a government inclined to abide by its norms. As here in Indonesia, a larger array of powers and ideals mediates this process. These include the efforts of intellectuals to derive generalizable political principles informed by the lessons of their own society's history. The process also includes the struggle of social groupings to project those principles into government, so that government can work with, rather than against, democratic civility.

There is no inevitable outcome to either of these processes. As Serif Mardin suggested, civilizational precedents may complicate efforts to provide a locally meaningful language of pluralism, freedom, and social dignity. However much official ideological guardians may say otherwise, however, the fate of a democratic civility is never merely determined by ancient precedent. Under the twinned circumstances of modern differentiation and cultural "globalization," intellectuals and politicians may look into their own historical experience and draw from it the lessons for a locally compelling language of civility. Not all such efforts will place as much emphasis on individual rights and privileges as in philosophical variants of Western liberalism. As the essays in this collection have shown, however, the real-and-existing democracies of the Western world have shown more variation on this point than political philosophers typically acknowledge.

Whether, over the long run, such civil precedents can be amplified and endure depends, of course, on more than their moral compellingness or intellectual allure. Though not merely a matter of crude power, civil rights and associations represent public claims by competing social groups, and the outcome of such claims depends on a constantly shifting balance of political, moral, and economic resources.[63] Thus, whether in Indonesia or elsewhere, it is impossible to predict the long-term outcome of struggles for civil democracy. At the very least, however, it is clear that the appetite for such a civil-ized politics is widespread.[64]

Drawing as it does not only on inherited discourse but on the changing practices of a modern way of life, we shouldn't be surprised to see family resemblances of action and aspiration across cultures, as modern forms of life press diverse societies toward similar (though never identical) organizations and meanings. All this is to say that, though the discourse of civil democracy may be globalizing, its meanings and practice are not unitary, but dependent on their articulation with a local way of life.

This web of influences makes the theoretical understanding of civil society more daunting than structural-determinists might have hoped. However, by underscoring the recurring influence of civil organization on government, and government on civil ideals, the lesson should also be reassuring. It implies that the outcome of this struggle for political decency is not predetermined by ancient civilizational instincts. On the contrary, as in Indonesia, the effort depends on cultures and institutions that require perpetual recreation and that, as such, can be brought within human reach.

Notes

1. The research in Indonesia on which this chapter is based was supported by a grant from the Harry Frank Guggenheim Foundation. I wish to express my deep gratitude to the officers of the Foundation for their support.
2. Ernest Gellner, *Conditions of Liberty: Civil Society and Its Rivals* (New York: Penguin Press, 1994).
3. Serif Mardin, "Civil Society and Islam." In John A. Hall, ed., *Civil Society: Theory, History, Comparison* (Cambridge: Polity Press, 1995), p. 278. In an anthropological overview of Western civil society literature, Chris Hann at first reaches a similar conclusion, arguing that the ideal of civil society "developed in historical conditions that cannot be replicated in any other part of the world today," especially in as much as it assumes "the universality of modern western notions of the person." By the end of his essay, however, Hann sees a silver lining in the civil-society cloud, arguing, as I attempt in this book, that civil society "is not the unique product of the West after all; others have developed important elements of it." See Chris Hann, "Introduction: Political Society and Civil Anthropology." In Chris Hann and Elizabeth Dunn, eds., *Civil Society: Challenging Western Models* (London and New York, Routledge, 1996), pp. 1, 5, 20.
4. John A. Hall, *Powers and Liberties: The Causes and Consequences of the Rise of the West* (Berkeley: University of California Press, 1985).
5. Mardin, "Civil Society and Islam," p. 295.
6. See especially ibid., p. 290.
7. Alexis de Tocqueville, *Democracy in America*, translated by George Lawrence, edited by J.P. Mayer (New York: Anchor Books, 1969), p. 517.
8. Robert D. Putnam, *Making Democracy Work: Civic Traditions in Modern Italy* (Princeton, N.J.: Princeton University Press, 1993), p. 182.

9. Ernest Gellner, *Conditions of Liberty*, p. 28.
10. Ibid., p. 29.
11. See Augustus Richard Norton's excellent, *Civil Society in the Middle East* (Leiden: Brill, 1995).
12. Adam Seligman, *The Idea of Civil Society* (New York: The Free Press, 1992), pp. 156–58.
13. James Mackie, "Changing Patterns of Chinese Big Business in Southeast Asia," in Ruth McVey, ed., *Southeast Asian Capitalists* (Ithaca, N.Y.: Southeast Asia Program, Cornell University, 1992), pp. 161–90.
14. For anthropological critiques of the bounded-society model, see Fredrik Barth, "Towards greater naturalism in conceptualizing societies," and Ulf Hannerz, "The global ecumene as a network of networks." In Adam Kuper, *Conceptualizing Society* (London and New York: Routledge, 1992), pp. 17–33 and 34–56.
15. Anthony Reid, *Southeast Asia in the Age of Commerce, 1450–1680*, volume 2: *Expansion and Crisis* (New Haven, Conn.: Yale University Press, 1993).
16. Hall, *Powers and Liberties*; Gellner, *Conditions*; and Max Weber, *The City* (New York: The Free Press, 1958).
17. I should hasten to add that, though this was the primary context through which Islam spread, there were numerous instances of religious warfare at the local level.
18. See Stuart Robson, "Java at the Crossroads," in *Bijdragen tot de Taal-, Land-, en Volkenkunde*, 137:259–92 (1981).
19. Anthony Milner, "Islam and the Muslim State," in M.B. Hooker, ed., *Islam in South-East Asia* (Leiden: Brill, 1983), pp. 23–49.
20. Milner, "Islam and the Muslim State," and Mark R. Woodward, *Islam in Java: Normative Piety and Mysticism in the Sultanate of Yogyakarta* (Tucson: The University of Arizona Press, 1989).
21. Clifford Geertz, *The Religion of Java* (New York: Free Press, 1960); Woodward, *Islam in Java*.
22. Reid, *Southeast Asia in the Age of Commerce*, p. 253.
23. Ibid., p. 264.
24. Ibid., p. 263.
25. See R. Michael Feener, "In the Realm of the Fifth Caliph: Sufism and the State in the Sultanate of Buton"; Boston: Unpublished Paper, Department of Religious Studies, Boston University; and Andi' Zainal Abidin, "The Emergence of Early Kingdoms in South Sulawesi: A Preliminary Remark on Governmental Contracts from the Thirteenth to the Fifteenth Century," *Southeast Asian Studies* 20:4: (March 1983): 1–39.
26. Reid, *Southeast Asia*, p. 14.
27. Ibid., p. 75.
28. See Anthony J. Reid, *The Contest for North Sumatra: Acheh, the Netherlands, and Britain, 1858–1898* (Kuala Lumpur: Oxford University Press, 1969); and M.C. Ricklefs, *A History of Modern Indonesia since c. 1300*, second edition (Bloomington: Indiana University Press, 1993), pp. 143–45.
29. Sartono Kartodirdjo, "Agrarian Radicalism in Java: Its Setting and Development"; in Claire Holt, ed., *Culture and Politics in Indonesia* (Ithaca, N.Y.: Cornell University Press, 1972), p. 89.
30. Kartodirdjo, "Agrarian Radicalism," p. 113. This situation is comparable to that of the Muslim peasantry in Minangkabau, Sumatra a few decades earlier. Nineteenth-century Minangkabau had a denser array of Islamic institutions in place at the time of the European arrival than some other parts of the archipelago, such as Java. Protest movements thus took a more forcefully revivalist form

than was the case in Java. Otherwise, however, Islam in this region too served to broaden the horizons of the peasantry and provide a moral-political idiom for articulating resistance to the colonial advance.

31. See William R. Roff, *The Origins of Malay Nationalism*, second edition (Kuala Lumpur: Oxford University Press, 1994); and Clive S. Kessler, "Archaicism and Modernity: Contemporary Malay Political Culture," in Joel S. Kahn and Francis Loh Kok Wah, eds., *Fragmented Vision: Culture and Politics in Contemporary Malaysia* (Honolulu: University of Hawaii Press, 1992), pp. 133–57.

32. See Sydney Jones, "The Contraction and Expansion of the 'Umat' and the Role of Nahdatul Ulama in Indonesia," in *Indonesia* 38 (1984): 1–20; and Robert W. Hefner, "Reimagined Community: A Social History of Muslim Education in Pasuruan, East Java." In Charles F. Keyes, Laurel Kendall, and Helen Hardacre, eds., *Asian Visions of Authority: Religion and the Modern States of East and Southeast Asia* (Honolulu: University of Hawaii Press, 1994), pp. 75–95.

33. See Andrée Feillard, *Islam et Armée dan L'Indonésie Contemporaine* (Paris: L'Harmattan, 1995).

34. See for example, Lance Castles, *Religion, Politics, and Economic Behavior in Java* (New Haven, Conn.: Southeast Asian Studies, Yale University, 1967); and Clifford Geertz, *The Social History of an Indonesian Town* (Cambridge, Mass.: MIT Press, 1965).

35. Cf. Resat Kasaba's essay on the internal politics of Turkish Sufi orders in this volume.

36. See Harry J. Benda, *The Crescent and the Rising Sun: Indonesian Islam under the Japanese Occupation, 1942–1945* (Dordrecht: Foris Publications, 1983 [1958]), pp. 20–31.

37. See Feillard, *Islam et Armée*, pp. 29–30.

38. On reformist and modernist Islam in late colonial Indonesia, see Deliar Noer, *The Modernist Muslim Movement in Indonesia, 1900–1942* (Kuala Lumpur: Oxford University Press, 1973).

39. See Christine Dobbin, *Islamic Revivalism in a Changing Peasant Economy: Central Sumatra, 1784–1847* (Copenhagen: Curzon Press, 1983), esp. pp. 128–41.

40. For an introduction to the most influential of the early modernists, see Ali Rahnema, *Pioneers of Islamic Revival* (London: Zed Books, 1994).

41. See James L. Peacock, *Muslim Puritans: Reformist Psychology in Southeast Asian Islam* (Berkeley: University of California Press, 1978); Alfian, *Muhammadiyah: The Political Behavior of a Muslim Modernist Organization Under Dutch Colonialism* (Yogyakarta: Gadjah Mada University Press, 1989); and Mitsuo Nakamura, *The Crescent Arises over the Banyan Tree: A Study of the Muhammadiyah Movement in a Central Javanese Town* (Yogyakarta: Gadjah Mada University Press, 1983).

42. For an example of one of the bolder attempts at contemporary recontextualization, see Abdullahi Ahmed An-Na'im, *Toward an Islamic Reformation: Civil Liberties, Human Rights, and International Law* (Syracuse, N.Y.: Syracuse University Press, 1990).

43. It is this Medinah experience to which many Muslim pluralists look today as a precedent for modern civil pluralism. See, for example, Nurcholish Madjid's, "Islamic Roots of Modern Pluralism, Indonesian Experience." In *Studia Islamika* (Jakarta) 1:1 (April-June 1994): 55–77.

44. One should remember, of course, that in Indonesia the nationalist community also included many non-Muslims.

45. See B.J. Boland, *The Struggle of Islam in Modern Indonesia* (The Hague: Martinus Nijhoff, 1983), pp. 15–23.

46. See Herbert Feith, *The Indonesian Elections of 1955* (Ithaca, N.Y.: Modern Indonesia Project, Interim Report Series, 1957).
47. On the failure of the constitutional Constituant Assembly and collapse of parliamentary democracy, see Adnan Buyung Nasution, *The Aspiration for Constitutional Government in Indonesia: A Socio-legal Study of the Indonesian Konstituante, 1956–1959* (Jakarta: Sinar Harapan, 1992).
48. See Robert Cribb, ed., *The Indonesian Killings of 1965–1966: Studies from Java and Bali* (Clayton, Victoria: Monash University, Centre for Southeast Asian Studies, 1991).
49. Jean L. Cohen and Andrew Arato, *Civil Society and Political Theory* (Cambridge, Mass.: MIT Press, 1992), p. ix.
50. Cohen and Arato, *Civil Society*, p. xv.
51. See Margot L. Lyon, *Politics and Religious Identity: Genesis of a Javanese-Hindu Movement in Rural Central Java* (Berkeley: University of California, Department of Anthropology, Ph.D. Dissertation, 1977); and Robert W. Hefner, "Politics and Social Identity: The 1965–1966 Killings and Their Aftermath," in Hefner, *The Political Economy of Mountain Java: An Interpretive History* (Berkeley: University of California Press, 1990), pp. 193–227.
52. Most of his writings from this period were collected in Nurcholish Madjid, *Islam, Kemodernan, dan Keindonesiaan* (Islam, Modernity, and Indonesian-ness) (Bandung: Mizan Press, 1987). Though, for reasons of space, I do not pursue the point here, there is a striking parallel between these leaders' ideas and those of some of the Christian civil activists Jose Casanova has described in his, *Public Religions in the Modern World* (Chicago: University of Chicago Press, 1994). Both decry the conquest of the state in the name of religion, but insist on the importance of religion in civil discourse and in the critique of government and market.
53. On this point, see Nurcholish Madjid, "Menuju Masyarakat Madani" (Toward a Madinah Society), in *Ulumul Qur'an* 2:7 (1996): 51–55; Moeslim Abdurrahman, "Muslim Civil Society di Indonesia: Siapakah yang memerankannya di masa depan?" (Muslim Civil Society in Indonesia: Who will be its actors in the future?), in Abdurrahman, *Semarak Islam, Semarak Demokrasi* (The Radiance of Islam is the Radiance of Democracy?) (Jakarta: Pustaka Firdaus, 1996), pp. 10–25.
54. See David Reeve, *Golkar of Indonesia: An Alternative to the Party System* (Singapore: Oxford University Press, 1985).
55. For a recent analysis on this irony, see Jamie Mackie and Andrew MacIntyre, "Politics," in Hal Hill, ed., *Indonesia's New Order: The Dynamics of Socio-Economic Transformation* (Honolulu: University of Hawaii Press, 1994), pp. 1–53.
56. Robert W. Hefner, "Islam, State, and Civil Society: ICMI and the Struggle for the Indonesian Middle Class," in *Indonesia* 56 (October 1993): 1–36.
57. Hefner, "Islam, State, and Civil Society," and 1987, "Islamizing Java? Religion and Politics in Rural East Java," in *The Journal of Asian Studies* 46:3 (August 1987): 533–54.
58. See "Islam: Coming in from the Cold?" in Adam Schwarz, *A Nation in Waiting: Indonesia in the 1990s* (Boulder, Colo.: Westview Press, 1993), pp. 162–93.
59. See Human Rights Watch/Asia, *The Limits of Openness: Human Rights in Indonesia and East Timor* (New York: Human Rights Watch, 1994).
60. See Madjid, "Menuju," and the special issue of *Ulumul Qur`an* dedicated to Islamic politics, "Islam Tidak Punya Sistem Politik?" (Does Islam not have a political system?), no. 2, vol. 4, 1993.

61. Ellis Goldberg , "Private Goods, Public Wrongs, and Civil Society in Some Medieval Arab Theory and Practice," in Ellis Goldberg, Resat Kasaba, and Joel S. Migdal, eds., *Rules and Rights in the Middle East: Democracy, Law, and Society* (Seattle: University of Washington Press, 1993), pp. 248–71.

62. Goldberg, pp. 256, 267. Henry Munson, Jr.'s *Religion and Power in Morocco* (New Haven, Conn.: Yale University Press, 1993) provides another example of the influence of contractual views of government among religious thinkers in the premodern Muslim world. Like Goldberg, however, he notes that sultans often managed to diminish the practical influence of such moral ideas. The fact remains that there are more diverse ideological precedents in premodern Muslim thought than recognized by many Western and Islamist writers.

63. Though emphasizing that up to now they have been dominated by Western individualistic values, the anthropologist Richard A. Wilson has made a similar argument concerning prospects for the generalization of human rights across cultures. See Wilson, "Human Rights, Culture and Context: An Introduction," in Wilson, ed., *Human Rights, Culture and Context* (London and Chicago: Pluto Press, 1997), pp. 1–27.

64. See Augustus Richard Norton's "Introduction" to his *Civil Society in the Middle East* on the appeal of democracy and civility in the contemporary Middle East. For a rich analysis of the relationship of this civil democratic Islam to other Islamist movements, see Dale F. Eickelman and James Piscatori, *Muslim Politics* (Princeton, N.J.: Princeton University Press, 1996).

Contributors

Brigitte Berger is professor of sociology emeritus, at Boston University and is currently completing a book on the family, democracy, and markets in Western social history.

Jose Casanova is professor of sociology at the New School for Social Research. His most recent works include *Public Religions in the Modern World*.

Daniel Chirot is professor of sociology at the University of Washington. His recent books include *Modern Tyrants: The Power and Prevalence of Evil in Our Age*.

John A. Hall is professor of sociology at McGill University. His books include *Powers and Liberties*, *Liberalism*, and *Civil Society: Theory, History, Comparison*.

Robert W. Hefner is professor of anthropology and associate director of the Institute for the Study of Economic Culture at Boston University and the author of several books on religion, politics, and economic change.

Resat Kasaba teaches international studies at the University of Washington. His latest book is a collection of essays, *Rethinking the Project of Modernity in Turkey*, co-edited with Sibel Bozdogan.

S. Gordon Redding is professor of management studies at the University of Hong Kong. His most recent works include *The Spirit of Chinese Capitalism* and *Capitalism in Contrasting Cultures*.

Adam B. Seligman is a member of the Institute for the Study of Economic Culture and associate professor of religious studies at Boston University. He is the author of *The Idea of Civil Society* and *Innerworldly Individualism*.

Robert P. Weller is a member of the Institute for the Study of Economic Culture and associate professor of anthropology at Boston University. His most recent books include *Resistance, Chaos, and Control in China* and *Unruly Gods: Divinity and Society in China*, co-edited with Meir Shahar.

Robert Wuthnow is Andlinger Professor of Sociology at Princeton

University and the author of many books on American religion, ethics, and social change.

Anton C. Zijderveld is dean of the Faculty of Letters and professor of sociology at Erasmus University, Rotterdam. He is the author of several books on culture, politics, and humor, and has just completed a book on the crisis of the European welfare state.

Index